AF872939

The Emergence of Humanitarian Intervention

How should the international community react when a government transgresses humanitarian norms and violates the human rights of its own nationals? And where does the responsibility lie to protect people from such acts of violation? In a profound new study, Fabian Klose unites a team of leading scholars to investigate some of the most complex and controversial debates regarding the legitimacy of protecting humanitarian norms and universal human rights by non-violent and violent means. Charting the development of humanitarian intervention from its origins in the nineteenth century through to the present day, the book surveys the philosophical and legal rationales of enforcing humanitarian norms by military means, and how attitudes to military intervention on humanitarian grounds have changed over the course of three centuries. Drawing from a wide range of disciplines, the authors lend a fresh perspective to contemporary dilemmas using case studies from Europe, the United States, Africa, and Asia.

Fabian Klose is a senior researcher at the Leibniz Institute of European History (IEG) in Mainz, Germany.

Human Rights in History

Edited by

Stefan-Ludwig Hoffmann, *University of California, Berkeley*
Samuel Moyn, *Harvard Law School*

This series showcases new scholarship exploring the backgrounds of human rights today. With an open-ended chronology and international perspective, the series seeks works attentive to the surprises and contingencies in the historical origins and legacies of human rights ideals and interventions. Books in the series will focus not only on the intellectual antecedents and foundations of human rights but also on the incorporation of the concept by movements, nation states, international governance, and transnational law.

Also in the series

Fehrenbach and Rodogno	*Humanitarian Photography: A History*
Fisch	*A History of the Self-Determination of Peoples*
Hoffmann	*Human Rights in the Twentieth Century*
Hong	*Cold War Germany, the Third World, and the Global Humanitarian Regime*
Snyder	*Human Rights Activism and the End of the Cold War: A Transnational History of the Helsinki Network*
Winter and Prost	*René Cassin and Human Rights: From the Great War to the Universal Declaration*

The Emergence of Humanitarian Intervention

Ideas and Practice from the Nineteenth Century to the Present

Edited by

FABIAN KLOSE

Leibniz-Institut für Europäische Geschichte, Mainz

CAMBRIDGE
UNIVERSITY PRESS

CAMBRIDGE
UNIVERSITY PRESS

University Printing House, Cambridge CB2 8BS, United Kingdom

One Liberty Plaza, 20th Floor, New York, NY 10006, USA

477 Williamstown Road, Port Melbourne, VIC 3207, Australia

314-321, 3rd Floor, Plot 3, Splendor Forum, Jasola District Centre, New Delhi-110025, India

79 Anson Road, #06-04/06, Singapore 079906

Cambridge University Press is part of the University of Cambridge.

It furthers the University's mission by disseminating knowledge in the pursuit of education, learning and research at the highest international levels of excellence.

www.cambridge.org
Information on this title: www.cambridge.org/9781107075511

© Cambridge University Press 2016

This publication is in copyright. Subject to statutory exception and to the provisions of relevant collective licensing agreements, no reproduction of any part may take place without the written permission of Cambridge University Press.

First published 2016

A catalogue record for this publication is available from the British Library

Library of Congress Cataloging in Publication data
The emergence of humanitarian intervention :
ideas and practice from the nineteenth century to the
present / edited by Fabian Klose, Leibniz Institut fur
Europaische Geschichte, Mainz.
pages cm
ISBN 978-1-107-07551-1 (Hardback)
1. Humanitarian intervention. I. Klose, Fabian.
JZ6369.E54 2016
327.1′1–dc23 2015017083

ISBN 978-1-107-07551-1 Hardback
ISBN 978-1-107-42831-7 Paperback

Cambridge University Press has no responsibility for the persistence or accuracy of URLs for external or third-party internet websites referred to in this publication, and does not guarantee that any content on such websites is, or will remain, accurate or appropriate.

Contents

Figures

Tables

Contributors

JOST DÜLFFER, University of Cologne

MANUEL FRÖHLICH, Friedrich Schiller University Jena

MICHAEL GEYER, Department of History, University of Chicago

ABIGAIL GREEN, Brasenose College, Oxford

FABIAN KLOSE, Leibniz Institute of European History, Mainz

STEFAN KROLL, Goethe University, Frankfurt

MAIRI S. MACDONALD, University of Toronto

NORRIE MACQUEEN, University of St Andrews

DAVIDE RODOGNO, The Graduate Institute, Geneva

JAN ERIK SCHULTE, Ruhr University Bochum

DANIEL MARC SEGESSER, University of Bern

BRADLEY SIMPSON, University of Connecticut

ANDREW THOMPSON, University of Exeter

JON WESTERN, Mount Holyoke College

Acknowledgements

The present book is the result of an existing network among international scholars in the field of humanitarianism and human rights as well as of the annual conference of the German Association for Historical Peace Research (Arbeitskreis Historische Friedensforschung) held in October 2012 at the Historisches Kolleg in Munich. I am most grateful to the German Foundation for Peace Research (DSF) for the generous funding of the conference and to the German Research Foundation (DFG), the History Department of the Ludwig-Maximilians-Universität Munich, and the German Association for Historical Peace Research for their significant support. I am indebted to all the scholars from different disciplines attending the conference for their perceptive remarks and contributions, which significantly helped to shape this book. Additionally, I would like to say thank you to Adrian Franco, who worked relentlessly as conference administrative assistant as well as conference *rapporteur*. Furthermore, I would like to thank Martin Aust at the Ludwig-Maximilians-Universität Munich, Brendan Simms at the University of Cambridge, and Tobias Grill at the Ludwig-Maximilians-Universität Munich for their important suggestions on various issues concerning the conference and the book. I am particularly grateful to Johannes Paulmann at the Leibniz Institute of European History in Mainz, Martin Geyer at the Ludwig-Maximilians-Universität Munich, and Andrew Thompson at the University of Exeter for their crucial and perceptive comments on earlier drafts of the manuscript. During the process of preparing this book for publication, I could rely heavily on the editorial work of Dona Geyer for which I am very grateful. Finally, I would like to thank Michael Watson at Cambridge University Press for his inestimable support in the publication process. Many thanks to all of you!

1

The emergence of humanitarian intervention

Three centuries of 'enforcing humanity'

Fabian Klose

> People begin to feel that not only is every nation entitled to a free and independent life, but also that there are bonds of international duty binding all the nations of this earth together. Hence, the conviction is gaining ground that if on any spot of the world, even within the limits of an independent nation, some glaring wrong should be done . . . then other nations are not absolved from all concern in the matter simply because of large distance between them and the scene of the wrong.[1]
>
> Giuseppe Mazzini, 1851

THE DILEMMA OF INTERVENTION: A HISTORICAL AND RECENT POLITICAL DEBATE

How should the international community react when a government transgresses humanitarian norms and violates the human rights of its own nationals? If a responsibility for protecting people from gross human rights violations exists, which international actor should be responsible for counteracting such crimes? Is it legitimate to interfere from outside in the internal affairs of a sovereign state to prevent mass atrocities and to stop crimes against humanity? These controversial questions are inherent

I would like to thank Andrew Thompson, Martin Geyer, and Johannes Paulmann for their perceptive comments on the draft of this chapter. My essay was supported by the German Research Foundation (DFG) for which I am deeply grateful.

1 Giuseppe Mazzini, 'On Nonintervention (1851)' in Stefano Recchia and Nadia Urbinati (eds.), *A Cosmopolitanism of Nations: Guiseppe Mazzini's Writings on Democracy, Nation Building, and International Relations* (Princeton University Press, 2009), 217–18.

to the issue of humanitarian intervention and reveal the existing conflict between two crucial pillars in international relations: the respect of state sovereignty and the defence of humanity. The debate revolves around the central problem of how to reconcile the humanitarian imperative with the idea of the inviolability of national sovereignty rights. This dilemma of intervention is not just a very recent one; it has a long history. Already at the beginning of the nineteenth century, an intense debate evolved over the issue of interfering in the rights of sovereign states 'in the cause of humanity'. In order to stop massive violations of humanitarian standards, the European Great Powers intervened repeatedly by military means in various regions of the world, such as West Africa, East Africa, North Africa, the Near East, and the Balkans; amazingly, these are almost the same 'geographic hot spots' of humanitarian intervention as those of the twentieth and twenty-first centuries. Fighting the transatlantic slave trade and protecting religious minorities became the two major impulses for the emergence of a new kind of interventionist doctrine. Thus the aim of the chapters in this book is to present the evolution of the practice and theory of humanitarian intervention over three centuries, from the nineteenth to the twenty-first century.

First and foremost, the dilemma of intervention is regarded as a hot topic in an ongoing international political debate. In his Millennium Report in 2000, the then United Nations (UN) Secretary-General Kofi Annan described trenchantly the problem by asking:

> I also accept that the principles of sovereignty and non-interference offer vital protection to small and weak states. But to the critics I would pose this question: if humanitarian intervention is, indeed, an unacceptable assault on sovereignty, how should we respond to a Rwanda, to a Srebrenica – to gross and systematic violations of human rights that offend every precept of our common humanity?[2]

Annan purposely referred to the two most fatal failures of the international community, in general, and the deployed UN Blue Helmets, in particular, to prevent mass atrocities against civilians – the genocide of approximately 800,000 Tutsis in Rwanda by Hutus in 1994 and the massacre of over 8,000 Bosnian Muslims by Serbian troops in the so-called UN safe haven of Srebrenica in July 1995 – in order to argue for the moral duty of intervening actively against such horrendous crimes.

[2] Kofi A. Annan, *'We the peoples': The Role of the United Nations in the Twenty-first Century. Report of the Secretary-General* (New York: United Nations, 2000), 48. For the full report, see www.unmillenniumproject.org/documents/wethepeople.pdf (last accessed on 18 May 2015).

Thus, the Secretary-General incorporated the central recommendations of two UN reports of inquiry concerning both cases, which acknowledged the complete failure of the UN system and demanded, as a lesson for the future, the development of an effective concept to protect humanity.[3] Ensuing from the humanitarian catastrophes in Rwanda and Srebrenica, the controversy revolves in general around the topics of the responsibility to act, the related serious doubts about the role of the UN, and the existing deficiency of international law. This debate was once more intensified by the inaction of the Security Council in the Kosovo crisis and the related North Atlantic Treaty Organization (NATO) military intervention without UN authorization in 1999.[4]

In response to the pending dilemma of intervention, the International Commission on Intervention and State Sovereignty (ICISS), set up by the Canadian government, proposed in December 2001 the idea of 'responsibility to protect' (R2P), which was based on an alternative, reframed concept of sovereignty.[5] In its final report, the ICISS argued that sovereignty not only gave states the right to control their own affairs but implied as well their primary responsibility to protect the people living within their borders:[6] 'Where a population is suffering serious harm, as a

[3] Report of the Secretary-General Pursuant to General Assembly Resolution 53/35. The Fall of Srebenica, 15 November 1999, UNGA A/54/549; Report of the Independent Inquiry into the Actions of the United Nations during the 1994 Genocide in Rwanda, 16 December 1999, UNSC S/1999/1257. For an eyewitness account by the Canadian Commander of the UN mission about the disastrous failure in Rwanda, see Roméo Dallaire, *Shake Hands with the Devil: The Failure of Humanity in Rwanda* (London: Arrow Books, 2004). For Kofi Annan's personal account on the failure of the UN in Rwanda and Srebrenica and the lessons to be drawn from it, see Kofi Annan, *Interventions: A Life in War and Peace* (New York: Penguin Press, 2012), 29–133. On the dilemmas of humanitarian interventions, see also Jonathan Moore (ed.), *Hard Choices: Moral Dilemmas in Humanitarian Intervention* (Lanham: Rowman & Littlefield, 1998); Luke Glanville, 'Ellery Stowell and the Enduring Dilemmas of Humanitarian Intervention', *International Studies Review*, 13, no. 2 (2011), 241–58.

[4] For a multidisciplinary study on the Kosovo crises and the related intervention, see Albrecht Schnabel and Ramesh Thakur (eds.), *Kosovo and the Challenge of Humanitarian Intervention: Selective Indignation, Collective Action, and International Citizenship* (Tokyo and New York: United Nations University Press, 2000); Aidan Hehir, *Humanitarian Intervention After Kosovo: Iraq, Dafur and the Record of Global Civil Society* (Basingstoke: Palgrave Macmillan, 2008).

[5] On this debate and related developments, see also Chapter 14 by Manuel Fröhlich in this book.

[6] The crucial new approach to sovereignty as responsibility, which the ICISS report follows, was articulated for the first time in the study by Francis M. Deng, Sadikiel Kimaro, Terrence Lyons, Donald Rothchild, and I. William Zartman, *Sovereignty as Responsibility: Conflict Management in Africa* (Washington: The Brooking Institution, 1996).

result of internal war, insurgency, repression or state failure, and the state in question is unwilling or unable to halt or avert it, the principle of non-intervention yields to the international responsibility to protect.'[7] In other words, when a state failed to uphold the fundamental rights of its people, its sovereignty was suspended, and the responsibility shifted to the international community, which could, as a last resort, even forcibly interfere.[8] This concept was celebrated as a crucial watershed, a promising normative advancement in international politics and gained international recognition at the UN World Summit in 2005. On the occasion of the sixtieth anniversary of the foundation of the UN, all UN member states officially affirmed their acceptance of 'the responsibility to protect its population from genocide, war crimes, ethnic cleansing and crimes against humanity'.[9]

Two recent conflict scenarios became test cases for the consistency and value of the new R2P formula in international politics. Following widespread attacks against civilians by the regime of Muammar al-Gaddafi in Libya, the UN Security Council issued its Resolution 1973 on 17 March 2011, in which it referred for the first time explicitly to the principle of the responsibility to protect[10] and authorized the UN member states 'to take

[7] International Commission on Intervention and State Sovereignty, *The Responsibility to Protect* (Ottawa: International Development Research Centre, 2001), xi, www.responsibilitytoprotect.org/ICISS%20Report.pdf (last accessed on 18 May 2015).

[8] For the development of the R2P concept, see Gareth Evans, *The Responsibility to Protect: Ending Mass Atrocity Crimes Once and For All* (Washington: The Brooking Institution, 2008); James Pattison, *Humanitarian Intervention and the Responsibility to Protect: Who Should Intervene?* (Oxford University Press, 2010); Anne Orford, *International Authority and the Responsibility to Protect* (Cambridge University Press, 2011); Ramesh Thakur, *The Responsibility to Protect: Norms, Laws, and the Use of Force in International Politics* (London and New York: Routledge, 2011); Cristina Gabriela Badescu, *Humanitarian Intervention and the Responsibility to Protect: Security and Human Rights* (New York: Routledge, 2011); Aidan Hehir, *The Responsibility to Protect: Rhetoric, Reality and the Future of Humanitarian Intervention* (Basingstoke: Palgrave, 2012); Melissa Labonte, *Human Rights and Humanitarian Norms, Strategic Framing, and Intervention: Lessons for the Responsibility to Protect* (London and New York: Routledge Chapman & Hall, 2013). On the development of the international law on the use of force since 1945 see especially: Claus Kreß, 'Major Post-Westphalian Shifts and Some Important Neo-Westphalian Hesitations in the State Practice on the International Law on the Use of Force', *Journal on the Use of Force and International Law*, 1, no. 1 (2014), 11–54.

[9] Resolution 60/1, 2005 World Summit Outcome, 24 October 2005, UNGA A/RES/60/1, 30, www.un.org/womenwatch/ods/A-RES-60-1-E.pdf (last accessed on 18 May 2015).

[10] The quote 'Recalling the Libyan authorities' responsibility to protect its population' is in Resolution 1970 (2011), 26 February 2011, UNSC S/RES/1970, 2, www.un.org/press/en/2011/sc10187.doc.htm (last accessed on 18 May 2015).

all necessary measures'[11] to protect the Libyan civilian population. As a result, NATO started to attack Gaddafi's forces with air strikes and thus contributed significantly to the victory of the opposition movement in the civil war. In a later interview, UN Deputy Secretary-General Jan Eliasson justified the armed intervention by arguing that Gaddafi's announced atrocities against civilians depicted a 'Srebrenica moment' that forced the international community to react.[12]

According to various reports of the international media, the recent civil war in Syria with the ruthless attacks against the civilian population also evokes memories of the Bosnian tragedy. For instance, both the desperate situation of the people in the besieged rebel stronghold of Homs and the appalling massacres of civilians in the town of Houla are repeatedly characterized as 'Syria's Srebrenica moment'.[13] Despite the ongoing humanitarian crisis, the international community shows no reaction similar to the Libyan case, is instead entirely divided over the issue, and abstains from the option of direct intervention. The UN Security Council remains paralysed by the division among the proponents and opponents of applying the R2P concept to the Syrian conflict. While the civil war continues to haunt the civilian population, the question of how to react to massive violations of human rights and ongoing humanitarian crises continues to be fiercely disputed within the sphere of international politics.[14]

[11] Resolution 1973 (2011), 17 March 2011, UNSC S/RES/1973, 3, www.un.org/press/en/2011/sc10200.doc.htm#Resolution (last accessed on 18 May 2015).

[12] '"Srebrenica-Moment": Der künftige UN-Vizechef über gute Gründe für Interventionen', *Die Zeit*, 22 March 2012. For a similar interpretation, see Brendan Simms, 'Road to Libya Runs through Srebrenica', *The Independent*, 29 May 2011.

[13] 'Syria's Srebrenica: Situation Grows Increasingly Grim in Rebel Stronghold of Homs', *Spiegel online International*, 23 February 2012, www.spiegel.de/international/world/syria-s-srebrenica-situation-grows-increasingly-grim-in-rebel-stronghold-of-homs-a-817145.html (last accessed on 18 May 2015); Michael Dobbs, 'Houla Massacre Evokes Memories of Srebrenica', *The Washington Post*, 2 June 2012, www.washingtonpost.com/world/europe/houla-massacre-evokes-memories-of-srebrenica/2012/06/02/gJQATaHs9U_story.html (last accessed on 18 May 2015); Fen Osler Hampson, 'Syria's Srebrenica Moment', *iPolitics*, 4 June 2012, www.ipolitics.ca/2012/06/04/fen-hampson-syrias-srebrenica-moment/ (last accessed 18 May 2015); Wolfgang Ischinger, 'Lehren aus Srebrenica', *Süddeutsche.de*, 28 August 2013, www.sueddeutsche.de/politik/moeglicher-militaereinsatz-in-syrien-lehren-aus-srebrenica-1.1756462 (last accessed on 18 May 2015).

[14] For this ongoing debate, see Michael Staack and Dan Krause (eds.), *Schutzverantwortung in der Debatte. Die 'Responsibility to Protect' nach dem Libyen-Dissens* (Opladen and Berlin, Verlag Barbara Buderich, 2015).

A SHORT- OR LONG-TERM HISTORY OF HUMANITARIAN INTERVENTION? DEFINITION AND THE STATE OF RESEARCH

Despite the recent intense political debate, the academic discussion about the issue of humanitarian intervention is much older. It reaches back to the work of scholars in the nineteenth and early twentieth centuries, in which there was already controversy over legal arguments for and against an interventionist doctrine.[15] However, against the backdrop of the ban on the use of force and intervention explicitly established in the UN Charter,[16] this debate at first waned noticeably after 1945, and prominent legal scholars such as Ian Brownlie even expressed serious doubts about the validity of the whole concept. By pointing to the political abuse of humanitarian rhetoric to justify forcible interference in the past, especially in the case of the German assault on Czechoslovakia in 1939,[17] Brownlie concluded that no genuine case of humanitarian intervention had ever occurred. Moreover, he called it a beneficial development in international law and politics that this 'institution has disappeared from modern state practice'.[18]

[15] For these early examples, see Henry Wheaton, *Elements of International Law: With a Sketch of the History of the Science* (Philadelphia: Carey, Lea & Blanchard, 1836), 82–94; Hermann Rotteck, *Das Recht der Einmischung in die inneren Angelgeheiten eines fremden Staates vom vernuftrechtlichen, historischen und politischen Standpunkt erortet* (Freiburg a. Br.: Adolph Emmerling, 1845); Augustus Granville Stapleton, *Intervention and Non-Intervention or The Foreign Policy of Great Britain from 1790 to 1865* (London: John Murray, 1866); Egide Arntz and Gustave Rolin-Jaequemyns, 'Note sur la Théorie du Droit d'Intervention', *Revue de Droit International et de Legislation Comparée*, 8 (1876), 673–82; William E. Lingelbach, 'The Doctrine and Practice of Intervention in Europe', *Annals of the American Academy of Political and Social Science*, 16 (July 1900), 1–32; Lassa Oppenheim, *International Law: A Treatise*, vol. 1: *Peace* (London: Longmans, Green, and Co.,1905), 181–90; Antoine Rougier, 'La Théorie de l'Intervention d'Humanité', *Revue Générale de Droit International Public*, 17 (1910), 468–526; Henry G. Hodges, *The Doctrine of Intervention* (Princeton: Banner Press, 1915); Ellery C. Stowell, *Intervention in International Law* (Washington: John Byrne & Co., 1921); P. H. Winfield, 'The Grounds of Intervention in International Law', *The British Year Book of International Law* (Oxford 1924), 149–62.

[16] See Article 2, para. 4 and para. 7 of the UN Charter.

[17] On this case, see Chapter 10 by Jost Dülffer in this book.

[18] Ian Brownlie, *International Law and the Use of Force by States* (Oxford: Clarendon Press, 1963), 340. An absolute exception was the prominent legal scholar Hersch Lauterpacht, who argued for the idea of humanitarian intervention as a way to protect human rights. See, Hersch Lauterpacht, *An International Bill of the Rights of Man* (New York and London: Columbia University Press, 1945), 169–78 and 207–13; Hersch Lauterpacht (ed.), Lassa Oppenheim, *International Law: A Treatise*, vol. 1: *Peace* (London and New York: Longmans, Green, and Co., 1948), 279–80; Hersch

The issue of humanitarian intervention regained momentum on the occasion of specific political events at the end of the 1960s and the beginning of the 1970s. The crisis in Biafra in 1968[19] and the military intervention of India to stop mass atrocities against the civilian population in East Pakistan in 1971 prompted academics to pay considerable attention to the notion once again. After these significant cases, they began to raise the question of whether the idea of forcible interference for humanitarian purposes fit into international law and earned any legal recognition.[20] Especially the last twenty years have witnessed a significant intensification of the debate within international law and political science. During this time, both disciplines have produced and are still producing a burgeoning body of literature on the topic.

While working intensively in the field, scholars such as J. L. Holzgrefe managed to offer a sustainable definition of humanitarian intervention. According to Holzgrefe, the term refers to 'the threat or use of force across state borders by a state (or group of states) aimed at preventing or ending widespread and grave violations of the fundamental human

Lauterpacht, *International Law and Human Rights* (London: Stevens & Sons Limited, 1950), 120–2.

19 See also Chapter 15 by Andrew Thompson, 348–49, in this book.

20 Already the US intervention in the Dominican Republic in 1965 evoked some echo in international law under the heading of 'humanitarian intervention': David S. Bogen, 'The Law of Humanitarian Intervention: United States Policy in Cuba (1898) and in the Dominican Republic (1965)', *The Harvard International Law Club Journal*, 7, no. 2 (Spring 1966), 296–315. Concerning the Biafra crisis, see: Michael Reisman and Myers S. McDougal, 'Humanitarian Intervention to Protect the Ibos' in Richard B. Lillich (ed.), *Humanitarian Intervention and the United Nations* (Charlottesville: University of Virginia Press, 1973), 167–95. This legal memorandum was prepared as a petition to the UN in September 1968 and circulated after its submission for discussion among international legal scholars. Laurie S. Wiseberg, 'Humanitarian Intervention: Lessons from the Nigerian Civil War', *Revue des droits de l'homme*, 70, no. 1 (1974), 61–98. For the whole debate on the occasion of India's invasion in East Pakistan, see Lillich, *Humanitarian Intervention*; Thomas M. Franck and Nigel S. Rodley, 'After Bangladesh: The Law of Humanitarian Intervention by Military Force', *The American Journal of International Law*, 67, no. 2 (April 1973), 275–305; Jean-Pierre L. Fonteyne, 'The Customary International Law Doctrine of Humanitarian Intervention: Its Current Validity Under the U.N. Charter', *California Western International Law Journal*, 4 (1973), 203–70. For additional articles on the subject, see B. de Schutter, 'Humanitarian Intervention: A United Nations Task', *California Western International Law Journal*, 21, no. 3 (1972), 21–36; Howard L. Weisberg, 'The Congo Crisis of 1964: A Case Study in Humanitarian Intervention', *Virginia Journal of International Law*, 12 (1972), 261–76; Farooq Hassan, 'Realpolitik in International Law: After Tanzanian-Ugandan Conflict: "Humanitarian Intervention" Reexamined', *Willamette Law Review*, 17 (1981), 859–912.

rights of individuals other than its own citizens, without the permission of the state within whose territory force is applied'.[21] Although this definition slightly varies in one form or another throughout the literature, most scholars agree on three key features in defining the term: the transboundary interference in the domestic affairs of a foreign state, the predominant humanitarian purposes, and the coercive nature of the engagement. Thus, most studies focus purely on the use of military force as humanitarian intervention and distinguish it clearly from other forms of civil humanitarian action, such as aid and relief operations by governmental and non-governmental agencies.[22] Accordingly, the various activities of prominent international organizations such as the Office of the United Nations High Commissioner for Refugees (UNHCR), the International Committee of

[21] J. L. Holzgrefe, 'The Humanitarian Intervention Debate' in J. L. Holzgrefe and Robert O. Keohane (eds.), *Humanitarian Intervention: Ethical, Legal, and Political Dilemmas* (Cambridge University Press, 2004), 18. This definition follows closely the general definition of the term 'intervention' as articulated by R. J. Vincent, who characterizes 'intervention as that activity undertaken by a state, a group within a state, a group of states or an international organization which interferes coercively in the domestic affairs of another state'. R. J. Vincent, *Nonintervention and International Order* (Princeton University Press, 1974), 3–13, here 13. For a general approach on the issue of intervention and its various types, see Hedley Bull (ed.), *Intervention in World Politics* (Oxford University Press, 1986); Andrew M. Dorman and Thomas G. Otte (eds.), *Military Intervention: From Gunboat Diplomacy to Humanitarian Intervention* (Aldershot: Dartmouth Publishing Company, 1995); S. Neil MacFarlane, *Intervention in Contemporary World Politics* (New York: Routledge, 2002); Martha Finnemore, *The Purpose of Intervention: Changing Beliefs about the Use of Force* (Ithaca and London: Cornell University Press, 2003).

[22] Sean D. Murphy, *Humanitarian Intervention: The United Nations in an Evolving World Order* (Philadelphia: University of Pennsylvania Press, 1996), 8–20; Adam Roberts, *Humanitarian Action in War: Aid, Protection and Impartiality in a Policy Vacuum* (Oxford: Routledge, 1996), 19–31; Francis Kofi Abiew, *The Evolution of the Doctrine and Practice of Humanitarian Intervention* (The Hague, London and Boston: Kluwer Law International, 1999), 18; Nicolas J. Wheeler, *Saving Strangers: Humanitarian Intervention in International Society* (Oxford University Press, 2003), 1–2; Jennifer M. Welsh (ed.), *Humanitarian Intervention and International Relations* (Oxford University Press, 2006), 3; Simon Chesterman, *Just War or Just Peace? Humanitarian Intervention and International Law* (Oxford and New York: Oxford University Press, 2003), 2–3; Pattison, *Humanitarian Intervention*, 24–30; Wilfried Hinsch and Dieter Janssen, *Menschenrechte militärisch schützen: Ein Plädoyer für humanitäre Interventionen* (Munich: C.H. Beck, 2006), 29–34; Taylor B. Seybolt, *Humanitarian Military Intervention: The Conditions for Success and Failure* (Oxford University Press, 2007), 5–6; Eric A. Heinze, *Waging Humanitarian War: The Ethics, Law, and Politics of Humanitarian Intervention* (Albany: State University of New York Press, 2009), 7–10; Aidan Hehir, *Humanitarian Intervention: An Introduction* (Basingstoke: Palgrave, 2010), 11–21; Thomas G. Weiss, *Humanitarian Intervention: Ideas in Action* (Cambridge and Malden: Polity Press, 2012), 6–15.

the Red Cross (ICRC), Médecins Sans Frontières (MSF)[23], CARE, and Oxfam are characterized as 'humanitarian aid', 'humanitarian protection', and 'humanitarian assistance' rather than as 'humanitarian intervention'.[24] As a matter of fact, various authors address the growing dilemma of intermingling military coercion and humanitarian action in this context. Thus 'coercive humanitarianism' can indeed undermine and endanger the genuine humanitarian enterprise.[25] For this reason, Didier Fassin and Mariella Pandolfi argue for a precise methodological distinction: 'We need to be clear that the work of humanitarian organizations cannot be likened to the action of military forces. It is therefore important that analysis does not add to the confusion of categories that reigns on the ground by blurring the issues and by placing all actors and all logics on the same level.'[26]

The existing literature on international law and political science takes a distinctly normative approach in addressing the topic of humanitarian intervention. Among legal scholars, the overarching concern deals with the lawfulness of this kind of intervention. They concentrate on the questions of whether and under which legal conditions it is permissible to forcibly intervene in the name of humanity. In short, does a right to interfere in the internal affairs of sovereign state for humanitarian purposes exist according to the body of international law? Their foremost attention is on the legal dilemma of intervention, which rests on competing claims of state sovereignty as a guiding principle in international

[23] See also Thompson, Chapter 15, 348.

[24] For these humanitarian actions and the related organizations, see United Nations High Commissioner for Refugees (ed.), *The State of the World's Refugees: Fifty Years of Humanitarian Action* (Oxford University Press, 2000); Larry Minear, *The Humanitarian Enterprise: Dilemmas and Discoveries* (Bloomfield, Conn.: Kumarian Press, 2002); Fabrice Weissman (ed.), *In the Shadow of 'Just Wars': Violence, Politics, and Humanitarian Action* (London: Cornell University Press, 2004); David P. Forsythe, *The Humanitarians: The International Committee of the Red Cross* (Cambridge University Press, 2005); Michael Barnett and Thomas G. Weiss (eds.), *Humanitarianism in Question: Politics, Power, Ethics* (Ithaca: Cornell University Press, 2008); Michael Barnett, *Empire of Humanity: A History of Humanitarianism* (Ithaca and London: Cornell University Press, 2011); Johannes Paulmann, 'Conjunctures in the History of International Humanitarian Aid during the Twentieth Century', *Humanity*, 4, no. 2 (Summer 2013), 215–38.

[25] See Minear, *Humanitarian Enterprise*, 99–118; Didier Fassin and Mariella Pandolfi, 'Introduction: Military and Humanitarian Government in the Age of Intervention', in Didier Fassin and Mariella Pandolfi (eds.), *Contemporary States of Emergency. The Politics of Military and Humanitarian Intervention* (New York: Zone Books, 2010), 9–25; Didier Fassin, *Humanitarian Reason: A Moral History of the Present* (Berkeley and Los Angeles: University of California Press, 2012), 223–42.

[26] Fassin and Pandolfi, 'Introduction', 14.

relations and on the evolving idea of the promotion of human rights. In order to illuminate this problem, some law scholars purposely trace the legal origins of an interventionist doctrine back to the Christian medieval tradition of just war. In addition, they analyse the further development of the notion according to the emergence of natural law theory in the work of such prominent figures as Hugo Grotius and Emerich de Vattel during the seventeenth and eighteenth centuries and in relation to the growth of positive law in the nineteenth century.[27] By integrating early historical precedents in their legal analysis, they discuss whether a doctrine of humanitarian intervention existed in customary international law prior to 1945. Nevertheless, legal research remains definitely focused primarily on the discourse on forcible interference under the legal paradigm of the UN Charter and on the very recent debate about the development of the concept of intervention from a right to intervene to a responsibility to protect.[28] The NATO intervention in Kosovo in 1999, which had no UN mandate, thereby serves as the prime case study for discussing the two contesting issues of the legality and legitimacy of humanitarian intervention and the impact on the body of international law.[29]

[27] For references to historical precedents, see Murphy, *Humanitarian Intervention*, 33–64; Wilhelm G. Grewe, *The Epochs of International Law* (Berlin and New York: De Gruyter, 2000), 487–96; Abiew, *Evolution of the Doctrine*, 21–59; Chesterman, *Just War*, 7–44; Mark Swatek-Evenstein, *Geschichte der 'Humanitären Intervention'* (Baden-Baden: Nomos, 2008); Hans Köchler, *The Concept of Humanitarian Intervention in the Context of Modern Power Politics: Is the Revival of the Doctrine of 'Just War" Compatible with the International Rule of Law?* (Vienna: International Progress Organization, 2001); Stephen Kloepfer, 'The Syrian Crisis, 1860–1861: A Case Study in Classic Humanitarian Intervention', *The Canadian Yearbook of International Law*, 23 (1985), 246–60; Istvan Pogany, 'Humanitarian Intervention in International Law: The French Intervention in Syria Re-Examined', *International and Comparative Law Quarterly*, 35 (January 1986), 182–90; Christian Hillgruber, 'Humanitäre Intervention, Grossmachtpolitik und Völkerrecht', *Der Staat*, 40, no. 21 (2001), 165–91. Stefano Recchia and Jennifer M. Welsh (eds.), *Just and Unjust Military Intervention: European Thinkers from Vitoria to Mill* (Cambridge University Press, 2013).

[28] Fernando R. Tesón, *Humanitarian Intervention: An Inquiry into Law and Morality* (Dobbs Ferry, N.Y.: Transnational Publishers, 2005); Thakur, *Responsibility to Protect*; Orford, *International Authority*.

[29] Louis Henkin, 'Kosovo and the Law of "Humanitarian Intervention"', *The American Journal of International Law*, 93, no. 4 (October 1999), 824–8; Jonathan I. Charney, 'Anticipatory Humanitarian Intervention in Kosovo', *The American Journal of International Law*, 93, no. 4 (October 1999), 834–41; Richard A. Falk, 'Kosovo, World Order, and the Future of International Law', *The America Journal of Law*, 93, no. 4 (October 1999), 847–57; Sean D. Murphy, 'The Intervention in Kosovo: A Law-Shaping Incident?', *Proceedings of the Annual Meeting* (American Society of International Law), 94 (5–8 April 2000), 302–04; Allen Buchanan, 'Reforming the International Law of

As far as the analytical timeframe of research is concerned, political science focuses more exclusively on the twentieth and twenty-first centuries. Political scientists put the issue of humanitarian intervention in the context of contemporary world politics, including geostrategic considerations, and analyse it according to the various schools of thought in international relations. In investigating the political dilemma of intervention, recent studies tend to take an integrative approach that merges the various ethical, moral, and legal perspectives into a more multidimensional analysis.[30] Crucial remain the questions about the role of international society and how it should react to gross violations of human rights. Broad agreement exists among scholars of law and political science that the emergence of a new world order after the end of the Cold War constitutes the decisive caesura. For decades, the idea of military intervention for humanitarian purposes was stalemated by superpower confrontation; therefore, only a very few cases occurred, such as India's invasion of East Pakistan to stop mass atrocities against the civilian population in 1971, Vietnam's in Kampuchea (the later Cambodia) to close down 'the killing fields' of the Khmer Rouge in 1978, and Tanzania's in Uganda to overthrow the murderous regime of Idi Amin in 1979. However, the 1990s witnessed a real 'explosion of intervention with largely humanitarian justifications'.[31] The end of the East–West conflict, induced by the collapse of the Soviet Union, enabled the UN to become a more active key player in the realm of international peace and security. Due to the outbreak of a series of new conflict scenarios, UN involvement in various humanitarian crises around the world, stretching

Humanitarian Intervention' in J. L. Holzgrefe and Robert O. Keohane (eds.), *Humanitarian Intervention: Ethical, Legal, and Political Dilemmas* (Cambridge University Press, 2004), 130–73; Katariina Simonen, *The State versus the Individual: The Unresolved Dilemma of Humanitarian Intervention* (Leiden and Boston: Martinus Nijhoff Publishers, 2011); Ciarán Burke, *An Equitable Framework for Humanitarian Intervention* (Oxford and Portland: Hart Publishing, 2013).

30 For this multidimensional approach, see especially Wheeler, *Saving Strangers*; Welsh, *Humanitarian Intervention*; Holzgrefe and Keohane, *Humanitarian Intervention*; Heinze, *Waging Humanitarian War*; Anne Orford, *Reading Humanitarian Intervention: Human Rights and the Use of Force in International Law* (Cambridge University Press, 2003).

31 Weiss, *Humanitarian Intervention*, 3. For the focus on the period since 1990, see, for example, MacFarlane, *Intervention*, 49–83; Michael C. Davis, Wolfgang Dietrich, Bettina Scholdan, and Dieter Sepp, *International Intervention in the Post-Cold War World: Moral Responsibility and Power Politics* (Armonk and London: M. E. Sharpe, 2004); Seybolt, *Humanitarian Military Intervention*; see also Thompson, Chapter 15, 344–46.

from Iraq to the former Yugoslavia and to Somalia, significantly increased in the post–Cold War era.[32]

As a result, the genealogy outlined by these interpretations views humanitarian intervention above all as a recent invention and denies the existence of a long, complex history of the idea of protecting humanitarian norms by force. To a great extent, the predominant normative approach found in the existing literature leaves little room for historical interpretation and marginalizes the relevant cases of the past centuries.[33] Most studies thus refer only very briefly if at all to historical precedents such as the interference of the Great Powers in the Greek War of Independence in 1827 and in the Civil War in Lebanon in 1860–1.[34] Apart from these interventions in the Ottoman Empire, some authors such as Gareth Evans, former co-chair of the ICISS, even characterize the four hundred years from the Peace of Westphalia in 1648 to the Holocaust as a time of 'institutionalizing indifference' in which very few examples of

[32] For a list of the various UN military operations in the 1990s, see Weiss, *Humanitarian Intervention*, 46. On the new role of the UN, see also Elizabeth G. Ferris, *The Challenge to Intervene: A New Role for the United Nations?* (Uppsala: Life & Peace Institute, 1992); Murphy, *Humanitarian Intervention*; Thomas G. Weiss, David P. Forsythe, and Roger A. Coate, *The United Nations and Changing World Politics* (Boulder: Westview Press, 2004), 47–92; Adam Roberts, 'The United Nations and Humanitarian Intervention', in Welsh, *Humanitarian Intervention*, 71–97; Lidwien Kapteijns, 'Test-firing the "New World Order" in Somalia: The US/UN Military Humanitarian Intervention of 1992–1995', *Journal of Genocide Research*, 15, no. 4, (2013), 421–42.

[33] Two exceptions are the articles by Chaim Kaufmann and Robert Pape, and Oded Löwenheim, in which the political scientists have explicitly chosen historical precedents as their case studies. See Chaim D. Kaufmann and Robert A. Pape, 'Explaining Costly International Moral Action: Britain's Sixty-Year Campaign against the Atlantic Slave Trade', *International Organization*, 53, no. 4 (Autumn 1999), 631–68; Oded Löwenheim, '"Do Ourselves Credit and Render a Lasting Service to Mankind": British Moral Prestige, Humanitarian Intervention, and the Barbary Pirates', *International Studies Quarterly*, 47, no. 1 (March 2003), 23–48.

[34] Besides the mentioned reference to historical precedents in law literature, only a few books in political science devote just a few pages to the cases. For example, see Wheeler, *Saving Strangers*, 45–6; Holzgrefe, *Humanitarian Intervention Debate*, 45; Martha Finnemore, 'Constructing Norms of Humanitarian Intervention' in Peter J. Katzenstein (ed.), *The Culture of National Security: Norms and Identity in World Politics* (New York: Columbia University Press, 1996), 153–85, here 161–72; Finnemore, *Purpose of Intervention*, 58–69; Hinsch and Janssen, *Menschenrechte militärisch schützen*, 17–20; Weiss, *Humanitarian Intervention*, 35–7. Also the Supplementary of the ICISS report of 2001 refers very briefly to the precedents of the nineteenth century: International Commission on Intervention and State Sovereignty, *The Responsibility to Protect: Research, Bibliography, Background.* Supplementary Volume to the Report of the ICISS (Ottawa: International Development Research Centre, 2001), 16–17, www.bits.de/NRANEU/docs/ICISS1201supplement.pdf (last accessed on 18 May 2015).

state intervention into foreign territory can be said to have occurred for humanitarian purposes or any reason beyond immediate economic and security interests, thanks to the unchecked operation of the Westphalian principles of sovereignty.[35]

However, this perspective seeks a counterargument: if the purity of humanitarian purposes is the sole criterion defining the concept of humanitarian intervention, then it never existed and will never exist. It is an absolute myth that states would risk or have ever risked the lives of their soldiers just to follow the altruistic call of humanity. From the past to the present, humanitarian intervention was and is almost invariably driven by a mixture of various intentions of the interfering parties. As we argue in this book, the humanitarian consideration was and still is just one motive among many, including economic, geostrategic, and security issues.[36]

Furthermore, to characterize the period from the late seventeenth to the early twentieth century as an age of 'humanitarian indifference' means to overlook completely the burgeoning body of historical research on the history of humanitarianism and early human rights. As recent studies show explicitly, this period witnessed a true 'humanitarian revolution'[37] in the sense that people started to feel sympathy for their fellow human beings, not only within their own country, but across borders and even on distant continents. Far from being indifferent, individuals were mobilized by a sentimental and moral 'humanitarian narrative' that motivated them to care for strangers and remedy their woes.[38] This new sensibility triggered a real wave of humanitarian reform within the societies of Western

[35] Evans, *Responsibility to Protect*, 15–19. For a similar interpretation, see Brownlie, *International Law*, 338–42.

[36] On the mix of various motives for humanitarian intervention, see also Michael Walzer, *Just and Unjust Wars: A Moral Argument with Historical Illustrations* (New York: Perseus Books, 2000), 101; Vincent, *Nonintervention*, 10–12; Wheeler, *Saving Strangers*, 37–9, 47; Pattison, *Humanitarian Intervention*, 156–61; Weiss, *Humanitarian Intervention*, 7–9; Andreas Krieg, *Motivations for Humanitarian Intervention: Theoretical and Empirical Considerations* (Heidelberg and New York: Springer, 2013).

[37] In this book we refer to the term 'humanitarian revolution' in the sense of the revolutionary emergence of humanitarian sensibility and activities rather than as a decline in violence, as it is interpreted by Steven Pinker, *The Better Angels of Our Nature: The Decline of Violence in History and Its Causes* (London and New York: Viking Press, 2011), 129–88.

[38] Frank J. Klingberg, 'The Evolution of the Humanitarian Spirit in Eighteenth-Century England', *The Pennsylvania Magazine of History and Biography*, 66, no. 3 (July 1942), 260–78; Shelby T. McCloy, *The Humanitarian Movement in Eighteenth-Century France* (New York: Haskell House, 1972); M. J. D. Roberts, *Making English Morals: Voluntary Associations and Moral Reform in England, 1787–1886* (Cambridge University Press, 2004); Norman S. Fiering, 'Irresistible Compassion: An Aspect of Eighteenth-Century

Europe and North America and led to the foundation of various new humanitarian movements at the end of the eighteenth and the beginning of the nineteenth centuries. In this context, the international efforts to abolish slavery and to protect religious minorities are primarily described as the epitome and driving force of the crystallization of humanitarian sentiments in international politics. However, the relationship between the 'humanitarian revolution' and state intervention to enforce the newly created norms has been indeed neglected by historians for a long time. They either referred to the historical cases very briefly, if at all, or emphasized other aspects of interventionist politics, such as anti-revolutionary and imperial purposes.[39] Thus, it is one of the crucial aims of this book to investigate the entangled history of emerging humanitarianism and interventionism as well as to relate both historiographies to each other.[40]

Sympathy and Humanitarianism', *Journal of the History of Ideas*, 37, no. 2 (April–June 1976), 195–218; Karen Halttunen, 'Humanitarianism and the Pornography of Pain in Anglo-American Culture', *The American Historical Review*, 100, no. 2 (April 1995), 303–34; Thomas Haskell, 'Capitalism and the Origins of Humanitarian Sensibility, Part 1', *The American Historical Review*, 90, no. 2 (April 1985), 339–61; Thomas Haskell, 'Capitalism and the Origins of Humanitarian Sensibility, Part 2', *The American Historical Review*, 90, no. 3 (June 1985), 547–66; Thomas Laqueur, 'Bodies, Details, and the Humanitarian Narrative', in Lynn Hunt (ed.), *The New Cultural History* (Berkeley: University of California Press, 1989), 176–204; Samuel Moyn, 'Empathy in History: Empathizing with Humanity', *History and Theory*, 45 (2006), 397–415; Lynn Hunt, *Inventing Human Rights: A History* (New York: W.W. Norton & Company, 2007); Richard D. Brown and Richard Wilson (eds.), *Humanitarianism and Suffering: The Mobilization of Empathy* (Cambridge University Press, 2009); Lynn Festa, 'Humanity without Feathers', *Humanity*, 1, no. 1 (2010), 3–27.

39 While Carole Fink does not refer to the military interventions in the Ottoman Empire at all, Paul Gordon Lauren mentions them briefly. Mark Mazower refers to the concept of humanitarian intervention in his recent book only in the context of the twentieth century and the end of the Cold War. See, Carole Fink, *Defending the Rights of Others: The Great Powers, the Jews, and International Minority Protection* (Cambridge University Press, 2004), 3–38, here especially 8–9; Paul G. Lauren, *The Evolution of International Human Rights: Visions Seen* (Philadelphia: University of Pennsylvania Press, 2011), 71–6; Mark Mazower, *Governing the World: The History of an Idea* (London: Allen Lane, 2012), 378–96. Matthias Schulz and Jürgen Osterhammel also refer briefly to the issue of humanitarian intervention but focus more on anti-revolutionary and imperial purposes of interventionist policy. See, Matthias Schulz, *Normen und Praxis: Das Europäische Konzert der Großmächte als Sicherheitsrat 1815–1860* (Munich: Oldenbourg, 2009), 73–88, 524–31, and 577–620; Jürgen Osterhammel, 'Krieg im Frieden: Zu Formen und Typologien imperialer Interventionen' in Jürgen Osterhammel, *Geschichtswissenschaft jenseits des Nationalstaats: Studien zu Beziehungsgeschichte und Zivilisationsvergleich* (Göttingen: Vandenhoeck & Ruprecht, 2001), 283–321, here especially 315–21.

40 This is a guiding theme for all of the chapters in this book, but on this issue see especially Chapter 2 by Michael Geyer and Chapter 15 by Andrew Thompson.

Very recent studies provide the first important steps towards a genuine history of humanitarian intervention, based on archival research, and sketch the genealogy of the concept's long history. The pioneering prelude to this trend is the book *Freedom's Battle: The Origins of Humanitarian Intervention* by the political scientist Gary Bass, in which he addresses the various interventions of the Great Powers in the Ottoman Empire during the nineteenth century.[41] Bass begins his narrative with the Greek War of Independence in 1821, moves then to European intervention in the civil war in Syria in 1860–1, and finally discusses the political agitation that occurred during the Bulgarian crisis in 1876–7. His perspective is clearly dominated by his focus on the role of leading contemporary figures such as the prominent British philhellene Lord George Gordon Byron, the French emperor Napoleon III, and the British Prime Minister William Ewart Gladstone. Although Bass anticipates some features of humanitarian intervention in the nineteenth century, his purpose is political rather than historical. His main concern is to vindicate and promote empathically the concept of humanitarian intervention. Thus he presents the historical precedents as a guideline, descended linearly from the past, for today's policy-making and presents a lesson he argues should be drawn from past ages: 'The nineteenth century shows how the practice of humanitarian intervention can be managed.'[42] By concentrating primarily on his political agenda, Bass unfortunately leaves unexcavated vital aspects of nineteenth-century humanitarian intervention in their manifold relations to the emerging concept of humanitarianism, the development of international law, and the assumptions of colonialism and imperialism.

Like Bass, the historian Davide Rodogno focuses in his book *Against Massacre: Humanitarian Interventions in the Ottoman Empire 1815–1914*[43] on the various cases in which the Great Powers intervened

[41] Gary Bass, *Freedom's Battle: The Origins of Humanitarian Intervention* (New York: Alfred A. Knopf, 2008). The articles of Davide Rodogno and Michael Marrus, published nearly at the same time as Bass's book, also focus on the history of humanitarian intervention. See, Davide Rodogno, 'Réflexions liminaires à propos des intervention humanitaires des Puissances européenes aux XIXe siècle', *Relations Internationales*, 131 (July–September 2007), 9–25; Michael R. Marrus, 'International Bystanders to the Holocaust and Humanitarian Intervention' in Richard Ashby Wilson and Richard D. Brown (eds.), *Humanitarianism and Suffering: The Mobilization of Empathy*, (Cambridge University Press, 2009), 156–74.

[42] Bass, *Freedom's Battle*, 360.

[43] Davide Rodogno, *Against Massacre: Humanitarian Interventions in the Ottoman Empire 1815–1914* (Princeton University Press, 2012).

in the Ottoman Empire during the nineteenth century, while adding the dimension of non-intervention. Rather than promote a political agenda and draw analogies to today's problem of humanitarian intervention, Rodogno clearly takes a genuine historical perspective. His approach becomes particularly evident by his reference to commonly used terms of the nineteenth century such as 'massacre', 'atrocity', and 'extermination', instead of using modern concepts such as human rights, genocide, or even ethnic cleansing.[44] The aim of this political, diplomatic history is to show the significant genealogical roots of the concept in the exclusive context of the manifold intertwined relations of the European powers to the Ottoman Empire. In doing so, Rodogno places the intervention issue in the larger matrix of the so-called Eastern Question and in relation to geostrategic, imperial factors. For him, nineteenth-century humanitarian intervention proved to be a selective practice used to protect exclusively Christian minorities and 'took place in a clearly defined geographical area of the globe – the Ottoman Empire.'[45] However, there remains the question about other interventions for protecting non-whites and non-Christians in various other regions of the world. For instance, how can the efforts to stop the transatlantic slave trade or to defend the rights of Jewish minorities throughout the nineteenth century be placed in this context? In their recently published volume, Bronwen Everill and Josiah Kaplan have compiled essays by historians and scholars of international relations on the practice of humanitarian intervention and aid. The geographical focus of the book shifts exclusively to the African continent, particularly to select cases in sub-Saharan Africa. Seeking to investigate the continuities and evolutions since the colonial era, Everill and Kaplan deliberately chose a rather broad conceptual approach, one that 'sees humanitarian military interventions as part of a series of related activities – or "interventions" – in African societies, which includes military action, economic aid, political support and state-building and assistance'.[46] However, by subsuming assistance for refugees, medical campaigns to combat leprosy, various forms of charity, famine relief, and discourses on good governance under the term of humanitarian intervention, the editors run the risk of blurring the term and losing

[44] Ibid., 4. [45] Ibid., 264.

[46] Bronwen Everill and Josiah Kaplan, 'Introduction: Enduring Humanitarianisms in Africa', in Bronwen Everill and Josiah Kaplan (eds.), *The History and Practice of Humanitarian Intervention and Aid in Africa* (Basingstoke and New York: Palgrave Macmillan, 2013), 3.

its conceptual precision. Both editors acknowledge the analytic importance of a long-term historical perspective, but nearly all of the chapters in the volume concentrate on case studies from the second half of the twentieth century.

In their book *Humanitarian Intervention: A History*, Brendan Simms and David Trim offer a broader, more comprehensive history of humanitarian intervention.[47] The edited volume, which consists almost solely of contributions by historians, presents for the very first time a long-term perspective covering the period from the sixteenth to the twentieth century. Besides European interventions in the Ottoman Empire and Africa, the editors incorporate non-European interventions and thus significantly extend the geographical scope of the book to a global dimension. They place their narrative mainly in the context of shifting geopolitical coordinates over four hundred years and seek to dismiss the 'Westphalian paradigm' of absolute territorial sovereignty. In their opinion, the volume confirms that 'the concept of Westphalia as originating a system of states whose sovereignty was absolute simply is not true'.[48] Accordingly, it was possible to merge geopolitical and humanitarian concerns to some extent, thereby creating the space in which humanitarian intervention could take place.

With respect to the methodological question of how far back the history of humanitarian intervention can be mapped out, both editors deliberately decided to include early modern precedents. For them, the early modern period constitutes a time of 'incubation', in which the notions of the common interest of 'Christendom' provided a crucial starting point for doctrines to evolve first during the Enlightenment and then during the nineteenth century into the ideas of today.[49] Accordingly, Simms and Trim argue: 'Precisely because of the frequency of such interventions, "human rights" emerged as a term and legal concept in the mid-nineteenth century and the term "humanitarian intervention" emerged in the late nineteenth century.'[50] At this point the *longue-durée* approach of the volume seems to be overstretched and far too linear,

[47] Brendan Simms and David J. B. Trim (eds.), *Humanitarian Intervention: A History* (Cambridge University Press, 2011).

[48] David J. B. Trim, 'Conclusion: Humanitarian Intervention in Historical Perspective' in ibid., 381.

[49] Brendan Simms and David J. B. Trim, 'Towards a History of Humanitarian Intervention' in ibid., 21.

[50] Ibid., 22.

especially with respect to the recent controversial debate among historians about the origins of the human rights concept and its relation to humanitarianism.[51] Historical precedents of humanitarian intervention indeed contributed significantly to the emergence of humanitarian norms in international law, but this was not tantamount to the rise of the human rights concept in a modern sense. For instance, prominent advocates of a legal doctrine of humanitarian intervention such as the Swiss legal scholar Johann Caspar Bluntschli and his German colleague Aegidius Arntz referred in their works to the protection of '*Menschenrechte*'[52] and '*droits de l'humanité*'[53] as a justifiable reason to interfere. However, without defining the content and nature of these aforementioned rights, they left the term completely vague and did not codify these rights, as was later realized in the Universal Declaration of Human Rights in 1948. Abolitionists could passionately fight against the transatlantic slave trade and demand military intervention against this violation of common sense humanity, but at the same time endorse the paternalistic concept of a mission to civilize the Africans without granting them equal rights.[54] For instance, William Wilberforce, one of the leading abolitionists, was recorded as expressing this view significantly in a parliamentary debate on the abolition of the slave trade in April 1791 with these words:

> The Negroes, he [Wilberforce] said, were creatures like ourselves: they had the same feelings, and even stronger affections than our own; but their minds were uninformed, and their moral characters were altogether debased. Men, in this state, were almost incapacitated for the reception of civil rights. In order to become fit for the enjoyment of these, they must, in some measures, be restored to that level from which they had been so unjustly and cruelly degraded. To give them power of appealing to the laws, would be to awaken in them a sense of the dignity of their nature. The first return of life after a swoon, was commonly a convulsion, dangerous, at once, to the party himself, and to all around him.

[51] For this recent debate on the origins of human rights, see: Hunt, *Inventing Human Rights*; Samuel Moyn, *The Last Utopia: Human Rights in History* (Cambridge, Mass. and London: Belknap Press, 2010), 11–43; Stefan-Ludwig Hoffmann, 'Introduction: Genealogies of Human Rights' in Stefan-Ludwig Hoffmann (ed.), *Human Rights in the Twentieth Century* (Cambridge University Press, 2011), 1–26.

[52] Johann Caspar Bluntschi, *Das moderne Völkerrecht der civilisierten Staten als Rechtsbuch dargestellt* (Nördlingen: C.H. Beck, 1872), 20, 265, 269.

[53] Gustave Rolin-Jaequemyns, 'Note sur la Théorie du Droit d'Intervention: À propos d'une lettre de M. le professeur Arntz', *Revue de Droit International et de Législation Comparée*, 8 (1876), 675.

[54] Vanessa Pupavac, 'Between Compassion and Conservatism: A Genealogy of Humanitarian Sensibility' in Fassin and Pandolfi, *Contemporary States of Emergency*, 129–49.

Such, in the case of the Slaves, Mr. Wilberforce feared might be the consequence of a sudden communication of civil rights.[55]

There are good reasons to argue that the history of humanitarian intervention is entangled with the emergence of humanitarianism and human rights in manifold ways. However, we have to be careful to avoid the random mixing-up of the different concepts, because the relationship between humanitarianism and human rights does indeed constitute a 'troubled rapport'.[56]

THREE CENTURIES OF HUMANITARIAN INTERVENTION: GUIDING RESEARCH THEMES AND OUTLINE OF THE BOOK

The timeframe of this book is set in the decisive formative period of the concept of humanitarian intervention and its development over the last three centuries. Despite our choice to start our study in the nineteenth century, we do not approach the European intervention in the Greek War of Independence as the prelude for the development of the idea of defending humanitarian norms by military force. Although there can be no doubt about the importance of the various European interventions in the Ottoman Empire, we do not focus here on these already well-studied cases. The book proposes another moment as the start of humanitarian intervention policy: rather than linking it exclusively to the protection of Christian minorities, we trace the origins of the concept to the milieu of the struggle against the transatlantic slave trade at the turn from the eighteenth to the nineteenth century. More than two decades before the European powers intervened for the first time in the Ottoman Empire, Great Britain sent Royal Navy squadrons to the West African coast to intercept slave ships. Their mission was to end coercively the trade in human beings, thus constituting a military campaign that lasted over sixty years and became the longest humanitarian intervention in history.[57] In this context the British government tried to gain the approval of other nations for an international ban of the slave trade, which was

[55] Wilberforce quote is found in the parliamentary debate of 18–19 April 1791 as recorded in Great Britain, Parliament, House of Commons (ed.), *The Debate on a Motion for the Abolition of the Slave – Trade, in the House of Commons on Monday and Tuesday, April 18 and 19, 1791* (London 1791), 37.

[56] See Michael Geyer, Chapter 2, in this book.

[57] Ch. D. Kaufmann and R. A. Pape, 'Explaining Costly International Moral Action: Britain's Sixty-Year Campaign against the Slave Trade', *International Organization*, 53 (Autumn 1999), 631–68.

achieved at the Congress of Vienna in 1815. As we argue, it was through the efforts to enforce this ban that an international moral consensus was created and a new practice of protecting humanitarian norms collectively was established in international politics. Furthermore, we identify a key transition in the nineteenth century: the departure from the early modern concept of protection on the grounds of religious affinity to the practice of defending humanitarian norms for all individuals regardless of their religious affiliation and on the basis of an evolving notion of a common humanity.

After illustrating the development of this new concept over the course of the nineteenth century as the genuine 'century of humanitarian intervention', the book seeks to build a bridge to experiences of 'enforcing humanity' in the twentieth and twenty-first centuries. In contrast to the vast majority of the existing literature, we deconstruct the notion of 'humanitarian intervention' as a pure phenomenon that only emerges successfully after the end of the Cold War. In seeking to investigate the long-term development, we analyse the concept against the backdrop of crucial historical epochs stretching from the ages of colonialism and imperialism via the interwar years in the first half of the twentieth century to the emerging East–West conflict after 1945. Finally, we pose the critical question whether the end of the Cold War in the 1990s really marks the beginning of a new era of humanitarian intervention and thereby incorporate very recent developments in international politics regarding the cases of Libya and Syria.

To cover four different geographical regions – namely Europe, America, Africa, and Asia – means that the book is methodologically oriented to the concept of transnational and global history. However, even though the historical approach clearly dominates this book, it is not exclusively grounded in the discipline of international history. Acknowledging the multidimensional character of the topic and emphasizing the enrichment of research from different perspectives, the book adopts a broad multidisciplinary approach. Scholars of international law, sociology, political science, and international history in the United States, Great Britain, Canada, Germany, and Switzerland provide, for the first time together, innovative insights into the concept of humanitarian intervention and thus strengthen an integrative approach to the theme.

With regard to the definition of humanitarian intervention, we basically adopt the aforementioned social-science proposal featuring the three key elements of transboundary interference in the domestic affairs of foreign state, predominant humanitarian purposes, and the coercive nature of the engagement.[58] For the purpose of broadly illustrating the idea of 'enforcing humanity' as well as mutual impacts, interactions, and tensions between various strategies, we include forms of coercive diplomacy rather than focus exclusively on direct military action. In addition, we keep in mind the specific historical circumstances in which direct military intervention was rejected. For instance, due to the exhaustion caused by the First World War, nations became utterly suspicious in the interwar period of any international military engagement on the behalf of suffering strangers. This then made it possible for other reactions to humanitarian crises to evolve significantly.[59]

To illustrate a history of humanitarian intervention over a time span of three centuries means that care must be taken in selecting the case studies to be presented. We have deliberately chosen episodes that represent decisive steps in the further development of the theory and practice of humanitarian intervention, episodes that have been often neglected by historical research so far. As mentioned earlier, we only briefly refer to already well-studied cases such as those in the Ottoman Empire. By choosing this approach, we seek to address the significant entanglement of various actors (e.g. humanitarian activists, politicians, and military personnel in a global perspective); of political, legal, military, civilian, and cultural relations; and of national, international, and transnational perspectives. It is also the book's aim to focus on the interdependence and conjunctures of humanitarian crises, international public opinion, and coercive intervention. Furthermore, by investigating the emergence of humanitarian intervention over three centuries, we aim to integrate the topic of enforcing humanitarian norms in two entangled and growing fields of research, namely the broader history of humanitarianism as well as the newer historiography of human rights. In contrast to the already existing literature on humanitarian intervention, this collection of work combines for the first time not only different geographical regions but also various historical epochs and academic disciplines in a single book.

The book combines a thematic with a chronological order and is arranged in five main sections. By discussing the theoretical approach and legal discourse on issues of sovereignty and humanitarian intervention (Part I) and the two major impulses for intervention, namely the battle against the slave trade and the protection of religious minorities (Part II), the book describes the nineteenth century as the decisive

[58] Holzgrefe, *Humanitarian Intervention Debate*, 18; Vincent, *Nonintervention*, 13.

[59] On this development, see especially Chapter 9 by Davide Rodogno in this book.

formative period for the idea of 'enforcing humanity'. In Chapter 2, Michael Geyer links the central issue of armed intervention to the major umbrella themes of humanitarianism and human rights and discusses the various related dilemmas. He suggests a historical baseline to assess, compare, and problematize contemporary definitions of humanitarian intervention without blurring concepts of human rights protection and humanitarianism. In his examination of current political definitions of humanitarian intervention, Geyer compares these with the historical lineage of forcible intervention in theory and practice, on the one hand, and the long tradition of humanitarianism and the protection of rights, on the other.

In Chapter 3, Daniel Marc Segesser discusses the tensions between the principle of state sovereignty and the idea of intervention on humanitarian grounds in the evolving body of nineteenth-century international law. His chapter focuses on the controversial discourse of legal scholars starting with the position taken by Henry Wheaton, as published in his influential work on the *Elements of International Law* in 1836. Segesser shows that the legal debate on how to react to major violations of humanitarian norms intensified once again in the context of the outbreak of massive violence in the Balkans in the second half of the nineteenth century. In the decades that followed, prominent legal scholars such as Johann Caspar Bluntschli, Gustave Rolin-Jaequemyns, and Aegidius Arntz advocated the concept of humanitarian intervention to end mass atrocities, thereby provoking the frank dissent of colleagues who spoke out in favour of the absolute protection of state sovereignty.

In Chapter 4, Stefan Kroll takes a close look at the problem of justifying international intervention in the period from the second half of the nineteenth to the beginning of the twentieth century. He argues that the interpretation of state sovereignty was never understood as absolute, neither in practice nor in theory. Furthermore, Kroll identifies a substantial shift in leading principles of international legal order. The idea of an international community as a new legal principle emerged and provided a benchmark to legitimate the collective action taken by the European powers for humanitarian causes. However, as Kroll shows in the case of the protection of Christian minorities and of the bogus defence of religious freedom, this emerging interventionist norm could also be abused to legitimate practices of cultural hegemony and imperial expansion.

In Part II, the major impulses for humanitarian intervention in the long nineteenth century – namely the fight against the slave trade and the protection of religious minorities – are discussed and compared against the backdrop of emerging colonialism and imperialism. In my own Chapter 5, I emphasize the close entanglement of civil society action, humanitarian norm-setting, and military intervention. The Congress of Vienna in 1815 and its Declaration for the Abolition of the Slave Trade is regarded as the central starting point for the concept of protecting a humanitarian norm coercively. By referring explicitly to the evolving 'humanitarian narrative', British abolitionists successfully mobilized national as well as international public opinion and thus greatly influenced the decision made in the Austrian capital to declare an international ban of the slave trade by all European powers. Furthermore, I argue that the significant interaction between civil society and international politics made it possible for the new practice of enforcing humanitarian norms by military means to finally become established in the aftermath of the Vienna summit. In this respect, the various cases of intervention by the Great Powers of Europe to protect Christian minorities in the Ottoman Empire did not mark, in and of themselves, the first practical implementation of the idea of humanitarian intervention.

In Chapter 6, Mairi MacDonald addresses the moral hazards of humanitarian intervention by taking a close look at the supposedly pretended last great step to complete the century-long campaign against the slave trade. On the pretext of humanitarianism, the Brussels General Act Relative to the African Slave Trade of July 1890 justified the military conquest of the interior of Africa and proclaimed colonial rule as the best way to accomplish the declared objective of protecting the aboriginal populations from slavery. Focusing on the prime movers of the conference, the United Kingdom and Belgium, this chapter explores the close link between coercive humanitarianism and the colonial projects of the European powers. As MacDonald argues, the humanitarian goals of eliminating the slave trade by 'civilizing' the interior of Africa provided the best cover for colonial conquest and exploitation. She raises the question of whether military intervention, as justified on the grounds of humanitarianism, establishes a contradiction in itself, if not an actual invitation to abuse.

In Chapter 7, Abigail Green deals with the second major impulse for humanitarian intervention in the nineteenth century, namely the protection of religious minorities. By exploring responses of coercive diplomacy to the Jewish question, especially to Jewish minority rights in Morocco and Romania during the 1860s and 1870s with reference to the Congress of Berlin (1878) and the Conference of Madrid (1880), she describes the key transition from the concept of protection on the grounds of religious affinity in early modern times to nineteenth-century practices of humanitarian intervention. According to Green, the experience of Jewish activists to promote civil and religious liberty in Romania and Morocco suggests that interference through coercive diplomacy was primarily a product of the international system, with religious affinity only a secondary factor. Thus her argument challenges articulated assumptions about humanitarian intervention in the nineteenth century as being essentially directed by Christian powers against the Muslim Ottoman Empire for the sole purpose of aiding Christian minorities.

In Part III, the book seeks to bring together the experiences of 'enforcing humanity' over the course of two centuries. Jon Western pursues this objective in Chapter 8 by comparing nineteenth-century public attitudes and concepts of humanitarianism in light of mass atrocities to the public attitudes concerning similar phenomenon in the twentieth century. Examining the different cases of international response to the Greek War of Independence in the 1820s, the intervention of the United States in Cuba in 1898, and the response of the US government to the Bosnian war from 1992 to 1995, Western analyses the complex mutual impacts of public opinion and foreign policy decision-making. In particular, he asks why the public was outraged in some instances of mass atrocity and not in others, what role media reports and elite cues played in influencing public attitudes about mass atrocities, and to what extent public attitudes have influenced state behaviour across time and place.

Actually, the first half of the twentieth century seemed to experience a complete halt in the further development of the concept of humanitarian intervention. Due to the heavy toll that the First World War took on Europe – socially, economically, and politically – nations became very wary of any proposed international military engagement on the behalf of peoples in far-off lands. For this reason, the interwar period is described as the 'eclipse of humanitarian intervention'.[60] Nevertheless, the reluctance of governments to interfere directly and militarily left the door open for the development of other types of reaction to humanitarian crisis. Thus Davide Rodogno focuses in Chapter 9 on the activities of the Near East Relief (NER) organization and its humanitarian politics on the fringes of the newly independent Turkish state in aftermath of the First World War. The chapter, based on archival sources often overlooked by historians, describes how this organization intended to relieve and

[60] Marrus, 'International Bystanders', 164–8.

rehabilitate the victims of 'crimes against humanity', specifically the ex-Ottoman Armenian civilians scattered in what would become Soviet Armenia, Syria and Lebanon (under French mandate), and Greece. The chapter highlights the ambitions and inconsistencies of various NER projects; it critically examines the paternalistic and quasi-colonial posture of the NER relief workers and leaders. Rodogno concludes by explaining the way in which NER activities prefigured international development politics and practices undertaken by the UN Relief and Rehabilitation Administration (UNRRA) and other UN agencies in the aftermath of the Second World War.

The interwar period not only yielded new forms of intervention but also new risks of abuse. In Chapter 10, Jost Dülffer addresses the dark sides of humanitarian intervention on the eve of the outbreak of the Second World War. His analysis focuses on the abuse of the concept of interfering for humanitarian purposes and its potential of being instrumentalized for an aggressive foreign policy. Dülffer argues that Nazi Germany used the rhetoric of the protection of German minorities to legitimate the assaults on the sovereignty of Austria, Czechoslovakia, and Poland in the period between 1937 and 1939. Although the National Socialist goal to return the German populations scattered throughout these neighbouring countries to the fold of the Greater German Empire were driven purely by racist, economic, and military strategic reasons, the argument that Germans were being suppressed beyond the borders of the Reich served as a dangerous diplomatic weapon that paved the way to military aggression. Thus, the concept of armed intervention for humanitarian purposes was significantly discredited and rejected as a useful diplomatic tool after the Second World War. As previously mentioned, the German case also compelled prominent legal scholars such as Ian Brownlie to dismiss utterly the validity of the whole concept of humanitarian intervention even as late as the 1960s.[61]

In order to break up existing caesuras, we scrutinize whether the Cold War era really meant the complete absence of humanitarian interventionist practice (Part IV). In the recent debate on humanitarian intervention, the East–West confrontation is mainly regarded as a stalemate, in which military interventions in the name of humanity were rather limited, if not completely impossible. By taking a close look at the role of the UN and its peacekeeping missions during the Cold War period, we challenge this

[61] Brownlie, *International Law*, 340.

notion and present instead a more multifaceted picture. In Chapter 11, Norrie MacQueen first looks back to the often-neglected pre-UN origins of international peacekeeping during the interwar period and the related role of the League of Nations. He explicitly connects this history with the evolution of the peacekeeping concept within the UN system in the 1950s under UN Secretary-General Dag Hammarskjöld. Focusing on the significant UN interventions in the Congo (1960–4) and in West New Guinea (1962–3) MacQueen explores the further development of the UN peacekeeping model against the backdrop of humanitarian intervention without neglecting to address the contradictions and tensions between the concepts.

Jan Erik Schulte picks up this theme in Chapter 12 and affirms the need to include the issue of UN peacekeeping in the broader context of the history of humanitarian intervention. He argues that UN operations during the East–West confrontation displayed various crucial elements believed to be constitutive ones for the concept of interfering for humanitarian purposes after 1989/90. Schulte explicitly refers to UN interventions during the Cold War as major preconditions for the genesis of the concept and the practice of humanitarian intervention. While linking Cold War experiences with developments of the post-Cold War era, he also illustrates that the changes in UN peacekeeping and the development of the rather multidimensional missions of the 1990s were gradual. Thus his analysis includes the prominent and controversial cases of UN involvement, starting in 1992, in Somalia and the former Yugoslavia and the far-reaching consequences.

In Part V, we finally ask whether the end of the Cold War does indeed mark the often-proclaimed starting point for a 'new century of humanitarian intervention' and thus leads directly to the concept of the 'responsibility to protect' in the twenty-first century. Bradley Simpson examines this alleged new interventionist attitude with regard to the international intervention in East Timor in 1999, which is considered a paradigmatic case in humanitarian intervention due to its timing (in the aftermath of the NATO intervention in Kosovo) and to the humanitarian justifications evoked by international politicians. In Chapter 13, Simpson challenges this notion and argues that most countries, including Australia and the United States, were motivated more by the fear that the devastation of East Timor might fatally undermine both Indonesian political stability and the credibility of the UN rather than by a newly evolving humanitarian sensibility. According to Simpson, the lessons that East Timor holds for both the history and future of humanitarian intervention are therefore much more sobering and limited than the humanitarian rhetoric surrounding the case study would suggest.

Manuel Fröhlich discusses the most recent case of military intervention in the name of human rights. In Chapter 14, Fröhlich examines the recent concept of R2P in the light of an attempt in the twenty-first century to reframe and reform the concept of what hitherto has been termed 'humanitarian intervention'. He investigates the origin of R2P and looks at the transformation process of the concept from its publication in 2001 to its first implementation in 2011. The case of Libya is looked at closely since it was the first time that the use of military intervention was justified by the argument of an international responsibility to react. Fröhlich examines the way the concept of responsibility evolved before, during, and after the military intervention. His conclusion offers important findings on the state of affairs of R2P and the possibility and rationale of normative change regarding the use of force and the protection of populations by the international community.

In the final chapter, Chapter 15, Andrew Thompson reflects on the main themes that emerge from this book. In doing so, he also describes how an examination of the past helps us better understand both current and future humanitarianism. Thompson presents lines of enquiry that are essential if we are to link the experiences of three centuries of 'enforcing humanity' and the relationship between humanitarian intervention and connected discourses. At the beginning he explores the various meanings of what role humanitarians played and play in relation to the course of history, the often unclear and vast areas of their engagement, and their entanglement with other discourses, in particular the debates on human rights. Furthermore, Thompson underscores how important it is to delineate genealogies and to agree upon major episodes concerning intervention in the 'cause of humanity'. He investigates the troubled relationship between power, paternalism, and humanitarianism, and emphasizes the need to investigate carefully various models for justifying intervention and the groups defining them. At the same time, he argues, it is imperative to pay attention to the logic of humanitarian legitimacy, which appears to have been far more selective and bound to 'geographies' or 'ethnographies' of care.

PART I

THEORETICAL APPROACH AND LEGAL DISCOURSE ON THE CONCEPT OF HUMANITARIAN INTERVENTION

2

Humanitarianism and human rights

A troubled rapport

Michael Geyer

In his Millennium Report to the UN in 2000, '*We the Peoples': The Role of the United Nations in the 21st Century*, Kofi Annan, the then Secretary-General of the UN, asked emphatically: 'If humanitarian intervention is, indeed, an unacceptable assault on sovereignty, how should we respond to ... gross and systematic violations of human rights that offend every precept of humanity?' He conceded that '[w]e confront a real dilemma. Few would disagree that both the defence of humanity and the defence of sovereignty are principles that must be supported.' But he weighed in unequivocally that 'surely no legal principle – not even sovereignty – can ever shield crimes against humanity ... Armed intervention must always remain an option of last resort, but in the face of mass murder it is an option that cannot be relinquished.'[1] Humanitarian crises, Annan argued, are the result of grievous human rights violations and, because of this underlying connection, justify forcible intervention. While the relief of human suffering is a humanitarian imperative, it is the grievous violation of rights that legitimates force. The causal link between humanitarian intervention and human rights violations is the foundation of Annan's justification of humanitarian intervention.

The link between human rights and humanitarianism or, more to the point, humanitarian intervention, is rarely put this unambiguously. More

[1] Kofi A. Annan, *We the Peoples: The Role of the United Nations in the 21st Century* (New York: United Nations, Dept. of Public Information, 2000), 48. Taken from www.un.org/millennium/sg/report/full.htm (last accessed on 11 November 2012). The report is no longer accessible on this website but can be found on www.un.org/en/events/pastevents/pdfs/We_The_Peoples.pdf (last accessed on 10 June 2014).

commonly, the language of humanitarian intervention invokes both moral sentiment and rights interchangeably and conflates morality and politics.[2] Many historians assume the equivalency of the two terms, human rights and humanitarianism.[3] Alternately, they agree with Sam Moyn that humanitarianism is an old phenomenon, whereas the phenomenon of human rights is a recent one.[4] So why should we bother to sort things out? Wouldn't it be enough to argue that the protection of populations from genocide, crimes against humanity, and war crimes is part and parcel of a humanitarian complex – 'a mode of governing that concerns the victims of poverty, homelessness, unemployment, and exile, as well as disasters, famines, epidemics, and wars' – which 'has become a potent force of our world'?[5] In fact, this complex has a surprisingly deep history and deserves a full historical exploration, because it allows us to explore the conceptual architecture of human rights and humanitarianism.

This chapter will argue that the difference between humanitarianism and human rights matters, for the relationship between the two, as I will demonstrate, is a troubled one. It is not just that the former reflects a sentiment of compassion and expects acts of solidarity, whereas the latter presupposes global norms either as customary law or as codified in international law. The trouble rather lies with the quintessential question of all politics of violence: Who decides the exception? The stakes of the answer to this question are, as Carl Schmitt put it, that '[n]o form of order, no reasonable legitimacy or legality can exist without protection and obedience. The *protego ergo obligo* is the *cogito ergo sum* of the state'[6]: I protect and thus obligate the protected.

[2] Stefan-Ludwig Hoffman, *Moralpolitik: Geschichte der Menschenrechte im 20. Jahrhundert*, Geschichte der Gegenwart (Göttingen: Wallstein, 2010). The American edition is more circumspect: Stefan-Ludwig Hoffmann, (ed.), *Human Rights in the Twentieth Century: A Critical History* (Cambridge University Press, 2011). See also Jan Eckel and Samuel Moyn (eds.), *Moral für die Welt? Menschenrechtspolitik in den 1970er Jahren*, Schriftenreihe der FRIAS School of History (Göttingen: Vandenhoeck & Ruprecht, 2012).

[3] Lynn Hunt, *Inventing Human Rights: A History* (New York and London: W.W. Norton, 2007).

[4] Samuel Moyn, 'Empathy in History, Empathizing with Humanity', *History & Theory*, 45, no. 3 (2006), 397–415; Samuel Moyn, 'Human Rights and "Neoloberalism"', http://imperialglobalexeter.files.wordpress.com/2013/12/samuel-moyn.gif (last accessed 2 February 2014) and originally on the hhr-blog http://hhr.hypotheses.org/215 (last accessed 18 May 2015).

[5] Didier Fassin, *Humanitarian Reason: A Moral History of the Present* (Berkeley: University of California Press, 2012), X, XI.

[6] Carl Schmitt, *The Concept of the Political*, trans. Georg Schwab (University of Chicago Press, 1996), 52. To complicate matters, Schmitt also argues that 'humanity as such cannot

The question is, therefore, who has 'the authority to decide'?[7] In carefully calibrating the relationship between human rights and humanitarianism, Annan found a solution to the problem that would have displeased Schmitt profoundly. He turned the tables by obligating or, in any case, trying to obligate the protector rather than the one who is protected. His means to the end was human rights. The difference between humanitarianism and human rights lies in the answer to the question whether states can be obligated to protect or whether they obligate the protected. This is not the end of the problems with humanitarian intervention, but it is a starting point for solving Annan's dilemma.[8]

Schmitt's question and Annan's answer also help to clarify some rather curious paradoxes that have arisen in recent historiography. The latter establishes mainly three things beyond reasonable doubt.[9] First, there is a long and well-established theory, as well as practice, of forcible intervention, notwithstanding the concurrent development of the principle of non-intervention that would seem to obviate the very act.[10] Second, there is indubitably a deep history of humanitarian intervention, but both the thought and practice of intervention happen in the absence (and, indeed, the studied rejection) of the name of 'humanitarian intervention'.[11] Third, recent research also establishes an elusive lineage of initiatives that use the language of obligation (rather than of rights) – and this, on the one hand, in a world of (human) rights and, on the other, in an 'anarchical society' of states that may acknowledge rights but does not know obligations.[12]

wage war' (54) and that a world state would, by necessity, be 'based exclusively on economics and on technically regulating traffic' and thus resemble more a 'social entity of tenants in a tenement house' (57).

7 Ibid., 47. Surprisingly, theorists of humanitarian intervention are rather more concerned with establishing the fact of exception than thinking through its political effect. Didier Fassin and Mariella Pandolfi (eds.), *Contemporary States of Emergency: The Politics of Military and Humanitarian Interventions* (New York and Cambridge, MA: Zone Books, 2010).

8 Nicholas J. Wheeler, *Saving Strangers: Humanitarian Intervention in International Society* (Oxford University Press, 2000), 299.

9 Andrew C. Thompson, 'The Protestant Interest and the History of Humanitarian Intervention, c.1685 – c.1756' in Brendan Simms and D. J. B. Trim (eds.), *Humanitarian Intervention: A History* (Cambridge University Press, 2011), 67–88.

10 R. J. Vincent, *Nonintervention and International Order* (Princeton University Press, 1974).

11 Thompson, 'The Protestant Interest'.

12 Hedley Bull, *The Anarchical Society: A Study of Order in World Politics* (New York: Columbia University Press, 1977).

In this context, the most bothersome issue for historians is the remarkably discontinuous nature of the construct of humanitarian intervention. It's not simply that the theory and practice of humanitarian interventions are highly discontinuous, that theory and practice move at different speeds and often asynchronously, and that the notions and words that capture the phenomenon change repeatedly. There is also much more talk than practice, but even talk is not consistent over time; every humanitarian moment creates its own history. In short, the past of humanitarianism and human rights is oddly fragmentary and conditional and resists a continuous narrative.[13] It is tempting to disregard the disjointed nature of the humanitarian complex and create a continuous narrative.[14] Alternatively, we might reduce the variety to a single epistemology.[15] The altogether better solution consists in using the paradox of the fragmentary and conditional nature of humanitarian interventions (and of humanitarianism and human rights in general), on the one hand, and the persistence of such initiatives over a very long time, on the other, in order to reconstruct what one author calls the 'architecture of concepts'.[16] This refers to ways of thinking or 'labels' that help us process the sporadic nature of humanitarian interventions and the torturous process of getting from thought to practice and back and of labelling the present in the light of the past. One of these 'labels' – and this is not at all meant to diminish his status – is 'Hugo Grotius'. A certain architecture of humanitarian intervention, that is, the human-rights-oriented architecture, will reliably produce Grotius as a way of thinking, although the 'historical' Grotius is only remotely linked to the 'concept'.

Political scientists will be troubled by the persistence of forcible (humanitarian) intervention despite the presumptive rise of non-intervention as a condition for the sovereignty of the nation state. The much-debated 'Westphalian Model' has not kept states from intervening

[13] Kenneth Cmiel, 'The Recent History of Human Rights', *American Historical Review*, 109, no. 1 (2004), 117–35.

[14] D. J. B. Trim, 'Humanitarian Intervention in Historical Perspective' in Brendan Simms and D. J. B. Trim (eds.), *Humanitarian Intervention: A History* (Cambridge University Press, 2011), 381–401.

[15] R. J. Vincent and Peter Wilson, 'Beyond Non-Intervention?' in Ian Forbes and Mark Hoffman (eds.), *Political Theory, International Relations, and the Ethics of Intervention* (New York: St. Martin's Press in association with the Mountbatten Centre for International Studies, University of Southampton, 1993), 122–30.

[16] Peter De Bolla, *The Architecture of Concepts: The Historical Formation of Human Rights* (New York: Fordham University Press, 2013).

in each other's affairs.[17] To be sure, humanitarian intervention has been an intermittent, yet recurring state practice, but the recourse to the idea of 'organized hypocrisy' or some such subterfuge is not a convincing way of interpreting the phenomenon.[18] While it is a fiction that 'in the Westphalian order both state sovereignty and the rule of non-intervention are treated as absolute norms', the 'reality' is not simply made up of less sovereignty and more intervention.[19] Rather, in a world of sovereign states, humanitarian interventions are the 'exception' – and for that very reason they are so very carefully defined. The 'authority to decide' is just too important to leave to the profession of moral standards or beliefs to which one's own behaviour does not conform. While an intermittent feature of state practice, humanitarian interventions are a constitutive feature of the modern world of states. There is so much talk about humanitarian intervention because defining the phenomenon decides who protects, who obliges, and who is obligated. Interventions establish (international) order. *Protego ergo obligo.*

THE CARE OF HUMAN SOCIETY

The first foray into the conceptual architecture of 'humanitarian intervention' takes us back well before the moment when we confidently can speak of 'humanitarianism' or 'humanitarian intervention' without either obfuscating the instructive particularity of the early-modern example or diluting the force that these terms eventually capture in the late nineteenth century and again in the late twentieth century.[20] We take our cue from Charles Owen, Presbyterian minister and political dissenter, and his *Alarm to protestant princes and people* ... (1725), which puts forth a voluble case for intervention to defend a population against oppression and tyrannical rule. 'Kings', he argues, 'besides the care of their own kingdom, have lying upon them the Care of human society. Hence it is, that the Powers of the Earth enter into Alliances and Leagues to guard Men against the Oppression of their own Governours and others.'[21]

17 Trim, 'Humanitarian Intervention in Historical Perspective'.

18 Stephen D. Krasner, *Sovereignty: Organized Hypocrisy* (Princeton University Press, 1999).

19 Aidan Hehir, 'Intervention: From Theories to Cases', *Ethics and International Affairs*, 9 (1995), 1–14, here 6.

20 A contrasting view: Brendan Simms and D. J. B. Trim (eds.), *Humanitarian Intervention: A History* (Cambridge University Press, 2011).

21 Thompson, 'The Protestant Interest', 67–88, here 67.

In actual fact, Owen is pleading for the support of Protestant co-religionists, who had come under attack in the city of Thorn in the Polish-Lithuanian Commonwealth.[22] It is a bit of a publicity stunt, because the rights of Protestants and Catholics in their respective areas of settlement had been acknowledged in the Treaty of Oliva (1660) and were guaranteed by the signatories, most prominently Prussia and Sweden. The crisis was resolved without intervention. Still, the plea for intervention is of interest, because it demonstrates that specific cases – an intervention to quell anti-Protestant riots in Thorn – were framed in the very general language of legitimacy of rule, which not everyone agreed with but everyone understood. It also makes clear that protection against arbitrary and violent rule was a commonly understood element of the early-modern negotiation of the limits of (absolute) sovereignty. Owen's rhetoric is alarming and inflammatory, and his solutions (retaliatory measures such as the removal of Catholics from Protestant countries) may raise eyebrows, but it is the conceptual language of the 'care for human society' that concerns us here.

Among Owen's references is Hugo Grotius, whose magisterial work *De jure belli ac pacis* sets the standards for much of the debate in his time on war and peace, in general, and on 'war ... undertaken on the Account of others', in particular.[23] Grotius, of course, is only one name among many on a by now well-established and oft-repeated list of contributors to a lively debate, and some would say he was an extravagant compiler of the extant knowledge of the time. He definitely needs to be seen in context, even if this context cannot be provided here.[24] It is rather more relevant

[22] Heinz Duchhardt, *Altes Reich und europäische Staatenwelt, 1648–1806*, Enzyklopädie deutscher Geschichte (Munich: R. Oldenbourg, 1990); Malcolm D. Evans, *Religious Liberty and International Law in Europe*, Cambridge Studies in International and Comparative Law, vol. 6 (Cambridge University Press, 1997).

[23] Hugo Grotius, *The Rights of War and Peace, edited and with an Introduction by Richard Tuck*, 3 vols. (Indianapolis, IN: Liberty Fund, 2005).

[24] Richard Tuck, *The Rights of War and Peace: Political Thought and the International Order from Grotius to Kant* (Oxford University Press, 1999); Richard Tuck, 'Grotius, Hobbes, and Pufendorf on Humanitarian Intervention' in Stefano Recchia and Jennifer M. Welsh (eds.), *Just and Unjust Military Intervention: European Thinkers from Vitoria to Mill* (Cambridge University Press, 2013), 96–112. About extravagance, see Hersch Lauterpacht, 'The Grotian Tradition in International Law', *British Yearbook of International Law*, 23 (1946), 1–53. Grotius is an intriguingly selective digest of preceding knowledge; see Knud Haakonssen, 'Hugo Grotius and the History of Political Thought', *Political Theory*, 13, no. 2 (1985), 239–65. The best scholarly introduction is Benedict Kingsbury, 'Introduction: Grotian Thought in International Relations' in Hedley Bull, Benedict Kingsbury, and Adam Roberts (eds.), *Hugo Grotius and International Relations* (Oxford University Press, 1990). With special reference to 'War in Behalf of Others', see

that his writing in *De jure belli ac pacis* took on emblematical value; it quickly became the authority that buttressed a certain kind of conceptual architecture, which was modified and adumbrated in changing political contexts. On the matter of intervention, Grotius had rather less to say than many of his predecessors. He approached the issue twice in *De jure belli ac pacis*, in a shortish chapter on war 'undertaken on the Account of others', which he squeezed in toward the end of Book II after a tone-setting chapter on 'Exhortations not rashly to engage in a War' and again in an earlier, rather longish, and at first sight surprising chapter, 'Of Punishment'. In the rush to talk about humanitarian intervention, historians of the subject do not always clearly separate the two modes of intervention although they deal with two different actions.

Like many before him and after, Grotius averred that making war is predicated on an inherent right to self-defence.[25] That is, war is just because it is conducted in self-defence. The latter complicates the reasoning about intervention, because coming to the help of a neighbour is not strictly speaking self-defence. Nonetheless, it is permissible and indeed laudable. As he boldly proclaims at the outset, 'every Man is authorized to maintain, not only his own Right, but also that of another Person'. You help your own first and then your allies, but you may also help others, if you can, 'upon the score of friendship' and due to 'that Relation that all Mankind stand in to each other'.[26] Still, caution prevails, he explains, because '[w]ar ... is so horrible, that nothing but mere Necessity, or true Charity, can make it lawful'.[27] Intervention is an act of exceptional necessity - or charity. 'It is another question', as Grotius delicately put it, whether this principle includes '[w]ar with another Prince, in order to relieve his Subjects from their Oppression under him'.[28] This was a much-debated and mostly negated question in Protestant circles, which Grotius answers in the affirmative. ('I may make War upon a Man, tho'he and I are of different Nations, if he disturbs and molests his own country.')[29] This argument was vigorously disputed by his learned contemporaries and successors, such as Pufendorf, Wolff, and Vattel.[30] Grotius

Paul A. Neuland, 'Traditional Doctrine on Intervention in the Law of Nations', unpublished PhD thesis, Georgetown University (1972), 53–61.

25 Tuck, *Rights of War and Peace.*

26 Grotius, *Rights of War and Peace,* [Book] II, [chapter] 25, [section] 1, §1.

27 Ibid., II, 25, 9, §3. 28 Ibid., II, 25, 8, §1. 29 Ibid., II, 25, 8, §3 & 4.

30 Richard Devetak, 'Between Kant and Pufendorf: Humanitarian Intervention, Statist Anti-Cosmopolitanism and Critical International Theory', *Review of International Studies*, 33, Supplement S1 (2007), 151–74; Jennifer Pitts, 'Intervention and Sovereign Equality: Legacies of Vattel' in Stefano Recchia and Jennifer M. Welsh (eds.), *Just and Unjust*

was circumspect. He insisted that the sovereignty of princes is absolute vis-à-vis their own subjects; in other words, he strenuously opposed the right of subjects to resist unjust rule.[31] However, he insisted that sovereigns are not absolute in relation to each other. '[I]f the Injustice be visible ... Tyrannies over Subjects, as no good Man living can approve of, the Right of human Society shall not be ... excluded.'[32] What binds sovereigns is the society of sovereigns and its principle of *protego* – 'guardianship' – that legitimates them as rulers.[33] Belligerent guardianship is therefore an integral aspect of sovereign rule. This is so because sovereigns act within an international society of sovereigns, whose interests and common values and, above all, whose legitimating rationale for sovereignty bind them.

By contrast, the section on punishment and, in this context, on war for the purpose of 'inflicting Punishment' is both extensive and abrasive.[34] Grotius declares that the right of sovereigns ('Kings') 'to exact Punishment' knows no borders if 'grievous Violations of the Law of Nature or Nations' are at issue.[35] Indeed, it is the mark of true sovereigns – being subject to no one – to dispense justice; they may also 'exact Punishment' on behalf of strangers.[36] At first, this looks like a case for a roving regime of universal justice, not least because Grotius, like his predecessors, invokes Hercules, who has 'freed the Earth of ... Tyrants ... unjust Men, and insolent Princes' (he adds: 'not with an ambitious Design of gaining them for himself') and is praised for 'the general Care he took of Mankind'.[37] However, Grotius took his argument in a quite unexpected direction (at least for us moderns). Herculean wars were wars against '[e]very Thing that was monstrous and wicked'; they were 'justly undertaken against those who are inhuman'.[38] Grotius singles out patricide, cannibalism, human sacrifice, and piracy, because 'so great a Depravity of Mind has cut [the perpetrator] off from Human Society and makes him to me, and all the World, a Foe'.[39] He turns universal jurisdiction literally into the hunt for inhuman 'Man': '[T]he justest War is that which is

Military Intervention: European Thinkers from Vitoria to Mill (Cambridge University Press, 2013), 132–53. Vattel's main point is that, if the injury to subjects is major and if the injury affects all subjects, the latter are effectively released into a lawless state of nature; and this is what sovereign rule cannot tolerate. Grotius, *Rights of War and Peace*, II, 25, 8, §2, n. 9.

31 Grotius, *Rights of War and Peace*, I, 4, §11.

32 Ibid., II, 25, 8, §2.

33 On guardianship: Ibid., II, 25, 8, §3.

34 Ibid., II, 20, 38.

35 Ibid., II, 20, 40, §1.

36 Ibid., II, 20, 40 §1.

37 Ibid., II, 20, 40, §2.

38 Ibid., II, 20, 40, §3. Grotius quotes Valerius Maximus. Punishing strangers may indeed be preferable over punishing one's own subjects, because it allows for more judicious action.

39 Ibid., II, 20, 40, §3. Grotius quotes Seneca.

undertaken against wild rapacious Beasts, and next to it is that against Men who are like Beasts.'[40] The care for humanity is distinctly the punishment of the wicked and monstrous, 'the Unjust', who have put themselves beyond human society.

The chapter ends on yet another unexpected note. Grotius's determination to deliver Beastly Men to justice is the mere inverse of his rejection of civic difference and religious division – any kind of religious dissent and division, including divisions between Christians and non-Christians – as reasons for punitive wars.[41] Inasmuch as universal justice can be imagined, it rests in God and, more so, the fear of God – any God. Hence, the 'Corruption of Religion is an Injury to all the World'. The chapter on war as punishment concludes with a ringing endorsement of Plato, 'when he is for inflicting Death upon all who despise Religion'.[42] The threat of death to non-believers is directed against no one in particular, but for that very reason potentially against everyone. The problem, however, is universal justice, for 'in the universal Society of Mankind, the Execution of Right is very difficult, as being to be performed [in the absence of civil institutions] no other Way than by the Use of Arms'.[43] For Gropius, the universal society of mankind is the only 'anarchical society' there is. In this kind of society, justice is necessarily violent.

In effect, Grotius constructs two worlds.[44] The first is a world of conditional sovereignty in an international society of sovereigns. Might is balanced by legitimacy, and the latter is articulated in the adherence to the *ius gentium*, above all the laws of war. This society of mutually obligated sovereigns comes as a surprise, if we believe in the idea of a 'Westphalian Model', in which sovereign power trumps a regime of shared customs and laws.[45] The second is a much harsher, anarchic world, which is typically projected beyond Europe but may also emerge within it. It is in this world that punitive intercessions enforce the rights of the 'universal Society of Mankind' – waging wars to ascertain norms and values against those rulers whose heinous actions do not simply violate

[40] Ibid., I, 4, §3 echoes with II, 25, 8, where the phrase *ius humanae societatis* appears. As in section 20, it is not 'the others' that matter, but the crimes committed (which in this case are the sacrifice of strangers, infanticide and cannibalism, and feeding human flesh to horses).

[41] Ibid., II, 20, 44 and 45. [42] Ibid., II, 20, 51, §2. [43] Ibid., II, 20, 44, §6.

[44] Kingsbury, 'Introduction: Grotian Thought'.

[45] The exemplary formulation of this position is by Leo Gross, 'The Peace of Westfalia, 1648–1948', *American Journal of International Law*, 42, no. 1 (1948), 20–41. For a critical view, see, for example, Heinz Duchhardt, ''Westphalian System': Zur Problematik einer Denkfigur', *Historische Zeitschrift*, 269, no. 2 (October 1999), 305–15.

but obviate them. Grotius's suggested solution for these grievous violations haunts forcible interventions throughout early modern and modern history. Punitive intercession is predicated on the inhumanity of rulers, and indeed peoples, as the cause of intercession. Its goal is to punish and expurgate. This is the opposite of what might reasonably be considered a human rights intervention, which at the very least would act in anticipation of a cosmopolitan legal order.[46] Still, the concept of punitive intervention is worth holding onto, because it will reappear in various guises all the way into the present. Grotius distinguishes these punitive interventions from wars on account of others, though grievous violations are at stake in both cases and the examples oddly overlap.[47] The latter essentially establish the conditions for intervention in a society of shared norms or, more specifically, meta-norms that underwrite the principle of sovereignty; and yet, Grotius's impeccable logic for what we might call 'humanitarian intervention' remains difficult to understand.[48] It is because of his deference to sovereign power that he argued for the possibility of intervention (though ultimately the act remains voluntary), for the violation of sovereign obligations (that is, to protect) violates all sovereigns. Sovereignty obligates sovereigns in relation to each other, because the violation of the principle of sovereignty affects all. They have in common the *ius gentium* as explicit reference points and the (natural) laws of the 'universal society of Mankind' as implicit ones.[49]

The element of an obligated, entangled, or embedded sovereignty has attracted considerable attention among scholars both of the Westphalian Peace and of early modern 'humanitarian intervention'.[50] They reject unequivocally the idea of a 'Westphalian Model' as modern-day fiction.[51]

46 Jürgen Habermas, 'Bestiality and Humanity: A War on the Border between Legality and Morality', *Constellations*, 6, no. 3 (1999), 263–72, here 69.

47 Grotius, *Rights of War and Peace*, II, 40, 3 and II, 25, 8.

48 R. J. Vincent, 'Grotius, Human Rights, and Intervention' in Hedley Bull, Benedict Kingsbury, and Adam Roberts (eds.), *Hugo Grotius and International Relations* (Oxford University Press, 1990), 241–55.

49 However, this commonality must be balanced against the difference between legal philosophy and political thought. Arnaud Blin, *1648, la paix de Westphalie ou la naissance de l'Europe politique moderne*, Questions à l'histoire (Brussels: Complexe, 2006), 51–77.

50 Andreas Osiander, *The States System of Europe, 1640–1990: Peacemaking and the Conditions of International Stability* (Oxford University Press, 1994); Simms and Trim, *Humanitarian Intervention: A History*; Stefano Recchia and Jennifer M. Welsh (eds.) *Just and Unjust Military Intervention: European Thinkers from Vitoria to Mill* (Cambridge University Press, 2013); Luke Glanville, 'The Antecedents of "Sovereignty as Responsibility"', *European Journal of International Relations*, 17, no. 2 (2011), 233–55.

51 Andreas Osiander, 'Sovereignty, International Relations, and the Westphalian Myth', *International Organization*, 55, no. 2 (2001), 251–87.

Rather than establishing the principle of sovereignty and non-intervention, the Westphalian arrangement consisted in a complex regime of law, based on the *fundamentum* set by the Peace Treaties of 1648, which established the architecture of peace (and peacemaking) for the time to come. More ambivalently and tenuously, these treaties also established the concept of intercession and anchored it in the concept of protection. It is this architecture of an obligated sovereignty, with its reference point in a self-constituted, consensual, and 'universal' *droit public de l'Europe*, that makes the early modern debate so extraordinarily evocative.[52]

The issue of intervention remained contested, but it was a crucial part of the treaty architecture of post-Westphalian Europe. It emerged from the urgent need to find a way, on the one hand, of containing the rampant violence of religious conflict without abandoning co-religionists and, on the other, of championing the cause of co-religionists without short-changing state interests. We might note first that the prerequisite for these arrangements was a comprehensive amnesty (*perpetua oblivio et amnestia*: Art. II Peace of Osnabrück and §2 of the Peace of Münster, respectively). Hence, the issue of war crimes was mute. Instead, the future maintenance of peace was at stake, and to that end the autonomy (*libertas*) of rulers was both strengthened and bound over in a regime of mutual obligations.[53] In order to understand this regime we need to distinguish between the arrangements of the internal affairs of the Holy Roman Empire and the arrangements with external powers (France in the Treaty of Münster and Sweden in the Treaty of Osnabrück).

No doubt, the most spectacular case of intervention under the aegis of Westphalia was the deposition of rulers within the confines of the Holy Roman Empire.[54] Although possible reasons for such deposition were outright tyranny and misrule – which did not quite measure up to the punishment of Beastly Men but certainly did mean the removal of persistently abusive rulers – more likely the issue at stake was taxation, and the conflict was between local estates and local rulers.[55] These incidents fit

[52] Heinhard Steiger, 'Konkreter Friede und allgemeine Ordnung: Zur rechtlichen Bedeutung der Verträge vom 24. Oktober 1648' in Heinz Duchhardt et al. (eds.), *1648: Krieg und Frieden in Europa*, Ausstellungskatalog zur 26. Europarataustellung, 3 vols. Vol. 1: *Politik, Religion, Recht und Gesellschaft* (Münster: 1998), 437–46.

[53] However, it should be noted that the issue of sovereignty was not formally raised. Osiander, *States System of Europe*, ch. 2.

[54] Werner Trossbach, 'Fürstenabsetzungen im 18. Jahrhundert', *Zeitschrift für historische Forschung*, 13 (1986), 425–54.

[55] James Allen Vann, *The Making of a State: Württemberg, 1593–1793* (Ithaca, NY: Cornell University Press, 1984).

the concept of 'humanitarian intervention' very well and are used to demonstrate the longevity of the concept. However, the salient point of these interventions is that that they occurred in a system of courts, above all the Imperial Aulic Council (Reichshofrat) and the Imperial Cameral Tribunal (Reichskammergericht), and thus settled conflicts short of military intervention. The surprise here is neither that the reign of a ruler could be cut short – because rulers were members of the Holy Roman Empire and subjected themselves to the complex constitutional regime of nestled authority – nor that there was a shared understanding, beyond religious divisions, of what 'bad government' and grievous offenses entailed. It is rather that these courts also showed a 'distinct receptivity to the urgency of cases involving immediate human misery' and that 'peasants also seized the Cameral Tribunal'.[56] Their court battles over liberty and property have led some scholars to argue that what we find here are not simply cases of humanitarian relief of distress, but the origins of human rights.[57] It is one thing, namely a humanitarian concept, to protect subjects from misrule (and to settle conflicts in court short of military intervention); it is another thing for subjects to claim rights and liberties, and to have these claims verified in court rather than by force in revolt. This would suggest that the rights claims of individuals and groups stood a better chance of being upheld in a highly structured society of autonomous rulers who sought protection in a higher law. The security of rulership they gained obligated them to adhere to the law, as expressed by the constitutional arrangement of the Holy Roman Empire.

In contrast to the Holy Roman Empire, it would seem plausible that Europe, with its established and emerging powers, was defined by its war-making ability.[58] Sweden and France, as contracting parties of the Westphalian Peace, and Great Britain, as an outside power (the Netherlands and Spain concluded a first Treaty of Münster in 1648, not to be confused with the aforementioned treaty), certainly did not feel limited in their sovereignty. Yet, they were bound not only by treaties, but also by the conventions, precedents, and understandings that held Europe together.

[56] Osiander, 'Sovereignty, International Relations', here 275.

[57] Peter Blickle, *Von der Leibeigenschaft zu den Menschenrechten: Eine Geschichte der Freiheit in Deutschland* (Munich: Beck, 2003); Wolfgang Schmale, *Bäuerlicher Widerstand, Gerichte und Rechtsentwicklung in Frankreich: Untersuchungen zu Prozessen zwischen Bauern und Seigneurs vor dem Parlament von Paris (16.–18. Jahrhundert)*, Ius commune, special issue 24 (Frankfurt a. M.: Vittorio Klostermann, 1986).

[58] Charles Tilly, *Coercion, Capital, and European States, AD 990–1990*, Studies in Social Discontinuity (Cambridge, MA: B. Blackwell, 1990).

When they broke these regime rules, they were keenly aware of doing so. Nothing demonstrates the working of this regime better than the tenuous settlement of religious difference and division. The Westphalian Peace established that every region must have religion, but rulers and ruled may have different ones and there may be more than one religion in a territory. What had been the exception in the Augsburg Peace of 1555, with its guiding principle of *cuius regio, eius religio* (literally exemptions and reservations), became the grudgingly tolerated norm for the Holy Roman Empire after 1648. This rule was reinforced by a regime of treaty-based guardianships or protectorships, in which major powers guaranteed the security of their co-religionists – with intervention as the ultimate threat.[59] The rulers of France, Great Britain, and Sweden and the Habsburg rulers in their own lands (though not as emperors of the Holy Roman Empire) de facto exempted themselves from the rule. They reserved the principle of non-intervention in relation to themselves, while ascertaining the right themselves to intervene on behalf of others. They did not, however, escape the strictures of their fellow sovereigns when they broke the arrangement, as France did with the expulsion of the Huguenots and the Habsburgs did by supporting the Salzburg archbishop in expelling the Protestants from his territory.

But much as religious conflicts persevered, the concept of guarantees also expanded. It spilled over into a long list of treaties from Oliva (1660), Nijmegen (1678), Ryswick (1697), Dresden (1745), Paris (1763), and Hubertusburg (1763) to the London Protocol (1814), the Vienna Settlement (1815), and the Treaty of Turin (1816). The Treaty of Kutchuk-Kainardji (1774) established Russia as the guarantor of Orthodox Christianity in the Ottoman Empire, thus cutting into the French Protectorate of all Christians that dated back to the Franco-Ottoman Alliance of 1536. All these treaties have in common that they limited the autonomy of sovereigns and that these limitations were guaranteed by extraneous powers, though all of these guarantees were the concessions of rulers rather than the rights of subjects.[60] The potential to intervene and (the threat of) intercession were thus written into the European order. They were not the exception in response to an emergency, but part and parcel of the contractual web that obligated sovereigns to act; they held the European order in place. *Protego ergo obligo*. The concept of

[59] Jürgen Luh, 'Unheiliges Römisches Reich: Der konfessionelle Gegensatz 1648 bis 1806', originally presented as PhD thesis (Verlag für Berlin-Brandenburg, 1995).

[60] Jennifer Jackson Preece, *National Minorities and the European Nation-States System* (Oxford University Press, 1998), 58.

guardianship defined early modern 'humanitarian intervention', which rather looked like what Charles Owen had in mind when he wrote 'that the Powers of the Earth enter into Alliances and Leagues to guard Men against the Oppression of their own Governours and others'.[61]

Owen was calling for a regime of guardians, in which sovereigns become caretakers – protectors, defenders – for religious and, more specifically, Protestant minorities, with the goal of protecting them against abuse. Then again, Charles Owen had a somewhat different arrangement in mind than the one just described, and long before Owen, British political opinion had been rather sceptical of the Westphalian arrangement, which it considered a sell-out of the Protestant cause.[62] Great Britain was not part of the arrangement, though it began to pursue the role of defender of Protestants within the Westphalian framework.[63] In any case, Owen's idea of intervention was far more activist, far more unilateral, and far more committed to the Protestant cause than that of many of his contemporaries. He made the case for a crusade, rather than for humanitarian intervention. It was not a higher law – be it natural law or treaties – that obligated a sovereign; it was the commitment to the Protestant cause as it was expressed by public opinion. This kind of politics of intervention had been building ever since the sixteenth century and was initially focused against the Catholic French king's 'tyrannie towards his people'.[64] By the late seventeenth century, it had become a general defence of Protestantism in Europe – within the Holy Roman Empire and without – with apocalyptic overtones. It is curious that this kind of politics had all the elements of a 'humanitarian' intervention in defence of a persecuted minority, except that it was singularly focused on the perceived mistreatment of fellow Protestants and on advancing the British cause. It was an intervention on behalf of 'friends' rather than of strangers. Its most characteristic mark was the public agitation for the principle that the obligation to fellow Protestants trumps reason of state. Indeed, the language of public obligation is a distinctly British language. It was motivated by the moral outrage in the face of the suffering of fellow

[61] Thompson, 'The Protestant Interest', 67.

[62] Steven C. A. Pincus, *Protestantism and Patriotism: Ideologies and the Making of English Foreign Policy, 1650–1668*, Cambridge Studies in Early Modern British History (Cambridge University Press, 1996).

[63] Thompson, 'The Protestant Interest'.

[64] D. J. B. Trim, '"If a prince use tyrannie towards his people": Interventions on Behalf of Foreign Populations in Early Modern Europe' in Simms and Trim, *Humanitarian Intervention: A History*, 29–66.

Protestants, rather than religious toleration. In this sense, British-style 'humanitarian intervention' was a destabilizing element in a Westphalian architecture that put a premium on stability.

We have moved away from the question of humanitarianism and human rights and yet have come so remarkably close. It is indeed not useful to think of any of these early modern practices as either humanitarian in spirit or human-rights-based in practice. They were neither. However, the concept of early modern intervention demonstrates the power of the obligation to protect and the power of the obligations that protection engendered. It establishes the difference between intervention on behalf of others, punitive intervention against others, and the empowerment of others to make their own legal claims against unjust rule. Last but not least, it suggests that the alleviation of human suffering and abuse short of war is not only imaginable but can indeed be achieved in international society, even if the achievement consists in a rather cumbersome judicial regime and a modestly effective system of guardianship that polices the weak while being unable to stop the powerful. This kind of intervention, based on the principle of guardianship, ought to be separated from punitive or 'Herculean' interventions, which we have not pursued in any detail here. Suffice it to say that such interventions were more frequent than Grotius's recondite text would suggest. An exploration of this subject is better reserved for a genealogy of what became 'crimes against humanity' in the 20th century.

RETURNING TO THE MILLENNIUM REPORT AND THE PROBLEM OF HUMANITARIAN INTERVENTION

The contemporary debate on humanitarian intervention began to take off in the early 1990s in the context of an escalating series of interventions that were legitimated as serving a humanitarian purpose.[65] At the time, participants were surprised to discover that such 'humanitarian interventions' were now available as a viable option of international politics. While they acknowledged that interventions had occurred in the era of the Cold War and that there was an even longer trail leading back into the distant past, the scholarly community firmly believed that, despite all precedents, humanitarian interventions were an altogether novel phenomenon. Inasmuch as there was a prehistory, it was treated as qualitatively

[65] Aidan Hehir, *Humanitarian Intervention: An Introduction* (Houndmills, Basingstoke, Hampshire and New York: Palgrave Macmillan, 2010).

different. Thus, it was generally recognized that humanitarian interventions had their ancient roots in just-war theory.[66] In addition, the interventions generated a huge debate on the 'Westphalian Model' of state sovereignty, which concluded that the current model and the historical reality were two quite different things.[67] Everyone was preoccupied by what appeared to be a new condition of international relations after the Cold War and decided that new conditions needed a new theory and a new practice. This new theory and this new practice were captured by the label 'humanitarian intervention'. The label was hotly contested. 'Saying "humanitarian intervention" ... is a little bit like crying "fire" in a crowded theater: it can create a clear and present danger to everyone within earshot.'[68] The debate was about the future of international relations, not about the past.

The ahistoricity of this 1990s debate did not sit well with historians. They quickly discovered that there was a history of humanitarian interventions after all. They expressed their amazement that anyone could possibly have overlooked the rich history of humanitarian intervention in the first place.[69] In the past few years, a rapidly growing wave of articles, books, and conferences has come to see humanitarian intervention as a long-standing practice of international relations. It is typical for this kind of historiography to push the origins ever further back in time. If initially the nineteenth century was seen as the point of departure, simply because this is when the term 'humanitarian intervention' was used for the first time, the temporal boundaries have since been pushed back into the sixteenth century. No doubt, they can be pushed even further back, much as they can be pushed across space into non-Western cultures and civilizations. For at bottom, intervention on behalf of the weak, the oppressed, or the suffering is, as Aristotle would have put it, a virtue of humanity.

However, the historical argument we are concerned with here is rather more pointed. It contends not simply that humanitarian interventions have a long history, but that these humanitarian interventions are human rights interventions. Thus, D. J. B. Trim and B. Simms in their *Humanitarian Intervention: A History* (2011) have defined humanitarian

[66] Simon Chesterman, *Just War or Just Peace?: Humanitarian Intervention and International Law* (New York: Oxford University Press, 2001).

[67] Krasner, *Sovereignty: Organized Hypocrisy.*

[68] Robert O. Keohane, 'Introduction' in J. L. Holzgrefe and Robert O. Keohane (eds.), *Humanitarian Intervention: Ethical, Legal and Political Dilemmas* (Cambridge University Press, 2003), 1–11, here 1.

[69] Simms and Trim, *Humanitarian Intervention.*

intervention as an 'action by governments (or, more rarely, by organizations) to prevent or to stop governments, organizations, or factions in a foreign state from violently oppressing, persecuting, or otherwise abusing the human rights of people within that state'. They identify the key problem as being 'how to protect human rights and safeguard human security' and think of it as being 'of truly ancient vintage'.[70] It so happens that they thus stumble into a debate that has gotten historians hot under the collar. Trim and Simms think not only that the theory and practice of humanitarian intervention is 'old' but that human rights are, too, and thus set themselves up for a debate with Sam Moyn, who has argued the opposite.[71] The two schools offer rival but perfectly sensible points of departure for a history of humanitarian intervention and possibly even of human rights; the question is what difference it makes to start at one point or the other.

I would suggest, following Trim and Simms, that rights-based interventions are indeed very old, dating back to 'Westphalia' and its conceptual architecture of guardianship. It is worth emphasizing the rights-based nature of sovereign relations in Europe at the time, not least because doing so allows us to study how an 'international society' works. But there is no meaningful way to think of the Westphalian order as a human-rights-based order, and the Westphalian order itself collapsed in the age of revolutions. Revolution and Restoration produced a quite different international order – much less of an international society and much more of a highly organized system of states.[72] However, this system of states produced quite frequent interventions and lively controversies on the subject. It is debatable if any of these interventions should be called 'humanitarian' and can be called human-rights-based interventions.[73] The term itself, 'humanitarian intervention', only appears in the late nineteenth century in a conspicuous shift away from an earlier rhetoric that invoked 'humanity'.[74] But neither interventions in the name of

[70] Ibid., 1. They reference Wheeler, *Saving Strangers*.

[71] Samuel Moyn, *The Last Utopia: Human Rights in History* (Cambridge, MA: Belknap Press of Harvard University Press, 2010).

[72] Matthias Schulz, *Normen und Praxis: Das Europäische Konzert der Grossmächte als Sicherheitsrat, 1815–1860*, Studien zur internationalen Geschichte (Munich: R. Oldenbourg, 2009).

[73] See the chapters in this volume.

[74] Davide Rodogno, *Against Massacre: Humanitarian Interventions in the Ottoman Empire, 1815–1914: The Emergence of a European Concept and International Practice* (Princeton University Press, 2012).

humanity nor humanitarian interventions are rights-based, despite repeated efforts (mostly from the conservative side) to formalize a law of intervention, and the liberal interventions are explicitly not human-rights-based. Not only was the language of human rights rejected, the substance of these 'humanitarian' interventions contradicted the basic precepts of the 'rights of man'. (I am not concerned here with the additional problem that the conceptual architecture of human rights in the late eighteenth century differs from the one in the late twentieth century.)[75] Inasmuch as these interventions were rights-based, they were based on a right to intervention by hegemonic states rather than a right to protection by oppressed subjects.[76]

It is hard even today to speak of a human-rights-based regime of humanitarian intervention. What does exist is a set of theories and a lively debate on the subject that dates back to the 1980s.[77] Thinking about a human-rights-based international order goes back further than Sam Moyn would like to suggest, beginning perhaps in the very early twentieth century, though here most of the empirical work has yet to be done.[78] By 1945, the elements of such an order had been articulated in a curious recovery of Hugo Grotius as inspiration for the present time, above all for his 'subjection of the totality of international relations to the rule of law'.[79] Hersch Lauterpacht was a key figure in this context, although he was by no means the only one. '[T]he urge to find the spiritual counterpart to the growing power of the modern State ... [and] the menacing shape of unbridled sovereignty of the State ... [as] the promoter of international anarchy' were the driving force.[80] This led him to embrace what he called 'dictatorial interference', should members of the UN contravene their 'obligation [qua members of the UN] ... to

[75] Peter De Bolla, *The Architecture of Concepts: The Historical Formation of Human Rights* (New York: Fordham University Press, 2013).

[76] Mark Swatek-Evenstein, *Geschichte der 'humanitären Intervention'*, Rheinische Schriften zur Rechtsgeschichte (Baden-Baden: Nomos, 2008).

[77] The best summary is J. L. Holzgrefe and Robert O. Keohane (eds.), *Humanitarian Intervention: Ethical, Legal and Political Dilemmas* (Cambridge University Press, 2003).

[78] Bruno Cabanes, *The Great War and the Origins of Humanitarianism, 1918–1924*, Studies in the Social and Cultural History of Modern Warfare (Cambridge University Press, 2014). It is an indication of the confusion over humanitarianism and human rights that Cabanes is out to prove that the origins of human rights can be found in the humanitarianism emerging from the First World War.

[79] Lauterpacht, 'Grotian Tradition', 19.

[80] Hersch Lauterpacht, 'The Law of Nations, the Law of Nature and the Rights of Man', *Transactions of the Grotius Society*, 29 (1943), 1–33, here 21.

respect human rights and fundamental freedoms ... Any Member disregarding that obligation would be acting contrary to one of the fundamental purposes of the Charter.'[81] But the reality of the UN was quite different from what Lauterpacht had projected as a new law-based and, indeed, human-rights-based international order.[82]

Especially if we look at humanitarian interventions in the 1990s, the human rights underpinnings of the concept of humanitarian intervention were remarkably underdeveloped. We find a rhetoric of human rights, but very little substance. Neither was there a legal or, for that matter, institutional framework for interventions, and inasmuch as it existed, it was circumvented, as in Kosovo 1999. Nor was there an understanding that the rights to be defended were those of the oppressed rather than the rights for intervention by hegemonic states. A human rights language was frequently used, but it was, strictly speaking, human rights rhetoric without a legal or institutional underpinning. Of course, humanitarians were not happy about the rhetoric either. Although interventions were meant to alleviate suffering and the case for intervention was strenuously put forth to rebut the 'realist' case for defending state or national interests in the public arena, the practice of intervention actually imperilled the humanitarian effort. And this is quite apart from the more principled challenge to the prevailing sentiment, especially in Europe, that considered humanitarianism as the antidote to military action. Add to this the sceptics and naysayers, who considered humanitarian interventions a mere excuse for heavy-handed neo-imperialism, and one gets some sense of how heated the debate was. The bottom line is that the majority of interventions were 'penal', if we think in term of Grotius, and 'dictatorial', if we think in terms of Lauterpacht; they were enacted by hegemonic states, but as hegemonic actions they typically did not reflect state interests, at least not in the way realist politicians (like Henry Kissinger) or academics (like John Mearsheimer) would define the latter. As humanitarian actions they were 'hegemonic' in the Schmittian sense of *protego ergo obligo* and thus could properly be called neo-liberal. This only changed with the concept of the 'responsibility to protect' (R2P) and the ensuing efforts to make it part of international law.[83] However, the

[81] Hersch Lauterpacht, *International Law and Human Rights* (London: Stevens, 1950), 166–7.

[82] On the context see Martti Koskenniemi, *The Gentle Civilizer of Nations: The Rise and Fall of International Law, 1870–1960* (Cambridge University Press, 2002).

[83] Alex J. Bellamy, *Responsibility to Protect: The Global Effort to End Mass Atrocities* (Cambridge: Polity Press, 2009); Aidan Hehir, *The Responsibility to Protect: Rhetoric,*

initiative still lacks the support of the international society for R2P that would allow us to consider human rights interventions as an intrinsic element of the present international order. The one example of human rights intervention we have witnessed, the humanitarian intervention in Libya in 2011, was a peculiar mix of principled action and national interest.[84] As intervention in the spirit of R2P, it was an abject failure.

What we have instead is the hegemonic license to intervene, which is sometimes sanctioned by international bodies and sometimes not and is human-rights-based mostly in the old humanitarian sense of a right to intervene and to protect some privileged group of sufferers.[85] This hegemonic license is what has been called humanitarian intervention ever since the nineteenth century.[86] For good reasons – the quest for self-determination and equality among states being foremost[87] – this hegemonic license had been nearly suppressed in the long struggle for self-determination that culminated in decolonization, and what was left was neutralized in the Cold War. (While the theory of non-intervention and the equality of states dates back to the eighteenth century, the practice of non-intervention and, even more so, the equality of states is short-lived. If anything, non-intervention is the 'hypocrisy' of the Cold War state-system.) The resulting suppression of the right to intervention explains at least in part the oblivion into which the history of humanitarian intervention had fallen by the early 1990s, when it began to re-emerge in full force.

The absence of a human rights framework for humanitarian interventions is acknowledged in the one authoritative study that would have benefited from using historical precedents, the exploration of *The Responsibility to Protect* by the International Commission on Intervention and State Sovereignty (ICISS). This study focused narrowly on the post–Second World War period and came to a quite dismal conclusion. The post-1945 interventions – ten of them are mentioned – are all characterized by the lack of human-rights or even humanitarian justifications.

Reality and the Future of Humanitarian Intervention (Basingstoke and New York: Palgrave Macmillan, 2012).

84 Hehir, *The Responsibility to Protect*, 12.

85 Ian Brownlie, an early opponent of humanitarian intervention, speaks of 'a general license to vigilantes and opportunists to resort to hegemonial intervention'. Ian Brownlie, 'Thoughts on Kind-hearted Gunmen' in Richard B. Lillich (ed.), *Humanitarian Intervention and the United Nations* (Charlottesville: University Press of Virginia, 1973), 139–48, here 48.

86 For a very different assessment, see Gary J. Bass, *Freedom's Battle: The Origins of Humanitarian Intervention* (New York: Alfred A. Knopf, 2008).

87 Jörg Fisch, *Das Selbstbestimmungsrecht der Völker: Die Domestizierung einer Illusion*, Historische Bibliothek der Gerda-Henkel-Stiftung (Munich: Beck, 2010).

Worse, '[h]umanitarian justifications were most robust in cases where purely humanitarian motives were weakest'. Referring to a Danish study on the past 150 years of humanitarian intervention, the ICISS concluded that '[t]he cases from this period demonstrate that powerful states have a long history of fabricating and employing tendentious legal arguments to rationalize intervention in weaker states ... [M]ost of the self-proclaimed humanitarian interventions were of dubious legitimacy.'[88] The ICISS report conceded that the terms of the debate had begun to shift in the 1990s and that, 'according to virtually everyone's definition', military interventions had become 'more legitimate than the earlier cases', but the basic architecture had not changed.[89]

In short, where historians see human rights, the ICISS rather feared hypocrisy. And if hypocrisy is the historical pattern for humanitarian intervention, it is not a good idea to argue with history, which is why the argument for a responsibility to protect turned out to be so singularly ahistorical. To be sure, the members of the committee may have collectively suffered from the same historical amnesia as the other participants in the debate. More likely, they considered humanitarian interventions in the recent and the distant past to be a license to intervene for other purposes. On the basis of this, they decided to disregard the record of past interventions, seen in this critical light, in order to argue in favour of a major initiative to make human rights interventions a new international order. The oblivion of history was the best way of salvaging their case. Humanitarian intervention had to be novel, in order not to be tarnished by the negative example of historical precedent.

In this context, we can now return to Kofi Annan's Millennium Report and the place of humanitarian intervention in this report. Supplementing the Millennium report with the ICISS 2001 report on the responsibility to protect, we can discern the conceptual architecture for human rights interventions.[90] Annan's Report was meant to prepare the UN for an age of globalization. While his main claim was put forward with due modesty – 'to identify the main challenges that we face, as we enter the twenty-first

[88] International Commission on Intervention and State Sovereignty, *The Responsibility to Protect: Research, Bibliography, Background. Supplemental Volume to the Report of the International Commission on Intervention and State Sovereignty* (Ottawa: International Development Research Centre, 2001), 67.

[89] Ibid., 117.

[90] International Commission on Intervention and State Sovereignty, *The Responsibility to Protect: Report of the International Commission on Intervention and State Sovereignty* (Ottawa: International Development Research Centre, 2001).

century; and to sketch out an action plan for addressing them' – the actual language and the substance of the report exceeded that modesty.[91] The wink to *We the Peoples* and, hence, the preamble of the UN Charter, itself modelled on the constitution of the United States, is as obvious as the invocation of President Roosevelt's Atlantic Charter with the reference to 'Freedom from Want' and 'Freedom from Fear' as the two main headings of the document, to which Annan added in a twenty-first-century turn 'the freedom of future generations to sustain their lives on this planet'. Both linguistically and in substance, the Millennium Report aimed at (re-) constituting the role of the UN in the post–Cold War world – defining it, perhaps, in an American spirit, but also setting the UN apart, if more implicitly, from any particular national interest, including that of the United States. The UN, so the thrust of the document, would become the main global forum not simply of humanitarian action but of globalization and its political effects. Human rights would be the higher law to guide this role. It would be the rule of law for the government of peoples. No doubt, there are more modest ways to read the Millennium Report; it is, after all, a carefully crafted diplomatic document. However, the strong interpretation that has been suggested here was fully articulated for everyone to read – and not just in the section of the report on humanitarian intervention.

A look at recent historical studies about the origins and the development of the UN quickly disabuses us of the idea that human rights had always been among its founding principles.[92] Hence, Annan's attempt to make human rights the constituting principle of the UN was a departure from the humanitarian interventions of the 1990s and was set against the hegemonic interventions of the nineteenth century. The UN would still be a platform to advance national (and imperial) interests, but if human rights were indeed at the centre of the enterprise of intervention, national interest would have to be articulated within a framework of rights as the prerequisite of learning 'how to govern better, and – above all – how to govern better together'.[93] In a nutshell, the Millennium Report aimed at better government of, for, and by 'the peoples', all peoples, under the rule of a (higher, human-rights) law that empowered peoples rather than hegemonic states. All this makes it a quite remarkably audacious – although some would also say, foolhardy – document.

[91] Annan, *We the Peoples*.
[92] Mark Mazower, *Governing the World: The History of an Idea* (New York: Penguin Press, 2012); Moyn, *The Last Utopia*.
[93] Annan, *We the Peoples*, 7.

There are many good reasons for why humanitarian intervention should have been part of this report. In a narrow reading of the document, we might think of the section on humanitarian intervention as a post-facto justification of the many 'humanitarian interventions' of the 1990s, and we might even consider it an effort to set in motion a political debate among 'the peoples' as to what this intervention is and what it does after a decade of ad-hoc actions.[94] The introduction of the issue in the Plenary Session of the General Assembly preceding the Millennium Report suggests that much. We might also reason that it was a response to a new wave of popular, non-governmental human-rights activism and, more specifically, humanitarian-intervention activism in the wake especially of the events in the former Yugoslavia and in Rwanda, both of which Annan invoked in his report.[95] In particular, the intervention in Kosovo is often considered to be the trigger for Annan's initiative; however, the timing does not quite work out.[96] In any case, humanitarian intervention had become a pressing political issue in the emergent post–Cold War world and a much-debated concept and action program.[97] There were multiple and competing definitions of 'humanitarian intervention' – some narrowly focused on the use of force by (any) group of states, some embedding force in a broader consideration of humanitarian action, some rejecting or, contrariwise, elevating the use of force beyond states, and some separating intervention sharply from humanitarian action, which others did not.[98] There were contrary opinions about the politics of intervention, including what role the UN should play, because it was not at all self-evident that the UN would or should be the initiator and arbiter of humanitarian interventions, quite apart from the question of who in the UN would do what.[99] Last but not least, there was massive concern mostly among smaller and poorer nations about the breach of sovereignty implied in humanitarian intervention, though the less visible rejection of the Millennial concept of humanitarian intervention by both

[94] Hehir, *Humanitarian Intervention.* [95] Wheeler, *Saving Strangers.*

[96] See the special issue on the 'Kosovo War' (so named in the introductory essay) in *International Affairs*, 85, no. 3 (2009).

[97] Aidan Hehir, *Humanitarian Intervention after Kosovo: Iraq, Darfur and the Record of Global Civil Society* (Basingstoke and New York: Palgrave Macmillan, 2008).

[98] See the not entirely unbiased discussion of the various positions in Holzgrefe and Keohane, *Humanitarian Intervention.*

[99] Bruce Cronin and Ian Hurd (eds.), *The UN Security Council and the Politics of International Authority* (London and New York: Routledge, 2008).

old and new great powers (United States, Russia, China, India, Brazil) deserves a lot more attention than it has received.[100]

It was a reflection of the ongoing public debate that the reference to humanitarian intervention was very detailed in the Millennium Report.[101] It occurs in the section on 'Freedom from Fear' and is set in the context of a discussion about new security threats (freshwater scarcities, severe forms of environmental degradation) that points to a new way of thinking about security less in terms of defending territory and more in terms of 'protecting *people*', an idea – 'human security' – that had come to capture the attention of civil-society activists and academics.[102] In the Millennium Report, humanitarian intervention is carefully placed between the section on 'prevention', which addresses the root causes of violence (such as 'the condition of poverty'), and the section on 'protection' of vulnerable populations ('the brutalization of civilians particularly women and children'), thus 'asserting the centrality of international humanitarian and human rights law'. The report's overriding concern is about measures to strengthen peace operations – 'post-conflict peace-building', economic sanctions, and arms reductions. The Secretary-General of the UN thus inserted the issue of humanitarian intervention into the ongoing discussion about the post–Cold War security environment and developed a programmatic stance on advancing human security, in which forcible humanitarian intervention was only one and, indeed, the ultimate means of preventing harm and maintaining peace in an age of globalization.

The Millennium Report debate and initiative were derailed or in any case transformed soon after by the politics of 9/11. It was written for an international society that did not (yet) exist. It may have been initiated in the hope that this society could be written into reality, but this hope was in vein. The Millennial conceptual architecture was, however, taken up and reshaped in pursuit of the initiative on the responsibility to protect.[103] The ICISS report gives some useful pointers with regard to the latter. The crucial innovation of R2P is that it rejects the language of humanitarian intervention; instead it licenses a right to intervene and speaks of a triple responsibility to prevent,

[100] Christopher Clapham, 'Sovereignty and the Third World State', *Political Studies*, 47, no. 3 (1999); Paul Taylor, 'The United Nations in the 1990s: Proactive Cosmopolitanism and the Issue of Sovereignty', *Political Studies*, 47, no. 3 (1999); Jean L. Cohen, 'Whose Sovereignty? Empire Versus International Law', *Ethics & International Affairs*, 18, no. 3 (2004).

[101] Annan, *We the Peoples*.

[102] Shannon D. Beebe and Mary Kaldor (eds.), *The Ultimate Weapon is No Weapon: Human Security and the New Rules of War and Peace* (New York: Public Affairs, 2010).

[103] Ramesh Chandra Thakur, *The Responsibility to Protect: Norms, Laws, and the Use of Force in International Politics* (Milton Park, Abingdon and New York: Routledge, 2011).

react, and rebuild. It thus gives the right to claim security and protection to the people who need it. This is the pivotal distinction between humanitarian license and human rights claims.[104] Those seeking support have claims; states have duties to protect: *Obligo ergo protego*.

What matters is Kofi Annan's stance, namely the assertion that a global age needs a new kind of security, the key to which is the global rule of law based on human rights and the capacity of the UN to initiate action, by force, if necessary, in order to protect peoples against grievous human rights violations. At the very least, a historically saturated analysis of humanitarian interventions should be able to do what Kofi Annan did, when he suggested that globalization in the late twentieth century requires – and facilitates – a new kind of international government and new kinds of (humanitarian) intervention. Of course, Annan may be wrong, but the connections he makes are worth generalizing. The novelty of the 1990s (and its debate on humanitarian interventions), he reasons, is not that there suddenly were interventions, when none had existed before; it is that interventions played a different role in a globalized world, as opposed to, say, the European international society of the seventeenth century or, for that matter, the European state system of the nineteenth.[105] The environment of international relations shapes the nature of sovereignty. The resulting question is what, at any given point in time, the international conditions for sovereignty were and are. This concern for the changing condition of sovereignty remains crucial, even if we countenance, as Kofi Annan did, the possibility of imperial hypocrisy ('gratuitous interference'), on the one hand, or the possibility of provocation ('secessionist movements ... provoke governments into committing gross violations of human rights in order to trigger external intervention'), on the other.[106] The question of sovereignty *is* the crux of the matter. But the sovereignty in question has always been rather more tenuous and circumscribed than theory (and post–Second World War politics) would have it – and the concept of humanitarian intervention is a perfect lens through which to observe these conditioning factors.[107]

104 International Commission on Intervention and State Sovereignty, *Responsibility to Protect*, 16–17. 'The right to intervene necessarily focuses attention on the claims, rights, prerogatives of the potentially intervening states much more so than on the urgent needs of the potential beneficiaries of the action.'

105 James N. Rosenau, 'The Concept of Intervention', *Journal of International Affairs*, 22, no. 2 (1968), 165–76; James N. Rosenau, 'Intervention as a Scientific Concept', *The Journal of Conflict Resolution*, 13, no. 2 (1969), 149–76.

106 Annan, *We the Peoples*.

107 Martha Finnemore, *The Purpose of Intervention: Changing Beliefs about the Use of Force*, Cornell Studies in Security Affairs (Ithaca, NY: Cornell University Press, 2003).

3

Humanitarian intervention and the issue of state sovereignty in the discourse of legal experts between the 1830s and the First World War

Daniel Marc Segesser

> The sovereignty of states is the basis for interstate relations. In this context sovereignty means that *states* are only subordinate to international law, i.e., they are *völkerrechtsunmittelbar*. Furthermore, there is the duty to respect the sovereignty and independence of other states. There is a *ban on intervention*, the duty to respect territorial integrity and to keep the peace.[1]

This doctrinal statement stems from a book edited by Wolfgang Graf Vitzthum and reflects a position that is still very common among specialists of international law on the European continent. Law in general, and in this specific case international law, is understood as an essential factor for the stability within a state and as a precondition for a functioning system of international relations. Already in 1984, however, Jörg Fisch showed that international law suffers from a central problem. On the one hand, it is a law between equals, following the principle of the equality of states. On the other hand, there are serious factual inequalities between the members of this society of nations that cannot be disposed of once and for all just by decreeing legal equality (*Rechtsgleichheit*).[2] This also holds

[1] Wolfgang Graf Vitzthum (ed.), *Völkerrecht*, 4th ed. (Berlin: De Gruyter, 2007), 189. Translation by the author. The original reads: 'Grundlage für die zwischenstaatlichen Beziehungen ist die Souveränität der Staaten. Souveränität bedeutet zunächst, dass *Staaten* nur dem Völkerrecht untergeordnet, d.h. *völkerrechtsunmittelbar* sind. Ausserdem besteht die Verpflichtung, die Hoheitsgewalt und Unabhängigkeit anderer Staaten zu achten. Es gilt das *Verbot der Intervention*, die Pflicht zur Achtung der Gebietshoheit sowie zur Friedenswahrung.'

[2] Jörg Fisch, *Die europäische Expansion und das Völkerrecht* (Stuttgart: Steiner, 1984), 505.

true for the set of problems relating to humanitarian intervention, as most recent studies on the history of that topic have shown, despite all their differences in detail.[3]

Against this backdrop, the present chapter aims to look at the discourse of legal experts roughly between the 1830s and the beginning of the First World War. Following a tradition that aims to historicize law more than has been done so far, especially on the European continent,[4] this chapter focuses on how legal experts of the period looked at the concept of state sovereignty and in what situation – if any – they considered an armed or unarmed intervention possible, legitimate, or legal. Furthermore, the question will be considered how the debates on the issue of intervention in general and humanitarian intervention in particular[5] were linked to similar ones on the idea of an international criminal court or a specific mission of European countries in the world. As Robert Kolb pointed out in a short note on that question in 2003, there was no absolute ban in the nineteenth century, and interventions occurred frequently. Doctrinal backing was split, but, as will be shown, this divide did not run along the well-known fault line between Anglo-Saxon and Continental writers, as Kolb has claimed.[6]

[3] Davide Rodogno, *Against Massacre: Humanitarian Interventions in the Ottoman Empire, 1815-1914: The Emergence of a European Concept and International Practice* (Princeton University Press, 2012); Brendan Simms and David J. B. Trim (eds.), *Humanitarian Intervention: A History* (Cambridge University Press, 2011); Mark Svatek-Evenstein, *Geschichte der 'Humanitären Intervention'* (Baden-Baden: Nomos, 2008); and Gary Jonathan Bass, *Freedom's Battle: The Origins of Humanitarian Intervention* (New York: Alfred A. Knopf, 2008).

[4] Considerable progress has been made in this field over the last years as is shown in Marcel Senn and Lukas Gschwend, *Rechtsgeschichte II – Juristische Zeitgeschichte*, 3rd edn (Zurich: Schulthess, 2010), 1–7; Thomas Vormbaum, 'Zum Geleit', *Journal der Juristischen Zeitgeschichte. Zeitschrift für die Rechtsgeschichte des 19. bis 21. Jahrhunderts*, 1 (2007), 1, or Diethelm Klippel, 'Rechtsgeschichte' in Joachim Eibach and Günther Lottes (eds.), *Kompass der Geschichtswissenschaft: Ein Handbuch* (Göttingen: Vandenhoeck & Ruprecht, 2002), 126–41.

[5] As was already recognized by the French jurist Antoine Rougier ('La Théorie de l'Intervention d'Humanité', *Revue Générale de Droit International Public*, 17 (1910), 525), it is almost impossible to extract clearly the motive of any intervention. It is therefore also difficult to make a clear cut between what an intervention in general and a specifically humanitarian intervention is. In this chapter, the two terms will therefore be used in the way they were used by the corresponding authors.

[6] Robert Kolb, 'Note on Humanitarian Intervention', *Revue Internationale de la Croix-Rouge*, 85 (2003), 121–4.

ARMED INTERVENTION, THE UNITED NATIONS, AND LEGAL ROOTS OF THE PRESENT-DAY DEBATE

On the one hand, state sovereignty and the principle of non-intervention is a central pillar of present-day international law, as inscribed in Article 2 of the UN Charter of 1945.[7] Ever since the seventeenth and eighteenth centuries, governments and legal scholars – such as Samuel Pufendorf or Emerich de Vattel – have claimed that no one had the right to intervene in the domestic affairs of others.[8] On the other hand, the idea that it was necessary to help the oppressed has remained present in international political and legal discourse since the sixteenth century. Starting then, humanitarian interventions took place time and again at least up to the First World War. After that, fewer (humanitarian) interventions occurred, but it would probably be better to speak of the period between 1914 and 1990 as an intermezzo rather than to claim that the Westphalian system was breached after 1990.[9] In 2005, an initiative was established within the UN under the heading of 'responsibility to protect', in which sovereignty is claimed to be a right, but one that also includes the responsibility to prevent international macro-criminality, such as genocide, war crimes, or crimes against humanity. In this context, the international community is considered to have the responsibility to intervene if a state does not fulfil its primary responsibility. As the current case of Syria shows, however, there is no agreement as to whether a right to armed humanitarian intervention exists at all, let alone the extent to which it exists, despite the fact that this case is immediately preceded by that of Libya in 2011.[10] At that time, the UN Security Council resolution allowed states or regional organizations (read NATO) to 'take all necessary measures ...

[7] Cf. Charter of the United Nations, Chapter I, Art. 2, headings 2 (principle of sovereign equality of all members) and 7 (ban on intervention) under www.un.org/en/documents/charter/chapter1.shtml (last accessed 8 July 2015).

[8] Rodogno, *Against Massacre*, 5; Brendan Simms, '"A False Principle in the Law of Nations": Burke, State Sovereignty, [German] Liberty, and Intervention in the Age of Westphalia', in Simms and Trim, *Humanitarian Intervention*, 90–1; Otto Kimminich and Stephan Hobe, *Einführung in das Völkerrecht*, 7th edn (Tübingen: A. Francke Verlag, 2000), 41.

[9] Rodogno, *Against Massacre*, 5; Simms, 'A False Principle', 89–90.

[10] Cf. United Nations Security Council Resolution 1674 of April 28, 2006 (S/RES/1674), www.un.org/en/sc/documents/resolutions/2006.shtml (last accessed 8 July 2015) on the movement R2P, and United Nations Security Council Resolution 1973 of 17 March 2011 (S/RES/1973), www.un.org/en/sc/documents/resolutions/2011.shtml (last accessed 8 July 2015) regarding the right to intervene in Libya.

to protect civilians and civilian populated areas under threat of attack' and 'all necessary measures to enforce compliance'.[11] Nevertheless, the right to intervene in order to protect was and is controversial.[12]

The debate on humanitarian intervention was a matter of similar controversy in the nineteenth century, too.[13] In this context, it is worth looking exemplarily at the book *Elements of International Law*, published by Henry Wheaton simultaneously in London and Philadelphia in 1836, a volume that remained very influential for a long time.[14] In his study, Wheaton referred to Emerich de Vattel and defined sovereignty as an 'internal constitution, which governs itself independently of foreign powers', but which could be qualified or even limited in various degrees by treaties or alliances.[15] The rights of a state – especially that of self-preservation and the increase of its dominion and resources – did not exist independently of other states. There were limits that were defined by the equal corresponding rights of other states growing out of the same right of self-preservation. In his 1836 edition, Wheaton expressed his conviction, however, that the difficult questions that were arising belonged rather to the science of politics than that of public law.[16] The section pertaining to this was enlarged in the English re-edition of 1866, which was based on the last re-edition made by Wheaton himself in French in 1848 just before his death. It now contained further comments on the

[11] Points 4 and 8 on p. 3 of United Nations Security Council Resolution 1973 of 17 March 2011 (S/RES/1973), www.un.org/en/sc/documents/resolutions/2011.shtml (last accessed 8 July 2015) regarding the right to intervene in Libya.

[12] On the current debate on the responsibility to protect, see Philip Cunliffe (ed.), *Critical Perspectives on the Responsibility to Protect: Interrogation Theory and Practice* (New York: Routledge, 2011), or Cristina G. Badescu, *Humanitarian Intervention and the Responsibility to Protect: Security and Human Rights* (New York: Routledge, 2010). On the debate on humanitarian intervention, see also Jeff L. Holzgrefe and Robert O. Keohane (eds.), *Humanitarian Intervention: Ethical, Legal, and Political Dilemmas* (Cambridge University Press, 2003).

[13] See Davide Rodogno, 'Réflexions luminaires à propos des interventions humanitaires des Puissances européennes au XIXe siècle', *Relations Internationales*, 131 (2007), 13–25; Michael Marrus, 'International Bystanders to the Holocaust and Humanitarian Intervention' in Richard Asby Wilson and Richard D. Brown (eds.), *Humanitarianism and Suffering: The Mobilization of Empathy* (Cambridge University Press, 2009), 158–64, and Fabian Klose, Chapter 5 in this book.

[14] George Grafton Wilson, 'Henry Wheaton and International Law' in Henry Wheaton, *Elements of International Law* (1866), edited with notes by George Grafton Wilson (Oxford: Clarendon Press, 1936), 13a.

[15] Henry Wheaton, *Elements of International Law with a Sketch of the History of the Science* (Philadelphia: Carey, Lea & Blanchard, 1836), 51.

[16] Ibid., 82–3.

right to interfere in order to prevent the undue aggrandizement of a particular state, while declaring that an interference with 'the internal development of a country, or its acquisition of colonies and dependencies at a distance from Europe' was not acceptable.[17] Wheaton gave several examples of intervention throughout history that he considered to be political, such as in the context of the wars of reformation or by the Holy Alliance after 1815. Only in the case of the Greek struggle for independence against the Ottoman Empire at the end of the 1820s did he accept the right to interference, but to his mind, it would have been enough to refer to the right of the Greeks to self-defence, rather than to take up issues such as the interest of European commerce or of humanity to put an end to what he called a 'bloody contest'.[18] In his 1836 edition, Wheaton summed up his ideas by claiming that 'no foreign state can lawfully interfere with the exercise of [the] right ... to freely exercise all its sovereign rights in any manner not inconsistent with the equal rights of other states, [except] by some special compact, or by such a clear case of necessity as immediately affects its own independence, freedom and security'.[19] The 1866 edition expressed the point even more adamantly, claiming that 'non-interference is the general rule, to which cases of justifiable interference form exceptions limited by the necessity of each particular case'.[20] In Wheaton's work, humanitarian motives were only mentioned by way of and with reference to the attempts of the Ottoman government to suppress Greek independence. Nevertheless, he was aware that interventions took place and could be justified in some very restricted cases. It was essential for Wheaton to show that an amalgamation of political motives and legal justification could result in forms of intervention that he did not consider justified by international law. With time, the debate on the legitimacy and legality of humanitarian interventions intensified, not only as a consequence of interventions mainly in the Ottoman empire, but also in regard to the abolishment of the slave trade[21] and in the context of the growing interest of lawyers in matters of international relations and international law, starting in the mid nineteenth century.[22]

[17] Wheaton, *Elements* (1866), 77.

[18] Wheaton, *Elements* (1836), 91–4; id., *Elements* (1866), 95–7.

[19] Wheaton, *Elements* (1836), 95.

[20] Wheaton, *Elements* (1866), 100.

[21] See Fabian Klose, Chapter 5; Fabian Klose, 'Humanitäre Intervention und internationale Gerichtsbarkeit: Verflechtung militärischer und juristischer Implementierungsmassnahmen zu Beginn des 19. Jahrhunderts', *Militärgeschichtliche Zeitschrift*, 72, no.1 (2013), 1–21; and Rodogno, *Against Massacre*, 63–140.

[22] Martti Koskenniemi, *The Gentle Civiliser of Nations: The Rise and Fall of International Law 1870–1960* (Cambridge University Press, 2001), 11–178.

LEGAL EXPERTS FAVOURABLE TO HUMANITARIAN INTERVENTION AND CRITICAL OF AN UNRESTRICTED STATE SOVEREIGNTY

Among the first to bring forward some arguments critical of unrestricted state sovereignty and favourable, at least to some extent, to humanitarian intervention was Johann Caspar Bluntschli, a Swiss lawyer and professor at the University of Heidelberg. In his book on international law, he defined sovereignty in a manner similar to Wheaton as 'independence … from a foreign state [and] the freedom … to decide one's own will within the state independently'. In contrast to his American colleague, sovereignty for Bluntschli was not only limited by that of other states, but also by what he called the 'necessary world order of humans' (*nothwendige menschliche Weltordnung*).[23] Interference and intervention in political matters was therefore not acceptable to Bluntschli, who noticed that the practice of the states was not yet fully in agreement with the principles of international law that guaranteed the independence of states regardless of their form of government. However, recent developments in Italy had shown that most European powers were ready to accept that there was no general right to intervention, as had been believed at the congresses of Laibach and Verona in 1821 and 1822, respectively.[24] If human rights or international law in general were violated in the context of political struggles, Bluntschli considered an intervention lawful:

> If, as a consequence of struggles regarding a state's constitution, those rights of humans that are generally recognized as absolutely essential or international law in general are violated, an intervention for the protection of these rights is justified in the same manner as would be the intervention of civilized states in any case where the violation of law constitutes a public danger.[25]

Here Bluntschli went well beyond Wheaton's arguments and spoke of a right to intervene, limited to so-called civilized states, in cases where

[23] Johann Caspar Bluntschli, *Das moderne Völkerrecht der civilisirten Staten als Rechtsbuch dargestellt*, (Nördlingen: C.H. Beck'sche Verlagsbuchhandlung, 1868), 84. Translation by the author. The original of the first part of the quotation reads: 'Unabhängigkeit … von einem fremden State [und] der Freiheit, … seinen eigenen Staatswillen selbst zu bestimmen.'

[24] Ibid., 265–7.

[25] Ibid., 268. Translation by the author. The original reads: 'Werden in der Folge der Verfassungskämpfe das allgemein als nothwendig anerkannte Menschenrecht oder das Völkerrecht verletzt, dann wird auch eine Intervention zum Schutze desselben aus denselben Gründen gerechtfertigt, wie das Einschreiten der civilisirten Staten überhaupt bei gemeingefährlichen Rechtsverletzungen.'

the violations of law posed a danger to public safety. Again and in a manner similar to Wheaton, Bluntschli pointed to the problems of Christian minorities in the Ottoman Empire as a possible reason for legitimate humanitarian intervention.[26]

After the end of the Franco-Prussian War, the issue of humanitarian intervention found itself clearly in the shadow of a debate on how to deal with violations of international legal norms and the possibility of further codification.[27] In this context, the president of what was to become the International Committee of the Red Cross (ICRC), Gustave Moynier, suggested that an international criminal court be created to handle violations of the Geneva Convention of 1864. Although Moynier did not mention intervention of any kind, his proposal headed in a similar direction. It called for a limitation of the principle of state sovereignty in a manner similar to that of Bluntschli and of the Mixed Commissions for the Abolition of the Slave Trade.[28] More than just asking for an intervention to stop the violations of fundamental rights of international law or for the creation of mere commissions to decide the fate of humans on the basis of prize or property laws, Moynier proposed the creation of an international court as an institution of the civilized states to combat violations of law dangerous to public safety.[29] His proposal was not received very well by most of his colleagues: Francis Lieber criticized that this would restrict the autonomy of the nation states too much, and both Carl Lueder and Heinrich Triepel claimed that no state would be ready to accept such an infringement of its sovereignty, especially not in case of war.[30] Although some colleagues such as Gustave Rolin-Jaequemyns,

[26] Ibid., 268–9. In the last re-edition of 1878, p. 270, Bluntschli also pointed to the fact that Russia had intervened in favour of Christians in the Balkans in recent times (1877/78).

[27] See Daniel Marc Segesser, *Recht statt Rache oder Rache durch Recht? Die Ahndung von Kriegsverbrechen in der internationalen wissenschaftlichen Debatte 1872–1945* (Paderborn: Schöningh, 2010), 86–102. Geoffrey Best, *Humanity in Warfare: The Modern History of the International Law of Armed Conflicts* (London: Weidenfeld and Nicolson, 1980), 128–215.

[28] Klose, 'Humanitäre Intervention', rightly criticizes Jenny S. Martinez, *The Slave Trade and the Origins of International Human Rights Law* (Oxford University Press, 2012), 6, for calling these commissions the 'first international human rights courts'.

[29] Gustave Moynier, 'Note sur la Création d'une Institution Judicaire Internationale propre à prévenir et à réprimer les Infractions à la Convention de Genève', *Bulletin International des Sociétés de Secours aux Militaires Blessés*, 11 (1872), 122–31. See Bluntschli, *Völkerrecht* (1868), 268.

[30] Letter, Francis Lieber to Guillaume-Henri Dufour, 10 April 1872, published in French translation in Gustave Rolin-Jaequemyns, 'Note sur le Projet de M. Moynier, relatif à l'Etablissement d'une Institution Judiciaire Internationale, Protectrice de la Convention,

Achille Morin, and Frantz von Holtzendorff encouraged Moynier not to give up, the latter soon dropped his proposal, possibly because he considered the challenges of the Brussels Conference on the codification of the laws of war and of the developments in the Balkans in the 1870s to be more important. At this stage, neither the community of lawyers nor the governments seemed ready to accept the idea of a court restricting state sovereignty.[31]

Although Moynier did not call for states to intervene when, in the wake of the insurrection in Herzegovina in 1875, a debate on how to deal with atrocities ensued, he did suggest in a letter to Johann Caspar Bluntschli that the recently created *Institute of International Law* ought to intervene by forming a commission to keep track of any violations of international law.[32] Bluntschli agreed, and together with the secretary-general of the institute, Gustave Rolin-Jaequemyns, the two men issued an international appeal to the warring parties to refrain from any atrocities. They thereby became the lawyers' voice in the public outcry reverberating through the European press[33] over several massacres that also became known as the Bulgarian horrors.[34] In light of criticism often levelled in the past against its own troops primarily by liberal lawyers in Western Europe who formed the core of the *Institute for International Law*, the Russian government made great efforts in its attempt to show the extent to which it adhered and would continue to adhere to the rules of the laws of war, while at the same time highlighting violations by the regular and

avec lettres de MM. Lieber, Ach. Morin, de Holtzendorff et Westlake', *Revue de Droit International et de Législation Comparée*, 4 (1872), 330–2; Carl Lueder, *Die Genfer Konvention: Historisch und kritisch-dogmatisch mit Vorschlägen zu ihrer Verbesserung. unter Darlegung und Prüfung der mit ihr gemachten Erfahrungen und unter Benutzung der amtlichen, theilweise ungedruckten Quellen* (Erlangen: Verlag von Eduard Besold, 1876), 431–3; Heinrich Triepel, 'Die neuesten Fortschritte auf dem Gebiete des Kriegsrechts', *Zeitschrift für Literatur und Geschichte der Staatswissenschaft*, 2 (1894), 211–12.

31 Rolin-Jaequemyns, 'Note sur le Projet', 332–44; Jean de Sennarclens, *Gustave Moynier: Le Bâtisseur* (Geneva: Slatkine, 2000), 217–30.

32 Letter, Gustave Moynier to Johann Caspar Bluntschli, 7 May 1877, quoted in Sennarclens, *Moynier*, 230–1.

33 See the study of Florian Keisinger, *Unzivilisierte Kriege im zivilisierten Europa? Die Balkankriege und die öffentliche Meinung in Deutschland, England und Irland 1876–1913* (Paderborn: Schöningh, 2008), which unfortunately is rather weak on the debates regarding the uprisings and the war from 1875 to 1878.

34 Jörg Fisch, *Europa zwischen Wachstum und Gleichheit 1850–1914* (Stuttgart: Ulmer, 2002), 220; Barbara Jelavich, *Russia's Balkan Entanglements, 1806–1914* (Cambridge University Press, 1991), 159–73; Rodogno, *Against Massacre*, 142–51; Segesser, *Recht*, 102–3.

irregular forces of the Ottoman Empire.[35] It will not come as a surprise that the issue of humanitarian intervention came up again in this context. In a long article in the *Revue de Droit International et de Législation Comparée*, Gustave Rolin-Jaequemyns discussed the current Balkan crisis, criticizing the British government for its failure to support a common European intervention.[36] As had been clearly shown, there was a right to collective intervention of European states in Ottoman affairs in order to guarantee peace and stability, Rolin-Jaequemyns continued. Although there was no obligation, the Belgian lawyer argued that it was the duty of the major European powers to use their authority within justified limits to uphold the interests of humanity and international peace. While the Holy Alliance had gone too far in its policy of intervention in the past, the great powers had to go further in the case of the Ottoman Empire, since it had shown itself to be unable to guarantee the basic legal rights of its inhabitants. State sovereignty could not be used as a tool to protect a state from its duties towards its inhabitants.[37]

Aegidius Arntz, a liberal German academic who taught civil, natural, and international law at the University of Brussels, supported Rolin-Jaequemyns and stressed that it was important to find a way between the absolute prohibition of intervention and regulation that left too much room for abuse. Presenting several examples – among them one of a despot who sent his subjects to the stake for no reason – Arntz was sure that no European power would tolerate such behaviour on its doorsteps. In such cases, he believed, an intervention was legitimate, especially if it was undertaken collectively.[38] Rolin-Jaequemyns completely agreed with Arntz and emphasized that, as a citizen of a small country, he was in no fear that this rule could one day be used against his own country, because

35 Peter Holquist, 'The Russian Empire as a "Civilized Nation": International Law as Principle and Practice in Imperial Russia, 1874–1917', unpublished paper to the 118th Annual Meeting of the American Historical Association, Washington, DC, 2004, 18; Jelavich, *Russia's Balkan Entanglements*, 143–6, 170–3; Vladimir V. Pustogarov, *Our Martens: F. F. Martens: International Lawyer and Architect of Peace* (Den Haag: 2000), 114–27; Gerrit Gong, *The Standard of 'Civilization' in International Society* (Oxford: Clarendon Press, 1984), 100–6.

36 Gustave Rolin-Jaequemyns, 'Le Droit International et la Phase Actuelle de la Question d'Orient', *Revue de Droit International et de Législation Comparée*, 8 (1876), 357–61. See Rodogno, *Against Massacre*, 168–9, for the reason why no collective intervention took place.

37 Rolin-Jaequemyns, 'Droit International', 367–70.

38 Gustave Rolin Jaequemyns, 'Note sur la Théorie du Droit d'Intervention – À propos d'une lettre de M. le professeur Arntz', *Revue de Droit International et de Législation Comparée*, 8 (1876), 673–5.

'its only effect is to remind all states, small or large, that even though they are independent, they are not alone in the world, but are part of humanity, and as such they have obligations that correspond to their rights'.[39] Rolin-Jaequemyns and Arntz were not alone in their views. In the same year, Edward S. Creasy claimed that

as a general rule, all ... Intervention is unlawful, [but] may be justifiable, and even a duty, in certain exceptional cases ... [such as] a grievously oppressed people, which has never amalgamated with its oppressors as one nation, and which its oppressors have systematically treated as an alien race, subject to the same imperial authority, but in other respects distinct, the distinction being the distinction between privileged and burdened, between honoured and degraded, between fully protected and ill protected by law in primordial rights of security for person and property – and the distinction being hereditary, permanent and practical.[40]

Similarly, the French lawyer and diplomat Édouard Engelhardt argued that, under certain conditions, an intervention was legal and legitimate according to the rules of international law.[41]

Although, as we shall see, many lawyers became more critical in regard to humanitarian intervention in the following years and up to the beginning of the First World War, quite a few still upheld the idea that interventions and even more so humanitarian interventions could be legitimate or legal. Among them were William Edward Hall and Thomas Joseph Lawrence, two English specialists of international law; Lassa Oppenheim, a lecturer of international law born in Germany who taught at the London School of Economics; and Antoine Rougier, a French lecturer from the University of Caen who later became professor of general administrative as well as civil law at the University of Lausanne in Switzerland. Hall claimed that, although states were under an obligation to respect the independence of others, there were some cases in

[39] Rolin-Jaequemyns, 'Note sur la Théorie', 682. Translation by the author. The original reads: '[sa] seule portée est de rappeler à tous les États, petits ou grands, que malgré leur indépendance, ils ne sont pas seuls au monde, qu'ils font partie de l'humanité et que, comme tels, ils ont des obligations corrélatives à leur droits'.

[40] Edward S. Creasy, *First Platform of International Law* (London: John van Voorst, Paternoster Row, 1876), 303–4 did not take up the issue of the then current violations of principles of international law in the Balkans but, referring to Wheaton, pointed to the events in Greece at the end of the 1820s, calling these 'an intervention justifiable on behalf of the interests of humanity' (300).

[41] Édouard Engelhardt, 'Le Droit d'Intervention et la Turquie', *Revue de Droit International et de Législation Comparée*, 12 (1880), 364–5.

which this respect was clearly incompatible with 'a due satisfaction of the superior right',[42] among which Hall counted the right to self-preservation, to oppose wrongdoing and to fulfil engagements.[43] For Hall, massacres, brutality in civil wars, or religious persecution were acts with no direct relationship to international law but were 'so inconsistent with the character of a moral being as to constitute a public scandal, which the body of states, or one or more states as representative of it, are competent to suppress'.[44] It was clear to Hall that any intervention based on such reasons nevertheless had to be authorized by what he called 'the body of civilised states accustomed to act together for common purposes'.[45] While Hall did not refer to the case of the Ottoman Empire, Thomas Joseph Lawrence did and thereby stressed the point much more than did Hall that interventions justified on the grounds of humanity were legitimate under very exceptional circumstances, such as when a contest had been marked by the most horrible barbarities for years (as in the case of the Ottoman oppression of Christian minorities in the empire).[46] Already in his first edition, Lawrence did not consider such interventions legally justified and in his later editions even called such interventions 'destitute of technical legality, but ... morally right and even praiseworthy to a high degree'.[47] Although he did not want to give up his position fully, Lawrence clearly mitigated his position because it had lost support at the beginning of the twentieth century. For his part, Lassa Oppenheim stressed that there might be a legal right to intervention. Such an intervention was, however, always dictatorial, as it was a forceful interference (yet fell short of war). It was only admissible under certain clearly defined conditions, that is, if sovereignty was not fully established, if there was a need to protect one's own citizens, if based on an international treaty, or if universally recognized principles of international law had been violated.[48] Intervention might also be admissible in default of the rights aforementioned. In the past, many had taken place for good reasons such as humanitarian motives; nevertheless, Oppenheim doubted whether

[42] William Edward Hall, *International Law* (Oxford: Clarendon Press, 1880), 241.
[43] Ibid., 241–2. [44] Ibid., 245. [45] Ibid., 247.
[46] Thomas Joseph Lawrence, *The Principles of International Law* (London: Macmillan, 1895), 132–3.
[47] Thomas Joseph Lawrence, *The Principles of International Law*, 4th rev. edn (London: Macmillan, 1911), 129.
[48] Lassa Oppenheim, *International Law: A Treatise*, 2 vols. (London: Longmans, Green and Co., 1905), vol. 1: *Peace*, 183–4.

there is really a rule of the Law of Nations which admits such interventions ... Yet, on the other hand, it cannot be denied that public opinion and the attitude of the Powers are in favour of such interventions, and it may perhaps be said that in time the Law of Nations will recognise the rule that interventions in the interests of humanity are admissible provided they are exercised in the form of a *collective* of the Powers.[49]

Oppenheim's colleague Antoine Rougier was one of the few legal specialists in France to support humanitarian intervention on a legal basis. Having studied the arguments brought forward in favour of almost unlimited state sovereignty, he confessed that they had not convinced him, although he agreed that there would almost be no reason for intervention in the case of two states on a similar level of civilization.[50] However, in all other cases involving the violation of fundamental human rights, such as the right to life, the right to freedom, or the right to a legal process, humanitarian intervention remained legally possible and justified if the inhuman character of the acts causing an intervention was the main motive prompting a power or several of them act.[51] Rougier was aware that motives for intervention would always be mixed, but for him it was possible that the humanitarian aspect always constituted the major reason, as in the cases of Syria, the Ottoman Empire, or Morocco.[52]

LEGAL EXPERTS CRITICAL OF HUMANITARIAN INTERVENTION

The idea of humanitarian intervention was not only received favourably, of course. There were many who voiced sharp criticism, and also those who favoured it clearly stated that such an intervention was only lawful under certain, very restricted conditions. Among the first to take a highly critical position towards the idea of humanitarian intervention was August Wilhelm Heffter, professor of law at the Friedrich Wilhelms University in Berlin from 1833 to 1880. In his 1844 study on the international law of contemporary Europe, he stressed the fact that all sovereign states, whether great or small, had the same rights and were therefore entitled to take whatever measures they wanted within the bounds of international law. Although equal before international law and having the right to a self-determined development, states had to accept a certain inequality also in legal matters as a consequence of the political situation in Europe. However, this did not mean that states had a right to extend

49 Ibid., 186–7. 50 Rougier, 'Théorie', 480–97. 51 Ibid., 497–525.
52 Ibid., 525–6.

their sovereignty beyond their own borders.[53] For Heffter, no state had any justification, in general, to intervene in the affairs of any other. He only accepted a very few exceptions, such as cases in which a government agreed to such an intervention, the sovereign rights of another state were violated, or an unlawful intervention had to be stopped. Furthermore, Heffter also accepted intervention by common consent to clear up an erratic situation inside a state or in a certain region and to re-establish international peace and order. In Heffter's view, the only aim of a lawful intervention was to assert an existing right or to compensate for the violation of law. In this context he warned his readers not to get carelessly involved in an intervention, even in cases of religious persecution or the reprobation of intolerance.[54] Only in later editions of his work did Heffter therefore explicitly accept the lawfulness of the intervention by the European powers in Greece at the end of the 1820s, and he never expressed any opinion on the lawfulness of the interventions in the Ottoman Empire in the 1870s.[55] This aspect was only taken up in the eighth edition, published in 1888 by Friedrich Heinrich Geffcken after Heffter's death in 1880. In his commentary placed in a footnote, Geffcken quoted the Berlin Treaty of 1878, which 'in Art. 23, 61, 62 establishes a comprehensive and collective right to intervention into the domestic affairs of Turkey, it remaining doubtful, whether this is the right means to remedy the existing grievances'.[56]

Théophile Funck-Brentano, a French sociologist, and Albert Sorel, a French historian, who together published an introduction to international law in 1877, were also sceptical about the lawfulness of intervention, although they were well aware that, throughout history, governments had considered such a course of action to be either necessary or profitable and had claimed a right to it.[57] Funck-Brentano and Sorel did not agree with such an interpretation. For them, states were sovereign and therefore did not accept any higher authority apart from certain customary laws based

[53] August Wilhelm Heffter, *Das Europäische Völkerrecht der Gegenwart* (Berlin: Verlag von E. H. Schroeder, 1844), 43–60.

[54] Ibid., 85–9.

[55] August Wilhelm Heffter, *Das Europäische Völkerrecht der Gegenwart auf den bisherigen Grundlagen*, 4th edn (Berlin: Verlag von E. H. Schroeder, 1861), 95.

[56] August Wilhelm Heffter: *Das Europäische Völkerrecht der Gegenwart auf den bisherigen Grundlagen*, 8th edn by Friedrich Heinrich Geffcken (Berlin: Verlag von H. W. Müller, 1888), 116, translation by the author.

[57] Théophile Funck-Brentano and Albert Sorel, *Précis du Droit des Gens* (Paris: Plon, 1877), 212–4.

on common interest and reciprocal obligations. The right to intervention was not one of these, and therefore Funck-Brentano and Sorel saw it not as a matter of law but as a matter of political fact.[58] Placing the right to sovereignty above all else, they concluded: 'Intervention is therefore not a right, because there is no right, which is against the law [*pas de droit contre le droit*]; and the sovereignty of the states is an essential principle of international law.'[59]

Nevertheless, Funck-Brentano and Sorel did not rule out the fact that there might be a necessity for intervention, as nations depended on each other and developments within one nation could threaten its neighbours. Intervention could therefore be reasonable, legitimate, and just, but never a matter of law. It was a political act, even an act of war, which at that time was not considered illegal in any way, but one that for Funck-Brentano and Sorel lay outside the focus of international law.[60]

Only a few years later, Paul Pradier-Fodéré, a French judge from Lyon, came to similar conclusions. Defining sovereignty as the supreme right of a nation to specify its internal organization free from any foreign interference, he made it clear that, to his mind, there was no right of intervention (*droit d'intervention*).[61] In the same manner as Funck-Brentano and Sorel, to whom he referred, Pradier-Fodéré stated that 'there is no right which is against the law [*pas de droit contre le droit*]. Law, this is independence; intervention is a violation of independence. There can be no right to violate an absolute legal principle.'[62] Looking more specifically at humanitarian reasons, Pradier-Fodéré at first stated that violations of the laws of humanity almost never took place in Europe and North America, although anti-Semitic violence was still a fact, especially in Eastern Europe. This was, however, to be considered an accidental return to barbarian customs of the past.[63] Discussing the arguments brought forward by his colleagues,[64] he finally concluded that, even in cases of violations against the laws of humanity, an intervention was to be

58 Ibid., 215.

59 Ibid., 216. Translation by the author. The complete original reads: 'L'intervention n'est donc pas un droit, car il n'y a pas de droit contre le droit; et la souveraineté des États est un principe essentiel du droit des gens.'

60 Ibid., 216–23.

61 Paul Pradier-Fodéré, *Traité de Droit International Public Européen et Américain*, 9 vols. (Paris: A. Durand et Pedone-Lauriel Éditeurs, 1885–1906), vol. I (1885), 232–4, 547.

62 Ibid., 547. Translation by the author. The original reads: 'il n'y a pas de droit contre le droit. Le droit c'est l'indépendance; l'intervention, c'est la violation de l'indépendance. Il ne peut y avoir un droit à violer un droit absolu.'

63 Ibid., 651–2. 64 Ibid., 652–62.

considered an illegal use of violence against the independence of a nation because 'inhuman acts, however condemnable they are, do not give third-party states a right to intervention as long as they [the acts] neither endanger nor threaten any other states, for no state can be a judge in regard to the conduct of others'.[65] Pradier-Fodéré went even further and claimed that, as equals, states were not allowed to take criminal legal action against each other. Without mentioning it explicitly, he hereby clearly opposed the proposal of Gustave Moynier to create an international criminal court.[66] Similarly straightforward was the evaluation of Franz von Liszt, professor of criminal and international law in Berlin, who, based on the fact that states alone were the subject of international law and that their territorial integrity had to be protected, also claimed that interventions were violations of international law. Liszt would accept only a very few exceptions, such as the case of the Ottoman Empire, where international treaties gave the European powers the right to intervene in support of Christian minorities on the Balkans and of the Armenians.[67]

Pasquale Fiore, professor of constitutional and international law at the University of Naples, was also adamant that interventions were not legal. They had to be considered a violation of international law.[68] Nevertheless, in the 1890 edition of his book on international law, he claimed that the community of nations as a collective entity had a right and a duty to make sure that the rules of international law were respected: 'An unjustified refusal to carry out a duty of humanity, if it causes real harm to other states, can legitimize a collective reprehension with the aim to guarantee the common interest.'[69] Such reprehension, however, had to be carried out by peaceful means such as retribution, reprisals, or pacific blockade; only if all such means had been used to no avail could states collectively resort to war.[70] In the re-edition of 1911, the passage on the right and

[65] Ibid., 663. Translation by the author. The original reads: 'les actes d'inhumanité, quelque condamnables qu'ils soient, tant qu'ils ne portent aucune atteinte, ni aucune menace aux droit d'autres États, ne donnent à ces derniers aucun droit d'intervention, car nul État ne peut s'ériger en juge de la conduite des autres.'

[66] Ibid., 664.

[67] Franz von Liszt, *Das Völkerrecht systematisch dargestellt*, 2nd edn (Berlin: Verlag von O. Haering, 1902), 52–9, referring to Article 61 of the 1878 Treaty of Berlin.

[68] Pasquale Fiore, *Le Droit International codifié et sa sanction juridique* (Paris: Chevalier-Maresq et Cie Éditeurs, 1890), 153–5.

[69] Ibid., 162–3. Translation by the author. The original reads: 'Le refus injustifié d'accomplir un devoir d'humanité peut, lorsqu'il cause un dommage réel aux autres États, légitimer une remontrance collective ayant pour but la garantie des intérêts communs.'

[70] Ibid., 295–303.

duty of the community of nations was omitted to make sure that the rules of international law were respected.[71] Fjodor Fjodorowitsch Martens, a Russian diplomat and specialist of international law, and Henry Bonfils, professor of international and commercial law at the University of Toulouse, also supported the view that intervention was not lawful. However, the former scholar limited this to cases between civilized nations, while the latter stated that non-intervention was a duty for all states, but a duty that political leaders did not respect if it was considered an obstacle to their ambitions or interests.[72]

CONCLUSION

As has been shown, throughout the nineteenth century and the first decade of the twentieth there were diverging opinions on the legitimacy and legality of interventions in general and humanitarian interventions in particular. All of the legal experts mentioned in this chapter considered the sovereignty of nations to be a central aspect of international law. However, some accepted that there was more than sovereignty and that therefore even sovereign states were subordinate to the rules of international law and to international obligations. Whether or not an intervention was considered legitimate was often linked to judgements on the developments of the time. This was especially true in regard to the Ottoman Empire, which early on was considered a power to be brought within the circle of the civilized nations of Europe, although it was almost never considered to have reached the same stage of civilization as European powers had.[73] Some legal scholars, and by far not only those from Anglo-Saxon countries, had a tendency to accept the idea of intervention in cases where rules of international law had been violated. Johann Caspar Bluntschli, Gustave Rolin-Jaequemyns, and Gustave Moynier therefore supported the Russian intervention in the Balkans in the years 1875 to 1878 as a means to strengthen the rules of international law, also in regard to the laws of humanity. Others, especially men from France and Prussia such as August Wilhelm Heffter, Théophile Funck-Brentano, and Albert Sorel, and most adamantly Paul Pradier-Fodéré and Franz von

[71] Pasquale Fiore, *Le Droit International codifié et sa sanction juridique*, Nouvelle édition (Paris: A. Pedone Éditeur, 1911), 307.

[72] Fjodor Fjodorowitsch Martens, *Traité de Droit International*, 3 vols. (Paris: Librairie Maresq, 1883–1887), vol. I (1883), 394–8; Henry Bonfils: *Manuel de Droit International Public (Droit des Gens)* (Paris: Arthur Rousseau, Éditeur, 1894), 153–67.

[73] Gong, *Standard*, 106–19.

Liszt, condemned almost any sort of intervention as a violation of international law. In this they were at the forefront of a movement that was gaining strength and ran parallel to debates on the equality before the law within states,[74] to a growing defensiveness about territorial changes and the right to self-determination,[75] and to a growing rivalry among large powers seeking to remain masters of their own destiny at a time when social Darwinism had begun to raise its head.[76] With the beginning of the First World War, other aspects in international law began to dominate, and the issue of intervention in general and humanitarian intervention in particular disappeared for some time from the discourses on international law.[77]

The claim that there is an absolute ban on any sort of intervention, as quoted at the beginning of this chapter, must be understood in this context. Furthermore, it is important to analyse carefully the content of the concept of state sovereignty by looking at the historical context and considering the different definitions given to the term by those involved. To decree the equality of states in a world of inequalities is not enough. What is needed is a careful analysis of the aims of the actors involved. The same must be done in the context of the debate on the necessity or impossibility of creating an international criminal court as suggested by Gustave Moynier in 1872 and realized with the founding of the International Criminal Court (ICC) in 2002. The argument that humanitarian intervention and the activities of the ICC are instruments of neocolonialism[78] in the same way that the 'civilizing mission' was in the nineteenth century[79] is therefore not completely untrue. However, it is linked to a certain and specific understanding of state sovereignty, which at the time discussed here was only applied fully to nations that were accepted as civilized ones. Therefore, in the future, the debate on the concept of state sovereignty needs to be historicized even more than has been done so far.

[74] See, Fisch, *Europa*, 27–37.

[75] See Jörg Fisch, *Das Selbstbestimmungsrecht der Völker: Die Domestizierung einer Illusion* (Munich: Verlag C. H. Beck, 2010), 119–39.

[76] On the growing rivalry amongst the Great Powers before 1914, but without reference to social Darwinism, see the recent work by Christopher Clark, *The Sleepwalkers: How Europe Went to War in 1914* (London: Allen Lane, 2012).

[77] Marrus, 'International Bystanders', 164–72.

[78] See W. Douglas Smith, 'The International Criminal Court: The Long Arm of Neocolonialism?', *International Affairs Review*, 1 November 2009, at http://iar-gwu.org/node/87 (last accessed 3 August 2015). The term 'neocolonialism' goes back to Kwame Nkrumah, *Neo-Colonialism: The Last Stage of Imperialism* (London: Nelson, 1965).

[79] See Rodogno, *Against Massacre*, 12–5.

4

The legal justification of international intervention

Theories of community and admissibility

Stefan Kroll

The legal justification of international intervention in the nineteenth century was generally based on the principle of international community.[1] The legal principle of international community did not stand in opposition to the principle of sovereignty but could be understood instead as an extension of its meaning. In a community of states, which is characterized by interdependent interests and shared normative expectations, the right and obligation to intervene was considered a necessary practice to react against violations of international norms. In this sense, the practice of intervention was understood as an expression of sovereignty rather than just as an unjustified form of interference into sovereignty. It follows from this that the international law of intervention does in the end not stand between national independence and international solidarity, the 'two poles of the society of nations', as Rolin-Jaequemyns and others have put it.[2] Instead, the international law of intervention is the extension of sovereignty in light of a society of states, which began to consider itself, at least in the eyes of influential legal scholars, more and more as an international community.

David Philpott described sovereignty as 'supreme legitimate authority within a territory', understanding supreme authority as implying

[1] This chapter was written during a Fellowship at the Max Planck Institute for the Study of Religious and Ethnic Diversity in Göttingen. The author wishes to thank Sara Dezalay and Fabian Klose for their invaluable comments on earlier drafts.

[2] Gustave Rolin-Jaequemyns, 'Note sur la Théorie du Droit d'Intervention, à propos d'une lettre de M. le professeur Arntz', *Revue de Droit International et de Législation Comparée*, 8 (1876), 677, translation by the author; Ellery C. Stowell, *Intervention in International Law* (Washington, DC: J. Byrne, 1921), v.

'independence from unwanted intervention by an outside authority'.[3] Many similar definitions may be found in the literature. However, the concurrent existence of a right – and in some cases even an obligation – to intervene, underlines that the principle of undisputed independence was not absolute. On the contrary, the nature of sovereignty as a legal principle needs to be understood as far more complex. The right to intervene was not just an exception to the rule of non-intervention, but an extension of an understanding of sovereignty. The principle of sovereignty, which is usually thought of as being exclusively based on the idea of the autonomous existence of an isolated nation state, is, however, also buttressed by a consciousness of collectivity shared by sovereign international actors. Based on this consciousness, intervention becomes the use of international force in cases where the normative principles, upon which the international community is established, have been severely violated.

To substantiate this argument, the chapter is organized in three sections. Section one shows that the justification of international intervention in the nineteenth century was based on a substantial shift of the leading principles of the international legal order. Without limiting the relevance of the principle of sovereignty, the international community emerged as an international legal principle of comparable weight. While a characteristic feature of the post-Westphalian international legal order was that the central measure of legitimate action was sovereignty, the international community emerged as a legal principle that constituted an auxiliary benchmark of legitimate action. Section two looks at the application of the concept of international community in the case of humanitarian intervention, in particular the case of religious minority protection. The protection of religious minorities is one of the main examples of legitimate international intervention in nineteenth-century international legal discourse. Even though the legal debates show elements of an original humanitarian interest, they also serve as an example of unequal interpretations of the doctrine of humanitarian intervention. Section three veers back to the legal theoretical perspective. Legal justifications of international intervention were heavily influenced by normative logics that did not form part of the legal imagination. Epithets such as 'economic', 'political', or 'humanitarian' interventions confirm the bearing of ostensibly non-legal characteristics on the motivation and

[3] Daniel Philpott, 'Sovereignty: An Introduction and Brief History', *Journal of International Affairs*, 48, no. 2 (1995), 357.

justification of international interventions. The use of alternative normative logics in a legal language signifies an expansion of the legal system as part of an evolutionary process of differentiation that can be illustrated with the metaphor of a semi-legal field. Even though international legal theorists of the nineteenth century argued in favour of the priority of the rule of non-intervention and the barriers for an exception of this rule were conceptualized as very high, there were approaches that introduced legitimate forms of intervention which cannot be considered as entirely legal or illegal but which exemplify how the border between law and non-law was shifted in international legal theory. Using the example of humanitarian interventions, I show how concepts of 'intervention politics' and 'admissible interventions' were introduced in order to legitimize forms of intervention that, on the one hand, were disputed in light of the pure principle of international sovereignty but, on the other, extended (or signalled an extension of) the legal field of international intervention.

THE POSSIBILITY OF A RIGHT AGAINST A RIGHT

The central challenge, which all legal concepts of international interventions share, was expressed by nineteenth-century international legal scholars Henry Bonfils and Paul Fauchille in their conclusion that 'a right of intervention is impossible and cannot be possible, since there cannot be a right against a right'.[4] The logical inconsistency of a violation of the right of sovereignty by the right of intervention was proved unable to withstand the complex reality of international legal relations, however.[5] Nevertheless, even though the right to intervene is in fact one against the right of state sovereignty, it is also based on legal grounds. The legal justification of international intervention was rendered possible by the fact that the meaning of sovereignty was never absolute, neither in practice nor in theory.[6] Even in the nineteenth century, during which

[4] Henry Bonfils and Paul Fauchille, *Lehrbuch des Völkerrechts für Studium und Praxis*, 3rd edn (Berlin: Carl Heymanns Verlag, 1904), 155, translation by the author.

[5] Karl Hettlage, 'Die Intervention in der Geschichte der Völkerrechtswissenschaft und im System der modernen Völkerrechtslehre', *Niemeyers Zeitschrift für Internationales Recht*, 30 (1927), 39.

[6] D. J. B. Trim, 'Conclusion: Humanitarian Intervention in Historical Perspective' in Brendan Simms and D. J. B. Trim (eds.), *Humanitarian Intervention: A History* (Cambridge University Press, 2011), 381; Stephen Krasner, 'Compromising Westphalia', *International Security*, 20, no. 3 (Winter 1995), 115–51; Stephen D. Krasner, *Sovereignty: Organized Hypocrisy* (Princeton University Press, 1999).

European international law was predominantly understood as a positivist legal regime applied among European states,[7] legal universalisms of natural legal rationale never completely disappeared. On the one hand, international law was based on the principle of Westphalian sovereignty, which consequently implied an absolute rule of non-intervention. On the other hand, legal historian scholarship has confirmed that no undisputed principle or positivist rule of non-intervention ever existed.[8]

On the contrary, nineteenth-century international legal theorists developed varied doctrines of legitimate interventions: political interventions to protect the 'Balance of Power',[9] economic interventions to govern state bankruptcies and international debt,[10] humanitarian interventions to protect co-nationals and co-religionists. While the political and moral aspirations which motivated these doctrines seem to be obvious, their legal foundation is not as self-evident. The key heuristic to justify international intervention was to formulate a legal principle that could stand alongside the principle of sovereignty and thus be used to deduce legitimate norms of intervention.[11] For nineteenth-century international legal scholars, this alternative was formulated as the idea of the international community of states.

[7] Georg Friedrich von Martens, *Einleitung in das positive Europäische Völkerrecht auf Verträge und Herkommen gegründet* (Göttingen: Johann Christian Dieterich, 1796); Johann Ludwig Klüber, *Droit des gens moderne de l'Europe, avec un supplément contenant une bibliothèque choisie du droit des gens* (Stuttgart: Cotta'sche Buchhandlung, 1819).

[8] Miloš Vec, 'Intervention/Nichtintervention: Verrechtlichung der Politik und Politisierung des Völkerrechts im 19. Jahrhundert' in Ulrich von Lappenküper and Reiner Marcowitz (eds.), *Macht und Recht: Völkerrecht in den internationalen Beziehungen* (Paderborn: Ferdinand Schöningh, 2010), vol. XIII, 147, 156.

[9] Miloš Vec, 'De-juridifying "Balance of Power": A Principle in 19th Century International Legal Doctrine', Conference Paper no. 5/2011, European Society of International Law Conference Paper Series, Tallinn Research Forum, 26–8 May 2011, 1–15, http://ssrn.com/abstract=1968667 (last accessed on 18 May 2015).

[10] Lea Heimbeck, Die Abwicklung von Staatsbankrotten im Völkerrecht: Verrechtlichung und Rechtsvermeidung zwischen 1824 und 1907 (Baden-Baden: Nomos, 2013).

[11] For the evolution of these rights in the context of the debate on so-called fundamental rights of states, see Miloš Vec, 'Grundrechte der Staaten: Die Tradierung des Natur-und Völkerrechts der Aufklärung', *Rechtsgeschichte. Zeitschrift des Max-Planck-Instituts für Rechtsgeschichte*, 18 (2011), 66–94; Kristina Lovrić-Pernak, *Morale internationale und humanité im Völkerrecht des späten 19. Jahrhunderts: Bedeutung und Funktion in Staatenpraxis und Wissenschaft* (Baden-Baden: Nomos, 2013).

A central source for the deeper understanding of the international community as a legal principle in the nineteenth century is Robert von Mohl's essay '*Die Pflege der internationalen Gemeinschaft als Aufgabe des Völkerrechts*'.[12] In this essay, Robert von Mohl discussed two principles as the main pillars of international law: the sovereignty of states and the international community. For Mohl, sovereignty was just the first step of international legal evolution and, as such, the basis of equal international relations. The second step was the international community. Mohl discussed the international community as the legal frame for the protection of the common interests of states. In his terminology the international community is the international legal instrument to achieve what he called 'human purposes'.[13] He did not specify, however, what such human purposes encompassed in concrete terms. Mohl basically argued that they are a set of intellectual and physical characteristics that we all aspire to and consider in the organization of our lives.[14] As a means to satisfy these 'needs', Mohl underlined two necessities: individual independence and the community with others.[15] He eventually applied this heuristic to the field of international relations: state sovereignty and the international community as the two fundamental and interrelated goals of international law.

On the basis of this idea of international community, international legal theorists argued that an inseparable component of sovereignty was therefore something we today might call an international 'responsibility to protect'.[16] From this it follows that the idea of international community did not reify the tension between independence and solidarity but emphasized the role of solidarity as an element of responsible independence. In this sense, what came to be known as the community of states or the *Rechtsgenossenschaft der Völker*[17] or the *société humaine*[18] was

[12] Stefan Kroll, 'Community, Enforcement and Justification: The International Law of Intervention in World-Societal Perspective', *SSRN eLibrary* (11 May 2012), 15–6, http://papers.ssrn.com/sol3/papers.cfm?abstract_id=2056626 (last accessed on 18 May 2015).

[13] Robert von Mohl, 'Die Pflege der internationalen Gemeinschaft als Aufgabe des Völkerrechts' in Robert von Mohl (ed.), *Staatsrecht, Völkerrecht und Politik*, vol. I: *Staatsrecht und Völkerrecht* (Tübingen: Laupp & Siebeck, 1860), 585, translation by the author.

[14] Ibid., 581–2. [15] Ibid., 583.

[16] Luke Glanville, 'Ellery Stowell and the Enduring Dilemmas of Humanitarian Intervention', *International Studies Review*, 13 (2011), 241–58.

[17] Hermann Strauch, *Zur Interventions-Lehre: Eine völkerrechtliche Studie* (Heidelberg: Carl Winter's Universitätsbuchhandlung, 1879).

[18] Antoine Rougier, 'La théorie de l'intervention d'humanité', *Revue Générale de Droit International Public*, 17 (1910), 468–526.

the legal source on which the right (and sometimes even duty) to intervene was based.

I have argued elsewhere that the idea of international community was the expression of a 'consciousness of collectivity' at the international level, which provided the key heuristic to justify interventions in cases where the security or the normative values of the community were at stake.[19] This consciousness of collectivity finds expression especially in the question of unilateral and collective intervention. Martha Finnemore has argued that, in the nineteenth century, international interventions did not have to be multilateral in order to be considered legitimate, while this would be the situation today.[20] Furthermore, Finnemore has underlined a qualitative difference between current and past multilateralism. While nineteenth-century multilateralism would have been 'strategic' and driven by 'non-humanitarian' aims, she argues that today's multilateralism is 'deeply political and normative, not just strategic'.[21] However, community-based doctrines of intervention show that nineteenth-century theories of intervention were also driven by shared political and normative expectations, including an expectation of multilateral action.

As a consequence of being based on the principle of community, most cases of legally justified international interventions were required to be performed collectively rather than unilaterally. In this context it is important to note first of all that self-help – the basic example of unilateral action – was usually not classified as an intervention in the legal debate, but rather as war in a classical sense.[22] The major challenge for legal authors was to define the cases in which an intervention on behalf of others was legitimate and the form, unilateral or collective, in which it had to be carried out.[23] Especially in cases of intervention in which the legitimacy of the motivation was disputed, as in the case of humanitarian intervention, collective action was requested.[24] This was based on a

[19] Kroll, 'Community, Enforcement and Justification', 12.

[20] Martha Finnemore, *The Purpose of Intervention: Changing Beliefs about the Use of Force* (Ithaca, NY and London: Cornell University Press, 2003), 53.

[21] Ibid., 80–1.

[22] Albert Friedrich Berner, 'Intervention (völkerrechtliche)' in Johann Caspar Bluntschli and Karl Brater (eds.), *Deutsches Staats-Wörterbuch* (Stuttgart and Leipzig: Expedition des Staats-Wörterbuchs, 1860), 341.

[23] Carole Fink, *Defending the Rights of Others: The Great Powers, the Jews, and International Minority Protection, 1878–1938* (New York: Cambridge University Press, 2004); Nicholas J. Wheeler, *Saving Strangers: Humanitarian Intervention in International Society* (New York: Oxford University Press, 2000).

[24] Hettlage, 'Die Intervention in der Geschichte', 67.

rationale that we know also from contemporary discourses on the right of intervention. As the legitimacy of humanitarian intervention was generally disputed, collective action was understood as a mechanism to avoid abuses of the right of intervention by powerful states, in the sense that the collective intervention of several powers led to a situation where those powers would monitor each other.[25]

Altogether, the legal idea of an international community was conceptualized as the basic element of the justification for international interventions. The right and duty to intervene was developed not as a right against the principle of the sovereignty of the nation state but rather as an extension of it. Given that sovereignty was the fundamental basis of the Westphalian international legal system, the principle of international community had to be coined similarly as a legal source of highest rank. The major challenge in this context was to justify this principle, which originated in legal philosophy,[26] as being a legal principle in the positivist legal sense that was predominant during that period. In fact, the emergence of a legal principle of international community which actually had the potential to complement the understanding of sovereignty in that period is a strong hint that the common attribution of positivism to the nineteenth century defines the era too narrowly. On the contrary, even though the legal scholars of that era were keen to hail themselves as positivists, the nature of their legal arguments was much wider than these actors themselves might have recognized.

HUMANITARIAN INTERVENTION AND THE PROTECTION OF RELIGIOUS MINORITIES

The process of law-making does not merely consist of the formal deduction of normative structures. The application, adoption, and reinterpretation of norms by legal actors form an inseparable part of the genesis of normative meaning. As I will show by the case of the humanitarian protection of religious minorities, the application of normative rules often leads to a substantial reinterpretation of their normative content or

[25] Friedrich Heinrich Geffcken, *Das Recht der Intervention* (Hamburg: Verlag von I. F. Richter, 1887), 5–6.

[26] Miloš Vec, *Recht und Normierung in der Industriellen Revolution: Neue Strukturen der Normsetzung in Völkerrecht, staatlicher Gesetzgebung und gesellschaftlicher Selbstnormierung* (Frankfurt a. M.: Vittorio Klostermann, 2006), 52.

purpose. The discussed principle of community might be used to pursue strategic and individual interest, as the sociologists of justification Boltanski and Thévenot have observed in the case of the principle of common humanity: 'A principle we shall call the principle of common humanity? In the light of this principle, cannot the application to humanity of an ordering principle at all be viewed as an unjustifiable act of "domination" that only serves the "personal interests" of those who would benefit from it?'[27]

While many legal historian writings have underscored the hegemonic use of the principle of intervention, others have ardently argued in favour of a 'genuine humanitarianism', which was not an expression of imperial practices of intervention.[28] Michael R. Marrus seems to take a middle position when describing the nineteenth century as 'an age of liberal imperialism, in which solid, bourgeois governments acted confidently on the world's stage, certain not only of their own right to rule, but also of their beneficent objectives in doing so'.[29] This 'liberal imperialism' was upheld by the 'liberal conscience' of a new generation of international lawyers to accept the practice of intervention 'when the interests of humanity were being infringed by the excess of a barbarous or despotic government'.[30]

I will contribute to this debate of intervention and hegemony by discussing humanitarian intervention for the protection of religious minorities in the nineteenth century as a particularly relevant case, in which the humanitarian principle was an expression of humanitarian interests but at the same time was used to legitimize unequal practices of intervention. The international legal literature of the nineteenth century examines several circumstances under which humanitarian intervention may be legal. Among those reasons, the protection of religious minorities stands as one of the most discussed cases.

Just as disputed as the legitimacy of humanitarian intervention in general was that of intervention on the basis of religious protection; it

[27] Luc Boltanski and Laurent Thévenot, *On Justification: Economies of Worth* (Princeton University Press, 2006), 38.

[28] Gary J. Bass, *Freedom's Battle: The Origins of Humanitarian Intervention* (New York: Alfred A. Knopf, 2008), 5.

[29] Michael R. Marrus, 'International Bystanders to the Holocaust and Humanitarian Intervention' in Richard Ashby Wilson und Richard D. Brown (eds.), *Humanitarian Suffering: The Mobilization of Empathy* (Cambridge University Press, 2009), 162.

[30] Martti Koskenniemi, *The Gentle Civilizer of Nations: The Rise and Fall of International Law, 1870–1960* (New York: Cambridge University Press, 2001), 95.

was simply not considered to be a generally shared international legal rule. The centrality of the issue during the nineteenth century is documented by the fact, however, that hardly any chapter on humanitarian intervention in an international law treatise could refrain from taking a position in regard to the issue of religion during that period.

At this point it is important to note that the approaches regarding religious protection differed according to the different strands, legal and non-legal, of discourse on the issue of humanitarian intervention. This book as a whole underscores the point that the protection of minorities in the nineteenth century was not only targeted at whites and Christians,[31] but that interventions were carried out also in the interest of Jewish minorities (Green) as well as against the slave trade (Klose and Macdonald). Gary Bass has similarly argued 'that nineteenth century's humanitarian interventions were about more than just rescuing fellow Christians'.[32] Still, it should be noted that he based this argument on an examination of humanitarian activism. Bass emphasized how humanitarian 'activism' confirmed the existence of a 'genuine humanitarianism'.[33] As this contribution shows, it is rather doubtful whether international lawyers of this period can be counted as humanitarian activists, for the legal discourse was still characterized by an 'ethnocentric cast'.[34] Davide Rodogno recently formulated the need to study more carefully 'the extent to which the intervening states responded to the suffering of others regardless of their ethnic or religious identity'; however, he also pointed out that only 'when the victims were Christians under the rule of an "uncivilized" state did the European powers consider the possibility of undertaking humanitarian intervention'.[35]

In the international legal discourse, humanitarian intervention for the protection of religious minorities was discussed in the context of religious freedom. At the end of the nineteenth century, Franz von Liszt observed that the protection of religious freedom among Christian states was a common rule within Europe since the Peace of Westphalia. According to Liszt, it was not necessary to regulate religious freedom by bilateral agreements among European powers.[36] However, in the context of

[31] Finnemore, *The Purpose of Intervention*, 53. [32] Bass, *Freedom's Battle*, 347.

[33] Ibid., 6. [34] Marrus, 'International Bystanders', 163.

[35] Davide Rodogno, *Against Massacre: Humanitarian Interventions in the Ottoman Empire, 1815–1914. The Emergence of a European Concept and International Practice* (Princeton University Press, 2012), 11, 34.

[36] Franz von Liszt, *Das Völkerrecht systematisch dargestellt* (Berlin: Verlag von O. Haering, 1902), 184.

international relations with Latin American and non-Christian Asian states, religious freedom did not have this taken-for-granted status, but was an essential part of the bilateral treaties with those governments. In this context, Liszt strongly emphasized the necessity to enshrine the protection of religious freedom in agreements with non-Christian states.[37] A closer look at bilateral agreements of European and non-European powers during the nineteenth century shows that religious freedom in these agreements was protected only asymmetrically in the interest of the Christian citizens of European origins who had recently arrived and were residing temporarily in non-European countries.

This asymmetric regulation of religious freedom was typical of the overall process of the so-called European expansion and the unequal relations between Europeans and non-Europeans at the end of the nineteenth century. Religious freedom was meant to protect Christian traders, missionaries, and consuls in non-Christian regions and not to support peaceful inter-religious coexistence. The unequal treaties of European powers with, for example, China (1844, 1847, and 1858) or Japan (1858) demonstrate that not only the right to have and to develop the Christian faith was protected by treaties asymmetrically but also the right to practice a religion in public and to establish suitable places for these purposes and even the right to engage in missionary activities. It is only in the context of European/non-European relations that European international legal scholars seem to have shared the view that intervention to protect these asymmetrical rights of a particular community might be necessary and justified.

Against this background, how did international legal theorists coin religion as a just ground for intervention? William E. Hall dedicated a chapter of his influential textbook on international law to the issue of intervention. In this chapter, he formulated a substantial critique of the right of humanitarian intervention and, in this context, of the legality of intervention on religious grounds. In his view, religious reasons had 'ceased to be recognised as an independent ground' for intervention.[38] Hall held the perspective that religion might have been a legitimate ground for intervention in the pre-Westphalian order within Europe but could not maintain this status any longer because of the risk of arbitrary abuses. It therefore was to be considered only in combination with other legitimating reasons for intervention. This argument was consistent with

[37] Ibid., 185.
[38] William Edward Hall, *International Law* (Oxford: Clarendon Press, 1880), 246.

Liszt's argument that religious freedom had not been an issue of inner-European debate since the Peace of Westphalia.

According to Hall, only Robert Phillimore, an English international law scholar and politician, seems to have 'sanction[ed] the intervention on the ground of religion' in the nineteenth-century debate.[39] Phillimore indeed argued that a just ground for intervention was 'to protect Persons, subjects of another State, from persecution on account of professing a Religion not recognised by that State, but identical with the Religion of the Intervening State'.[40] Taking the contemporary case of Russian intervention into the Ottoman Empire (the Crimean War, 1853–1856) as a vantage point, Phillimore discussed three paths to justify intervention on religious grounds.

The first case was the intervention of a Christian state into another Christian state on behalf of a Christian minority. This case, which is said to have originated in the time of the Reformation, 'has ... been practiced, and cannot be said ... to be a violation of international law'. However, it was only to be practiced in extreme cases and would not qualify or limit the general rule of non-interference.[41] The second case, which is more important in the context of this chapter, was the intervention of a Christian state into a Muslim state. Phillimore approached this case with a suggestive question, which already implied that there is a qualitative difference to the intervention of Christians in a Christian state:

> Is the rule of law altered by the fact that the persons in whose behalf the right of Intervention is claimed, are the subjects of a Mahometan or Infidel State?
>
> The true answer seems to be that the rule is not changed, but that there is a much wider field for the application of the exceptional principle of interference.[42]

Just a few sentences before, Phillimore had mentioned that the reverse, the 'Mohametan Intervention with Christian States', had yet to emerge, 'but would be subject on principle to the same law'.[43] This "true answer" makes clear that there is less equality in the practice of different cases of co-religious protection than an international legal order based on the principle of sovereignty and equality would actually require.

This becomes even more evident in his discussion of a third way to justify intervention on religious grounds, namely the case of bilateral treaties that guarantee religious freedom for Christian states in non-

[39] Ibid., 247.

[40] Robert Phillimore, *Commentaries upon International Law* (Philadelphia: T. & J. W. Johnson Law Booksellers, 1854), 315.

[41] Ibid., 340. [42] Ibid., 341. [43] Ibid.

Christian environments, which I have touched upon earlier in this section. Should those treaties be violated, interventions were considered legitimate, according to Phillimore. In line with the asymmetrical nature of the regulations enshrined in these unequal bilateral treaties, Phillimore's chapters also confirm that, in practice, only the intervention of Christians in non-Christian regions was considered a legitimate intervention and not vice versa.[44]

We can find another perspective on the role of bilateral treaties as a basis for interventionist practices in Hermann Strauch's 1879 commentary on the international law of intervention. Strauch refuted the existence of a common doctrine of intervention on behalf of Christians and religious minorities in principal.[45] However, he emphasized the practical importance of so-called revisionary rights (*Einmischungsrechte*). These revisionary rights, according to Strauch, were based on bilateral treaties and would have the potential to enlarge the right of intervention beyond its regular limits. Strauch argued that, in practice, revisionary rights had been applied and ethically justified only in the regions of south-eastern Europe (Turkey) and other foreign regions in the world (East Asia).[46] Thus, Strauch identified an ethically justified practice to interfere into the affairs only of those states that were considered in the international legal literature at the time to be semi- or uncivilized nations. Even though the absence of a Christian legacy was not the only reason to consider a society as uncivilized in the second half of the nineteenth century,[47] it still was an important factor. So Strauch's hint about 'cultural backwardness' (*zurückstehende Kultur*) was *inter alia* another justifying argument for the legitimacy of intervention in non-Christian regions.

INTERVENTION POLITICS AND ADMISSIBLE INTERVENTION

Strauch was convinced – and this again was typical for international legal writing in the period of European expansion[48] – that interventions by European civilized states were an important instrument to develop the administrative and legal structure of 'culturally backward' states. As a consequence of such interventions, these societies might at some point be awarded full sovereignty, and this, again, would confirm intervention as

[44] Ibid., 341–5. [45] Strauch, *Zur Interventions-Lehre*, 14. [46] Ibid., 22–3.

[47] Stefan Kroll, *Normgenese durch Re-Interpretation: China und das europäische Völkerrecht im 19. und 20. Jahrhundert* (Baden-Baden: Nomos, 2012), 9–18.

[48] Jörg Fisch, *Die europäische Expansion und das Völkerrecht* (Stuttgart: Steiner, 1984).

a practice of solidarity with regard to human development and prove the 'foolishness' of the principle of non-intervention: '*Die erwähnte Interventions-Politik bezeugt also durch ihre Existenz die Solidarität menschheitlicher Entwicklung und zugleich die ganze Thorheit des Geschrei's der Ritter des Nicht-interventions-Prinzips*.'[49]

As the quote underlines, Strauch's term for this kind of necessary intervention into non-European world regions was a 'politics of intervention'. Paradoxically, he derived the legal source of the politics of intervention from the multilateral Berlin Treaty of 1878. Paradoxically, indeed, for this treaty, which contained important regulations with regard to the issue of intervention and the protection of religious minorities, did not regulate the religious freedom of the Christian co-nationals of European powers alone but claimed the equality of all religions in the legislation and public administration in various Balkan states 'without any exception', as Franz von Liszt rightly observed.[50] In Strauch's interpretation, this imposition of political and legal institutions introduced a common revisionary right ('*ein Einmischungsrecht allgemeiner Art*') with regard to the legislation pertaining to religious freedom in these regions.[51] According to Strauch, this common revisionary right was the legal formalization of intervention politics, and Strauch was convinced that the necessity of intervention politics would become even more visible in the future, as the European expansion into Asia advanced.[52]

Altogether, the Treaty of Berlin was interpreted by Strauch not as the introduction of a universal rule on religious freedom but as a legal justification for intervention politics that partook in nineteenth-century civilizing missions in the non-European world. In this context, it is important to note as well that religious freedom in the Berlin Treaty was not regulated in a single universal article but in various separated regulations that protected religion in the respective countries.[53] In other words, even though each article addressed religion in a broad sense and not just the Christian faith, the equal and universal protection of all religions in all signatory states was obviously never intended.

Another version of the idea of intervention politics was formulated by Lassa Oppenheim, one of the most influential international legal theorists of the early twentieth century. In volume one of his famous international law textbook, Oppenheim introduced the distinction between 'rightful'

[49] Strauch, *Zur Interventions-Lehre*, 26.
[50] Liszt, *Das Völkerrecht*, 185.
[51] Strauch, *Zur Interventions-Lehre*, 24.
[52] Ibid., 25.
[53] Fink, *Defending the Rights of Others*, 37.

and 'admissible' interventions. According to this, an intervention can be legitimate, even if a right of intervention is not acknowledged. A rightful intervention 'is always based on a legal restriction upon the independence or territorial or personal supremacy of the State concerned'.[54] To illustrate his argument, Oppenheim named examples of rightful interventions as being cases involving the possible right of a suzerain to intervene into a vassal state or a protectorate, the protection of citizens abroad, the violation of international treaties, the unilateral action of another state in dealing with an international affair, and finally, the violation of universally recognized principles of international law.[55]

Admissible albeit not rightful interventions, according to Oppenheim, occur in at least two undisputed cases. 'Although they violate the independence ... of the State concerned ... such interventions in default of right ... are generally admitted and excused' in a case of self-preservation or in the interest of the balance of power.[56] While the former case is a rather obvious consequence of an international system that is based on the existence of sovereign nation sates, the latter deserves closer consideration in the context of this chapter. According to Oppenheim, the 'equilibrium between the members of the Family of Nations is an indispensable condition of the very existence of international law. If the States could not keep another in check, all Law of Nations would soon disappear.'[57] *In fine*, intervention for the protection of the balance of power was articulated in close connection with the more general legal concept of international intervention, which I have discussed in section one and which was based on the idea of an international community and the protection of its normative order. In Oppenheim's interpretation, the balance of power is understood less as a mechanism of international hegemony than as a form of international police action in the name of international legal principles.

Oppenheim followed therein with a third case of admissible intervention, one that was, however, disputed among jurists: the case of humanitarian intervention for the protection of religious groups as described earlier. Oppenheim named cases that confirmed the practice of these kinds of interventions and came to the conclusion that, even though there was no acknowledged international legal rule which allowed for intervention in the interest of religious minorities, 'it cannot be denied that public opinion and the attitude of the Powers are in favour of such

[54] Lassa Oppenheim, *International Law: A Treatise*, 2 vols. (New York: Longmans, Green, and Co., 1905), vol. I: *Peace*, 183.

[55] Ibid., 183–4. [56] Ibid., 185. [57] Ibid.

interventions'.[58] This reference to the importance of public opinion and international practice was complemented, finally, in the following section in which Oppenheim came to the overall conclusion that all intervention was '*de facto* a matter of policy just like war'.[59]

In sum, Strauch and Oppenheim developed two distinct concepts of a politics of intervention that shared the heuristic of the legitimacy of necessary interventions even in cases in which there is no commonly accepted right of intervention. This does not mean that these kinds of intervention stand outside the law. On the contrary, these two concurrent approaches could be read as attempts to outline a semi-legal field, within which the evolution of certain legal concepts becomes visible.[60] These concepts are not entirely legal or illegal, but something in-between. The orientation taken by these concepts, however, is deemed to be geared towards integration within the legal system. This was very obvious especially in the work by Oppenheim. In other words, coining non-legal logics, such as politics and ethics, in a legal language within the context of humanitarian intervention is, in fact, an attempt to integrate these logics into the legal imagination, rather than to exclude them.

All told, the main purpose for allowing humanitarian intervention on religious grounds in international law during the nineteenth century was to protect Christian co-religionists within non-Christian environments. This was a consequence of the European expansion that took place in the second half of that century. The introduction of necessary forms of intervention showed how the line between legal and non-legal normative concepts had shifted in the international legal debate. At the beginning of the twentieth century, the relevance of religion as a just ground for intervention was not disputed either, but its place in the legal theory debate varied. While H. G. Hodges or Ellery Stowell discussed it in the context of humanitarian intervention,[61] Antoine Rougier concluded in his *Théorie de l'intervention d'humanité* that intervention on religious grounds requires a specific theoretical treatment that differs from the case of humanitarian intervention.[62] However, in principle, its ability to justify intervention was not questioned.

[58] Ibid., 186. [59] Ibid., 187.

[60] The metaphor of a semi-legal field is an adaption of the 'semi-autonomous social field', which is discussed in context of classical legal pluralism; see Sally Falk Moore, 'Law and Social Change: The Semi-autonomous Social Field as an Appropriate Subject of Study', *Law & Society Review*, 7, no. 4 (1973), 719–46.

[61] H. G. Hodges, *The Doctrine of Intervention* (Princeton: The Banner Press, 1915), 95; Stowell, *Intervention in International Law*, 54.

[62] Rougier, 'La théorie de l'intervention d'humanité', 56.

CONCLUSION

Here I have explored the legal justification of international intervention as it was coined and debated in the nineteenth century. I showed that the idea of international community served as a principle from which the justification of intervention was developed. Even though the right of international intervention was referred to as a violation of national sovereignty in many legal theoretical sources, its conceptualization was based on the idea of international community and was understood as the extension of a principle of Westphalian sovereignty, which was specified by the concept of an autonomous, but isolated nation state. Taking this as a vantage point, I discussed the protection of religious freedom and religious minority groups as a field of humanitarian intervention in which the application of the right of intervention could be further studied. On the one hand, this specific type of intervention and the debates surrounding it showed that the right to intervene could be used asymmetrically to protect the interests of certain groups or states. On the other hand, legal theorists reacted to these developments by introducing new categories of necessary and legitimate forms of intervention. Even though these kinds of intervention politics and admissible interventions could not be described as entirely legal or illegal during that period, the attempt to frame them in the legal terms of treaties helped integrate these novel doctrines into the international legal system rather than exclude them. I used the metaphor of a semi-legal field to illustrate that, on the whole, the legal justification of humanitarian intervention in these nineteenth-century cases was neither entirely integrated nor excluded from the international legal order but formed a transitional case revealing the dynamics of the shifting boundaries of the legal system. Altogether, the doctrine of (humanitarian) intervention emerged as a novel normative concept during the course of the nineteenth century and was gradually integrated into the legal discourse. The legal language was particularly desirable for contemporary actors, as it served as an instrument to formulate a justification narrative for the unequal use of the instrument of intervention. This unequal application of a normative principle in the name of a common humanity appears to be the main reason why the right of humanitarian intervention is legally disputed and ethically deceptive to the present day.

PART II

FIGHTING THE SLAVE TRADE AND PROTECTING RELIGIOUS MINORITIES

Major impulses for humanitarian intervention in the nineteenth century

5

Enforcing abolition

The entanglement of civil society action, humanitarian norm-setting, and military intervention

Fabian Klose

> I was not aware till I had been some time here [in London] of the degree of frenzy existing here about the slave trade. People in general appear to think that it would suit the policy of the nation to go to war to put an end to that abominable traffic; and many wish that we should take the field on this new crusade.[1]
>
> Lord Wellington, July 1814

When evaluating the Congress of Vienna of 1814/15, historians traditionally concentrate on the negotiations to redraw the political map of Europe and on the establishment of an order meant to ensure peace on the continent in the wake of the Napoleonic Wars.[2] As a result of their experiences with France's aggressively hegemonic aspirations, which had thrown the entire continent into bloody military confrontation for more than twenty years, the victorious Great Powers of Great Britain, Austria, Prussia, and Russia – expanded in 1818 to include France in the Concert of Europe – strove during the Vienna summits to create a lasting,

I would like to thank Andrew Thompson, Martin Geyer, and Johannes Paulmann for their perceptive comments on the draft of this chapter. My essay was supported by the German Research Foundation (DFG) for which I am deeply grateful.

[1] Letter, 'Wellington to Henry Wellesley, 29 July 1814' in A. W. of Wellington (ed.), *Supplementary Despatches, Correspondence, and Memoranda of Field Marshal Arthur Duke of Wellington* (London: Murray, 1862), vol. IX, 165.

[2] On the Congress of Vienna and its importance, see, for example, H. Nicolson, *The Congress of Vienna: A Study in Allied Unity, 1812–1822* (London: Constable, 1947); P. W. Schroeder, *The Transformation of European Politics, 1763–1848* (Oxford: Clarendon Press, 1994), 517–82; A. Zamoyski, *Rites of Peace: The Fall of Napoleon and the Congress of Vienna* (New York; HarperCollins, 2007), 260–441.

stable, and peaceful order based on the idea of a political balance of power.[3] In this context, the practice of intervention was attributed a clear function after 1815: the Great Powers would jointly intervene under all circumstances to put down revolts and revolutions that posed a danger for them and the newly created international order.[4] The Holy Alliance, a coalition of the Continental powers of Prussia, Austria, and Russia, clearly committed itself to this anti-revolutionary principle of intervention in the 'Protocole pour déterminer le droit d'intervention des grandes Puissances' (Troppau Protocol), signed 19 November 1820 in what was then the Austrian city of Troppau.[5] This is interpreted as the attempt 'to commit all of Europe to a reactionary model of rule and society'.[6]

However, in the case of Great Britain, historians attest that the great maritime power followed a strict policy of non-intervention, one that enjoyed the support of a broad domestic consensus and whose most vehement advocate was the long-time British foreign secretary Lord Castlereagh. This foreign-policy paradigm of non-intervention is said to have eroded only in the period from 1815 to 1827 in connection with the Greek struggle for independence from the Ottoman Empire and the question about possible intervention by the other great European powers. According to the argument presented by John Bew, Great Britain was drawn into concerted European intervention out of 'the necessities of *Realpolitik*', specifically out of the fear that unilateral action on the part of Russia would cause a disadvantageous shift in the balance of power in the Mediterranean region so vital for Great Britain.[7]

[3] P. W. Schroeder (ed.), *Systems, Stability, and Statecraft: Essays on the International History of Modern Europe* (Basingstoke and New York: Palgrave Macmilan, 2004), 37–57, 223–41; M. Schulz, *Normen und Praxis: Das Europäische Konzert der Großmächte als Sicherheitsrat 1815–1860* (Munich: Oldenbourg, 2009), 46–58.

[4] On this, see Th. G. Otte, 'Of Congresses and Gunboats: Military Intervention in the Nineteenth Century' in A. M. Dorman and Th. G. Otte (eds.), *Military Intervention. From Gunboat to Humanitarian Intervention* (Aldershot: Dartmouth, 1995), 19–52; J. Osterhammel, 'Krieg im Frieden: Zu Formen und Typologie imperialer Interventionen' in Jürgen Osterhammel, *Geschichtswissenschaft jenseits des Nationalstaats: Studien zu Beziehungsgeschichte und Zivilisationsvergleich* (Göttingen: Vandenhoeck & Ruprecht, 2001), 295–8.

[5] The 'Protocole pour déterminer le droit d'intervention des grandes Puissances' is found in L. B. Descamps and L. Renault (eds.), *Recueil International des Traités du XIXe Siècle, Tome Premier 1801–1825* (Paris: Arthur Rousseau, 1914), 803–5.

[6] Schulz, *Normen und Praxis*, 81, 584.

[7] J. Bew, '"From an Umpire to a Competitor": Castlereagh, Canning, and the Issue of International Intervention in the Wake of the Napoleonic Wars' in B. Simms and D. J. B. Trim (eds.), *Humanitarian Intervention: A History* (Cambridge University Press, 2011), 117–38, here 119.

However, to associate the practice of intervention only with the Congress of Vienna and to interpret it as having derived strictly from the concerns of power politics is to overlook another aspect taking shape in the shadows of the congress, one that would become firmly established in nineteenth-century international politics, namely, the use of military intervention to enforce an internationally stipulated humanitarian norm. In addition to the various territorial provisions, the congress also produced the 'Déclaration des 8 Cours, relative à l'Abolition Universelle de la Traite des Nègres', with which the Great Powers established for the first time a universal ban on the slave trade in international law. For a long time, this document received relatively little attention and was characterized only as a vague declaration of intentions, devoid of any major impact.[8]

It will be shown here that the international ban of the slave trade, as declared by the Congress of Vienna, not only created an international humanitarian norm but also conceived the corresponding international apparatus to enforce it. Great Britain was the central force driving this, which represented a major departure from its foreign-policy paradigm of non-intervention. The London government championed a new practice of intervention that innovatively combined the use of military and legal means on the international level. In this context, we detect a notable entanglement of civil society action, humanitarian norm-setting, and military intervention. By mobilizing public opinion in Great Britain, the abolitionists succeeded first to commit their own government to a policy of intervention against the slave trade and then to have this translated into foreign policy action by the United Kingdom. This perspective throws a new light on the early nineteenth-century practice of intervention and makes it more than just a reactionary instrument used by the crowned heads of the Holy Alliance to retain power. It possessed another, completely different aspect that has been rarely considered until recently. Under the influence and the pressure of civil society activists, the state began to intervene in the defence of humanitarian norms. Therefore, it is the central argument of this contribution that the origins of the governmental practice of humanitarian intervention, which more recent research on the nineteenth century have linked exclusively to the protection of

[8] Gratifying exceptions are H. Berding, 'Die Ächtung des Sklavenhandels auf dem Wiener Kongress 1814/15', *Historische Zeitschrift*, 2 (1974), 266–89; I. Clark, *International Legitimacy and World Society* (Oxford University Press, 2007), 37–60; T. Weller, '... répugnant aux principes d'humanité'. 'Die Ächtung des Sklavenhandels in der Kongressakte und die Rolle der Kirchen' in H. Duchhardt and J. Wischmeyer (eds.) (Göttingen: Vandenhoeck & Ruprecht, 2013), 183–213.

Christian minorities in the Ottoman Empire,[9] should be traced to the milieu of the Congress of Vienna and the context of the struggle against the transatlantic slave trade.

DEMANDING INTERVENTION: THE ENTANGLEMENT OF CIVIL SOCIETY ACTION AND INTERNATIONAL POLITICS

The famous African American civil rights leader and historian W. E. B. Du Bois called the transatlantic slave trade 'the most magnificent drama in the last thousand years of human history'.[10] From the end of the fifteenth century to the middle of the nineteenth, Europeans shipped over 11 million Africans to America. The hunt and enslavement of human beings on the African continent alone cost countless lives even before the slave ships set sail, and it is estimated that another 1.5 million people died during the *middle passage*, the infamous crossing of the Atlantic.[11] The transatlantic slave trade reached its highpoint in the 1780s when over 80,000 Africans were transported annually on European ships to America.[12] Besides France, Great Britain was the undisputed leader in the flourishing economic system of the transatlantic slave trade.

Yet it was also in the United Kingdom during the heyday of human trafficking across the Atlantic that a small group of people began to organize civil resistance to this well-established economic system of human trade. On 22 May 1787, various abolitionists met at the house of the publisher James Philipps in London to form the Committee for Effecting the Abolition of the Slave Trade.[13] With regard to the strategic focus of their newly

[9] Above all, see G. Bass, *Freedom's Battle: The Origins of Humanitarian Intervention* (New York: Knopf, 2008); M. Swatek-Evenstein, *Geschichte der 'Humanitären Intervention'* (Baden Baden: Nomos, 2008); B. Simms and D. J. B. Trim, *Humanitarian Intervention*, 111–225; D. Rodogno, *Against Massacre: Humanitarian Interventions in the Ottoman Empire, 1815–1914* (Princeton University Press, 2012).

[10] W. E. B. Du Bois, *Black Reconstruction in America: An Essay Toward a History of the Part Which Black Folk Played in the Attempt to Reconstruct Democracy in America, 1860–1880* (New York: Russell & Russell, 1966), 727.

[11] D. Eltis, 'The Volume and Structure of the Transatlantic Slave Trade: A Reassessment', *The William and Mary Quarterly*, 58 (January 2001), 17–46; H. S. Klein, 'The Atlantic Slave Trade: Recent Research and Findings' in H. Pietschmann (ed.), *Atlantic History: History of the Atlantic System, 1580–1830* (Göttingen: Vandenhoeck & Ruprecht, 2002), 301–20.

[12] Klein, 'Atlantic Slave Trade', 198.

[13] Th. Clarkson, *The History of the Rise, Progress, and Accomplishment of the Abolition of the African Slave-Trade by the British Parliament* (London: Longman, Hurst, Rees, and Orme, 1808), vol. I, 255–8; F. J. Klingberg, *The Anti-Slavery Movement in England:*

founded organization, the members agreed to concentrate on the fight against the slave trade. They thought that such a focus would tackle the overall problem of slavery by the roots and would also decisively improve the hard living conditions of slaves in the colonies. By banning the transatlantic transport, the supply of new slaves would come to a complete halt and thus force slave owners in the colonies to treat the labourers already there more humanely and with better care.[14] The complete abolition of slavery was to become the long-term aim of this organization.

For the abolitionists, the crucial factor in deciding this focus was their estimation of the prospects for political success in effectuating their demands. By concentrating exclusively on the abolition of the slave trade, they deliberately avoided any involvement in complicated legal disputes over the property rights of the powerful plantation aristocracy to their slaves and the controversial legality of efforts by the London government to intervene in the legislation of the colonies.[15] By contrast, the regulation of any type of trade issue clearly fell under the jurisdiction of Westminister. Therefore, as the leading abolitionist Thomas Clarkson noted, a ban on human trafficking could be implemented by governmental means: 'By asking the government, again, to do this and this only, they were asking what it could really enforce. It could station its ships of war, and command its custom-houses, so as to carry any act of this kind into effect.'[16] Even in the founding phase of their organization, the abolitionists had a clear idea how to realize their humanitarian aims through a governmental policy of intervention.

Finally, in 1807, the major breakthrough for the movement was achieved under the leadership of Thomas Clarkson and William Wilberforce. After having conducted a decades-long campaign of distributing flyers and pamphlets in an effort to mobilize the British public to support a ban of the transatlantic slave trade, the abolitionists witnessed the passing of the Act for the Abolition of the Slave Trade by the British Parliament on 25 March 1807.[17] Under the threat of a painfully high

A Study in English Humanitarianism (New Haven and London: Yale University Press and Oxford University Press, 1926), 73.

[14] Clarkson, *History*, 284–6. [15] Ibid., 286–7. [16] Ibid., 287.

[17] S. Farrell, '"Contrary to the Principle of Justice, Humanity and Sound Policy": The Slave Trade, Parliamentary Politics and the Abolition Act, 1807' in S. Farrell, M. Unwin, and James Walvin (eds.), *The British Slave Trade: Abolition, Parliament and People* (Edinburgh University Press, 2007), 141–71. There has been an intensive research debate with various explanations concerning the background of British abolition. For an overview, see for example Th. Bender (ed.), *The Antislavery Debate: Capitalism and Abolitionism as a Problem in Historical Interpretation* (University of California Press, 1992).

penalty fee of 100 pounds per slave, every British subject was prohibited from participating in any way, directly or indirectly, in the slave trade. The particular significance of this legislation lay in the fact that the previous struggle against the transatlantic slave trade had been conducted by the abolitionists exclusively on the level of civil society activism and politics; through this law, it had now become the concern of the United Kingdom. The British state committed itself to use its means to combat human trafficking. Accordingly, the Abolition Act contained instructions to British authorities on the capture and seizure of the ships involved.[18]

Contrary to the ban on slave trade passed by the US Congress that same year, which Du Bois later dubbed the 'dead letter' due to the failure of implement it,[19] the British Abolition Act did not diminish into worthless political lip service. Instead, it served as the legal basis for the deployment of the Royal Navy off the West African coast to enforce militarily the ban of transatlantic human trade. For this purpose, the British admiralty sent two warships to African waters as early as 1808. In light of the more than 3,000-miles-long coastline from Cape Verde in today's Senegal down to Cape Frio in what is now Angola, this step was at first no more than a symbolic act, albeit one marking the start of the first and longest humanitarian intervention in history. Once the number of ships was increased in 1811 to that of a flotilla, Great Britain demonstrated its permanent military presence on the notorious slave coasts until the mid 1860s. At the highpoint of its involvement in the 1840s, the fleet consisted of more than thirty ships.[20]

The costs incurred by this military action were enormous for Great Britain. Chaim Kaufmann and Robert Pape speak of the 'most expensive international moral effort in modern world history'[21] and estimate the loss of life among the ranks of the Royal Navy at more than 5,000 and the economic cost of the abolitionist measures at an average of 1.8 per cent of

[18] Act of the British Parliament for the Abolition of the Slave Trade, 25 March 1807, in *British and Foreign State Papers* (BFSP), vol. V, 559–68.

[19] W. E. B. Du Bois, *The Suppression of the Atlantic Slave-Trade to the United States of America 1638–1870* (New York: Russell & Russell, 1965), 109.

[20] On the deployment of the Royal Navy against the slave trade, see Ch. Lloyd, *The Navy and the Slave Trade: The Suppression of the African Slave Trade in the Nineteenth Century* (London and New York: Longmans, Green, 1949); W. E. F. Ward, *The Royal Navy and the Slavers: The Suppression of the Atlantic Slave Trade* (London: Allen and Unwin, 1969); S. Rees, *Sweet Water and Bitter: The Ships that Stopped the Slave Trade* (University of New Hampshire Press, 2009).

[21] Ch. D. Kaufmann and R. A. Pape, 'Explaining Costly International Moral Action: Britain's Sixty-Year Campaign Against the Slave Trade', *International Organization*, 53 (Autumn 1999), 633.

the British state's annual national income in the period from 1808 to 1867.[22] The reasons for this extremely costly intervention policy reveal a significant conflation of economic, imperial, and moral motives.[23] Following the unilateral departure from the slave trade with the passage of the Abolition Act in 1807, it was clearly not in the interest of the British government to leave the economic advantages of the lucrative trade with African slaves to other nations and thereby risk a palpable competitive disadvantage for their own West Indian colonies. This argument is poignantly underscored by the fact that the British lobby of West-Indian plantation and slave owners began to support an aggressive stance against the slave trade after the national abolition occurred.[24] Apart from these economic interests, no British government could afford by this time to resist the domestic pressure created by the abolitionists. On the contrary, it was forced to integrate their humanitarian aims in its own foreign-policy agenda.[25] The fight against the slave trade thereby became one of the main paradigms of British foreign policy in the nineteenth century.

From the start, one key problem facing maritime intervention was the insufficiently clarified issue of a mandate. Were officers of the Royal Navy allowed to stop, search, seize, and turn over for court trial the slave ships of other nations along with British ones? This question involved the sensitive area of national sovereign rights and contained enough diplomatic dynamite to spark serious international complications. During the Napoleonic Wars, Great Britain legitimated its unilateral action against slave ships flying under foreign flags with reference to the right to search as set down in naval war law and turned over seized ships to be convicted in the British prize court that had been established in Freetown, Sierra

[22] For the purpose of comparison, the average aid from OECD countries between 1975 and 1996 only equalled 0.23 per cent of their gross national income. On the costs and the comparison, see ibid., 634–7.

[23] See especially, M. Mason, 'Keeping Up Appearances: The International Politics of Slave Trade Abolition in the Nineteenth-Century Atlantic World', *The William and Mary Quarterly*, 66 (October 2009), 809–32; Ph. D. Morgan, 'Ending the Slave Trade: A Caribbean and Atlantic Context' in D. R. Peterson (ed.), *Abolitionism and Imperialism in Britain, Africa, and the Atlantic* (Athens: Ohio University Press, 2010), 101–28; S. Drescher, 'Emperors of the World: British Abolitionism and Imperialism' in D. R. Peterson (ed.), *Abolitionism and Imperialism in Britain, Africa, and the Atlantic* (Athens: Ohio University Press, 2010), 129–49.

[24] E. Williams, *Capitalism and Slavery* (Chapel Hill: University of North Carolina Press, 1944), 175–6.

[25] Chaim Kaufmann and Robert Pape emphasize this dimension of domestic politics: Kaufmann and Pape, 'Explaining Costly International Moral Action', 649–61.

Leone for precisely this purpose.[26] With the peace agreement of 1814, this situation changed fundamentally, because in peacetime a new grounding in international law was needed to legitimize the capture and seizure of foreign ships and establish a corresponding legal jurisdiction.[27] In his general work on prize law, 'A Digest of the Law of Maritime Captures and Prizes', written at the time, Henry Wheaton, a judge at the Marine Court in New York, addressed the special legal situation involving ships confiscated in the fight against the slave trade. The renowned American jurist expressed the hope that a ban of the slave trade, which had already been passed at the national level by the British Parliament and the US Congress in 1807, would become an integral part of the 'conventional law of nations' as soon as possible.[28]

British abolitionists took a very similar stance and viewed the end of the Napoleonic Wars in April 1814 as an opportunity to realize their long-held dream. The national ban of the slave trade and its enforcement by the Royal Navy was to be transferred to the international level. Wilberforce and his fellow abolitionists were certain that an opportune moment had arrived to advance their cause by making their voices heard in the upcoming peace negotiations. To this end, they tried to commit their own government to their aims. On the initiative of the abolitionists, both the House of Commons and the House of Lords each sent a petition to Britain's prince regent George in which they called upon the British government to encourage other European countries to adopt a similar ban of the slave trade.[29] Thus, Parliament declared its strong affirmation of the abolitionist aims and at the same time assigned a clear task to the British delegation at the pending negotiations in Paris: the peace agreements with France were to be directly coupled with concrete abolition measures.

[26] See especially, T. Helfman, 'The Court of Vice-Admiralty at Sierra Leone and the Abolition of the West African Slave Trade', *Yale Law Journal*, 115 (2006), 1122–56.

[27] On this, see especially J. Allain, 'The Nineteenth Century Law of the Sea and the British Abolition of the Slave Trade', *British Yearbook of International Law*, 78 (2007), 348–54; M. Ryan, 'The Price of Legitimacy in Humanitarian Intervention: Britain, the Right of Search, and the Abolition of the West African Slave Trade, 1807–1867' in B. Simms and D. J. B. Trim, *Humanitarian Intervention* 234–5; L. Benton, 'Abolition and Imperial Law 1790–1820', *Journal of Imperial and Commonwealth History*, 39 (September 2011), 361–4.

[28] H. Wheaton, *A Digest of the Law of Maritime Captures and Prizes* (New York: R. M'Dermut & D. D. Arden, 1815), 227–30.

[29] 'Address of the House of Commons to the Prince Regent of Great Britain', 3 May 1814, in *British and Foreign State Papers* (BFSP), vol. III, 893; 'Address of the House of Lords to the Prince Regent of Great Britain', 5 May 1814, in ibid., 895–6.

The negotiations in Paris soon put a damper on such high hopes.[30] The leading British negotiator, Foreign Secretary Lord Castlereagh, was forced to acknowledge that France, under the leadership of the newly enthroned Bourbon king Louis XVIII, refused to fulfil British demands. Foreign Minister Talleyrand justified the French position by arguing that the conditions forced upon France were not in accord with the national honour of his country. Moreover, the major economic interests of French mercantile cities would cause them to clearly oppose immediate abolition, which – should it be implemented against the will of this influential group – could seriously endanger the acceptance and stability of the new French government.[31] In the end, the two countries were finally able to agree only on an additional article to the peace treaty, in which France pledged to be wholly responsible for the abolition of its slave trade after a five-year period and without British pressure.[32]

Castlereagh returned to London feeling confident in the overall success of the negotiations. The overwhelming majority of Parliament honoured this accordingly, enhanced also by the patriotic elation of victory after more than twenty years of war. His presentation of the peace treaty in the House of Commons prompted standing ovations.[33] Wilberforce, however, did not join the exuberant chorus of congratulations. He was shocked by the final agreement on the slave trade, as he noted in his diary.[34] He vented his boundless disappointment in the subsequent parliamentary debates, during which he called the celebrated treaty a 'death-warrant of a multitude of innocent victims, men, women and children'.[35] Instead of achieving the desired ban, the agreement enabled the French to resume their slave trade, with all of its catastrophic consequences in Africa, for the period of another five years.[36]

[30] On the 1814 peace of Paris, see also Zamoyski, *Rites of Peace*, 197–202.

[31] Report, 'Castlereagh to Liverpool', 19 May 1814, in Ch. K. Webster (ed.), *British Diplomacy 1813–1815: Select Documents Dealing With the Reconstruction of Europe* (London: G. Bell & Sons, 1921), 183–4.

[32] 'Additional Article to the Definitive Treaty of Peace Between Great Britain and France', 30 May 1814, BFSP, vol. III, 890–1.

[33] Parliamentary minutes on the topic of the peace treaty, 6 June 1814, in T. C. Hansard (ed.), *The Parliamentary Debates from the Year 1803 to the Present Time* (London, 1817), vol. XXVII, 1078.

[34] Diary entry by Wilberforce, 4 June 1814, in R. Wilberforce, *The Life of William Wilberforce* (London: John Murray, 1838), vol. IV, 186.

[35] Speech by Wilberforce, 6 June 1814, in Hansard, *Parliamentary Debates*, vol. XXVII, 1079.

[36] Ibid., 1078–82.

In reaction to this bitter setback, abolitionists began to organize public resistance by way of well-tested means. Wilberforce declared: 'Let the nation loudly and generally express its deep disappointment and regret, and most earnestly conjure both Houses, but especially the House of Commons, to use its utmost efforts in behalf of the unhappy Africans.'[37] In pamphlets, the anti-slavery movement sharply attacked the agreement that had been reached with France and specifically accused the British government of having thwarted its own policy.[38] It was argued that, on the one hand, the Royal Navy had been delegated the military authority to act against slave traders along the West African coast and the Vice-Admiralty Court in Sierra Leone had been set up specifically for the purpose of trying captured slave ships, freeing the slaves on board, and finally resettling them in the colonies. On the other hand, the resumption of the French slave trade was being tolerated, and thus the signing of the peace treaty endangered all of the hard-won progress achieved in the previous twenty-five years.[39]

The abolitionists encouraged the public to support petitions in which Parliament was being called upon explicitly to revise the controversial additional agreement.[40] In this way, the movement succeeded within a very short period to launch one of its most successful campaigns: a flood of more than 800 petitions with just under a million signatures from nearly all parts of the country swept the British Parliament.[41] Thoroughly surprised by this overwhelming reaction by the populace, even Great Britain's grand hero, the Duke of Wellington, had to admit during a brief visit to the homeland: 'I was not aware till I had been some time here [London] of the degree of frenzy existing here about the slave trade. People in general appear to think that it would suit the policy of the nation to go to war to put an end to that abominable traffic; and many wish that we should take the field on this new crusade.'[42] Instead of the

[37] Wilberforce, *Life of William Wilberforce*, vol. IV, 192.

[38] On this, see *Observations on That Part of the Late Treaty of Peace With France Which Relates to the African Slave Trade, Extracted From a Periodical Work For June 1814* (London, 1814).

[39] Ibid., 8–9.

[40] For example, see the petition of 17 June 1814, in ibid., 11–12.

[41] This is a surprisingly high figure for a total population of roughly twelve million. J. Walvin, 'The Public Campaign in England Against Slavery, 1787–1834' in D. Eltis and J. Walvin (eds.), *The Abolition of the Atlantic Slave Trade: Origins and Effects in Europe, Africa, and the Americas* (Madison: University of Wisconsin Press, 1981), 67–68. S. Drescher, 'Whose Abolition? Popular Pressure and the Ending of the British Slave Trade', *Past and Present*, 143 (May 1994), 160–2.

[42] Letter, 'Wellington to Henry Wellesley', 29 July 1814, in Wellesley, *Supplementary Despatches*, vol. IX, 165.

war-weariness that Wellington had expected among his fellow countrymen, he found instead a great willingness even to enter a new war in order to abolish the slave trade.

Buoyed by this sentiment, Wilberforce once again went on the offensive in Parliament. He cleverly used the personal presentation of a petition signed by 38,000 Londoners to initiate two further parliamentary petitions to the prince regent.[43] In these, the prince was asked by both chambers to exert his personal influence on the French government to force concessions and on the soon-to-convene Congress of Vienna to promote an absolute ban of the slave trade.[44] The abolitionists had succeeded yet again to get Parliament to commit to their aims. However, this time the pressure on the British government increased enormously, enhanced by the massive public support. Even the prince regent felt compelled to forward the petition of the British Parliament to the French king in a personal letter and to request the king's close cooperation on the matter of the slave trade.[45]

In his new role as envoy, Wellington himself carried this letter to Paris, where he, at London's behest, again commenced bilateral negotiations on changing the controversial additional agreement.[46] In this context, Great Britain even brought up the idea of forcing concession from countries that resisted a ban of the slave trade by issuing an import ban on their colonial products.[47] Furthermore, for the first time Wellington presented to Talleyrand specific proposals for a joint intervention against the slave trade. The navies of both countries were to be granted the right to mutual visitation of their merchant ships in a precisely demarcated zone north of the equator for the purpose of capturing slave ships and turning them over to the responsible admiralty court for proceedings.[48]

For their part, the abolitionists tried to establish a presence at the same time on the international level and thus intensified their direct contacts to leading statesmen.[49] Wilberforce kept up a lively correspondence with

[43] Presentation and speech by Wilberforce, 27 June 1814, in Hansard, *Parliamentary Debates* (1814), vol. XXVIII, 267–78.

[44] See, 'Address of the House of Commons to the Prince Regent of Great Britain', 27 June 1814, in BFSP, vol. III, 896–9, and 'Address of the House of Lords to the Prince Regent of Great Britain', 30 June 1814, in ibid., vol. III, 899–700.

[45] Letter, 'Prince Regent George to Louis XVIII', 5 August 1814, in ibid., vol. III, 900.

[46] On these negotiations, see, letter, 'Castlereagh to Wellington', 6 August 1814, in ibid., vol. III, 891–3; letter, 'Wellington to Castlereagh', 25 August 1814, in ibid., vol. III, 901–2.

[47] Letter, 'Castlereagh to Wellington', 6 August 1814, in ibid., vol. III, 901.

[48] Letter, 'Wellington to Talleyrand', 26 August 1814, in Ministère des Affaires Étrangères (hereafter MAE), MD A 23.

[49] B. Fladeland, 'Abolitionist Pressures on the Concert of Europe, 1814–1822', *The Journal of Modern History*, 38 (1966), 360.

influential personalities such as Talleyrand and even met the Russian czar Alexander I and the Prussian king Friedrich Wilhelm III in London, both of whom assured Wilberforce of their sympathy and support.[50] The abolitionist strategy strove to provide important policymakers with detailed information about the horrors of the slave trade and thus to influence accordingly their position, especially in connection with the upcoming Congress of Vienna. To this end, Thomas Clarkson produced a shortened version of his work 'Evidence on the Subject of the Slave Trade' that he had written originally for the British Parliament. This revised work was translated into Italian, Spanish, French, and German. In his preface, Clarkson explicitly addresses the assembled European rulers and appeals impressively to them to make the moment in which they themselves have been liberated from Napoleonic oppression also be the hour in which the African population is liberated from the evils of the human trade.[51] On just a few pages, Clarkson delivered a concise and graphic account of the entire problematic issue, which he concluded by calling on the heads of state at the Congress of Vienna to declare, in the name of humanity, the slave trade as a violation of international law.[52] The abolitionists distributed this publication among the various diplomats and delegates.

Thus the abolitionists did not limit their activities strictly to a national campaign to mobilize support. They also tried to firmly establish the slave trade on the agenda at the international level and sought in this way to create a political climate favourable to their cause for the negotiations in Vienna. At the congress, the greatest pressure clearly rested on the shoulders of the British government, whose own public expected it to achieve concrete results. Parliament's decree dictated a clear mandate to the British delegation, and Lord Liverpool, the prime minister, accurately described the burden of obligation: 'I had a letter from Wilberforce yesterday, which proves to me that the Abolitionists in this country will press the question in every possible shape. We must do therefore all we can, and at least be able to show that no efforts have been omitted on our

[50] Diary entry by Wilberforce, 11 June 1814, in Wilberforce, *Life of William Wilberforce*, vol. IV, 190, also 198–9.

[51] For example, see the German version: *Eine summarische Uebersicht der vor dem Ausschuß des Unterhauses des Großbritannischen Parlaments abgelegten Zeugnisse über den Gegenstand des Sclaven-Handels den verschiedenen Regenten in der christlichen Welt zugeeignet von Thomas Clarkson* (London, 1814), 5.

[52] Ibid., 33.

part to give effect to the Addresses of the two Houses of Parliament.'[53] The objective in the Austrian capital was to fulfil these high expectations, and seldom before in the history of British diplomacy did a delegation attend an international conference with such a clear mandate.[54] The abolitionists could congratulate themselves for having successfully mobilized the involvement of civil society and thereby secured a spot on the agenda of international politics for the issue of establishing and enforcing a ban of the slave trade.

THE CONGRESS OF VIENNA AND THE ESTABLISHMENT OF AN INTERNATIONAL HUMANITARIAN NORM

The Congress of Vienna, which began in September of 1814, was a summit attended by nearly all European rulers to negotiate the new political order on the European continent, essentially under the guidance of the Great Powers of Austria, Prussia, Russia, and Great Britain, following the end of the Napoleonic Wars. Consequently, the congress was clearly characterized by power politics and the related conflicts of interests among the Great Powers. There appeared to be no place here for humanitarian issues, such as those of the abolitionists. So it is remarkable that Castlereagh wasted no opportunity to discuss the question of an immediate ban of the slave trade and to encourage support from the representatives of the various delegations. Yet, all the while, his main objective remained the commitment of France to the ban.[55] For his part, Talleyrand unequivocally rejected British overtures, specifically the proposal for a mutual right of search, on the basis of the need to protect national interests.[56] Yet, at the same time and as a gesture of goodwill, he offered to further support British efforts for an international ban at the congress.

[53] Letter, 'Liverpool to Wellington', 2 September 1814, in Charles Petrie, *Lord Liverpool and His Times* (London: J. Barrie, 1954), 198–9.

[54] R. Coupland, *The British Anti-Slavery Movement* (London: Frank Cass & Co., 1964), 154.

[55] Letter, 'Castlereagh to Bathhurst', 9 October 1814, in BFSP, vol. III, 939; letter, 'Castlereagh to Liverpool', 25 October 1814, in Webster, *British Diplomacy*, 215–6.

[56] Letter, 'Talleyrand to Castlereagh', 5 November 1814, in BFSP, vol. III, 940–1; letter, 'Wellington to Castlereagh', 5 November 1814, in ibid., vol. III, 913–4. On the French position in negotiations at the Congress of Vienna, see also 'Instruction de Prince de Talleyrand pour les plénipotentiaires français au congrès de Vienne', 10 September 1814, MAE, MD F 677.

In line with this gesture and also with the aim of securing the favour of Great Britain in other important matters, such as those concerning Italy, the French foreign minister ended up being the one to put the issue of the slave trade on the official agenda of the Congress.[57] As a solution, he proposed the creation of a commission of representatives from Great Britain, France, Spain, Portugal, Russia, Prussia, Austria, and Sweden.[58] At first, this proposal was opposed by the two Iberian countries, who wanted only to permit representatives from the four colonial powers directly involved in the problem because they were concerned that a larger body would weaken their negotiating power. Arguing that human trafficking was an issue about the general morality and 'humanity' affecting all countries, the other six delegations rejected this objection, and the special eight-nation commission commenced its work in January 1815.[59]

Castlereagh immediately took the reins into his hands at the very first meeting.[60] Invoking the principles of Christianity and of common morality and humanity, he attempted to persuade the other countries to support a declaration for the immediate universal ban of the slave trade.[61] All members of the commission expressed their general approval. Only the Spanish and the Portuguese envoys demanded a special clause reflecting their view that each country should continue to be allowed to determine when the slave trade in their jurisdiction should finally be banned.[62] France also leaned in this direction and insisted on the five-year period of transition agreed upon in the Paris peace treaty. Castlereagh was forced to realize that it was not possible at that time to bring about an immediate ban. Therefore, he tried during the ensuing negotiations to prompt Portugal, Spain, and France to make concessions

[57] J. Reich, 'The Slave Trade at the Congress of Vienna: A Study in English Public Opinion', *Journal of Negro History*, 53 (April 1968), 136; M. Putney, 'The Slave Trade in French Diplomacy from 1814 to 1815', *The Journal of Negro History*, 60 (1975), 422.

[58] 'Propositions du Plénipotentiare de France', 10 December 1814, in BFSP, vol. III, 576–7.

[59] 'Protocole de la Conférence entre les Plénipotentiaires d'Autriche, d'Espagne, de France, de la Grande Bretagne, de Portugal, de Prusse, de Russie, et de Suède', 16 January 1815, in ibid., vol. III, 946–9.

[60] For a detailed account of these negotiations, see Ch. K. Webster, *The Foreign Policy of Castlereagh, 1812–1815: Britain and the Reconstruction of Europe* (London: Bell 1931), 413–24. One of the first accounts of these negotiations from the French perspective was *Histoire et Apologie du Congrés de Vienne, Livre IV, par M. de Flassan, Historiographe des Affaires etrangeres* (Paris, 1817), MAE, MD F 689.

[61] 'Protocole de la 1ère Séance Particulière Entre les Plénipotentiares des 8 Cours', 20 January 1815, in BFSP, vol. III, 949–51.

[62] Ibid., 952.

with regard to a zone north of the equator in which the slave trade was to be prohibited and to introduce the ban as soon as possible.[63] At the same time, the British foreign secretary proposed joint measures of maritime intervention[64] and recommended the creation of a permanent commission that would continue to address the issue of the slave trade once the Congress of Vienna ended.[65] In order to lend the necessary weight to its demands, the British delegation explicitly repeated the threat to ban the importation of colonial products that it had already made to France and thereby introduced to diplomacy the use of economic sanctions in peacetime.[66]

Castlereagh's proposals were supported for the most part by the continental powers of Russia, Prussia, and Austria – countries not involved in the slave trade – as well as by Sweden, which had signed a treaty in 1813 with Great Britain that abolished the slave trade in the Scandinavian country completely.[67] Whereas France tried to take as balanced a position as possible, the two Iberian countries resisted vehemently. In return for British compensation payments for seized slave ships amounting to £300,000[68] and the clearance of a war debt of £600,000, the Portuguese government agreed in a separate treaty signed on 22 January 1815, to ban its slave trade north of the equator, but it was not willing to make any further concessions.[69] Together with Spain, Portugal considered an immediate ban and the related measures to implement it as a serious violation of their national sovereign rights and interference in their economic interests.[70] Furthermore, both

[63] 'Protocole de la 2de Conférence Particulière Entre les Plénipotentiares des 8 Cours', 28 January 1815, in ibid., vol. III, 960. On the British negotiation strategy, see also 'Memorandum as to the Mode of Conducting the Negotiations in Congress for the Final Abolition of the Slave Trade', 1814, MAE, MD F 685.

[64] 'Protocole de la 2de Conférence', 961–2.

[65] 'Protocole de la 3ème Conférence Particulière Entre les Plénipotentiares des 8 Cours', 4 February 1815, in BFSP, vol. III, 964–5.

[66] Ibid., vol. III, 967. See especially Nicolson, *Congress of Vienna*, 215–6.

[67] 'Separate Article to the Treaty Between Great Britain and Sweden', 3 March 1813, in BFSP, vol. III, 886.

[68] On this, see 'Convention Between Great Britain and Portugal Relative to the Indemnification of Portuguese Subjects for Certain Detained Slave-Trade Vessels', 21 January 1815, in BFSP, vol. II, 345–8.

[69] 'Treaty Between Great Britain and Portugal for the Restriction of the Portuguese Slave Trade; and for the Annulment of the Convention of Loan of 1809 and Treaty of Alliance of 1810', 22 January 1815, in ibid., vol. II, 348–54.

[70] 'Protocole de la 1ère Séance', 20 January 1815, in BFSP, vol. III, 956–8; 'Protocole de la 3ème Conférence', 4 February 1815, in ibid., vol. III, 965.

countries declared that they would only be willing to completely abolish human trafficking after a period of eight years.[71]

As a result, the product of the negotiations in Vienna was a compromise to which the countries involved could finally agree, namely the 'Déclaration des 8 Cours, relative à l'Abolition Universelle de la Traite des Nègres', signed on 8 February 1815. In the spirit of the Enlightenment and in the name of all civilized states, the eight members of the commission condemned the slave trade as a glaring contradiction 'aux principes d'humanité et de la morale universelle'.[72] The declaration acknowledged the urgency of the matter and expressed explicitly the wish to end the scourge that devastated Africa, humiliated Europe, and haunted humankind. The signatory states affirmed their willingness to establish a universal ban as promptly as possible and with all available means, albeit on the condition that the particular interests of the various countries and their peoples be allowed the necessary consideration. For this reason, the joint declaration stated that a point in time for a universal end to the slave trade could not be determined; instead this had to be the business for negotiations between each of the powers. The declaration concluded with an appeal to all civilized nations to support this noble cause with all their might and to contribute to a successful outcome.

The Vienna declaration did not establish a legally binding ban, as the British delegation had striven to achieve; it was strictly a declaration of intent. Still, the government in London did not appear displeased with the results.[73] Even the abolitionists largely withheld their criticism and acknowledged Castlereagh's sincere efforts.[74] Indeed, the significance of the declaration should not be underestimated. Its inclusion in the Final Act of the congress reveals its special status in international law because this international condemnation of human trafficking was approved not only by the members of the eight-nation commission but also by all of the

[71] Letter, Wellesley to Castlereagh, 26 January 1815, in ibid., vol. III, 934–5; 'Les Plénipotentiaires Portugais aux Plénipotentiaires des Puissances Signataires du Traite de Paris', 6 February 1815, in ibid., vol. III, 972–4; 'Les Plénipotentiaires Portugais au Vicomte Castlereagh', 11 February 1815, in ibid., vol. III, 974.

[72] 'Declaration des 8 Cours, relative à l'Abolition Universelle de la Traite des Nègres', 8 February 1815, in ibid., vol. III, 971–2.

[73] Letter, 'Liverpool to Canning', 16 February 1815, in Wellesley, *Supplementary Despatches*, vol. IX, 565–7.

[74] Reich, 'Slave Trade at the Congress of Vienna', 142–3; In the parliamentary debates on the Congress of Vienna: 'Mr. Wilberforce expressed his satisfaction at what had been done respecting the Slave Trade', 20 March 1815, in Hansard, *Parliamentary Debates* (1815), vol. XXX, 305.

countries participating in the congress.[75] With this broad base of support, the declaration transfused a humanitarian idea to a concrete legal norm for the first time and established it in international law.[76] Although the Vienna declaration was not legally binding, it could be used well to exert moral pressure in later negotiations. Therefore, it may be referred to as one of the first important documents in history for international humanitarian law.

Everything achieved in the Austrian capital was soon called into question again by the return of one man: Napoleon. Even as the Great Powers convened, Napoleon dared an escape from his imposed exile on Elba and landed in southern France with the help of faithful followers on 1 March 1815, after which he seized the reins of power in France for another one hundred days.[77] Aware of public opinion in Great Britain, the French emperor instrumentalized the abolition issue with the intent to evoke sympathy and support from the other side of the channel.[78] On 29 March, he issued a decree banning the French slave trade that immediately went into effect.[79] His ultimate defeat at Waterloo on 18 June 1815 forever dashed Napoleon's dreams of power but did not abolish his decree on French abolition.

The Allies, led by Great Britain, demanded that Louis XVIII confirm the validity of this ban as the necessary condition to be reinstated on his Bourbon throne.[80] Under the circumstances, the French king had no choice but to concede. He could not take a back seat to the 'humanitarian' decision of the Corsican 'despot' and therefore was forced to promptly prohibit the French slave trade. Certainly it seems to be historical irony that a single decision made by Napoleon eclipsed the achievements of all the strenuous negotiations between London and Paris in the previous years. France had finally been forced to join the camp opposing the slave

[75] The declaration was included in Article 118 as no. 15 of the Final Act. See J. L. Klüber (ed.), *Schluß-Acte des Wiener Congresses vom 9. Juni 1815* (Erlangen: Palm u. Enke, 1818), 111.

[76] Berding, 'Ächtung des Sklavenhandels', 267–8; Clark, *International Legitimacy*, 42, 55–7.

[77] On this, see Zamoyski, *Rites of Peace*, 442–98.

[78] Putney, 'Slave Trade in French Diplomacy', 424; P. M. Kielstra, *The Politics of Slave Trade Suppression in Britain and France 1814–48. Diplomacy, Morality and Economics* (Basingstoke: Palgrave Macmillan, 2000), 56–7.

[79] 'Dècret Impérial Français, qui abolit la Traite des Noirs', 29 March 1815, in BFSP, vol. III, 196.

[80] See letter, 'Castlereagh to Stuart', 14 June 1815, in Wellesley, *Supplementary Despatches* (London, 1863), vol. X, 498; 'Protocole de la 15ème Confèrence entre les Plénipotentiaires des 4 Cours Alliées', 20 July 1815, in BFSP, vol. III, 196–7.

trade. In an article appended to the second Paris peace treaty of 20 November 1815, the French government explicitly agreed to respect the agreements reached in Vienna regarding the slave trade and to cooperate constructively in the subsequent conference planned in London and Paris on the international enforcement of the decisions.[81]

THE STRUGGLE FOR THE INTERNATIONAL ENFORCEMENT OF ABOLITION

Abolitionists could now refer directly to the Vienna declaration in their demands to enforce the humanitarian norm agreed upon. Because Spain strongly opposed any restriction of the slave trade, the country was increasingly targeted by the abolitionists.[82] The lawyer James Stephen, who had provided his brother-in-law Wilberforce with the decisive legal impulse for the Foreign Slave Trade Act in 1806 and is thus to be considered as the chief architect of the Abolition Act, published a pioneering pamphlet in 1816 titled 'An Inquiry into the Right and Duty of Compelling Spain to Relinquish her Slave Trade in Northern Africa'. In it, Stephen maintains that the Vienna declaration had made it the legal duty of the signatory countries to enforce a universal ban of the slave trade.[83] In light of the opposition put forth by the Spanish government, the pamphlet asked what steps the other European countries were authorized to take in order to enforce this obligation. In his commentary, the British jurist made direct references to the founding fathers of international law, Hugo Grotius and Emerich de Vattel, both of whom in their important works had each granted states the right to intervene in cases where natural law was being severely violated.[84] Since the slave trade was now recognized as a grievous contradiction of natural and international law, Stephen derived from it the right and the duty of other states to use means of force.[85] He concluded:

81 'Article Additionnel au Traite Définitif', 20 November 1815, MAE, MD A 23.

82 Fladeland, *Abolitionist Pressures*, 367. See also the report by Don Pedros Cevallos on the criticism of the Spanish throne that appeared in British newspapers, 10 November 1815, Archivo General de Simancas (hereafter AGS), ESTADO, Legajo 8176.

83 J. Stephen, *An Inquiry into the Right and Duty of Compelling Spain to Relinquish her Slave Trade in Northern Africa* (London, 1816), 13, 20, and 59.

84 Ibid., 18–20, 33.

85 According to Helmut Berding, no sanctions could be derived from the declaration of Vienna. See Berding, 'Ächtung des Sklavenhandels', 285. However, the writings of abolitionists like James Stephen disprove this argument, because they directly derive sanctions from the declaration.

To maintain the law of nature and of nations, to punish, or at least restrain, enormous violations of it, to succour an unhappy people oppressed by such offences, to promote by all the means in our power the social and moral improvement and happiness of other countries, are duties, and therefore rights, not peculiar to Great Britain ... but belong to all the branches of the human family, and pre-eminently to every civilized nation.[86]

Using this argument derived from natural and international law, Stephen provided one of the first justifications for forceful intervention against human trafficking, which he buttressed by pointing out pertinent aspects of realpolitik. Without a doubt, he noted, the United Kingdom had at its disposal the necessary maritime means, such as the naval fleet operating in West African waters, to be deployed against Spanish slave ships.[87] Stephen considered the danger that such action might provoke war with Spain as being highly improbable. The government in Madrid was said to lack the necessary financial and military resources just then; hence, it would not be in a position to counter British intervention with any serious resistance.[88] In closing, Stephen urged that the favourable opportunity be seized to demonstrate strength and, if need be, to stop the Spanish slave trade by force.[89]

Even more politically explosive was the issue involving military intervention for humanitarian reasons in connection with the trade of white slaves. Since the beginning of the sixteenth century, pirates of the North African Barbary States left their bases in Algiers, Tunis, and Tripoli to conduct raids throughout the Mediterranean region and hunt humans either to sell into slavery or to hold for ransom.[90] The British admiral Sir William Sidney Smith had already tried to draw attention to this special problem – quasi in the wake of the abolitionists and their campaign – just before the Congress of Vienna. In doing so, he had urged the European nations to conduct a joint naval operation and launch a military strike against the slave trade of the Barbary States.[91] He was able to participate

86 Stephen, *Inquiry into the Right*, 50. 87 Ibid., 69–70. 88 Ibid., 71–2., 78–9.

89 Ibid., 82.

90 On the history of the piracy and the slave trade conducted by the Barbary States, see D. Panzac, *Barbary Corsaires: The End of a Legend, 1800–1820* (Leiden: Brill, 2005); R. C. Davis, *Christian Slaves, Muslim Masters: White Slavery in the Mediterranean, the Barbary Coast, and Italy, 1500–1800* (Basingstoke: Palgrave Macmillan, 2003).

91 For this purpose, Admiral Smith also founded the philanthropic organization Society of Knights Liberators of White Slaves in Africa. On his activities, see J. Barrow, *The Life and Correspondence of Admiral Sir William Sidney Smith* (London: Richard Bentley, 1848), vol. II, 365–79; T. Pocock, *A Thirst for Glory: The Life of Admiral Sir Sidney Smith* (London: Pimlico, 1996), 219–22 and 228–30; W. S. Smith, *Mémoire sur la nécessité et*

as a private person in the congress itself thanks to influential friends and initiated an elaborate fundraiser among the gathered princes to benefit Christian slaves. Smith continued his private campaign after the end of the summit in Vienna, during which he cleverly linked the fate of the Christians in Muslim hands to that of the African slaves.[92]

Until then, Great Britain had paid little attention to piracy and the slave trade in the Barbary States, because this did not immediately affect the country. Starting at the end of the seventeenth century, the North Africans largely avoided any direct confrontation with the United Kingdom and its citizens because of the increasing strength of the Royal Navy. Instead, they concentrated their attacks on the ships of weaker nations, such as those of small Italian and German principalities, and on various coastal regions in the Mediterranean. Therefore, the Barbary States did not pose a threat to British interests. On the contrary, they were considerably advantageous for London insofar as they weakened potential trade competition, in addition to their role as important suppliers of provisions for the British garrisons stationed on Menorca and Gibraltar.[93] Owing to rivalry with the United States, the British deliberately tolerated the attacks on US merchant ships and permitted the North African buccaneers to pass through the Straights of Gibraltar, which the British controlled, so that they might raid ships sailing under the Stars and Stripes in the Atlantic.[94] These attacks hurt the US trade in the Mediterranean enormously. As a result, Washington decided to undertake two major military operations against the Barbary States, in 1801 and 1815, to protect its own citizens and national trade interests.[95]

les moyens de faire cesser les pirateries des états barbaresques, 31 August 1814, MAE, MD A5.

92 W. S. Smith, 'Relation des atrocités commises par les corsaires barbaresques dans l'adriatique et autres parties de la méditerranée', 1815, MAE, MD A5; Pamphlet 'Circulaire à Messieurs les souscripteurs au fonds charitabale pour l'abolition de l'esclavage des blancs aussi-bien que celui des noirs en Afrique', 20 April 1816, in ibid.; W. S. Smith, 'Souscription pour operer l'abolition de esclavage des blancs aussi-bien que des noirs en Afrique', 22 June 1816, in ibid.

93 J. L. Anderson, 'Piracy and World History: An Economic Perspective on Maritime Predation', *Journal of World History*, 6 (Fall 1995), 186–8.

94 R. W. Irwin, *The Diplomatic Relations of the United States with the Barbary Powers, 1776–1816* (Chapel Hill: University of North Carolina Press, 1931), 57–64.

95 The conflict between the United States and the Barbary States was ended for all practical purposes with a peace and friendship treaty in 1815. See 'Treaty of Peace and Amity Between the United States of America and the Dey of Algiers', 30 June 1815, in BFSP, vol. III, 45–51. On the Barbary Wars in general, see F. Lambert, *The Barbary Wars: American Independence in the Atlantic World* (New York: Hill and Wang, 2005);

London's policy of tolerating if not even instrumentalizing the Barbary States was put to the test in the course of the debates on international abolition that Great Britain itself had initiated. The more Great Britain focused its foreign policy on the fight against the transatlantic slave trade, the more the problem of Christian slaves in North Africa also became a serious test of its moral credibility.[96] Once even Admiral Smith, a man from the ranks of the Royal Navy, had skilfully linked the fates of the African and European slaves in his personal campaign, the British government came increasingly under pressure to explain, especially to Spain and Portugal, why the greatest sea power in the world took forceful action against Spanish and Portuguese slave ships but at the same time quietly accepted the enslavement of Christians by Muslim pirates.[97] The Spanish government seized upon this contradiction and rejected any further concessions in the fight against the transatlantic slave trade, while reminding Great Britain of its duty to white slaves: 'On the other hand, nothing can appear to be more flattering to the philanthropy of the British Government, in whose consideration the liberty of the Whites of Europe cannot be of less importance than that of the Blacks of Africa.'[98] The Spanish viewpoint implied that Great Britain's fight against the slave trade was not motivated very much by humanitarian considerations but was guided instead by the selective dictates of power politics. Finally, even Foreign Secretary Castlereagh expressed the conviction in a letter to the British ambassador in St. Petersburg 'that it is only by making the Slave Trade and the question of the Barbary Powers go pari passu, that we can fully meet the wishes of the Emperor [Russian czar] and the other powers, who press the latter point as one of universal interest'.[99]

In order to defend the credibility of its abolition policy and retain its foreign-policy influence, the government in London felt compelled also to push for the liberation of Christian slaves. Thus, from March to May

J. E. London, *Victory in Tripoli: How America's War with the Barbary Pirates Established the U.S. Navy and Built a Nation* (Hoboken: Wiley, 2005).

96 See especially O. Löwenheim, '"Do Ourselves Credit and Render a Lasting Service to Mankind": British Moral Prestige, Humanitarian Intervention, and the Barbary Pirates', *International Studies Quarterly*, 47 (March 2003), 23–48.

97 Webster, *Foreign Policy of Castlereagh*, 463.

98 Letter, 'Cevallos to British government', 7 April 1816, The National Archives (hereafter TNA), FO 84/1; Letter, Castlereagh, 7 June 1816, in ibid.

99 Letter, 'Castlereagh to Cathcart, British ambassador in St. Petersburg', 28 May 1816, in Ch. Vane (ed.), *Correspondence, Despatches and Other Papers of Viscount Castlereagh* (London: H. Colburn, 1853), vol. XI, 255. See also 'Extract from the Confidential Memorandum, 28 May 1816', TNA, FO 84/1.

1816, the British admiralty sent a squadron under the command of Lord Exmouth on a mission to the North African coast to reach a diplomatic solution.[100] The negotiations with the various Barbary rulers resulted in the purchased liberation by the British admiral of more than a thousand Sardinians, Sicilians, Neapolitans, Genoese, and Germans from slavery as well as new peace treaties, also in the name of Sardinia and the Kingdom of the Two Sicilies.[101] With Tunis and Tripoli a separate treaty was signed according to which future prisoners were no longer allowed to be enslaved but had to be treated as prisoners of war in accordance with humanitarian standards and were to be exchanged without any type of ransom payment.[102] Only Omar Bashaw, the self-confident dey of Algiers, vehemently rejected such a supplementary treaty, which also would have meant for him the end of the extremely lucrative trade with Christian slaves.

In England itself, the mission by Lord Exmouth was sharply criticized from various directions. In the *Times*, opinions were expressed that castigated the liberation of Christian slaves from other nations as the squandering of British tax revenue and military resources. There was no place for such 'quixotism' in view of constrictions facing Britain's own budgetary situation, and – should weaker countries consider using British protection against the Barbary States – then they should also pay for it.[103] Strong criticism of the negotiations conducted was also expressed by abolitionists, but for thoroughly different reasons. In Parliament, they accused the government of acknowledging the criminal practices of the North African pirates by paying ransoms and argued that such action seriously endangered the reputation of Great Britain at the international level.[104] In their opinion, the time had come to finally end the suffering

[100] C. Northcote Parkinson, *Edward Pellew* (London: Meuthen, 1934), 426–32; Panzac, *Barbary Corsaires*, 273–4; R. Perkins and K. J. Douglas-Morris, *Gunfire in Barbary: Admiral Exmouth's Battle With the Corsairs of Algiers in 1816 – the Story of the Suppression of White Slavery* (Homewell: Mason, 1982), 67–71.

[101] The various treaties are found in 'Treaties Between Great Britain and the Barbary States 1816' in BFSP, vol. III, 509–16; 'Treaties of Peace Between Sicily and the Barbary States (Concluded Under the Mediation of Great Britain)' in ibid., vol. III, 521–48; 'Treaties of Peace and Friendship Between Sardinia and the Barbary States (Concluded Under the Mediation of Great Britain)' in ibid., vol. III, 173–93.

[102] 'Declaration of the Bey of Tripoli Relative to the Abolition of Christian Slavery', 29 April 1816, in ibid., vol. III, 515–6; 'Declaration of the Bey of Tunis Relative to the Abolition of Christian Slavery', 17 April 1816, in ibid., vol. III, 513.

[103] *The Times*, 29 June 1816.

[104] See the parliamentary debates on 19 June 1816 in Hansard, *Parliamentary Debates* (1816), vol. XXXIV, 1147.

caused by the Barbary States. They did not think the solution to the problem lay in further diplomatic efforts, but in a well-aimed military strike by the Royal Navy.[105]

These domestic calls for the use of force did not miss their mark and eventually led London to punctuate its foreign-policy paradigm of abolition with military action. In July 1816, the British Admiralty ordered Lord Exmouth to sail once again to Algiers with a force consisting of fifteen warships and over 6,000 men. The specific occasion was the murder in the Algerian city of Bône of almost 200 Italian coral fishermen who had been under British protection. This was interpreted as a breach of the peace treaties that had just recently been signed.[106] This time the instructions for Lord Exmouth, whose fleet was reinforced by six Dutch warships, were very clear: under all circumstances and by the use of any means, the dey was to be forced to release immediately all Christian slaves and to end the slave trade once and for all. After the British ultimatum to this effect went unanswered and the Algerian shore battery hastily opened fire, the joint Anglo-Dutch fleet began to bombard Algiers on 27 August 1816. The devastating bombardment lasted for hours and destroyed almost the entire pirate fleet and a great deal of the city's fortifications.[107] Omar Bashaw was forced to accept unconditionally all British demands.[108] In addition to the release of 1,624 European slaves and reparation payments amounting to 382,500 Spanish dollars, the dey also had to sign the additional treaty on the unqualified end of Christian enslavement that he had rejected in May.[109] The military strike thus fulfilled all expectations. In contrast to the strictly national aim of the US operations a year earlier, the British had primarily liberated foreign citizens from slavery and, moreover, brought about a treaty from which all Christian nations profited.[110]

105 Ibid., 1149–50.

106 Order, British Admiralty to Lord Exmouth, 18 July 1816, TNA, FO 84/1; Parkinson, *Edward Pellew*, 437.

107 On the exact course of the attack, see Parkinson, *Edward Pellew*, 457–64; Perkins and Morris, *Gunfire in Barbary*, 107–32.

108 'Treaty of Peace Between Great Britain and Algiers', 28 August 1816, in BFSP, vol. III, 516; 'General Memorandum von Exmouth', 30 August 1816, in BFSP, vol. III, 519.

109 'Declaration of the Dey of Algiers Relative to the Abolition of Christian Slavery', 28 August 1816, in ibid., vol. III, 517.

110 Among the liberated slaves were only eighteen English people: the vast majority of those freed from captivity came from the Kingdom of the Two Sicilies, Sardinia, and Spain. For an exact listing, see Perkins and Morris, *Gunfire in Barbary*, 147.

The victory in North Africa unleashed a storm of enthusiasm. Upon their return, Lord Exmouth and his officers were showered with honours. The British prince regent awarded the admiral the title of viscount for his services, and the kings of Spain, the Netherlands, Sardinia, and the Two Sicilies each demonstrated their gratitude to the war hero by knighting him.[111] For the British government, the exceptional value of the military success lay, above all else, in its impact on foreign policy. In a private letter of thanks to Lord Exmouth, Foreign Secretary Castlereagh expressed this sentiment: 'You have contributed to place the Character of the Country above all suspicion of mercenary policy, the great atchievements of the War had not eradicated some lurking suspicion that we cherish'd Piracy as a commercial Ally; you have dispelled this cloud and I have no doubt the National Character in Europe will be Essentially Enobled by your Services.'[112] During a later debate in Parliament on the official tribute to the admiral and his Dutch allies, Castlereagh depicted the military strike against Algiers even as a 'war of justice and humanity', in which the British nation had intervened selflessly in defence of the rights of all European countries against the North African pirates.[113] The victory over the Barbary States was instrumentalized to prove the credibility of the United Kingdom's commitment to humanitarian aims in foreign affairs and sent at the same time the unequivocal signal that London would not hesitate to deploy the massive use of force in order to enforce the ban of the slave trade.[114]

Using the tailwind of its successful operations in the Mediterranean, the British government sailed forth with assertive calls to enforce universal abolition. On 28 August 1816, one day after the British triumph in Algiers, Great Britain invited France, Russia, Prussia, and Austria to conduct consultations on this in London.[115] In doing so, Britain referred explicitly to the agreements reached at the Congress of Vienna and the

[111] On the numerous honours, see Parkinson, *Edward Pellew*, 469–70; Perkins and Morris, *Gunfire in Barbary*, 155, 165–71.

[112] Private letter of thanks, 'Castlereagh to Exmouth', 30 September 1816, in Parkinson, *Edward Pellew*, 467.

[113] Speech, 'Castlereagh before the House of Commons', 3 February 1817, in Hansard, *Parliamentary Debates* (1817), vol. XXXV, 177–9. The same glorifying intent was also pursued by the contemporary publication of an unknown author *Triumph of Justice, or British Valour Displayed at the Cause of Humanity: The Recent Expedition to Algiers* (Manchester: J. Gleave, 1816).

[114] Löwenheim, 'British Moral Prestige', 42–4.

[115] 'Protocole No 1 des Conférences pour l'abolition de la Traite des Négres', 28 August 1816, TNA, FO 84/1.

supplementary protocol to the second Paris peace treaty. At the meeting, Castlereagh confronted the other participants with a plan to establish a temporary maritime league both to fight the North African pirates and to abolish the slave trade once and for all.[116] The framework and mission of the proposed alliance were clearly defined:

> It is submitted that as any attempt at African colonization or conquest might give rise to political as well as military difficulties of considerable magnitude, that the proposed defensive concert should be purely maritime, and that it should be solely directed to afford ... to each State a reasonable security for an unmolested enjoyment of the blessings of peace and a due observance of those civilized principles which the said regencies have lately been compelled by Lord Exmouth's operations to recognize.[117]

By stipulating that intervention would be conducted strictly as naval operations, the proposed plan attempted from the start to exclude the possibility of potential conflict among the various allies over claims to colonial territory in Africa. The explicit reference to Lord Exmouth emphasized the role played by the military strike against Algiers as a precedent for future policy using force to combat the slave trade. In order to realize the common goals, each of the parties was to contribute a certain number of warships to an international fleet that would enforce the international agreements by military means. Authority was to lie with a joint high command to be supervised by a commission to be located in Paris and made up of a representative from each of the five great powers. In addition to the passage on the mutual right to stop and search suspicious ships from the other treaty countries, the proposed plan also contained regulations on a joint legal prosecution of captured ships.

Such a plan to limit intervention strictly to naval operations offered relatively significant opportunities for the dominant sea power Great Britain to exert its influence. Since the British already dominated the high seas, this plan, which would also require states to surrender national sovereign rights, met with growing scepticism among the other participants at the conference. The French government viewed the plan first and foremost as yet another means by which Great Britain intended to enhance its maritime dominance and thereby tarnish France's national

116 'Annexe au Protocole de la 7éme Confèrence', 20 September 1816, TNA, FO 84/1; Memorandum, French ambassador in London, 'Abolition de la traite des négres', 1 November 1816, MAE, MD A15; Kielstra, *Politics of Slave Trade Suppression*, 64–7.

117 'Annexe au Protocole de la 7éme Confèrence', 20 September 1816, TNA, FO 84/1.

honour.[118] Such fears eventually led to the failure by the five countries to agree on any specific measures, even during the subsequent consultations that were held on a regular basis.[119] The concept of the joint military and legal enforcement of the slave-trade ban that had evolved over the course of diplomatic talks was now spelled out in very specific terms and served as the basis for all further negotiations.[120]

The meeting of the five Great Powers in Aachen in the fall of 1818 – at which it was decided, among other things, to withdraw the last allied occupational forces from French territory and thus return France to its place in the Concert of Europe – offered Castlereagh the welcome opportunity to present the plans for enforcing the ban on the slave trade once again.[121] The major aim of the British foreign secretary was to move the conference members to approve a 'right of mutual visit' in the case of suspicious ships. Castlereagh took particular care, especially in dealing with Britain's former enemy France, to deflect concerns about a possible restriction of national sovereign rights.[122] At the same time, he emphasized how crucial it would be, both practically and morally, to have the great naval power France participate in a system of joint operations at sea in order to effectively combat the slave trade.

Despite these efforts, Great Britain's proposals continued to find little favour among the other participants at the congress.[123] While Austria made its approval conditional on the stance taken by the other countries, the Russian delegation presented its own plan,[124] in which all Christian states would jointly establish a neutral institution to be seated on the African coast and outfitted with its own naval fleet and legal authority to

[118] 'Note sur le projet d'une ligue maritime pour assurer l'abolition de la traite et la repression de la piraterie des Barbaresques', n.d., MAE, MD A15.

[119] For the minutes of each of the negotiation sessions, which continued into 1819, see TNA, FO 84/1 and TNA, FO 84/2. French memorandum on the negotiations, n.d., MAE, MD A5.

[120] This aspect clearly qualifies the evaluation of these consultations as having been useless and unproductive, an argument put forth by Helmut Berding, Suzanne Miers, Wilhelm Grewe, and Maeve Ryan, to name a few. See Berding, 'Ächtung des Sklavenhandels', 281; S. Miers, *Britain and the Ending of the Slave Trade* (New York: Longman, 1975), 13–4; Ryan, 'The Price of Legitimacy', 237.

[121] Webster, *Foreign Policy of Castlereagh*, 462–4.

[122] Letter, 'Castlereagh to Duc de Richelieu with attached memorandum', 27 October 1818, MAE, MD A 24.

[123] Letter, 'Castelereagh to Bathurst', 23 November 1818, in BFSP, vol. VI, 65–6.

[124] 'Opinion du Cabinet d'Autriche sur la Question de la Traite des Nègres', in ibid., vol. VI, 75–6.

enforce the ban on the transatlantic slave trade.[125] The Russians had no problem with the idea of granting a right to visit and seize ships to such a body, which was to be under the collective supervision of the founding states, because it was convinced that this plan would ensure that the maritime and economic interests of no nation would be endangered. However, the practicality of implementing this visionary idea of an international enforcement agency was highly questioned, even by the British delegation.[126] Prussia and France both rejected outright any 'right to visit'. Both countries emphasized first and foremost the danger of misuse and viewed it as a potential source of conflict.[127] The French delegation in particular predicted that, in view of its long-existing rivalry with Great Britain, exercising the visitation right would lead inevitably to hostile conflict between the two countries.[128] The idea of a joint legal jurisdiction was also strictly rejected as a grave infringement of France's sovereign rights. In order to weaken the necessity of joint enforcement measures, Paris announced that it had already sent one if its own fleets to the coast of Senegal to combat unilaterally the French slave trade.[129] The outlook of surrendering sovereign rights and being incorporated into an enforcement regime dominated by Great Britain finally pushed Paris to implement unilateral military intervention against the French slave trade on the West African coast.[130]

Except for the joint letter to the king of Portugal calling for that country to set a date by which the Portuguese slave trade would be outlawed,[131] the negotiations in Aachen concluded without any concrete results. The Great Powers were not willing to approve a mutual right to visit each other's ships. Far too great were their concerns of sacrificing sovereign rights and also of enabling the already dominant sea power Great Britain favourable conditions by which to further expand its maritime hegemony. In the end, an agreement on measures of collective implementation failed to come about because joint public conviction to

125 'Opinion du Cabinet de Russie sur la Question de la Traite des Nègres', 7 November 1818, MAE, MD A 24.

126 Memorandum of the British Government in BFSP, vol. VI, 79.

127 'Opinion du Cabinet de Prusse sur la Traite des Nègres' in ibid., vol. VI, 76.

128 'Mémoire Français sur la Traite des Nègres' in ibid., vol. VI, 69–75.

129 Ibid., 74.

130 On the unilateral French intervention see: S. Daget, *La répression de la traite des Noirs au XIXe siècle. L'action des croisières françaises sur les côtes de l'Afrique (1817-1850)* (Paris: Éditions Karthala, 1997).

131 'Projet de Lettre de Cabinet des Souverains d'Autriche, de France, de la Grande Bretagne, de Prusse et de Russie à Sa Majesté le Roi de Portugal' in ibid., vol. VI, 85–6.

the humanitarian struggle against the transatlantic slave trade was far outweighed by considerations of realpolitik.[132]

Despite this failure to establish a means to enforce the ban of the slave trade on the multilateral level, international enforcement did eventually still occur. The model of combining military and legal enforcement that had been discussed at the Congress of Vienna and subsequent conferences found its way into the bilateral treaties between Great Britain and various other countries.[133] The first agreements in what would become a comprehensive international network were the legally binding treaties in 1817 with Portugal and with Spain, followed by one in 1818 with the Netherlands.[134] In these, each of the contractual parties granted its counterpart the 'right to visit' the merchant ships of the other in international waters during peacetime. In the view of British foreign secretary Castlereagh, this mutual right was crucial in the fight against the slave trade: 'It is the basis of the whole without which treaties to abolish it [the slave trade] are mere waste paper.'[135] The navies of each of the respective countries were thus permitted to stop and search vessels suspected of being slave ships in the zones agreed upon and to confiscate these ships should slaves be found illegally on board. These treaties also created 'Mixed Commissions for the Abolition of the Slave Trade'. It was the purpose of these commissions, which were scattered over the entire

[132] 'Protocole de la Conférence entre les Plénipotentiaires des 5 Cours, Aix-la-Chapelle', 19 November 1818, in ibid.

[133] F. Klose, 'Humanitäre Intervention und internationale Gerichtsbarkeit – Verflechtung militärischer und juristischer Implementierungsmaßnahmen zu Beginn des 19. Jahrhunderts', *Militärgeschichtliche Zeitschrift*, 72, no.1 (2013), 1–21.

[134] 'Additional Convention for the Purpose of Preventing Their Subjects from Engaging in Any Illicit Traffic in Slaves' between Great Britain and Portugal, 28 July 1817, TNA, FO 84/2; 'Tratado Para la Abolicion del Trafico de Negros' between Spain and Great Britain, 23 September 1817, Archivo General de Indias (hereafter AGI), ULTRAMAR, Legajo 32, N. 20; 'Treaty for Preventing Their Subjects from Engaging in Any Illicit Traffic in Slaves' between Great Britain and the Netherlands, 4 May 1818, in BFSP, vol. V, 125–35. For the international treaty regime against the slave trade, see E. A. Nadelmann, 'Global Prohibition Regime: The Evolution of Norms in International Society', *International Organization*, 44 (Fall 1990), 491–8; E. Keene, 'A Case Study of the Construction of International Hierarchy: British Treaty-Making Against the Slave-Trade in the Early Nineteenth Century', *International Organization*, 61 (Spring 2007), 311–39; Allain, 'Nineteenth Century Law of the Sea', 357–76; Mason, 'Keeping Up Appearances', 809–32; R. Law, 'Abolition and Imperialism: International Law and the British Suppression of the Atlantic Slave Trade' in D. R. Peterson (ed.), *Abolitionism and Imperialism in Britain, Africa, and the Atlantic* (Athens: Ohio University Press, 2010), 150–74.

[135] Letter, 'Viscount Castlereagh to Wellesley', 24 July 1817, TNA, FO 72/196.

Atlantic region, to adjudicate the cases of captured ships according to a standardized procedure. In this respect, the commissions are to be viewed as the beginning of international jurisdiction.[136] Under the leadership of Great Britain, an international regime to enforce the ban of the slave trade was thus developed,[137] based on the idea that an internationally stipulated norm was to be enforced with a combination of military means and international law.

CONCLUSION

As this chapter shows, the practice of humanitarian intervention on the part of the state – that is, state intervention to enforce the implementation of a humanitarian norm – originated in connection with the Congress of Vienna and the campaign against the transatlantic slave trade. Apart from strictly anti-revolutionary intervention determined by the interests of power politics, as has been associated to date with the peace order established in Vienna, an alternative policy of state intervention also emerged over the course of the summit. The main actor was Great Britain, which not only strongly advocated the establishment of a universal ban of the slave trade as an internationally accepted humanitarian norm but also fought in numerous diplomatic negotiations for the creation of a system of international enforcement. To buttress its credibility with regard to its new foreign policy paradigm of universal abolition, London discarded earlier foreign policy positions and was willing, as it demonstrated with the military strike against Algiers in the summer of 1816, to punctuate its policy with unilateral military operations and to charge ahead of other states. By and large, the British government's policy was influenced considerably by civil society. By successfully mobilizing public opinion, abolitionists were insistent in their calls for an active policy of intervention against the slave trade – first on the national and later on the

[136] Klose, 'Humanitäre Intervention'. For the Mixed Commissions, see also L. Bethell, 'The Mixed Commissions for the Suppression of the Slave Trade in the Nineteenth Century', *The Journal of African History*, 7 (1966), 79–93. The legal prosecution of the slave trade has been evaluated differently, especially in the most recent research literature. While Jenny Martinez views it as the 'origins of international human rights law', Lauren Benton evaluates this development especially as a 'project of consolidating the legal authority of empires'. See J. Martinez, *The Slave Trade and the Origins of International Human Rights Law* (Oxford University Press, 2012); Benton, 'Abolition and Imperial Law', 355–74.

[137] Nadelmann,'Global Prohibition Regimes', 491–8.

international level. In this way, civil society agitation became significantly intertwined with international policy in the early nineteenth century.

Although the new concept of intervention with its novel combination of military and legal means failed to take hold in the realm of multilateral cooperation, it eventually became firmly established by way of bilateral treaties. Through this international regime to enforce the ban of the slave trade, a new practice was established in international politics for governments to intervene collectively to protect humanitarian norms. In this respect, the various cases of intervention by the Great Powers of Europe to protect Christian minorities in the Ottoman Empire did not mark, in and of themselves, the first practical implementation of the idea of humanitarian intervention, as recent studies have proclaimed.[138] Instead, such intervention grew out of foregone diplomatic debates and foreign-policy practice, the cornerstone of which was laid earlier in nineteenth-century international politics in connection with the Congress of Vienna and the fight against the slave trade.

[138] See especially Bass, *Freedom's Battle*; Simms and Trim, *Humanitarian Intervention*, 111–225; Rodogno, *Against Massacre*.

6

Lord Vivian's tears

The moral hazards of humanitarian intervention

Mairi S. MacDonald

On 2 July 1890, Baron Lambermont reported that the United Kingdom's minister to Belgium had been unusually emotional when the two men met that day: 'He took my hands, tears pouring from his eyes, and showed me the telegram he had received from [Foreign Secretary] Lord Salisbury. After we had recounted the personal costs of our long and difficult campaign, we embraced.'[1]

What Hussey Crespigny Vivian showed his Belgian counterpart was the proof that the United Kingdom had just managed to complete the last great step in its century-long campaign to end the trade in African slaves. That battle had deployed military resources to forcibly interrupt the transport of enslaved Africans from the west coast of the continent and had been a major focus of Britain's multilateral and bilateral diplomacy, as well as a topic of considerable transnational interest, for many years.[2] When this meeting occurred, Britain and Belgium had invested nearly eight months in bringing the Brussels Anti-Slavery Conference to a successful conclusion. Even then, Lambermont and Vivian – representing,

[1] Lambermont to Leopold II, 2 July 1890, Archives du Palais Royal, Brussels [hereafter APR], Archives du Cabinet du roi Léopold II, Documents relatifs au développement extérieur de la Belgique, [hereafter DRDEB], vol. 72. Unless otherwise noted, all translations from French are by the author.

[2] See Fabian Klose, Chapter 5 in this book. The most thorough examination of the Brussels conference remains Suzanne Miers, *Britain and the Ending of the Slave Trade* (London: Longman, 1975). On the involvement of transnational groups and movements in 'anti-slavery internationalism', see for instance Daniel Laqua, 'The Tensions of Internationalism: Transnational Anti-Slavery in the 1880s and 1890s', *International History Review*, 33, no. 4 (2011), 705–26.

respectively, the host country and the visitor whose foreign policy was most closely identified with efforts to end the slave trade – had had to divide the final treaty to get it signed. The statement of principle and objectives was signed that day. Postponed to a subsequent process was the issue of how to equip the Independent Congo State (ICS) with the necessary means to carry out these objectives. The conference had indeed been long and difficult, and the anti-slavery campaign itself infinitely more so. Vivian's tears were no doubt tears of relief as well as joy.

To the postcolonial eye, tears of shame might have been more appropriate. The Brussels Treaty is breathtaking in its cynicism. On the pretext of eliminating a trade that by this time was focused on the capture and transport of human beings over the Sahara and the Indian Ocean towards slave markets in the predominantly Muslim states and empires of the Middle East, the seventeen powers that signed the treaty agreed to cooperate in the military conquest and colonial rule of the interior of Africa. Most shocking is the treaty's conceit that colonial rule was the best, even the only, way to accomplish the humanitarian objective of 'effectively protecting the aboriginal populations of Africa' and of 'assuring to that vast continent the benefits of peace and civilization'.[3] Yet this premise was deeply engrained in the minds of the proponents of the scramble for Africa. Even Belgium's King Leopold II, who cynically manipulated the international system to obtain and then enlarge his personal kingdom in central Africa, appears to have had a profound belief in the equation of European rule with civilization. Military conquest, economic exploitation, diplomatic manipulation and deception, cultural denigration and destruction: to this way of thinking, all were incidental to the civilizing mission, including its most explicitly humanitarian objective, namely that of freeing people from the slave trade.

As Henri Brunschwig famously observed about colonialism and the civilizing mission, 'people are not, generally speaking, conscious hypocrites'.[4] Rather than to focus on proving him wrong, even with so inviting a target as Leopold, it is more fruitful to investigate the consequences of this consensus. How did the humanitarian pretext affect the course of Leopold's conquest and exploitation of Congo? Did international

3 'General Act of the Brussels Conference relative to the African Slave Trade, etc. Signed at Brussels, 2nd July 1890', reproduced in Sir Edward Hertslet, *The Map of Africa by Treaty*, 2nd rev. edn (London: HMSO, 1896), 48–89 (Brussels Treaty), Preamble, 49.

4 Henri Brunschwig, *French Colonialism 1871–1914: Myths and Realities*, trans. William Glanville Brown (New York: Praeger, 1966), 167.

agreement about the humanitarian objectives of colonial rule in Congo create a moral hazard, and if so, whose actions were affected by it? The concept of moral hazard is drawn from economics, where it suggests that the existence of insurance to cover loss may provide an incentive to engage in riskier behaviour than would otherwise be the case. The political science of international relations broadens the concept slightly. Martha Finnemore uses it to describe the impact of the practice by some states of undertaking military intervention to recover debts owed to their citizens. In that case, citizens had no incentive to mitigate their own risk of loss from foreign investment because their state would back them up, with violence if necessary.[5] The concept has been applied occasionally in the literature concerning humanitarian intervention to suggest why rebel movements might engage in 'excessively risky or fraudulent' behaviour in cases where their actions against a government are backed up by international military intervention, resulting in even greater civilian suffering than would otherwise have been the case.[6]

I use the term slightly differently here to ask whether moral hazard helps explain Belgian and British reactions to allegations that Congo officials and companies were themselves creating conditions tantamount to slavery even as they purported to carry out the mandate of the Brussels Treaty. In particular, did the fact that the international community had given preliminary sanction to Leopold's actions in Central Africa as 'humanitarian' intervention provide officials with an incentive to behave more recklessly or cruelly in Congo than they might otherwise have done? Did this moral sanction of Leopold's ends incent diplomats to downplay evidence of depravity in the means he used? For Leopold, one of the most important benefits of international sanction for his ICS was that it enabled him to recruit labourers, police, and soldiers from the African colonies of friendly powers. Yet from the earliest days, there were reports that these recruits – men, and the women taken along with them – were subjected to wanton violence, inadequate sustenance and living conditions, lack of suitable medical attention, and arbitrary changes to their contracts of recruitment, including the rate of pay and the nature of the work itself. Many were drawn from Britain's West African colonies. The maltreatment of these recruits drew the attention of the British

[5] Martha Finnemore, *The Purpose of Intervention: Changing Beliefs About the Use of Force* (Ithaca, NY and London: Cornell University Press, 2003), 35.

[6] Alan J. Kuperman, 'The Moral Hazard of Humanitarian Intervention: Lessons from the Balkans', *International Studies Quarterly*, 52, no. 1 (March 2008), 49–80.

Colonial Office (CO), which in turn pressured the Foreign Office (FO) to take up their cause with ICS authorities. The interaction among these institutions lets us examine the different ways in which anti-slavery ends were used to justify means that were not far from the worst of the abuses the Brussels Treaty sought to eliminate. The record of how the British government approached these issues during the 1890s provides an enlightening backdrop to Roger Casement's extraordinary mission of investigation in 1903 and E. D. Morel's Congo Reform Movement, which ultimately pressured the FO to act against Leopold's reign of terror.[7] It also suggests a degree of caution is warranted when labelling international treaties 'humanitarian'.

THE PERILS OF SERVICE IN CONGO

The British government had its first clear indication in April 1889 that something was amiss in the treatment of Congo recruits. On 5 April, the Marquess of Salisbury, who was both prime minister and foreign secretary, instructed Lord Vivian to ask whether the ICS had any evidence to support allegations forwarded to him by the colonial secretary. Officials in the Gold Coast reported that it would be difficult to recruit Hausa for service in Congo, because the Sultan of Sokoto had forbidden any of his people to enlist 'in consequence of those sent to the Congo some years back not having returned'.[8]

Any further discussion of the Sultan's concerns was lost in the growing enthusiasm to convene an international conference that would take a secular approach to the slave trade in Africa. Britain and Belgium first discussed this project in September 1888. Charles Lavigerie, the cardinal of Algiers, had just concluded an enormously successful European speaking tour. Lavigerie spoke of the evils of the 'Arab Slave Trade' and called for the creation of a private army of a million men, answerable to the Pope, to fight against the traders still operating in central and eastern Africa.[9] Though both governments recognized that the public passion the

[7] Séamas Ó Siocháin and Michael O'Sullivan (eds.), *The Eyes of Another Race: Roger Casement's Congo Report and 1903 Diary* (Dublin: University College Dublin Press, 2003); Wm. Roger Louis and Jean Stengers (eds.), *E.D. Morel's History of the Congo Reform Movement* (Oxford: Clarendon Press, 1968).

[8] Salisbury to Vivian, 5 April 1889, no. 15 Africa, United Kingdom, National Archives [hereafter UKNA], Foreign Office (FO) 881/6009.

[9] On Lavigerie's campaign specifically and on the organization of religious and other anti-slavery societies across Europe generally, see Laqua, 'Tensions of Internationalism', 707–10.

cardinal had stirred was a force that could be harnessed to suit their purposes, neither had much enthusiasm for the solution he proposed. As constitutional monarch of a largely Catholic country and absolute sovereign of the new Congo State, Leopold was in a particularly difficult position. He was consequently very receptive to the British suggestion of bringing this new crusade into the realm of international law.[10] For their part, the British cited 'the altered political conditions of the African seaboard' as a reason to seek the support of the rest of Europe's powers in concerted action 'to effect the common object' of ending the trade, even though 'Her Majesty's Government would cheerfully continue to bear [its] burthen'.[11]

The proposal to convene an international conference with Belgium as its host languished until spring 1889. Several events renewed the impetus for this initiative. First, an Anti-Slavery Society was formed in Belgium in response to Cardinal Lavigerie's call, and it announced its intention to send armed men to establish fortified posts on Lake Tanganyika to prevent the export of slaves from the Congo State. This made the threat of Lavigerie's private army all too real in Brussels.[12] Second, by April 1889, the Anglo-German blockade of Zanzibar seemed to be on the verge of resolution, making conditions more favourable to international cooperation. Third, both the conference's proponent and its putative host had received indications that Germany would favour the proposal. With Germany's agreement, the British were confident that they would be able to induce France, Italy, and Portugal to participate as well, thereby incorporating 'Representatives of all the Christian Powers who are interested in the coast-line upon which the Slave Trade continues to exist'.[13]

The conference convened the following November. In this atmosphere of shared objectives – and of the delicate diplomatic and legal negotiations required to reach agreement on the means to carry them out – allegations that ICS officers were mistreating Africans were most unwelcome. A sternly worded dispatch from Assistant Under-Secretary of State T. V. Lister to renowned explorer and author V. Levitt Cameron made this clear. 'I am to inform you that substantial evidence would be required

[10] François Renault, *Cardinal Lavigerie: Churchman, Prophet and Missionary*, trans. John O'Donohue (London & Atlantic Highlands, NJ: Athlone Press, 1994), 369–72; Greindl to Leopold II, 3 September 1888, Archives du Ministère des affaires étrangères, Royaume de Belgique [hereafter BE MAE], Institut royal colonial belge (723)71.

[11] Salisbury to Vivian, 17 September 1888, no. 15 Africa, UKNA, FO 84/2010.

[12] Vivian to Salisbury, 9 March 1889, no. 18 Africa, UKNA, FO 881/6009.

[13] Lambermont to Leopold II, 13 April 1889, APR, DRDEB, vol. 72; Salisbury to Vivian, 17 April 1889, no. 17 Africa, UKNA, FO 881/6009.

to support accusations of so grave a character, and that without very strong proofs it would not be either proper or useful to bring the subject before the Slave Trade Conference', he wrote on 3 December. In fact, raising the issue was out of the question. Instead, the FO was doing everything it could to accommodate Leopold's escalating demands for Africans to serve Congo. On 8 December, Vivian wrote to Permanent Under-Secretary of State Sir Philip Currie to convey a new proposal from the Belgian king. In exchange for permission to establish posts in British colonies 'for recruiting coloured armed police for the Congo state', Leopold was offering 'free scope to establish communications and a British zone from the Victoria Nyanza to the free waters of Lake Tanganyika, and thence to Lake Nyassa and the Zambesi'. Leopold was freely mixing humanitarian and political objectives to convince his British allies to cooperate. The forward posts these 'armed police' were to establish would not only 'crush' the slave trade but also 'checkmate the Portuguese'. The CO expressed no objection but sounded a slight note of caution about the practicality of recruiting in the colonies south of the Zambezi, where African workers were being drawn to the South African gold fields by relatively high wages. Neither did the CO believe there was much prospect of recruiting Hausa from West Africa, despite their evident desirability: 'Although the colonies go to great expense in enlisting them they cannot obtain a sufficient number to meet their own requirements', it informed Currie.[14]

Subjects from all three of Britain's West African colonies were fair game.[15] Recruiting had begun in the Lagos, Gold Coast, and Sierra Leone colonies by August 1891, and expanded rapidly. Between 25 May and 18 June 1891, 639 men and 9 women embarked for Congo at Freetown, Sierra Leone. The recruiting agent, Freetown merchant A. T. Porter, put up posters around the town on 23 June, calling for a further '500 labourers and 100 women'.[16] This was not an insignificant number: the government census conducted in Sierra Leone in April 1891 counted

[14] T. V. Lister to V. Lovett Cameron, 3 December 1888, and Vivian to Sir Philip Currie, Private, 8 December 1888: both in UKNA, FO 541/37; Vivian to Leopold II, 8 December 1889, and Vivian to Leopold II, 15 December 1889, enclosing Herbert to Currie, 13 December 1889: both in APR, DRDEB, vol. 115.

[15] Britain distinguished between African inhabitants of its colonies, who were subjects and could consequently benefit from consular intervention, and those living in the protectorates it had acquired by treaty.

[16] Acting Governor J. J. Crooks to Lord Knutsford, 14 August 1891, no. 312, UKNA, FO 10/730.

fewer than 40,000 men in the entire colony and a total population of 74,835.[17] Porter may have been particularly energetic and successful in his recruitment efforts, but all three colonies were well represented within the African labour force in Congo.

In short order, colonial authorities began to hear terrible stories about how the recruits were being treated. The first major report came from Lagos colony and reached the Foreign Office at the end of June 1891. A local minister, the Rev. James Johnson, wrote to Acting Governor George Denton on behalf of four men who had asked him 'to respectfully solicit the interference and aid of the Lagos Government to relieve them of their distressed condition and get them sent home from the Congo Free State', and a number of others who told similar stories of 'much unkind, hard and cruel usage' by agents of the ICS and companies acting on its behalf. Many of these labourers were put to work to build the railway from Matadi to Stanley Pool. Building railways was always backbreaking work in the nineteenth century, and topography and climate made the Congo railway especially difficult. However, these labourers did not seem to be objecting to the nature of the work. Instead, they complained of the circumstances in which they were forced to work and of the abuse they suffered at the hands of their supervisors, which was resulting in the deaths of many of their colleagues. Johnson summarized the horrors suffered by the men from Lagos:

> [Their employer] neglected for about six weeks after their arrival at Matadi to house them, left them exposed to sun and rain and heat and cold at the wharf, fisted and imprisoned six of their number who had called on the Chief Agent at his office and demanded on their own behalf and on behalf of their fellows to be housed ... and also put them in chains, and afterwards led them out chained together in a gang to work, besides two others whose offence was that they had directed two of their friends, who had complained to them of being beaten by some Europeans, to the Superintendent's office, that they had fed them upon very poor fare, which, with the long exposure, had caused them all to suffer from frequent and serious illness; flogged some of their number to death, employed flogging to force work from them and punish what they were pleased to call offences, amongst which might be reckoned any expression of dissatisfaction with an officer's treatment if it came to his hearing from others telling him of it.

They also complained that their employer was unilaterally changing the terms of their contracts, 'against their will employing them as soldiers

[17] House of Commons Parliamentary Papers, 1893–4 [C.6857–14] Colonial reports – Annual, no. 64, Sierra Leone, Annual report for 1891.

whereas they had engaged them as labourers'. Part of their pay was withheld and applied, so they were told, to repaying the railway company for their subsistence. Finally they alleged that the company reneged from its promise of paying their return fare to Lagos.[18]

Complaints of both types – of neglect and abuse by overseers, on one hand, and of breach of contract, on the other – would recur frequently over the next three or four years, but the FO was slow to react effectively. The absence of a consular official on the ground significantly hampered its ability to investigate complaints. Instead, when the FO received colonial governors' complaints through the CO, it would relay them to ICS authorities in Brussels. This it did with Johnson's complaint from Lagos. Edmund van Eetvelde, Leopold's top official for Congo in Brussels, seemed very responsive, ordering Congo authorities at Boma 'to make a severe and minute inquiry into the alleged grievances'.[19] His quick action was due in part to the fact that, at the same time, officials in Sierra Leone were demanding that Congolese representatives post a bond as guarantee 'for due performance of contract'. This demand so outraged the Belgian king that Leopold ordered his officials to complain through both diplomatic and political channels.[20]

Both complaint and inquiry were resolved in favour of the ICS authorities. Colonial Secretary Henry Holland, Viscount Knutsford, instructed Sierra Leone's acting governor, J. J. Crooks, to waive the requirement for the deposit as his government had accepted the 'responsibility of [the] King on account of terms of contract'. The report of the ICS inquiry, when it finally reached London in late December 1891, also exonerated the employees of the Belgian Railway Company in nearly every respect. The Congo State's Procureur d'État, Auguste-Paul-Léon Rorcourt, conducted the inquiry, accepting all the explanations the company's (white) employees offered. The company had provided its itinerant labourers with plenty of shelter. Men were left outdoors only in the nicest weather and only because others had turned up unexpectedly, so not all could be accommodated in the limited housing available. Any man left outdoors was issued with two blankets. The company fed its black

[18] G. Denton (acting governor, Lagos) to Knutsford, 29 May 1891, enclosing Rev. James Johnson to Denton, 24 April 1891, UKNA, FO 10/730.

[19] Salisbury to Martin Gosselin (Brussels), 1 July 1893, no number, UKNA, FO 10/730; Gosselin to Salisbury, 23 July 1891, no. 56 Africa, UKNA, FO 10/730.

[20] D'Oultremont to de Worms, 12 July 1891; Currie (FO) to R. H. Meade (Colonial Office), 15 July 1891, enclosing de Chimay to Solvyns of 11 July 1891; J. J. Crooks (acting governor of Sierra Leone) to Knutsford, telegram, 16 July 1891: all in UKNA, FO 10/730.

labourers food that was just as good as that which was intended for whites. Even the very high mortality rate among the company's African labour force – 12 per cent per year – was, ultimately, the fault of the labourers themselves. Contrary to the allegations of the Lagos men, this death rate 'was not due to maltreatment, want of medical care, insufficient food, or even the climate'. The company's doctors knew the true causes: 'constitutional infirmity or advanced age of those hired; previous illness or deprivations; blacks' lack of attention to hygiene and cleanliness; their apathy, discouragement and being unaccustomed to regular work; their infamous morals, their habits of pederasty and masturbation; finally, illnesses that they bring with them from their countries of origin'.

The doctors would hold themselves and the company blameless. The fault lay entirely with the men, who failed to look after themselves and were afraid of European medicine. As to the allegations that labourers were beaten, sometimes to death, 'the inquiry reveals that it is possible that some men were struck, that is, that some of the overseers might, in a moment of ill humour, have permitted themselves to hit a man. But the witnesses affirm that no serious effect resulted.' After all, company doctors had never had to treat serious injuries. The ICS asserted that the inquiry's findings were corroborated in every particular by Major Parminter, a British officer in Boma. As staff in the British embassy in Brussels noted, however, Parminter 'was formerly in the service of the Independent State, and is now Managing Director of the Compagnie de la Commerce et de l'Industrie' – hardly a disinterested observer.[21]

The ICS investigation extended only one faint lifeline to the labourers. The prosecutor asked for permission to send a *commission rogatoire* to Lagos to take evidence there. Both the FO and the CO agreed to this, and the CO duly instructed the colonial authorities at Lagos to facilitate such an inquiry.[22] Meanwhile, more direct, though not much more impartial, evidence came in of the maltreatment of British subjects on the Congo railway. Responding to a wildcat strike in December 1891, A. T. Porter himself travelled to Matadi to investigate. His report attempted to balance the interests of the railway and its employees. Where he considered the workers' complaints to be justified, he sought and obtained promises from railway officials to improve matters. Concerning the rations fed to

[21] Gosselin to Salisbury, 23 December 1891, no. 83 Africa with enclosures, UKNA, FO 10/730.

[22] FO to CO, 11 January 1892; Knutsford to Sir Gilbert Carter (governor of Lagos), 12 January 1892: both in UKNA, FO 10/730.

the men, for instance, Porter noted: 'I had to admit that the quantity appeared to me sufficient, but the fish and meat were bad in quality and I considered them rotten and unfit for use.' Company secretary M. Goffin told him 'the Company could not do better'; Porter noted that he had heard this responsibility was to be taken over by a third party. Goffin was far less helpful on the question of the violence meted out to labourers. 'To the allegation that the men were ill-treated M. Goffin replied to me that the men were often insubordinate and when I said I had heard that the men were sometimes kicked, whipped and chained by their necks, M. Goffin shrugged his shoulders and said that was nothing.' Porter was more successful in extracting promises of increased medical supplies and revisions to the hours of work to be more appropriate to the climate.[23]

Yet the impartiality of Porter's report was also suspect because of his obvious pecuniary interest in keeping the railway supplied with labour. The CO reiterated its demand for effective British diplomatic representation in Congo. In response to Salisbury's rather routine query whether Knutsford accepted Porter's report, the colonial secretary was unusually blunt: 'Lord Knutsford has no means of testing the truth or value of Mr. Porter's report, which however might be done by the Vice Consul, who, it was stated in your letter of the 1st [March 1892], would at once be appointed at the Congo.' He would leave to Salisbury's discretion whether to wait for a report from this official before tackling the ICS authorities at Brussels about the mounting evidence of abuse. He noted, though, that if the vice consul were the usual sort of person appointed to such a position, 'he might scarcely possess sufficient independence to enable him to make a trustworthy report'. The FO responded that he would be a salaried official and consequently sufficiently independent to 'watch carefully the manner in which the engagés are treated by their employers'.[24]

It would be another year before the vice consul arrived in Boma. Meanwhile it was becoming increasingly clear that the explanations, promises, and new laws that the embassy in Brussels was able to extract

[23] John Bramston (CO) to FO, 10 March 1892, enclosing Sir W. H. Quayle Jones (acting governor of Sierra Leone) to Knutsford, 6 February 1892, in turn enclosing A. T. Porter to Quayle Jones, 3 February 1892, UKNA, FO 10/730.

[24] Lister (FO) to CO, 5 April 1892; Meade (CO) to FO, 11 April 1892; Lister (FO) to CO, 27 April 1892: all in UKNA, FO 10/730. The file contains a printed version of this correspondence that was evidently compiled to help the new vice consul prepare to take up his duties, dated January 1893.

from Belgian Ministry of Foreign Affairs and ICS government personnel were not satisfactory to the colonial officials trying to deal with the mounting volume of complaints from Congo recruits. Moreover, colonial officials were increasingly willing to take unilateral action to end the problem. Reporting on the results of the *commission rogatoire*, Lagos governor Sir Gilbert Carter told Knutsford: 'It is impossible to doubt from a persual [sic] of this evidence, making every allowance for the negro's disregard of the truth, that the men have been treated in a most disgraceful and inhuman manner, reflecting grave discredit on what is supposed to be a civilized administration.' Carter, who himself was not above justifying acts of war against recalcitrant Africans in his own colony as attacks on slavery in the interests of civilization, believed the allegations of substandard food, housing, medical treatment, and underpayment to be adequately supported by the evidence. As a result, he warned, 'I shall adopt every means in my power to discourage the acceptance of offers to labourers for service in the Congo State.'[25]

Gold Coast governor Sir Brandford Griffith was also increasingly impatient. In February 1891, his initial response to reports that labourers from Accra were subject to brutal and degrading treatment in Congo had been to write to the authorities in the ICS, seeking their assurance that the practices complained about were not 'allowed to take place in the Free State'. This would allow him to deny the reports and thus quash rumours, 'the existence of [which] has a tendency to disquiet the minds of such impressionable beings as the natives of West Africa are'. The ICS authorities obliged. Replying in June, van Eetvelde explained he was happy to 'reduce to their true importance' the Accra labourers' complaints. He enclosed the report of a quasi-judicial inquiry conducted for the chief prosecutor that he said proved 'the grievances complained of were not exempt from a certain exaggeration'. Griffith accepted van Eetvelde's formal assurance that 'all abuse has ceased, that measures necessary to prevent its return have been taken, and that the Accramen now declared themselves to be entirely satisfied with the way they are being treated'.

The arrival in Accra in late October 1891 of a Belgian steamer carrying thirty-nine labourers 'in a very bad state of health' and reporting a large number of deaths en route from Congo, mostly from dysentery, belied

[25] Carter (Lagos) to Knutsford, 6 June 1892, with enclosures, no. 183, UKNA, FO 10/730. On Carter's 1892 campaign against the Ijeba, see Toyin Falola, 'The End of Slavery among the Yoruba' in Suzanne Miers and Martin A. Klein (eds.), *Slavery and Colonial Rule in Africa* (Abingdon: Routledge, 1999), 234–5.

van Eetvelde's assurances that the Accra labourers were now happy and healthy. The resulting Gold Coast inquiry revealed further horrors: if a worker fell ill, his rations were cut, and he was offered only minimal medical care, consisting most often of gin and turpentine; discipline included severe flogging and being put to work in a gang of men chained together by their necks; moreover, punishments were meted out for the most trivial of slights and errors and regularly killed the offender. Writing to Knutsford in March 1892, Griffith was now more inclined to believe the accounts of the British subjects in his charge: 'There may have been exaggeration on the part of the labourers, although ... their complaints made from Matadi, in 1890, correspond with those now made upon their return to Accra.' He urged Knutsford to pressure the FO to send its Loanda-based consul, G. F. Annesley, to Matadi to conduct his own inquiry.[26]

However, in the Foreign Office, the most conservative approach to this evidence carried the day. In a minute on Carter's report, Sir Percy Anderson noted that the FO had no clear path because 'these blacks are such inveterate liars'. The governor of Sierra Leone had been persuaded not to pursue any further the complaints that had occasioned Porter's visit in December, but the governor of Lagos seemed to believe the depositions he had forwarded. The only course available to the FO, he argued, was complete inaction: 'evidently we can carry this case no further at present'. The FO communicated this decision to their CO colleagues – but only after a further month's delay.[27] Yet it was also becoming clear that the FO did not want to dig itself any deeper into a situation that risked unrest in the West African colonies and was beginning to affect public opinion in England. Sir Edmund Monson, who succeeded Vivian as British minister to Brussels in February 1892, wrote to the Belgian king at the end of August to convey the new foreign secretary's reaction to Leopold's wish to extend recruiting facilities in the British colonies. 'Lord Rosebery declared with no hesitation that he feared this would not be possible', he wrote.[28] In response to a letter from the Aborigines Protection Society in December, the FO emphasized that it believed the evidence of abuse to

26 Griffith to Knutsford, 7 March 1892, no. 53 Gold Coast, with enclosures including van Eetvelde to Griffith, 1 June 1891, no. 1918, and conclusion of Gold Coast commission of inquiry, 18 December 1891: all in UKNA, FO 10/730.

27 Anderson, minute, undated (c. 1 July 1892), on Carter to Knutsford, 6 June 1892, no. 183, both in UKNA, FO 10/730; Lister (FO) to CO, 8 August 1892, UKNA, FO 10/730.

28 Monson to Leopold II, 30 August 1892, APR, DRDEB, vol. 86.

be equivocal: 'The result of [British] enquiries has shown that though in some cases there has been ground for complaint in the majority there has been exaggeration.' However, the FO was taking positive action: at last, it was appointing a vice consul who would actually be resident in Congo. 'Her Majesty's Government trust that his presence on the spot will afford efficient protection to labourers imported from British territory', Lister assured the APS.[29]

Try as he might, however, Vice Consul Edward Bannister's presence 'on the spot' did not prove to be much more effective in protecting British subjects in Congo. Bannister ran into two problems, one as old as the Congo State and one rather new. The old problem was the attitude of the ICS authorities, who resented any inquiry or interference in how they conducted the business of the state. The new one was that labourers recruited from British West Africa were now subject to impressment into Congo's Force Publique as soon as they landed in Congolese territory.

The newer problem became apparent soon after Bannister arrived in Boma in April 1893. Men and boys recruited in the West African colonies 'leave their homes fully persuaded that they are to be employed as labourers'. But when they arrived at Boma, 'officers of the State proceed on board the steamer: the men are bundled ashore, and in a few days time are put into uniform, when they realise, for the first time, that they are soldiers and not labourers'. Bannister cited a group from Elmina who arrived in September 1893, but 'absolutely refused to quit the consulate' until the consul extracted a promise from the governor that they would indeed be used as labourers. 'When they find they have been duped', Bannister continued, 'they begin to get sulky, shirk their work, and give endless trouble to myself and the officers of the State.' The consul mentioned, almost in passing, the complaints of 'constant abuse and corporal punishment', including the lash of the 'whip of twisted hippopotamus hide' – the chicotte – used 'pretty freely ... at the sweet will of any one who chooses to make a complaint, and apparently in many cases for trivial offences'.[30] The focus of his report was contracts made under false pretences, and it was this aspect that most interested Consul Annesley as well as the FO in London. Not only was this a matter that might, in principle, be regulated by making representations to the ICS authorities in Brussels, it was also an issue that directly affected the legitimacy of

[29] Lister to Fox-Bourne, 20 December 1892, UKNA, FO 10/730.
[30] Edward Bannister to W. Clayton Pickersgill, 24 January 1894, enclosed in Pickersgill to Lord Rosebery, 16 March 1894, no. 14, UKNA, FO 10/730.

colonial authority in the British colonies, because the recruiting agents were careful to ensure that a district commissioner was present to witness the (fraudulent) contracts at the point of embarkation. Thus both the FO and the CO could agree on 'the necessity of putting a stop to these abuses', though Colonial Secretary Lord Ripon ventured his opinion that it might 'become a serious question whether the Governors of the West African Colonies should not be instructed to prohibit any emigration from them to the Congo Free State, unless very effectual steps are taken to put an end to the ill-treatment to which it is clear the unfortunate emigrants are exposed'.[31]

In his next dispatch to London, Bannister was much blunter, both about the conditions of which his constituents complained and about the unwillingness of local ICS officials to do anything to help. This time the complainants were fourteen men from Accra who had run away from the army post in Lengi where they had been stationed. The first, Emanuel Mensah, arrived 'severely flogged' at the consulate on 5 April. Bannister sent him to the ICS's chief medical officer, Dr Reytter, who confirmed the vice consul's view that Mensah's injuries were caused by the chicotte. Five days later, thirteen more Accra men arrived at the consulate. They reported they had been flogged for denying they knew where Mensah was and fled their post in fear when another Accra man died of chicotte wounds. The following day they were arrested at the consulate and charged with desertion and, in some cases, rape. They were eventually tried in a proceeding of which Bannister observed 'a greater travesty of justice it has never been my lot to witness': the accused were not permitted to call witnesses or even to testify in their own behalf, and their sentences were read immediately following their conviction, suggesting that the guilty verdict was a foregone conclusion.

Bannister's outrage at the treatment of the Accra labourers is palpable in this dispatch, and again he mentions that because they were recruited as labourers, it was wrong 'to treat these men as soldiers – "deserters from their post" and put them in chains after their having received a flogging, as if they were Belgian recruits, or slaves, and not British subjects'. However, Bannister's central concern was the deterioration in his relations with his ICS hosts. An exchange – which began with the governor flatly telling the consul that 'until my arrival in the Congo they had had no such trouble with their people, and ... any interference in these matters of

[31] Sanderson (FO) to CO, 21 April 1894; Wingfield (CO) to FO, 5 May 1894: both in UKNA, FO 10/730.

complaint endangered the discipline of his soldiers', and Bannister retorting that 'until my arrival the poor fellows had no one to complain to' – escalated to the point that the consul wrote to public prosecutor Rorcourt, accusing him of lying.[32]

The FO's reaction to Bannister's tale of woe was telling. Anderson's minute began in his usual haughty tone: 'This is a long story and very unpleasant reading. The Africans, even the British subjects, are notorious liars, and their stories cannot be relied on.' His concern was that the ICS authorities would formally complain about Bannister's intemperate language, though he noted that such a charge would be difficult to support because 'the Congo State authorities have so bad a case about the contracts, and generally the treatment of their men . . . The fact is that the men enlisted as labourers for two years and were made soldiers. The only excuse in the correspondence is the suggestion that "policemen" are labourers.' Lord Kimberley was slightly more sympathetic. On the one hand, he agreed that Bannister must be told that his letter to Rorcourt 'is utterly unjustifiable'. On the other, wrote the foreign secretary, 'the Congo Government must be made to understand that if any further attempt were made to turn men who enlist as labourers into soldiers [against] their will, we may have to put a stop to the engagement of men in our colonies'. In the rebuke that Anderson sent to Bannister, it was Kimberley who softened the blow by adding the proviso, 'whilst you acted quite rightly in interfering on behalf of these British subjects'. More importantly, the FO once again considered whether it could exercise extraterritorial judicial jurisdiction in Congo, although it did not pursue this option.[33]

In the Gold Coast, Griffith went ahead at the end of June 1894 to prohibit further recruitment for Congo service. In a January 1895 dispatch, Griffith made a point of emphasizing to Ripon that he could not doubt the accuracy of reports from Britain's own consular official in Congo. 'Your Lordship will notice that Mr. Bannister confirms the suspicion which I had formed that the term "policeman" was a euphemism for "soldier".' By February 1895, the Foreign and Colonial Offices finally agreed: 'It is impossible in the present circumstances to secure efficient

32 Bannister to Lord Kimberley, 17 June 1894, no. 1 Africa with enclosures, UKNA, FO 403/304 (print) and FO 10/730.

33 Minutes (Anderson and Kimberley) to Bannister to Kimberley, 17 June 1894, no. 1 Africa; Anderson to Bannister, 14 August 1894, no. 1; Frederick H. T. Streatfield to file, 30 August 1894: all in UKNA, FO 10/730.

protection for the labourers, and ... there is no alternative but to inform the Congo Free State Government that the recruitment of labourers will be prohibited in all the British West African Colonies ... unless sufficient and satisfactory guarantees are given.'[34] For British subjects, the nightmare was coming to an end. For the Congolese, as Bannister was already warning the FO, it would go on for many more years.

THE MORAL HAZARDS OF ENDING THE SLAVE TRADE

Belgian historian Jean Stengers once noted, 'one does not send choirboys to build a colony'. He asserted that the most egregious violence in Congo attended efforts to exploit it economically, not to conquer it in the first place.[35] Yet it is quite clear from the British records that the brutality and callousness of ICS authorities, from the highest to the least of the 'black sergeants' whom Bannister observed 'daily, walking about with chicote [sic] in hand, and with or without provocation using the same unsparingly on any one they may deem a fit subject to inflict it on', was a feature of the administration of the ICS from its earliest days.[36] The problems in Congo went beyond rapacious exploitation for the personal enrichment of the state's absolute monarch.

The question is whether this can be explained by reference to the idea of moral hazard. The evidence on this point is highly suggestive, if not conclusive. The consistent tone of self-justification evident in the reports of those conducting inquiries within the ICS does imply that Leopold's officials believed that any behaviour was permissible so long as it advanced his 'civilizing mission' in Congo. Even more suggestive is the fact that it is the king himself who gave the clearest indications that Belgian authorities appreciated the instrumental value of operating under an international agreement that endorsed their conquest of Congo as a humanitarian mission. Leopold struck this exculpatory note early and often. It was there in 1890 when he insisted that van Eetvelde could not sign the Brussels Treaty for the ICS unless the Berlin Act of 1885 was also amended to enable the Congo State to charge import duties. 'If you are asked,' he instructed, 'you will reply that you are guided by our previous declarations and that you have been ordered to conform your behaviour

34 Griffith to Ripon, 9 January 1895, unnumbered dispatch, UKNA, FO 403/304; Kimberley to Sir F. Plunkett (British minister at Brussels), 11 February 1895, no. 18 Africa, UKNA, FO 403/304.

35 Jean Stengers, *Congo: Mythes et réalités* (Brussels: Éditions Racine, 2005), 105.

36 Bannister to Pickersgill, 17 April 1894, enclosed in Bannister to Kimberley, 17 June 1894, no. 1 Africa, UKNA, FO 403/304.

to the logic of humanity and our desire, above all, to ensure that the Conference results only in effective works.'[37] By contrast, the British used the logic of humanitarianism to pressure Leopold into backing away from his over-zealous pursuit of his own private interest. For example, by December 1890, they suspected that it was the right to levy import duties, not the anti-slave trade treaty, that really mattered to the king. At a point when, absent compromise from Leopold, it looked like French and Dutch opposition might defeat the separate agreement on import duties, Lord Salisbury telegraphed to Vivian the instruction to 'immediately impress upon the Government of the King-Sovereign the grave responsibility and even the reproach which it must bear if the failure of the great humanitarian work accomplished by the Brussels Conference can be attributed to him'.[38]

Perhaps the clearest expression of Leopold's view that his own humanitarian desires excused the conduct of his agents in Congo came in a letter he sent to van Eetvelde in June 1897. Belgians who had lost their lives in Congo were martyrs, he asserted. The ICS's agents were engaged in a 'noble and devoted' mission: 'Faced with primitive savagery, gripped by bloody customs dating back thousands of years, [our agents] must reduce them gradually.' It was this barbarism, not European greed, which had led to the evils now being described in newspapers across Europe. The solution was equally obvious to him: Europeans must back up their authority with force:

> In these barbaric countries, I know, it takes strong authority to bring the indigenous people to the practices of civilization; to this end one must be both firm and fraternal ... But if, in view of the necessary domination of civilization, it is permitted to rely, as needed, on means that give it force, the supreme sanction of law, it is no less true that its end is a work of peace.

For Leopold, there was no question that a peaceful end justified violent means. Yet he went further to provide his agents with a positive incentive to enact harsh discipline against Africans, both their subordinates and civilians. It was the example of white officers and military discipline that would inculcate in the natives the appropriate 'horror of human trophies', he noted. Europeans would teach that 'the exercise of authority cannot be confused with cruelty'.[39]

[37] Leopold II to van Eetvelde, 22 June 1890, APR, DRDEB, vol. 108.
[38] Lambermont to Leopold II, 23 December 1890, APR, DRDEB, vol. 72.
[39] Leopold II to van Eetvelde, 16 June 1897, BE MAE, files compiled by the Institut Royal Colonial Belge [IRCB] (721)66.

If Leopold was telling his agents in Belgium that everything they did was by definition the humanitarian work of civilization, the resulting moral hazard does not seem to have extended to the British Foreign Office. The English were at least as contemptuous of their African subjects as were Leopold and his men. Their record demonstrates a shameful reluctance to take any effective action to protect the interests of their subjects. In this, the existence of the international treaty sanctioning Leopold's activities in Congo may have acted as a modest constraint. However, it seems more likely that the FO's moral cowardice stemmed from its pursuit of diplomatic advantage.

At the height of the scramble for Africa, Belgium and its king occupied a diplomatic position that was both inherently weak and relatively strong. Small, neutral, and owing its existence to the consent of far greater powers, Belgium's strongest card with the British was the fact that it was neither France nor Germany. Another signal advantage was Leopold's own royal status. The king was never shy about playing both of these cards, but the apogee of Leopoldian manipulation of this position may have been the Anglo-Congolese agreement of May 1894.[40] Wm. Roger Louis has described this agreement as Sir Percy Anderson's biggest blunder. Anderson, who had replaced Lister as assistant under-secretary in January 1894, was obsessed with the danger that France posed to Britain's African ambitions. In his narrow focus on trying to use Leopold's Congo as a buffer state to block French access to the headwaters of the Nile, Anderson overlooked the danger of concluding an arrangement with the Belgian king that seemed to slight German interests in East Africa. The British were forced to remove provisions of the agreement that offended Germany and France, and Leopold's greed for territory, plus the secrecy with which he conducted his elaborate diplomatic manoeuvres, brought Congo to the brink of war with France. This, in turn, could have seriously endangered Belgium in Europe despite its official neutrality.[41]

It is certainly true that Anderson, and more generally the FO, let fear of French ambitions in Africa create blind spots that affected their dealings with Leopold and with Imperial Germany. However, the FO's bigger blunder, in humanitarian terms at least, was its failure to take any

40 For a minute, and admiring, examination of Leopold's diplomacy in pursuit of what he famously called 'this magnificent slice of African cake', see Pierre van Zuylen, *L'Échiquier Congolais ou le secret du Roi* (Brussels: Charles Dessart, 1959).

41 Wm. Roger Louis, 'The Scramble for Africa: Sir Percy Anderson's Grand Strategy', in *Ends of British Imperialism: The Scramble for Empire, Suez and Decolonization* (London and New York: I. B. Tauris, 2006), 51–74.

effective measures to force Leopold to insist that his agents in Congo treat their African employees and the Congolese themselves according to the standards of the 'civilization' that justified their presence in Central Africa. Louis agrees that the agreement was a moral failure but says the problem was Anderson's inability to see far enough into the future to anticipate the 'revelations of the anti-Congo campaign'.[42] As we have seen, the FO already had plenty of evidence in 1894 regarding the brutality of the Congolese administration. Anderson missed an opportunity to act on the reports of abuse and maltreatment of British African subjects in the 1894 Anglo-Congolese agreement. The issue of recruitment was relegated to a set of accompanying notes. The British promise to permit the ICS to continue its recruitment made no attempt to constrain any of the practices associated with it.[43] That this was inadequate to deal with the ongoing problems, let alone their moral implications, is evident in the fact that, within a month, the governor of Britain's Gold Coast colony acted to end all recruitment there for service in Congo.

For the FO, the risk of behaving immorally was created by overwhelming ambition to win the diplomatic game, not by the pretext of a civilizing mission. When it did advert to the humanitarian objectives of the Brussels Treaty, it was as part of that game. As they had in 1890, British diplomats used Leopold's professed humanitarian motives to try to rein in the king's material ambitions. In March 1894, for instance, Rennell Rodd, the FO's special negotiator with the ICS authorities charged with crafting the Anglo-Congolese agreement, reported that Leopold was being difficult. The king's first response to the English initiative was to complain that 'he was invited to undertake the opening up of a vast territory, which would entail great expense and loss of life – the first years in African development being always the most difficult and unremunerative – only that others might step in hereafter to reap the benefits and profit of his labour'. Rodd pointed out in reply that this 'suggestion of the profit to be reaped from an occupation' was new to him, as 'His Majesty had continually put forward as his plea for desiring to occupy the country on the left bank of the Nile the necessity for guaranteeing the territories of the Congo State from the attacks of slave-raiders and predatory tribes'.[44]

[42] Louis, 'Grand Strategy', 74.

[43] Sir F. R. Plunkett (minister to Brussels) to Lord Kimberley, 12 May 1894, no. 69 Africa, UKNA, FO 403/201.

[44] Rennell Rodd to FO, 19 March 1894, 'Secret report on negotiations in Brussels', UKNA, FO 403/201.

African lives were pawns to both sides of the Anglo-Congolese relationship, but in different ways. For Leopold and his agents in ICS, they were a resource to be used and abused at will, in the interests of a commercial exploitation that was itself conducted on the pretext of replacing the depredations of slave-traders with the benefits of European civilization.[45] For the British FO, sending labour from elsewhere in West Africa was a diplomatic démarche: a way to keep Leopold happy. The CO cooperated, but only so long as there was no real threat to the authority or security of colonial administration in West Africa. The two branches of government ultimately agreed that the cost of compliance was too high, reflecting some credit on their humanitarian instincts. What reflects far less well is the fact that it took nearly another decade before public pressure forced the FO to send Roger Casement to investigate reports of murder and atrocity in the pursuit of profit, then another two years before his findings were confirmed by Leopold's own commission of inquiry and consequently endorsed by Casement's employer.[46]

CONCLUSION: THE MORAL HAZARDS OF HUMANITARIAN INTERVENTION

It is of more than purely academic interest to examine the history of military interventions justified on the grounds of humanitarian purpose. The idea in itself establishes a contradiction, if not an actual invitation to abuse. That one might kill so as to prevent a greater humanitarian disaster is a morally uncomfortable position – or at least it should be. As the responsibility to protect is invoked more and more to justify military intervention, how might we analyse and understand the moral difficulty in which it immerses those charged with carrying it out?

The notion of moral hazard is a useful tool with which to approach the murky waters of bad behaviour in a good cause because it helps distinguish among the reasons for such behaviour. In the case examined here, the humanitarian goals of eliminating the slave trade by 'civilizing' the interior of Africa through colonial conquest, exploitation, and rule provided cover for decidedly inhumane and uncivilized behaviour.

[45] International legal scholars also contributed to the evolving rationale for this exploitation, not only by Leopold but also by other colonial powers. See Andrew Fitzmaurice, 'Liberalism and Empire in Nineteenth-Century International Law', *American Historical Review*, 117, no. 1 (2012), 122–40.

[46] Ó Síocháin and O'Sullivan (eds.), *The Eyes of Another Race*, 28–30.

For Leopold's agents in Congo, the fact that the king was working so energetically to protect his, and consequently their, absolute freedom of movement created a moral hazard. It provided them with an incentive to behave in a more reckless manner than they might have had they not benefited from the sanction of their king and his co-signatories in Brussels.

Used this way, the idea of moral hazard also helps to nuance the increasingly common reduction of colonialism to racism.[47] It is not a shocking revelation that the discourse of late nineteenth-century colonialism was shot through with vile racial stereotypes. However, racism is not a sufficient explanation for the behaviour of individuals or of groups. More pragmatic explanations, such as colonial governors' fear of local unrest and instability, or foreign policymakers' interest in preserving their advantages in diplomatic relations, add an essential and detailed dimension. The concept of moral hazard can help to further distinguish actions motivated by self-interest and then rationalized by racism, such as dispossessing Africans from their land, from actions imbued with such brutality and inhumanity that one is inclined to search for something more to explain them.

Diplomatic manoeuvring blinded British officials to the moral risks of inaction in the face of evidence of what was happening in Congo. This was not, strictly speaking, a moral hazard: they had no incentive to disregard the atrocities being committed there. In fact, the incentives ran the other way. Being able to paint Congo as the work of the least choirboy-like of the European powers was a useful way to deflect attention from Britain's own colonial excesses. Still, the diplomacy of the scramble for Africa had its own deleterious effect on the humanity with which British diplomats and officials reacted to stories from Congo. Lord Vivian might well have wept from shame.

[47] See, for instance, Caroline Elkins, 'Race, Citizenship, and Governance: Settler Tyranny and the End of Empire', in Caroline Elkins and Susan Pedersen (eds.), *Settler Colonialism in the Twentieth Century: Projects, Practices, Legacies* (London and New York: Routledge, 2005), 203–22.

7

From protection to humanitarian intervention? Enforcing Jewish rights in Romania and Morocco around 1880

Abigail Green

DEFENDING THE DEFENCELESS: JEWISH RIGHTS AND THE OBLIGATIONS OF HUMANITY

On 14 May 1781, the Irish Whig politician Edmund Burke made a powerful intervention in the House of Commons on behalf of the Jewish inhabitants of the West Indian island of St. Eustatius, who had been disproportionately harshly treated by British forces during the conquest of that island from the Dutch.[1] In a landmark speech, he reflected on the particular complexities of the Jewish question as a problem for the international system. For, as Burke noted,

> [h]aving no fixed settlement in any part of the world, no kingdom nor country in which they have a Government, a community and a system of laws, [the Jews] are thrown upon the benevolence of nations and claim protection and civility from their weakness as well as from their utility ... Their abandoned state and their defenceless situation calls most forcibly for the protection of civilised nations. If Dutchmen are injured and attacked, the Dutch have a nation, a Government and armies to redress or revenge their cause. If Britons are injured, Britons have armies and laws, the laws of nations ... to fly to for protection and justice. But the Jews have no such power and no such friend to depend on. Humanity then must become their protector and ally.[2]

[1] On this episode, see Guido Abbattista, 'Edmund Burke, the Atlantic American War and the "Poor Jews at St. Eustatius": Empire and the Law of Nations,' *Cromohs* 13 (2008), 1–39. On Burke and intervention, see Brendan Simms, '"A False Principle in the Law of Nations": Burke, State Sovereignty [German] Liberty, and Intervention in the Age of Westphalia' in Brendan Simms and D. J. B. Trim (eds.), *Humanitarian Intervention: A History* (Cambridge University Press, 2011), 89–110.

[2] Michael R. Marrus, 'International Bystanders to the Holocaust and Humanitarian Intervention" in Richard Ashby Wilson and Richard D. Brown (eds.), *Humanitarianism and Suffering: The Mobilization of Empathy* (Cambridge University Press, 2009), 159.

Both Burke's assertion that the Jews were a people uniquely deserving 'the protection of civilised nations' and the explicitly humanitarian terms in which he made this case serve to illuminate a key transition in the evolution of humanitarian intervention from early modern traditions of intervention on grounds of religious affinity – epitomized by the historic right to protect Ottoman Christians granted France and, later, Russia under the Capitulations – to nineteenth-century practices of humanitarian intervention.[3] For, as Burke noted, Jews differed from the Protestant and Catholic minorities that were such a feature of post-Westphalian Europe and from the Christians of the Ottoman Empire, in that they could not look to neighbouring states and princes for protection on the basis of religious affinity. In the more universalist age of the Enlightenment, however, they might yet hope for the protection of 'civilised nations' through an appeal to common 'humanity'.

In seeking to apply such concepts to the international enforcement of Jewish rights, Burke was more than a century ahead of his time. As I have argued elsewhere, the Damascus Affair of 1840 marked the beginning of a tradition of active diplomatic intervention in the Jewish question by Britain and, to a lesser extent, other Western powers.[4] At first, this tradition found expression through the ad-hoc interventions of European diplomats in response to specific local incidents and through a certain degree of sensitivity to Jewish concerns in the corridors of power. In 1878, however, these concerns were written into international law with the Treaty of Berlin and its well-known provisions to safeguard religious equality and the status of minorities – provisions that were intended, among other things, to overcome the problems faced by Jews in newly independent Romania.[5] This outcome reflected years of public activism by Jewish leaders such as Sir Moses Montefiore, long-serving president of the Board of Deputies of British Jews, and his French counterpart Adolphe Crémieux, vice-president of the Consistoire Central and founder

[3] On early modern traditions of intervention in the 'Protestant interest', see Simms and Trim, *Humanitarian Intervention*, Part I.

[4] Abigail Green, 'Intervening in the Jewish Question, 1840–1878' in Simms and Trim, *Humanitarian Intervention*, 139–58; Abigail Green, 'The British Empire and the Jews: An Imperialism of Human Rights?' *Past & Present*, 199 (May 2008), 175–205.

[5] On the long-term implications of this development, see Carole Fink, *Defending the Rights of Others: The Great Powers, the Jews, and International Minority Protection, 1878–1938* (Cambridge University Press, 2004).

of the Alliance Israélite Universelle.[6] Their willingness to deploy the language of 'civilization' and 'humanity' in the cause of international Jewish relief and their ability to forge alliances with elements within Western public opinion that were sensitive to this language were critical to the success of men such as Montefiore and Crémieux in obtaining official support for Jewish rights abroad.[7] Moreover, as Burke had appreciated, the readiness of European powers to intervene on behalf of Jews – rather than Christians – marked a crucial departure from early modern norms: away from the protection of like-minded religious groups towards a willingness to defend the 'human rights' of individuals regardless of religious affiliation.[8] This transition from 'protection' to 'humanitarian intervention' and from the responsibilities accorded particular powers on behalf of religious communities to a collective, international commitment to promote the rights of individuals as a matter of principle is the focus of this chapter.

The practice of humanitarian intervention in the nineteenth century has attracted renewed attention in recent years, most importantly through the work of Gary Bass, Davide Rodogno, and an influential volume of essays edited by Brendan Simms and David Trim.[9] This new wave of scholarship has identified the abolition of the slave trade and the protection of religious minorities as the two humanitarian causes that prompted militarized interventions in this period. Bass and Rodogno in particular have focused on successive European interventions – and failures to intervene – on behalf of Eastern Christians, prompted by a combination of *realpolitik* and Western humanitarian outrage at reports of atrocities perpetrated by Ottoman forces or local Muslim communities.

6 On Montefiore, see Abigail Green, *Moses Montefiore: Jewish Liberator, Imperial Hero* (Cambridge, Mass.: Harvard University Press, 2010). On Crémieux, see S. Posener, *Adolphe Crémieux, a Biography* (Philadelphia: Jewish Publication Society, 1940) and Daniel Amson, *Adolphe Crémieux, L'Oublié de la Gloire* (Paris: Seuil, 1988).

7 On the forging of 'horizontal alliances' by Jewish leaders in this period, see David Sorkin, 'Montefiore and the Politics of Emancipation', *Jewish Review of Books*, 1, no. 2 (Summer 2010).

8 Use of the term 'human rights' in this context is controversial. For opposing views, see Lynn Hunt, *The French Revolution and Human Rights: A Brief Documentary History* (Boston: Bedford Books, 1996); Lynn Hunt, *Inventing Human Rights: A History* (New York: W.W. Norton, 2007); and Samuel Moyn, *The Last Utopia: Human Rights in History* (Cambridge, Mass.: Harvard University Press, 2010), especially chapter 1.

9 Gary J. Bass, *Freedom's Battle: The Origins of Humanitarian Intervention* (New York: Alfred A. Knopf, 2008); Davide Rodogno, *Against Massacre: Humanitarian Interventions in the Ottoman Empire, 1815–1914* (Princeton University Press, 2012); Simms and Trim, *Humanitarian Intervention.*

Despite their different emphases, both accounts take it as a given that a combination of uneven power relations in an age of empire and religious affinity ensured that interventions of this kind were restricted to Ottoman lands. In short, despite the universalist language of 'humanity' and 'civilization' used to justify such interventions, the practice itself remained distinctly limited. By contrast, the willingness of European powers to intervene on behalf of Jews represented a decisive shift towards the less selective application of humanitarian norms.

Surprisingly, however, the Jewish question has been largely overlooked by scholars working in this area, notwithstanding the important work of Carole Fink on the origins of international minority protection.[10] The lack of attention devoted to this theme serves to privilege militarized action over the broader ways in which humanitarian ideology intersected with various forms of coercive (and often collective) diplomacy, particularly in the later nineteenth century.[11] Yet this was a period marked by the striking integration of humanitarian concerns into the broader architecture of international agreements that emerged from a series of conferences and congresses held in the last quarter of the nineteenth century as European powers sought to carve up Africa and the Balkans. Thus the Treaty of Berlin (1878), and the General Acts of Berlin (1885) and Brussels (1890) demonstrate the willingness of European powers to use collective diplomacy as a mechanism for establishing international civilized norms in zones of informal and, increasingly, formal empire: by safeguarding civil and religious liberty for minorities and enforcing the abolition of the slave trade.[12] Once we consider collective action of this kind, it becomes clear that the provisions safeguarding civil and religious liberty in the Treaty of Berlin were merely one facet of a broader humanitarian agenda that began to be implemented through coercive diplomacy in the final quarter of the nineteenth century.

[10] Fink, *Defending the Rights of Others*.

[11] On the difficulties of defining humanitarian intervention as a historical practice, see D. J. B. Trim and Brendan Simms, 'Towards a History of Humanitarian Intervention' in Simms and Trim, *Humanitarian Intervention*, 2–7. On the origins of humanitarianism more generally, see Richard Ashby Wilson and Richard D. Brown (eds.), *Humanitarianism and Suffering: The Mobilization of Empathy* (Cambridge University Press, 2009), and Michael Barnett, *Empire of Humanity: A History of Humanitarianism* (Ithaca, NY: Cornell University Press, 2011).

[12] See, for instance, L. H. Gann, 'The Berlin Conference and the Humanitarian Conscience', and Suzanne Miers, 'Humanitarianism at Berlin: Myth or Reality?' both in Stig Förster et al. (eds.), *Bismarck, Europe, and Africa: The Berlin Africa Conference 1884–1885 and the Onset of Partition* (Oxford University Press, 1988), 321–31 and 332–45, respectively.

In this context, the Jewish question represents an illuminating case study. First, it crossed key boundaries between Western and Eastern Europe, and between Europe and the Muslim world, in ways that illuminate the realities of state power and global inequalities in unexpected ways. Second, it was crucially significant as an early example of intervention on behalf of a group who were (like enslaved Africans) 'not people like us'.[13] As such, it reinforced the claim that European powers acted in the cause of 'humanity' and 'civilization' to stop massacre and relieve suffering, rather than simply on behalf of fellow Christians in time-honoured fashion. Importantly too, concern for the plight of Jews ensured that Christian states, as well as Muslim ones, were called to account before the court of 'enlightened' public opinion. If the first great Mansion House meeting held in the name of persecuted Jews was prompted by the Damascus Affair (1840) and the emergence of blood liberal allegations in the Middle East, then the next two were occasioned by reports of anti-Jewish violence and persecution in Christian Europe (Romania, 1872; Russia, 1882). Interestingly, the first Jewish calls for international guarantees of freedom of conscience emerged in the context of the Mortara Affair (1858), which concerned the kidnapping of a forcibly converted Italian Jewish boy by Papal authorities. Canon Law, and not Sharia, was the target.[14]

Here, I explore some of these issues by contrasting international responses to atrocity reports and the broader question of Jewish minority rights in the Balkans and North Africa during the 1860s and 1870s, with particular reference to the parallel situations in Romania and Morocco, and the solutions presented to these problems at the Congress of Berlin (1878) and the Conference of Madrid (1880). The former holds a well-established place in accounts of nineteenth-century interventionism, while the latter has hitherto been seen as important only by scholars of late nineteenth-century Morocco. Yet, both were formal gatherings of the European Great Powers and other significant international players, notably the United States. Both addressed, in different ways, the question of citizenship rights and discrimination against religious minorities in historic zones of Muslim empire. Yet, it is important to note that the legal framework differed in each case. Thus, the Congress of Berlin considered the constitutional rights of religious minorities as part of a broader political package designed to redraw the boundaries of the Ottoman

[13] Green, 'Intervening in the Jewish Question'. [14] See Green, *Montefiore*, 278–81.

Empire and establish quasi-'European' states in the Balkans. The Conference of Madrid, by contrast, aimed to regulate the problem of foreign protection in Morocco – a problem that only emerged when the well-established practice of consular protection became a vehicle for European rivalry in the age of imperialism.

Crucially, these two international gatherings had very different outcomes. Berlin, as is well known, resulted in a treaty clearly endorsing the principle of religious equality in both the Ottoman Empire and the emerging nation states of the Balkans, while Madrid resulted only in a nonbinding declaration in favour of religious freedom, appended to the Madrid Convention and signed by the representatives of the Great Powers, with the notable exception of Morocco. Thus the Treaty of Berlin sought to apply 'modern' humanitarian norms throughout the formerly Ottoman Balkans, but the outmoded principle of 'foreign protection' was allowed to persist relatively undisturbed in Morocco. In other words, although international Jewish lobby groups invoked 'humanity' and 'civilization' in both cases, the international system appeared to favour a more actively interventionist approach in the Christian Balkans than in Muslim Morocco. This conclusion, which sits uneasily with the assumptions of Bass and Rodogno about the interplay between humanitarian intervention and religious affinity, merits further reflection.

PARALLEL PROBLEMS, DIFFERENT RESONANCES: JEWS IN THE BALKANS AND NORTH AFRICA

Modern Jewish historians have tended to treat the nineteenth-century history of Jews in Romania and Morocco as largely unrelated fields. The story of Romanian Jewry in this period appears quintessentially 'east European'. Here we have a 'traditionalist' (essentially Ashkenazi) Jewish community, exposed to the precocious pressures of anti-Jewish violence, state-sponsored persecution, and modern political anti-Semitism in a nationalist key.[15] By contrast, the history of Moroccan Jews in this period reflects a different set of concerns related to the realities of Jewish life in the Sephardic world: most obviously, debates about Jewish integration in

[15] The classic account remains Carol Iancu, *Les Juifs en Roumanie (1866–1919): De l'Exclusion à l'Emancipation* (Aix en Provence: Editions de l'Université de Provence, 1978), available in a slightly abridged translation as Carol Iancu, *Jews in Romania 1866–1919: From Exclusion to Emancipation* (New York: Columbia University Press, 1996). See also the account in Green, *Montefiore*, ch. 16.

Muslim society and the impact of imperialism on Muslim–Jewish relations.[16] These different approaches make sense in terms of twentieth-century developments but obscure the Balkan and Sephardic context in which Romanian Jewry emerged.[17] For Romania remained to some extent part of the Ottoman world right up to the Congress of Berlin, even as Russian and Austrian interference in the Danubian Principalities and the Paris–Bucharest axis nurtured by Romanian revolutionaries and intellectuals rendered the European context increasingly relevant. More generally, a comparison of the problems faced by Jews in Romania and Morocco presents very interesting parallels.

Both countries were home to very significant Jewish communities with a total population of more than 100,000 in the case of Romania and between 200,000 and 300,000 in the case of Morocco. Yet, the nature of these communities was very different. Jews and Muslims had coexisted in Morocco since Roman times, and, for the most part, the Jews of nineteenth-century Morocco traced their origins at least to the fifteenth century. Romania had also sustained a small Sephardic presence for centuries, but the eighteenth century saw a gradual influx of Ashkenazim from Galicia and south-western Russia into the Danubian Principalities. This influx gradually became a flood, and as it did, 'Romanian Jewry' moved further from its Balkan origins and closer to its east European neighbours. Thus the number of Jews in sparsely populated Moldavia doubled from 30,000 to 60,000 between 1803 and 1848; it doubled again in the next ten years. By 1859, there were nearly 120,000 Jews in Moldavia, compared with just over 9,000 in neighbouring Wallachia. While some had deep roots in the country, most were first-, second-, or third-generation immigrants.[18]

All this had obvious implications for intercommunal relations. The situation of Jews in Morocco was ambiguous. On the one hand, they lived as *dhimmis* enjoying protection but not equality under Muslim law,

[16] Above all, see Mohammed Kenbib, *Juifs et Musulmans Au Maroc, 1859–1948: Contribution à l'Histoire Des Relations Inter-Communautaires en Terre d'Islam* (Casablanca: Najah el Jadida, 1994). H. Z. Hirschberg, *From the Ottoman Conquests to the Present Time,* vol. 2 of *A History of the Jews in North Africa* (Leiden: E. J. Brill, 1981) provides a useful Zionist counterpoint. For an introduction to these historiographical debates, see Daniel J. Schroeter, *The Sultan's Jew: Morocco and the Sephardi World* (Stanford University Press, 2002), Introduction.

[17] On Balkan Jewry, see Esther Benbassa and Aron Rodrigue, *Sephardi Jewry: A History of the Judeo-Spanish Community, 14th–20th Centuries* (Berkeley: University of California Press, 1993).

[18] For general demographic statistics, see Iancu, *Jews in Romania*, 47.

owing additional taxes, and experiencing a range of ritualized humiliations, of which the requirement to walk barefoot outside specified Jewish quarters was the most glaring. On the other hand, Muslims and Jews honoured each other's saints and coexisted within a web of mutual obligation bridging the confessional divide.[19] They were outsiders, but they were insiders as well. This was less true in the Danubian Principalities. The small community of Jews in Wallachia may have been relatively acculturated, but the burgeoning Ashkenazi community in Moldavia was highly distinctive culturally and generated inevitable demographic and economic strains. These contrasting situations played out in the parallel but fundamentally contradictory debates about Jewish citizenship in Morocco and Romania that underpinned negotiations in Berlin and Madrid. The contradiction is striking precisely because of the key role played in both cases by Jewish activists in Western Europe and the United States in setting the terms of these debates and in formulating concerns about the situation of their co-religionists in the language of contemporary humanitarianism. In this context, both the Jewish press and an increasingly institutionalized and globally oriented Jewish lobby (epitomized by the Alliance Israélite Universelle, which boasted 345 local branches in 26 different countries by 1880) emerged as key factors in the formation of international public opinion.[20]

The international campaign on behalf of Moroccan Jews should be understood in the broader context of concerns for the status of religious minorities in Muslim lands. Newspaper articles describing the 'abject and despised state' of Moroccan Jewry and the 'system of persecution' to which they were subjected belonged to a well-established tradition of

[19] The classic account of Moroccan Jewish life remains Shlomo Deshen, *The Mellah Society: Jewish Community Life in Sherifian Morocco* (University of Chicago Press, 1989). On Muslim–Jewish coexistence, see also Emily Gottreich, *The Mellah of Marrakesh: Jewish and Muslim Space in Morocco's Red City* (Bloomington: Indiana University Press, 2007).

[20] Lisa Moses Leff, *Sacred Bonds of Solidarity: The Rise of Jewish Internationalism in Nineteenth Century France* (Stanford University Press, 2006), 164. See Eli Bar-Chen, *Weder Asiaten noch Orientalen: Internationale jüdische Organisationen und die Europäisierung "rückständiger" Juden* (Würzburg: Ergon, 2005) on transnational Jewish organizations. For a broader analysis, see Abigail Green, 'Nationalism and the "Jewish International": Religious Internationalism in Europe and the Middle East c. 1840–c. 1880', *Comparative Studies in Society and History*, 50, no. 2 (April 2008), 535–58; and Abigail Green, 'Old Networks, New Connections: The Emergence of the Jewish International' in Abigail Green and Vincent Viaene (eds.), *Religious Internationals in the Modern World: Globalization and Faith Communities Since 1750* (Basingstoke: Palgrave Macmillan, 2012), 53–81.

European travel writing about the Jews of the Orient.[21] Conversely, the steady stream of newspaper articles recounting brutal miscarriages of justice – 'the atrocities committed on and persecution of the industrious and peaceful Jewish people from the hands of the subjects of His Shereefian Majesty, without the least motive or provocation on their part' – must be contextualized in terms of everyday life in Morocco.[22]

As Sir John Drummond Hay, the British consul to Morocco, commented in 1880:

> In the journals of Europe narratives are published of the murders or other cruel treatment of the Jewish subjects of the Sultan, and the Israelite Associations in London and Paris have frequently urged the British and French Governments to use their good offices in behalf of their suffering co-religionists; but no humanitarian has yet raised his voice in behalf of the Mahommedan rural population, who are even more cruelly oppressed and ill-treated by Governors and Sheikhs than their Jewish fellow-subjects.[23]

There was truth in this, but it ignored the fundamental religious inequalities of life in Morocco and the ways in which contact with the West was beginning to disturb the traditional pattern of coexistence.

This disturbance took two forms. First, high profile interventions by foreign Jews – most prominently Montefiore's 1864 mission to Marrakesh – encouraged Moroccan Jews to challenge existing practices. This change manifested itself both through concerted acts of defiance and more random gestures of insubordination, which provoked clashes in Salé, Casablanca, Azemmour, Mogador, Fez, Meknes, the Gharb, and parts of the Atlas Mountains. Montefiore eventually felt impelled to remind Moroccan Jews of their duty to the Sultan, recognizing the extent to which the *dahir* of 1864 and its aftermath had undercut the Sultan's authority.[24] Here, the activities of the international Jewish lobby interacted with a second set of problems created by contact with the West, namely the emergence of a class of elite Jews employed by European firms

[21] 'The Jews of Morocco', *The Jewish Chronicle*, 21 October 1859, 6. For a sample of such European views, see the controversial work by Bat Ye'or, *The Dhimmi: Jews and Christians Under Islam* (Madison, NJ: Fairleigh Dickenson University Press, 1985).

[22] Matthews to the Grand Vizier of the Emperor of Morocco, 21 February 1880, Papers Relating to the Foreign Relations of the United States (FRUS), 6 December 1880, 796.

[23] Hay to the Marquis of Salisbury, received 22 March 1880, *Morocco*. No. 1. *(1880) Correspondence Relative to the Conference Held at Madrid in 1880 Respecting the Right of Protection of Moorish Subjects by the Diplomatic and Consular Representatives of Foreign Powers in Morocco* (House of Commons Parliamentary Papers, 1880), no. 67.

[24] For an account of these events see Green, *Montefiore*, ch. 14; and Kenbib, *Juifs et Musulmans Au Maroc*, ch. 3.

and consulates in the seaports who, as the protégés of foreign governments, were freed from the constraints of their status as *dhimmis* and placed entirely beyond the reach of Moroccan law. This had a profoundly destabilizing effect both on intercommunal relations and on the Moroccan polity, since the various foreign powers vying for influence in Tangier were inclined to increase the numbers of Moroccans under their protection as a way of extending their reach.[25]

Superficially, the numbers were tiny: no more than '1,000 of the wealthiest Jews, including their families'.[26] Irregular protection meant the potential impact of this was far greater. As Hay noted, the Italian consul in Tangier protected thirty of the wealthiest Jews and Muslims, together with their families; if the thirteen other foreign governments followed suit, a third of the total population of Tangier could end up benefiting from foreign protection, with only 'the poorest class of inhabitants' still subject to Moroccan law. 'This anomalous state of affairs might, on the same grounds, be extended to all the ports, the government of the country would become impossible, vexatious questions and interminable litigations would arise at the Tribunals of the different Consular officers, as well as with the Moorish authorities.'[27]

Conversely, Jewish lobbyists claimed that, while the number involved seemed small, 'the influence of this privilege is felt far beyond the area of protected persons and constitutes an effective restraint upon the lawless portion of the Moorish Population'.[28] First, they argued that, given the 'ill treatment humiliation and murderous outrages to which the Jews in Morocco are so frequently exposed', their constant appeals to the foreign consuls and their inability as *dhimmis* to obtain justice in Muslim courts, it was 'only through the good offices of the foreign consuls that the Jews in Morocco are enabled to preserve their lives and to secure their property'. Second, they argued that the widespread practice of foreign

[25] On the problem of foreign protection in Morocco, see above all Mohammed Kenbib, *Les Protégés: Contribution à l'Histoire Contemporaine du Maroc* (Rabat: Université Mohammed V, 1996).

[26] *Morocco. No. 1 (1880)*, 75; J. M. Montefiore, president of the London Committee of Deputies of British Jews, and John Simon, vice president of the Anglo-Jewish Association, to the Rt. Honorable Earl Granville, FO 99/196, The National Archives.

[27] Remarks of Sir J. Drummond Hay upon the Procès-Verbaux regarding Protection, Demands of the Moorish Government, Inclosure 1 in no. 67 in *Morocco. No. 1. (1880)*, 78.

[28] J. M. Montefiore, president of the London Committee of Deputies of British Jews, and John Simon, vice president of the Anglo-Jewish Association, to the Rt. Honorable Earl Granville, FO 99/196, The National Archives.

protection meant that, in places like Tangier, 'the difficulty of distinguishing in the street the unprotected from the protected Jew [was] sufficient to insure to nearly the whole Jewish population of the town an immunity from molestation'. When the Moroccan government, with the support of Hay and the British government, set about trying to impose strict limits on foreign protection at the Conference of Madrid, Jewish lobbyists mounted an international campaign to preserve the practice 'in the name of humanity'.[29] Heading a deputation to British Foreign Secretary Lord Granville, the MP Serjeant Simon asserted:

> this custom has grown up, and it has now become a necessity for the peace of the community, because but for the consular protection there would be constant disturbances arising on the part of a fanatical population on an unoffending, helpless portion of the community. The Jews would be the constant objects of attack. It is so now in the interior. Something has given rise to the impression that the Congress now sitting is about to withdraw protection from them . . . We do not ask Her Majesty's Government to give the Jews of Morocco any immunity, but we do say Great Britain has treaty rights, and we do ask the British Government not to abandon the Jews of Morocco to the fury of a barbarous population.

In this context, explicit and unfavourable parallels were sometimes drawn between the issues under discussion in Madrid and the guarantees of religious equality enshrined in the Treaty of Berlin.[30] Yet the situation in Romania was almost the reverse of that in Morocco. Rather than urging the Great Powers to preserve Jews from the disadvantages of local citizenship through the traditional medium of foreign protection (as was the case in Morocco), Jewish leaders expressed their outrage at the unwillingness of the Romanian government to recognize Jews as indigenous inhabitants entitled to full citizenship rights, in accordance with modern constitutional norms. In the decades after 1866, the deteriorating political situation for Jews in Romania led some 100,000 to claim Austrian protection, but no one (least of all the Austrians) regarded this as cause for celebration.[31] Indeed, in 1876, Austria-Hungary became the first of the Great Powers to sign a commercial agreement with Romania that allowed the government in Bucharest to treat Austrian Jews in

29 See, for instance, the account of the Jewish deputation received by Lord Granville in 'The Jews in Morocco', *The Jewish Chronicle*, 21 May 1880, 11.

30 'The Morocco Conference', *The Jewish Chronicle*, 28 May 1880, 5; 'The Morocco Conference', *The Jewish Chronicle*, 9 July 1880, 9.

31 Beate Welter, *Die Judenpolitik der rumänischen Regierung 1866–1888* (Frankfurt am Main: Peter Lang, 1989), 51. By contrast, there were only 4,763 Jews under foreign protection in 1859.

Romania in the same way and under the same laws as 'Romanian' Jews. The Balkan context is critically important for understanding why, between 1878 and 1880, international approaches to the Jewish question in Morocco and Romania moved in such decisively different directions. It is crucial to understand that the freedoms accorded religious minorities in the Balkans by the Treaty of Berlin – particularly Article 44 which dealt with the rights of religious minorities in Romania – need to be situated not only within the emergence of an increasingly active international Jewish lobby and the role this lobby played within the domestic politics of various European states, but also within the broader tapestry of ethno-religious conflict in this region.

As an international cause, the plight of Romanian Jewry galvanized European public opinion far more effectively than parallel concerns over Morocco. Here, the intertwined processes of Romanian unification and the birth of constitutional politics rendered 'the Jewish question' a lightning rod for deep-rooted political, social, and economic tensions, as malcontents attracted to the nascent Moldavian separatist movement blamed Moldavia's relative backwardness on the Jews. These accusations chimed so neatly with the interests of the fledgling Christian bourgeoisie that land-owning boyars, eager to regain their grip on power, were soon fanning the flames of anti-Jewish sentiment in the hope of overturning political union. The resulting combination of organized political resistance to Jewish emancipation and anti-Jewish rioting in towns such as Jassy and Bacău had a transformative impact on proceedings in the new parliament at Bucharest. This was because the largely Wallachian ministry needed the support of Moldavian deputies to govern, and the electoral law bestowed disproportionate influence on the urban and professional middle classes, who represented 3.5 per cent of voters but made up over a third of the new parliament. Conservatives could still count on the support of the over-represented boyar class, but radicals such as Ion C. Brătianu saw no option but to court the 'people'. This was a very precocious outbreak of modern, politically organized anti-Semitism, and leading Romanian politicians cynically played the anti-Jewish card as the best way of staying in power.[32]

[32] This interpretation draws on Welter, *Judenpolitik*, 37–9. See also Frederick Kellogg, *The Road to Romanian Independence* (West Lafayette, IN: Purdue University Press, 1995), 21; and Constantin Iordachi, 'The Unyielding Boundaries of Citizenship: The Emancipation of "Non-Citizens" in Romania, 1866–1918', *European Review of History*, 8, no. 2 (Autumn 2001), especially 161–2.

As a result, the Romanian Constituent Assembly of 1866 adopted two articles that effectively excluded Jews from Romanian citizenship. Article 6 paid lip service to religious toleration while no longer recognizing the possibility for native Jews to be naturalized under existing civil laws. Article 7 went further, clearly stating: 'Only foreigners of Christian religion may become Romanian.' This reflected the official view of the matter, namely that Jews were a foreign element and 'the Jewish question' in Romania was economic and demographic rather than cultural or religious. As Brătianu put it to the Chamber: 'The Jews have become a social plague ... It is only by administrative regulation that we can save ourselves from this disease and prevent the foreign proletariat from invading our country.'[33] Indeed, the Romanian Constitution of 1866 was followed by a decade of exclusionary legislation. A succession of interior ministers enjoined prefects to expel (Jewish) 'vagabonds' from the districts under their control, which gradually led to the exodus of Jews from the countryside through a combination of aggressive policing and economic measures that prevented them from engaging in traditional mainstays of Jewish economic activity. Once forced into the towns, Jews faced arrest for spreading crime and infection, while their ability to hold property and enter certain professions was again severely restricted. The resulting hardship and dramatic episodes of anti-Jewish violence produced a stream of atrocity reports that transfixed the 'civilized' world. Thus the plight of Romanian Jewry prompted much activity from abroad: regular protests from foreign consuls; telegraphic disapproval from Napoleon III; a mission by Sir Moses Montefiore in 1867 sponsored by all five Great Powers; the arrival in Bucharest of an American consul explicitly empowered to represent Jewish interests; parliamentary discussion in England, Italy, the United States, and Germany; the great Mansion House meeting of 1872 in London; and two groundbreaking conferences of international Jewish activists held in 1872 and 1876, respectively.

This degree of outrage and public concern far exceeded that generated by the smaller (but still significant) stream of atrocity reports from Morocco. The difference is only partly explained by the greater numbers involved. A telegram from Jassy in 1867, for instance, described 'upwards of 20,000 families in the greatest danger of our lives; men are pursued in the streets, thrown in chains, hunted we know not whither; about 300 families have already been ruined. Every moment threatens to

[33] Iancu, *Jews in Romania*, 38–9.

annihilate all.'[34] There was certainly nothing like this in Morocco, although observers such as Drummond Hay believed the threat of such disturbances was real. When the Jews of Fez appealed to Hay to ask the Sultan to issue an edict authorizing Jews to wear shoes when passing through the Muslim quarter of that city, he replied that while their complaint was justified, such a step would leave them vulnerable to 'an ebullition of Mahommedan fanaticism, which might place in jeopardy not only their lives and property, but also the safety and honour of their wives and children'.[35] On one level, the scapegoating of Jews by a constitutional government for political reasons in Romania was a very different phenomenon from the historic dependency of Moroccan Jews on the goodwill of a weak Sultan who was unable to protect them from unscrupulous local officials and popular resentments. Yet the level of mortality resulting from these atrocities, although significantly higher in Romania, was probably not of a radically different order. Ultimately, the second-class status of Jews in both countries rendered them vulnerable to arbitrary treatment by the authorities and victimization by the rest of society at a time of rapid social, economic, and political change precipitated, in both cases, by contact with the West.

BETWEEN PROTECTION AND HUMANITARIAN INTERVENTION: THE CONGRESS OF BERLIN AND THE CONFERENCE OF MADRID

In comparing international responses to parallel humanitarian dilemmas regarding the rights of Jews in Romania and Morocco, we need to bear two parameters in mind: on the one hand, the problem of religious affinity, and on the other, the place of these two different polities within the international system. While religious and cultural prejudice undoubtedly coloured the reception of atrocity reports from both countries, it is my contention that material assessments of the capacity of these states to adopt modern constitutional and bureaucratic forms as a prerequisite for membership in the international system was a more critical consideration.

Strategically, the position of these two Muslim empires was broadly comparable. Perched on the edge of the straits of Gibraltar, Morocco

[34] Telegram communicated to Lord Stanley by the Chief Rabbi, *Principalities*. No. 1 *(1877) Correspondence respecting the condition and treatment of the Jews in Servia and Roumania 1867–1876*, letter 30, 14.

[35] Hay to Granville, Tangier, 24 June 1880 (received July 2), *Morocco. No. 1. (1880)*, 137–9.

commanded the western gateway to the Mediterranean and the sea routes to Africa, India, Australia, and the Far East. Straddling the straits of the Bosphorus, the Porte commanded access to the Black Sea, the eastern Mediterranean and, more generally, to the land and sea routes connecting Europe with Asia and North Africa. Historians may be more familiar with the diplomatic contours of the Eastern Question and the impact of Great Power rivalries in the Balkans, but Britain's reliance on Morocco to provision its strategically vital naval base in Gibraltar meant that the British government was almost as concerned to limit the imperial ambitions of France and Spain in Moroccan North Africa as it was to limit Russian ambitions in the east.[36]

Yet there could be no real comparison between the international standing of these two polities. The Ottoman Empire had been recognized as a member of the Concert of Europe in 1856; Morocco had not. Both encompassed vast and geographically diverse territories that bordered the Mediterranean and participated in its maritime trade routes. Both were criss-crossed by mountain ranges and were home to urban civilizations and nomadic tribal cultures, in which the sultan's power rested heavily on his religious authority.[37] Importantly, however, the Ottoman state was underpinned by a sophisticated and increasingly effective machinery of government, which derived new strength and vitality from the modernizing Tanzimat reforms of this period.[38] Morocco, by contrast, lacked a 'state' in the modern sense of the word: the power of the sultan rested on a combination of personal charisma and the rudimentary bureaucracy of his peripatetic treasury, while the country remained divided between territory effectively controlled by the government (*blad al-makhzan*), and

[36] The classic account of the Eastern Question remains M. S. Anderson, *The Eastern Question, 1774–1923: A Study in International Relations* (London: Macmillan, 1966). On Moroccan foreign relations, see the monumental work by Jean-Louis Miège, *L'Ouverture,* vol. 2 of *Le Maroc et l'Europe (1830–1894)* (Paris: Presses Universitaires de France, 1961); Francis Rosebro Flournoy, *British Policy Towards Morocco in the Age of Palmerston (1830–1865)* (Baltimore, Md.: John Hopkins Press, 1935); and the more recent Khalid Ben-Srhir, *Britain and Morocco During the Embassy of John Drummond Hay, 1845–1886*, trans. Malcolm Williams and Gavin Waterson (New York: RoutledgeCurzon, 2005), which takes proper account of the Moroccan perspective.

[37] See Amira K. Bennison, *Jihad and Its Interpretations in Pre-Colonial Morocco: State-Society Relations during the French Conquest of Algeria* (London: RoutledgeCurzon, 2002); Selim Deringil, *The Well-Protected Domains: Ideology and the Legitimation of Power in the Ottoman Empire, 1876–1909* (London: I. B. Tauris, 2009).

[38] For a brief introduction to the problematic of modernization and reform in the Ottoman Empire, see M. Şükrü Hanioğlu, *A Brief History of the Late Ottoman Empire* (Princeton University Press, 2008).

the tribal 'land of dissidence' (*blad al-siba*). The influential British consul Sir Drummond Hay undoubtedly supported a modernizing political agenda in Morocco in ways that parallel Stratford Canning's influential support for change in the Ottoman Empire.[39] There was, however, no basis in Moroccan society for anything like the changes brought about by the Tanzimat, the Ottoman constitutional movement, or the Young Turk revolution. Indeed, without a bureaucracy to foster, the government had little incentive to sponsor the emergence of westernizing elites. These contrasting political realities limited the options available both to international Jewish lobby groups and to diplomatic actors when it came to protecting the rights of religious minorities.

The story of Jewish lobbying at the Congress of Berlin has been told several times, and historians have stressed the critical influence exerted by Bismarck's banker, Gerson von Bleichröder, and the fortuitous interaction between demands for Jewish emancipation in Romania and an influential German lobby of disappointed Romanian railway investors.[40] Of course, Bismarck's goodwill made a difference. Yet the resulting commitments to religious freedom and equality embedded within the constitutions of the new Balkan states were framed in general terms that reflected longer-term diplomatic patterns. The establishment of civil and religious equality was an absolutely central facet of the Tanzimat reforms, one that clearly reflected the agenda of European powers rather than a more internal drive to transform the Ottoman state.[41] Consequently, of the sixty-six articles in the Treaty of Berlin, eleven dealt with religious freedom and civil and political rights – not just in the new Balkan states, but in the rump Ottoman Empire itself. These, in turn, drew on a tradition stretching back through Article 23 of the 1856 Treaty of Paris to the Hatt-i Sherif of Gülhane. Even without the Bismarck–Bleichröder connection, decades of campaigning on behalf of oppressed Jews and Ottoman Christians had helped to render the treatment of religious and ethnic minorities a precondition of acceptance into

39 On Hay, see Ben-Srhir, *Britain and Morocco*. On Stratford Canning, see for instance Allan Cunningham, 'Stratford Canning and the *Tanzimat*' in William R. Polk and Richard L. Chambers (eds.), *Beginnings of Modernization in the Middle East: The Nineteenth Century* (University of Chicago Press, 1968), 245–64.

40 On Bleichröder's role, see above all Fritz Stern, *Gold and Iron: Bismarck, Bleichröder and the Building of the German Empire* (Harmondsworth: Penguin, 1977), ch. 14.

41 See, for instance, Selim Deringel, '"There Is No Compulsion in Religion": Conversion and Apostasy in the Late Ottoman Empire 1839–1856', *Comparative Studies in Society and History*, 42, no. 3 (July 2000), 547–75.

an international state system that was increasingly governed by Western norms.[42] Jewish lobbying and Western outrage at the persecution of Jews in Romania were certainly factors, but the logic of the emerging international system and the place of a reformed Ottoman Empire within it supported the introduction of these clauses into the Treaty of Berlin. For both the Ottoman Empire and the new states of the Balkans, internal 'modernization' and integration in the new international order went hand in hand. Without internal transformation, however, there could be no such integration. Thus, the nature of the Moroccan polity precluded European powers from taking a similarly principled stance on civil and religious liberty.

Contemporaries were certainly aware of the parallels. In an 1880 letter to the Grand Vizier protesting a series of recent anti-Jewish outrages, US Consul Felix Matthews warned the Moroccan government of the perils of following the Turkish example by persisting 'in misusing her non-Mohammedan subjects'.[43] Concerned as it was with the fate of Catholic missionaries and converts, the Papacy, too, saw Berlin as a precedent and formally requested support from the Catholic Powers in obtaining a commitment at Madrid 'on the affairs of Morocco relative to the religious freedom of the inhabitants there, similar to that which was adopted at the Congress of Berlin for the subjects of the Sublime Porte'.[44]As Cardinal Nina noted, if the Ottoman sultan could endorse religious toleration, then surely the Sharifian ruler of Morocco could do so as well.[45] While diplomats such as Matthews and Cardinal Nina emphasized the parallels between Morocco and the Ottoman Empire as Muslim polities, for Jewish activists the similarities with Romania appeared equally compelling. Yet, if we look at the actual negotiations in Madrid, it is clear that neither the Ottoman precedent nor the humanitarian concern directed towards Moroccan Jewry counted for much in the face of the British foreign policy commitment to Moroccan independence and broader concerns about the nature of the Moroccan state itself.

[42] This argument is further elaborated in Green, 'Intervening in the Jewish Question'.

[43] Matthews to the Grand Vizier of the Emperor of Morocco, 21 February 1880, FRUS, 6 December 1880, 796; Letter from Cardinal Nina, extracted in Protocol No. 12 of the session 26 June 1880, FRUS, 6 December 1880, 915; Károlyi, London, to Granville (received June 1) in *Morocco. No. 1. (1880)*, no. 105, 99–100.

[44] Note from the Chambers of the Vatican to the Ambassador Extraordinary of Austria-Hungary at the Holy See, 5 May 1880, *Morocco No. 1 (1880)*, 100.

[45] Letter from Cardinal Nina, extracted in Protocol No. 12 of the session on 26 June 1880, FRUS, 6 December 1880, 915.

On other occasions Britain consistently took the lead in forcing humanitarian concerns onto the diplomatic agenda, partly for ideological reasons but also thanks to the strength of the humanitarian constituency.[46] Jewish lobbyists such as Montefiore had taken care to build horizontal alliances with leading figures within this lobby, and these alliances still held. Yet when the Austrian Count Ludolf called on Sackville West, the British ambassador in Madrid, seeking 'a declaration in favour of religious liberty in Morocco in the sense of Article 62 of the Treaty of Berlin', he met with a polite rebuttal.[47] Crucially, Sackville West maintained that

> the impossibility of the Jewish subjects of the Sultan being placed upon religious equality with the Mussulman subjects, and referred to Sir John Drummond Hay's decided opinion that if the Sultan was forced by foreign Powers to take any such step, he (the Sultan) would be unable to restrain the fanaticism of the Mahommedan population, and that a general massacre of the Jewish inhabitants of the towns would ensue.[48]

There may have been truth in this, although the 1861 massacres of Christians in Syria hardly suggest that the threat of collective religious violence was unique to Morocco. Interestingly, however, neither Sackville West nor anyone else involved in the negotiations at Madrid stopped to consider why an argument that applied just as much to the Ottoman Empire as it did to Morocco should only carry weight when considering the institutional arrangements of the latter.

The diplomatic correspondence does not explain these double standards, but it is suggestive. The US consul was particularly uncompromising in his support for Moroccan Jews, and the US government categorically endorsed the Austrian proposals.[49] Yet, when considering the issue of protection for naturalized US citizens, even Felix Matthews accepted that '[i]t would be absurd to compare Morocco with Turkey, notwithstanding that the Ottoman Government still lacks many reforms and much morality to place it within the circle with Germany and other

46 See the argument in Miers, 'Humanitarianism at Berlin'.

47 Sackville West, Madrid, to Granville (received June 3) in *Morocco. No. 1. (1880)*, no. 107, 103.

48 Granville, Foreign Office, 5 June 1880, to Károlyi in *Morocco. No. 1. (1880)*, no. 109, 104.

49 Matthews to the Grand Vizier of the Emperor of Morocco, 21 February 1880, FRUS, 6 December 1880, 796; Evarts, Washington to Fairchild, 15 June 1880, FRUS, 6 December 1880, no. 578, 897.

civilized nations'.[50] In his view, the complete lack of bureaucracy and the prevalence of venality rendered Morocco 'an exception to all other nations'. Likewise, the tenor of Hay's reports led Foreign Secretary Granville to conclude that the government of Morocco was 'one of the worst in the world'.[51] Thus both sides of the argument agreed that Morocco was incapable of rising to the standard of 'civilized nations'. Whereas, Hay believed in bolstering the Moroccan state so that it could regain control of the situation (and protect its Jews), Matthews believed religious liberty would ultimately preclude the need for foreign protection, but that the plight of Moroccan Jews fully justified their exceptional status until it did so. Importantly, however, Matthews does not seem to have seen a contradiction between expressing support for religious toleration in general terms and the continuation of consular protection for the foreseeable future. Indeed, even Jewish lobbyists thought consular protection was the best defence of civil and religious liberty in Morocco, a country where early modern diplomatic norms remained the most appropriate way of proceeding.

Viewed in the light of developments at Madrid, humanitarian intervention in the Ottoman Empire and the insistence on enforcing supposedly European norms of religious freedom and equality acquires a somewhat different character. It is, of course, impossible to understand European interaction with either the Ottoman Empire or Morocco without taking into account both the problem of religious affinity and the broader power imbalances of the age of imperialism. Yet, these factors promoted very different outcomes in these different contexts precisely because Europeans believed that the Ottoman Empire could be more effectively held to 'civilized' standards than its North African counterpart. By contrast, diplomats such as Drummond Hay concluded that in 'barbarous' and unstable Morocco, a 'policy … of too active an interference on the part of the foreign Governments in such matters' was 'much to be deprecated'.[52] From this perspective, humanitarian interventions in the Ottoman Empire represented a kind of backhanded compliment for it

[50] Mathews, Tangier, to Evarts, FRUS, 6 December 1880, no. 505, 791.

[51] Granville, Foreign Office, to Hay, 15 June 1880, in *Morocco. No. 1. (1880)*, no. 118, 117.

[52] Memorandum of the Language held by Her Majesty's Representative at Tangier to the Anglo-Jewish Association in England respecting the Protection hitherto afforded to the Jewish Population in Morocco by the Foreign Representatives in *Morocco. No. 1. (1880)*, Inclosure 2 in no. 40, 56–7.

indicated the belief that, given time, this was a state that might aspire to full membership in the European state system.

Here the comparison with Romania is particularly instructive. Romania was a Christian country with a Jewish minority, and yet Romania, unlike Morocco, was forced to embrace the principle of civil and religious liberty, at least on paper. This reflected both the higher standards applied to a Christian and European polity and the broader diplomatic context. Ultimately, the situation in Romania confounded expectations both of Christian civilization and of constitutional democracy. 'I cannot believe that Your Highness' enlightened government authorises measures so contrary to humanity and civilisation', wrote Napoleon III to Prince Carol of Romania in 1867.[53] By contrast, atrocity reports from Morocco merely confirmed in-built prejudices, leading the powers at Madrid to accept that such a 'barbarous' polity could not be held to account. This tended to confirm the assessment of Jewish activists that, in a country like Morocco, traditional forms of consular protection were the only practical option and infinitely preferable to a hopeless but principled attempt to impose civil and religious liberty in a country lacking modern constitutional and bureaucratic forms.

All this suggests that we need to rethink assumptions about the impetus behind humanitarian interventions in the Ottoman Empire and the Balkans. The experience of Jewish activists when trying to promote civil and religious liberty in Romania and Morocco suggests that humanitarian intervention through coercive diplomacy was primarily a product of the international system. Religious affinity – though important – was only a secondary factor. Once we move beyond the immediate Eastern European context and think more carefully about the Jewish question in Romania, it is easier to appreciate the importance of constitutional forms within the emerging diplomatic structures of the late nineteenth century – and the extent to which civil and religious liberty served as a proxy for 'civilised values' in the international construction of new diplomatic norms. Comparing Berlin and Madrid, we can also see what a quite radical transformation this was.

[53] *Aus dem Leben König Karls von Rumänien: Aufzeichnungen eines Augenzeugen*, vol. I (Stuttgart: Verlag J.G. Gotta'schen Buchhandlung, 1894), 201.

PART III

TRANSFERRING A CONCEPT TO THE TWENTIETH CENTURY

8

Prudence or outrage? Public opinion and humanitarian intervention in historical and comparative perspective

Jon Western

When we consider the sources and implications of public attitudes and conceptions of humanitarianism in response to mass violence against civilian populations, a number of questions are raised: Why is the public outraged in some instances of mass atrocities and not in others? What is the source of public indignation and how are the demands for state action manifested? What role do media reports and elite cues play in influencing public attitudes? What is the relationship of moral arguments to prudent ones regarding public demands for, or against, state action to 'enforce humanity'? Finally, to what extent have public attitudes influenced state behaviour across time and place? To probe these questions, we will look here at the international response to three humanitarian crises over the past two centuries: the international response to the Greek crisis of the 1820s; the American war with Spain in Cuba in 1898; and the US response to the Bosnian War from 1992 to 1995.

It is important, first, to determine a basic analytical framework from which to examine the role of public opinion and foreign policy decision-making on war and intervention. Then, in a second step, this framework is examined in the context of the three humanitarian crises listed earlier. Obviously, it exceeds the scope of this contribution to provide the level of depth that each case deserves. So the intent here must be more limited. These cases will be used to identify a range of similarities and differences in how public opinion originates and manifests in response to emerging humanitarian crises. The third and concluding step will be to offer a few broad observations and implications drawn from the three cases.

UNDERSTANDING THE BASICS: PUBLIC OPINION AND FOREIGN POLICY

The relationship between foreign policy and public opinion is complex. The causal arrow often points in both directions with foreign policy driving public opinion and vice versa. Despite this complexity, we have some general understanding about what moves public attitudes and how they interact with foreign policy decisions.

First, in almost all societies, decisions for war and peace require some element of public support. For more than two millennia, from the Funeral Oration of Pericles to the Iraq War campaign of President George W. Bush's administration, leaders have understood the significance of public opinion in matters of war and peace. While decisions for war and peace are not made by public referendum, most leaders recognize that asking or compelling citizens to fight, kill, and die on behalf of the state – and to do so effectively – requires mobilization strategies to generate public support. These strategies often include shaping public discourse on the imperative for war and the righteousness of the cause. This is obviously true in democratic regimes with institutional checks and balances, direct citizen participation in voting, and relatively free and independent media. Democratic leaders are beholden to voters and must find ways to convince citizens to support the use of force.

The need for public support also holds for many autocratic regimes as well. While autocracies can and do use coercion and other elements of repression to maintain internal security, they routinely employ instruments of persuasion and public appeal to mobilize the resources and support for external security. Historically, the most powerful appeals tap into deeply entrenched identities such as religion, ethnicity, and race. Napoleon, for example, believed public opinion was a fundamental source of power, and, while it required great delicacy in managing, it was also a source of guidance:

> Public opinion is a mysterious and invisible power, to which everything must yield. There is nothing more fickle, more vague, or more powerful; yet capricious as it is, it is nevertheless much more often true, reasonable, and just than we imagine.[1]

1 Christopher J. Herold, *The Mind of Napoleon: A Selection from His Written and Spoken Words* (New York: Columbia University Press, 1969), 120.

Second, public attitudes develop along fairly well-understood patterns. Early public opinion scholars were split over the question whether public opinion was a top-down, elite-driven, and manipulated process or a bottom-up and spontaneous response to events.[2] This debate is much more refined today as most scholars recognize the influence of both elite cues and broader public norms in public attitudes. John Zaller's seminal work on the origins of mass opinion concludes that public opinion is a blend of predispositions and information, or more precisely, 'information to form a mental picture of a given issue, and predisposition to motivate some conclusion about it'.[3] Predispositions are a blend of beliefs in which *worldviews*, *principled beliefs*, and *causal beliefs* interact.[4] Worldviews reveal how an individual conceives of the general orientation of the world and understands the basic elements of political, social, and moral order. They are often rooted in broad religious traditions, such as Catholicism or Protestantism, or secular traditions, such as liberalism and romanticism. Worldviews help influence an individual's principled beliefs about what is right and wrong, be it slavery, torture, mass atrocities, discrimination, or the deliberate targeting of civilians. Finally, predispositions include rudimentary beliefs of causality about how things connect through cause and effect and beliefs about the right 'strategies for the attainment of goals'.[5] Individuals often have a general sense, based on their view of the world and understanding of past experiences, about what types of policies can work and what can't work in particular contexts. All of these predispositions contribute to the development of *latent public opinion* – the broadly embedded views of the collective public on identity, authority, legitimacy, power, and the appropriateness and utility of force.[6]

Information flows link with these predispositions in the formation of public opinion. The public can only interpret the nature and meaning of

[2] Walter Lippmann, *Public Opinion* (New York: Greenbook, 2010); Robert Page and Benjamin Shapiro, *The Rational Public: Fifty Years of Trends in Americans' Policy Preferences* (Chicago: University of Chicago Press, 1992); John Zaller, *The Nature and Origins of Mass Opinion* (Cambridge and New York: Cambridge University Press, 1992).

[3] Zaller, *Nature and Origins*.

[4] Judith Goldstein and Robert O. Keohane, 'Ideas and Foreign Policy: An Analytical Framework' in Judith Goldstein and Robert O. Keohane (eds.), *Ideas and Foreign Policy: Beliefs, Institutions, and Political Change* (Ithaca, NY: Cornell University Press, 1993), 9–10.

[5] Ibid.

[6] Jon Western, *Selling Intervention and War: The Presidency, the Media, and the American Public* (Baltimore: The Johns Hopkins University Press, 2005), ch. 1.

an event or respond critically to arguments about those events to the extent that it has knowledge or information. Information, however, is never unfettered from social or political norms and discourses. Events do not speak for themselves. The actors of information transmission – agents of the state, the media, nongovernmental organizations, and civil society – all filter information through a variety of lenses that often reflect the influence of their own predispositions on the information. In the end, the public is beholden to a variety of elites who provide their interpretation of the context and meaning of the event.

A number of factors influence how information is collected and disseminated.[7] On matters of war and peace – especially as they pertain to specific foreign policy crises – the state often has initial information and propaganda advantages to influence the information flows and thereby shape public opinion either for or against war and intervention. Especially early in a crisis, the state often has much more direct access to a foreign policy crisis abroad; it has institutions such as deliberative national security bodies, intelligence agencies, privileged and confidential diplomatic channels, and a host of analytical, technological, and procedural elements to collect, analyse, interpret, and disseminate information about foreign policy crises. Other elites in society are often dependent on the state to release elements of the information. This allows the state to produce the first cut of the narrative of a particular crisis and to establish the dominant discourse on it.

This initial state advantage, however, can be constrained by a number of factors. First, if the state itself is divided, the flow of information is often filtered and processed through multiple and competing lenses. Opposition forces can pick up on the competing information to challenge the state's initial narrative of the events. In addition, some opposition groups can collect their own independent information. This can be done by collecting information from an exile community, NGOs, missionaries, business travellers, and others with direct access to the region in crisis.

Furthermore, the independent media also influences information flows. How it influences information flows often depends on the case. Should the media convey contradictory information and narratives, then in these cases, it can be an accelerant and intensify demands for a response to a crisis by increasing public agitation and compressing the decision-making

[7] Ibid., ch. 2.

time. It can also be a cheerleader for the state, a defender of the status quo, and an impediment to action.[8]

Finally, the longer a crisis lasts and the more intense it becomes, the more difficult it is for the states to sustain information advantages. Longer crises often produce greater information flows and alternative analyses. They also suggest the failure or limits of initial policy response and increase the likelihood of elite dissensus and oppositional mobilization.

PUBLIC OPINION AND THE ORIGINS OF HUMANITARIAN THOUGHT

Despite the large historical arc of this book and the cases presented in this chapter, the combined factors of predispositions (latent public opinion) and information flows have historically influenced the direction, intensity, and duration of public opinion. Broadly speaking, since the latter half of the eighteenth century, we have seen the emergence of a number of movements in which people in one state have come to empathize with populations from another who are suffering from acute danger or extreme humanitarian crises.[9] While that process has moved in fits and starts since then, most societies today express outrage and engage in a range of strategies to mobilize against perpetrators of extreme violence if those perpetrators are in clear violation of expressed norms. Whether or not these broad views translate into expressed support for *direct military intervention* on behalf of victims and against perpetrators is often a function of how the conflict is framed and understood and the degree of political contestation over the information flows and the contextualized discourse of those crises.

As the earlier chapters in the book depict, humanitarian ideas emerged slowly throughout the latter half of the eighteenth century and throughout much of the nineteenth century. The confluence of emerging Enlightenment thought, coupled with new forms of political expression and communication, economic exchange and capitalism, new political identities and institutions, and an expanding range of religiously and morally based attitudes – including empathy and solidarity – conjoined to produce

[8] Daniel C. Hallin, 'The Media, the War in Vietnam, and Political Support: A Critique of the Thesis of an Oppositional Media', *The Journal of Politics*, 46, no. 1 (February 1984), 2–24.

[9] Michael Barnett, *Empire of Humanity: A History of Humanitarianism* (Ithaca, NY: Cornell University Press, 2011).

the broad 'humanitarian revolution'.[10] These forces were not simply principled expressions of sympathy; as Fabian Klose and others have demonstrated elsewhere in this book, the emergence of these broadly sweeping moral sentiments was prompted through a complex combination of ideational and material factors.[11]

The first and most notable sign of the humanitarian revolution emerged with the ideational and material contest over the abolition of the slave trade. Indeed, there is evidence that the effort by the British navy to interdict the international slave trade set a precedent that could be later used to endorse the use of force across borders for humanitarian purposes.[12] New norms and conceptions of appropriateness transmitted extensively from the efforts to abolish the slave trade. As Davide Rodogno notes in his findings:

> The abolitionists gave birth to the politics of pressure groups, including mass petitions, publication of magazines and tracts, holding public meetings, appealing to public opinion, and founding of voluntary societies. The importance of public opinion was included in the solemn public declaration of ministers of eight Europeans powers on February 8, 1815, regarding the Africa slave trade, which not had to be regarded, "by just and enlightened men, in all ages, as repugnant to the principles of humanity and of universal morality." The ministers of the principal European states mentioned that "the public voice in all civilized countries" demanded the suppression of slavery, and that the universal abolition of it was "conformable to the spirit of the age and the generous principles of the allied powers".[13]

While this often involved more rhetoric than action, it underscores that new ideas were emerging as conceptions of political participation expanded and ultimately as public opinion ultimately began to focus on

[10] Thomas Haskell, 'Capitalism and the Origins of Humanitarian Sensibility, Part 1', *The American Historical Review*, 90, no. 2 (April 1985), 339–61; Thomas Haskell, 'Capitalism and the Origins of Humanitarian Sensibility, Part 2', *The American Historical Review*, 90, no. 3 (June 1985), 547–66; Thomas Laqueur, 'Bodies, Details, and the Humanitarian Narrative', in Lynn Hunt (ed.), *The New Cultural History* (Berkeley: University of California Press, 1989), 176–204; Samuel Moyn, 'Empathy in History: Empathizing with Humanity', *History and Theory*, 45 (2006), 397–415; Lynn Hunt, *Inventing Human Rights: A History* (New York: Norton, 2007); Richard D. Brown and Richard Wilson (eds.), *Humanitarianism and Suffering: The Mobilization of Empathy* (Cambridge University Press, 2009); Lynn Festa, 'Humanity without Feathers', *Humanity*, 1, no. 1 (2010), 3–27.

[11] Fabian Klose, Chapter 5 in this book.

[12] Davide Rodogno, *Against Massacre: Humanitarian Interventions in the Ottoman Empire, 1815–1914* (Princeton University Press, 2012).

[13] Ibid., 7.

questions of humanitarian intervention. In the following, I elaborate on these factors in the context of three cases across time and place, namely the fight for Greek independence in the early nineteenth century, the American war with Spain and Cuba at the turn of the nineteenth and twentieth centuries, and the battle over intervention in Bosnia at the end of the twentieth century.

THE GREEK CRISIS AND THE RISE OF THE HUMANITARIAN DEBATE

While the humanitarian revolution began within the eighteenth-century humanitarian movement and continued throughout the nineteenth century, the fight over the international response to the Greek Revolution in the 1820s marked one of the first major dilemmas of humanitarian intervention amid great-power conflict.[14] The revolution began as an uprising by Greek nationalists against Ottoman rule in Wallachia and Moldavia in early 1821 and quickly spread to the Morea and elsewhere. The Greek insurgents used particularly brutal means, going from village to village to slaughter Muslims. In the first months, they killed at least 15,000 in the Morea.[15]

The Ottoman response was swift and furious. As many as 30,000 Greeks were killed in the first three months as the Ottomans carried out a scorched earth policy in which they destroyed Greek Orthodox churches, slaughtered Greeks in Constantinople and Smyrna, and executed prominent religious leaders, including the public hanging of the Patriarch of Constantinople in front of his church.

Throughout Europe, sympathies tended to support the Greeks in their struggle to overthrow Ottoman rule. Over the course of the next eight years, the pressure for international intervention on behalf of the Greeks ebbed and flowed. Public opinion was slow to galvanize but eventually was moved by a number of episodes of brutality and by the changing dynamics of great-power politics. In October 1827, six years after the initial uprising, the British joined Russian and French naval forces in Navarino Bay to defeat the Ottoman fleet. On two more occasions, Russia intervened, and in 1832, Greece successfully gained its independence.

[14] Gary J. Bass, *Freedom's Battle: The Origins of Humanitarian Intervention* (New York: Alfred A. Knopf, 2008).

[15] Ibid., 56.

The Castlereagh response: elite consensus and latent public opinion

At the outset, the Greek uprising was seen throughout most of continental Europe and in Great Britain not through the lens of a humanitarian crisis, but the dominant lens of whether or not it posed a strategic interest to the Great Powers. In the aftermath of the Napoleonic Wars and the Congress of Vienna, public opinion across the Continent tended to accept the necessity of the new order, which relied on ensuring a concert among the four victorious powers of Great Britain, Russia, Prussia, and Austria. Britain's Lord Castlereagh and Austria's Prince Metternich successfully manoeuvred the Great Powers through the negotiations at Vienna to end the Napoleonic Wars and pave the way for the Concert of Europe. Preserving the alliance system – and the stability it was intended to produce – became the dominant strategic logic of the day. To the extent that interventionism gained traction, the Holy Alliance endorsed an anti-revolutionary doctrine in the Troppau Protocol of 1820.[16]

Though Castlereagh himself was often unpopular, his attitudes – which were predominantly conservative and realist – probably reflected those of a wider public in Britain at the time. The experiences of both the American and French Revolutions helped generate the support behind conservative ideas and for a new concept of core British interests. The American Revolution cost the country its largest and most lucrative colony and was a blow to national pride. The French Revolution was met with a blend of anxiety and disdain. George Canning's *The Anti-Jacobin* gazette was one of many leading voices that focused on the excesses of the revolutionary process. The Reign of Terror and the Napoleonic era tainted liberal and republican ideas. King George III's articulation of British national interests in the context of the uncertainty and chaos of the French Revolution and his commitment to defeating Napoleon galvanized his support at home.

In this new strategic landscape, Castlereagh committed British engagement with the Continent in a way that his eighteenth-century predecessors were unwilling and unable to do. Some critics, such as Henry Wheaton, objected to the Castlereagh's closeness to the Holy Alliance, while others objected to the extensive Congresses.[17] Nonetheless, little of the criticism

[16] John Bew, 'From an Umpire to a Competitor', in Brendan Simms and D. J. B. Trim (eds.), *Humanitarian Intervention: A History* (Cambridge University Press, 2013), 117–38.

[17] Henry Wheaton, *Elements of International Law*, 8th edn, (Boston: Little, Brown, and Cox, 1866).

influenced or penetrated Castlereagh's thinking. Castlereagh's conservative Tory Party dominated the politics at the time, and he wielded extensive powers over foreign policy and within parliament. The Whigs and other opposition leaders were generally weak and ineffective. Newspaper circulation in the early 1820s was increasing but still lacked critical mass. The largest newspaper, the *Times*, was viewed as the most credible but often provided the government the opportunity to set the initial narrative.

The first major test to Castlereagh's system was the Spanish Revolution in 1820 and 1821, which set the tone for his initial response to the Greek uprising a year later. King Ferdinand's rule had become widely unpopular as the country's empire deteriorated. Although the country was nearly bankrupt and the empire had lost colonies in the Caribbean and South America, Ferdinand mustered on as though nothing was amiss. In early January 1820, a military rebellion broke out at Cadiz with officers demanding the promulgation of the republican constitution of 1812. Ferdinand failed to respond to the challenge, the revolt escalated, and he was forced eventually to accept the republican constitution.

Tsar Alexander I of Russia objected to the revolutionary elements behind the military insurrection and hinted at intervention. While Castlereagh was not sympathetic to the uprising, he believed intervention would inevitably create friction and jeopardize the Holy Alliance. In a flurry of diplomatic exchanges, he convinced Alexander that the revolution in Spain was of no significant threat to the alliance. Furthermore, while the alliance had been developed to control revolutionary power – namely the militarized form that had developed in France – it should not be used to control the 'democratic principles' present in this case.[18]

Castlereagh's effort successfully diffused the situation. Even though Castlereagh thus sided with the nascent republican forces, his concern was principally with preserving the system, not with supporting the revolution.

Similarly, at the beginning of the Greek Revolution, Castlereagh had little sympathy for the Greeks; as in Spain, his major concern rested with Russia. Russia's traditional religious kinship and empathies for the Greek Orthodox Christians were stirred with the onset of violence. Following the public execution of the Patriarch, representatives of the major powers met to discuss whether or not to rebuke the Ottoman leadership. The crisis escalated after the Ottomans detained Russian vessels travelling

[18] Charles Webster, *The Foreign Policy of Castlereagh*, (London: G. Bell and Sons, 1925), 238.

through the Bosphorus Straits.[19] Fearing the escalation would lead to a Russo-Turkish War (and ultimately to the breakdown of the new settlement), Castlereagh devised a two-prong strategy in which Britain would simultaneously get the Russians to step back from war and convince the Turks to moderate their violence against the Greeks. The pro-Turkish British ambassador in Constantinople worked on the latter aim. Meanwhile, Castlereagh pressed Tsar Alexander to refrain from war. Alexander was under pressure from the Russian public and other elites to support the Greeks. He argued that, despite his own anxious desire to preserve the tranquility of Europe, he had to contend with a strong tide of public opinion and public prejudice and therefore to consider the feelings of the great mass of his people, for whom every consideration conspired to make a war with Turkey inviting and popular. However, Alexander also saw the revolutionary process as a threat, and Castlereagh exploited this sentiment to change Alexander's position.

Back at home, the events unfolded without much public scrutiny. There was a nascent movement to support the Greeks, but to the extent the public or media focused on the initial crisis, it tended to be more anti-Russian than pro-Greek. European attitudes were similarly more concerned with the broad strategic implications. Prince Esterhazy of Austria wrote: 'The public here, of course, look on the question as one of Liberalism, but they are not prepared to see the liberty of Greece bought at the price of Russian supremacy in the Mediterranean.'[20]

With limited public engagement, British policy was driven by Castlereagh's views. He had already conveyed his position on non-intervention during the Spanish Revolution, and his position remained unchanged. The integrity of the Holy Alliance and the broader system of the Concert of Europe was more important than the exigencies of the Greeks' situation. In his dispatch to Bagot, he warned:

> It is impossible not to feel the appeal; and if a statesman were permitted to regulate his conduct by the counsels of his heart instead of the dictates of his understanding, I really see no limits to the impulse, which might be given to his conduct, upon a case so stated. But we must always recollect that his is the grave task of providing for the peace and security of those interested immediately committed to his care; that he must not endanger the fate of the present generation in a speculative endeavor to improve the lot of that which is to come. I cannot, therefore, reconcile it to my sense of duty to embark in a scheme of new modeling the position of the Greek population in those countries at the hazard of all the

[19] Ibid., 354, 355. [20] Ibid., 362.

destructive confusion and disunion which such an attempt may lead to, not only within Turkey but in Europe.[21]

The combination of prudence and the appeal to a higher, overarching sense of morality – the stability of the system – helped persuade Tsar Alexander to step back from intervention and war with the Ottomans in February of 1822. At the time, Castlereagh had hoped the crisis would subside.

The Chios massacre, crisis duration, and the changing political and strategic landscape

Less than four months later, the trajectory of the British and international response changed. First, in March 1822, the Ottomans launched a major attack on the island of Chios and slaughtered most of the residents by particularly brutal means. The British press coverage of Greece pivoted and escalated dramatically and triggered the first major unified press response against Castlereagh's position. The bloodshed at Chios would later be depicted by the French painter Delacroix in his 1824 masterpiece *The Massacre of Chios*. The massacre galvanized the philhellenic movement into a more focused and coherently mobilized community. The second event that transformed the British and international response was the suicide of Castlereagh in August of 1822. Castlereagh's successor, George Canning, shared Castlereagh's opposition to intervention, but his position would gradually change, in part because of the duration of the crisis and his declining relationship with Metternich abroad and Wellington at home.

The plight of the Greeks only slowly resonated within British public opinion. Aided by the advocacy of Greek diaspora communities, romantic visions of ancient Greece had fuelled the emergence of a broad philhellenic movement in the decades before the outbreak of violence in 1821. Highly celebrated archaeological finds at Bassae and the acquisition by the British Museum of slabs from the Ionic cella frieze at the Temple of Apollo Epicurius were displayed in 1815. A year later, the Elgin Marbles from the Parthenon were acquired by the British Museum and brought to London amid both fanfare and criticism.[22]

[21] Ibid., 376–7.
[22] Dorothy King, *The Elgin Marbles: The Story of the Parthenon and Archeology's Greatest Controversy* (London: Hutchinson, 2006)

The massacre of Chios transformed the disparate philhellenic movement into a more focused and coherent advocacy community. Lord Byron and the Romantics led the campaign to challenge the British government's indifference to the Greeks. Their effort was not cast simply as an appeal to support the Greek insurgents but as a broader appeal to recast the Greek struggles as one in which humanity was fighting against both liberalism and conservatism. For the Romantics, identity and culture were the antidotes to the crass materialism and egoism of the Enlightenment and utilitarian notions of political economy. Other progressive Europeans and Americans also held romanticized visions of ancient Greece and joined in support of the Greek struggle. The London Greek Committee provided the organizational capacity to mobilize support. It collected and disseminated the accounts of violence from the diaspora community and worked to influence press accounts of the cause. Byron not only championed the revolution at home but also joined and eventually died in the struggle. His death fuelled more attention and sympathy for the cause.

Still, this campaign on behalf of the Greeks only slowly and probably only marginally had an effect. George Canning assumed the office of foreign secretary following Castlereagh's death and shared his predecessor's views on intervention and the perseveration of the Holy Alliance. Nonetheless, a number of factors contributed to the shift in Canning's position and British policy. First, the crisis continued unabated throughout his tenure. As it lingered, the Whigs and the critical press gained more voice and challenged Canning on the crisis regularly. Unlike Castlereagh, he did not command that same level of control over the government or parliament and was thus more susceptible to scrutiny and challenge. Second, Canning confronted a constant threat from Russia to intervene. In an effort to avert Russian intervention in 1826, he brokered a compromise agreement with Russia to support Greek autonomy within the Ottoman Empire. This eventually locked Britain into supporting Greek independence following the Ottoman rejection of the compromise. Third, Canning's relationship with Metternich was strained from the beginning and deteriorated significantly between 1822 and 1827. The strain soured Canning's commitment to the alliance. Hence, by 1827, the preservation of the alliance did not hold the same constraint vis-à-vis Greece that it had for Castlereagh in 1822. Finally, the opposition had challenged the narrative about the effects of Greek independence. The continued insurgency in the face of the brutal methods employed by the Ottomans convinced most people that Greek independence was inevitable. As the crisis intensified with mounting atrocities, public sentiment in Britain and France moved towards support for Russia to impose peace on the region and to back Greek independence.[23]

In the end, Canning changed his views in response to political, strategic, as well as public pressure. No singular event or atrocity triggered the intervention, but the cumulative slow burn of the crisis, the changing strategic landscape, and the diplomatic fatigue and frustration all played a role.

THE SPLENDID LITTLE WAR: THE SPANISH–AMERICAN WAR OF 1898

Seventy-five years after the Greek uprising began, the United States went to war against Spain to liberate Cuba from Spanish rule. Like the international response to the Greek uprising, a mixture of strategic, political, and humanitarian factors motivated the American response in Cuba. While it is difficult to parse out the independent effects of each factor, the humanitarian elements were more pronounced and more direct in influencing the decision-making in 1898 than they were in 1827.

American strategic designs on Cuba date back to the founding fathers. Thomas Jefferson wrote to President Monroe in 1823 that Cuba would be the most attractive possible addition to the United States. In the latter half of the nineteenth century as the United States planned a canal through Latin America, many believed it was a strategic imperative to control Cuba and the deep-water shipping lanes on its southern coast.

Yet, despite these grand strategic designs, humanitarian considerations played a central role in the decision for war in 1898. The Cuban insurrection that began in 1872 was violently repressed by the Spanish. This sent thousands of Cubans to the United States, where the exile community spent the next twenty years campaigning for American support for the Cuban Revolution. Exile communities along the East Coast (New York, Boston, Philadelphia, Baltimore, and Washington) generated a significant amount of sympathy for the Cuban cause. Presidents Grant through Cleveland were frequently criticized for failing to do more to aid the cause.

In 1895, Spanish Prime Minister Canovas feared that if the insurrection continued, the United States would eventually launch an invasion of Cuba. In order to put an end to the insurrection, he appointed General

[23] Ibid., 619.

Valeriano Weyler, an army hardliner, to resolve the situation. Weyler set a two-year timeframe to defeat the insurrection and chose an aggressive counter-insurgency strategy. His first policy upon assuming command was to decree the 'reconcentration' of rural populations into fortified towns and villages and to destroy the agricultural output that supplied the insurgents. The violent campaign was brutal and the reconcentrated peasants quickly overwhelmed the capacity of the towns and villages. Hunger, disease, and suffering escalated.

This corresponded with the rise of what came to be known as 'yellow journalism' in the United States. William Randolph Hearst and Joseph Pulitzer were engaged in a fierce battle for readership in New York City. This battle produced the infamous yellow journalism in which news reporting moved towards more sensational depictions. Both Hearst and Pulitzer saw an opportunity in Cuba, and so both sent reporters and photographers to the island to report on the policies of General 'the Butcher' Weyler. The reports from the field depicted extreme brutality and indignity and whipped up extensive public demands on the US government to do something to protect the Cubans. Other newspapers picked up on the stories, and reports of Weyler's atrocities spread across the country. Isolationist newspapers even sympathized with the Cubans, and editorials began to conclude that the United States would have to support the Cuban rebels with arms and intervention if necessary.[24]

At the time, neither President Cleveland nor his successor, President McKinley, had any inclination to support an American war against Spain for Cuba. Cleveland feared war would create economic turmoil in an economy struggling to regain its footing from the recession of 1893/94. Upon taking office, McKinley lamented that Cleveland had dropped the Cuba problem in his lap. Like Cleveland, McKinley believed war would be a disaster for the economy. He also had a deeper aversion to war. He was a Civil War veteran, had served as a corporal in the Union Army, and witnessed the Battle of Antietam, the bloodiest battle of the war. His recollection of that battle had a profound influence on his reluctance for war.

McKinley's ability to control the narrative was limited by a very active US media with direct and proximate access to the events unfolding in Cuba. It was also limited by dissensus within his administration. McKinley's key defence advisers were generally timid and passive on the

[24] Ernest R. May, *Imperial Democracy: The Emergence of America as a Great Power* (New York: Harper Torchbooks, 1961), 69–70.

question of Cuba – with one notable exception. His Assistant Secretary of the Navy, Theodore Roosevelt, saw the world through the lens of America's emerging global role. He believed the United States had an obligation, not to the Cubans, but to the future of US power to gain control of Cuba. He publicly and privately criticized McKinley's passivity on Cuba, and his voice often overwhelmed the voices of restraint within the administration.

McKinley's opposition to war (and his reluctance to push back on Roosevelt's views) was tempered by the fact that he was also disturbed by the Spanish conduct. McKinley frequently expressed sympathies for the Cubans in his public speeches. As Warren Zimmerman notes, 'McKinley was a follower not a leader of public opinion. As it shifted toward war, he shifted with it, though to Roosevelt's exasperation, he agonized all the way.'[25]

The press's role was pivotal not only for laying the broader attitudinal conditions for war, but also for accelerating the proximate triggering events. It simultaneously depicted the barbarities of the Spanish and the sympathies of the Cubans. On 9 February 1898, the *New York Journal* – Hearst's newspaper – printed a letter intercepted from the Spanish minister in Washington. The minister labelled McKinley a weak 'would be politician' and nothing more than a 'bidder for the admiration of the crowd'.[26] A week later, the *USS Maine* exploded and sunk in Havana Harbor, killing 268 US sailors. The initial reports indicated that the cause was a spontaneous combustion explosion in the boiler room. That finding would be confirmed eight decades later by an investigation led by US Admiral Hyman Rickover. However, amid the heightened tensions and inflamed situation at the time, the sensational press speculated that it must have been a torpedo or a mine.

McKinley, who was still trying to avoid war, lost the battle in effect when his close friend Senator Redfield Proctor reported on his recent trip to Havana. Proctor was an influential businessman and a moderate. His impassioned speech on the floor of the US Senate sealed the decision for war.[27] He reported that the violence and conditions for the Cuban population were worse than he could imagine and that all of the people

[25] Warren Zimmerman, *First Great Triumph: How Five Americans Made Their Country a World Power* (New York: Farrar, Straus and Giroux, 2002), 254.

[26] Ibid., 256.

[27] David F. Trask, *The War with Spain in 1898* (Lincoln, NE: University of Nebraska Press, 1996), 36.

were 'struggling for freedom and deliverance from the worst misgovernment of which I ever had knowledge'.[28] Leading politicians looked at the speech as the most influential one to affect public opinion in more than a half century. Less than a month later, McKinley delivered his war message to Congress and the United States went to war.

To be sure, American elites had long a strategic eye on Cuba, and in 1898, McKinley was forced into a war that would advance those interests. However, public opinion approved of war not out of an interest in strategic expansion, but out of support for the Cubans. Public attitudes were fuelled by an aggressive press that often exaggerated and embellished already disturbing facts. It is perhaps the clearest case in American history where public and political outrage over the treatment of human beings moved a reluctant president to war.

Of course, it is an unfortunate irony of this case that the Americans ultimately did not allow the Cubans to control their own destiny. Not only did they fail to integrate the Cuban rebels into the military campaign, they also kept them out of the Spanish surrender at Santiago and excluded them from the Paris peace talks in 1899. In the end, the public interest in Cuba waned after the passage of the Platt Amendment. Humanitarian impulses helped feed the war, but Americans' appetite for it was soon satiated.

WE DON'T HAVE A DOG IN THAT FIGHT: THE BOSNIAN WAR, 1992–1995

Nearly a century after the war with Spain, Americans were again confronted with images of enormous pain and suffering. The Bosnian War began in late March of 1992 and lasted until the fall of 1995. In that time, more than 100,000 people were killed, more than 2 million were displaced, and Europe again witnessed extreme violence – rape camps, concentration camps, and the siege of Sarajevo.

The initial reaction of the US government was that the conflict was fuelled by age-old ethnic hatreds about which little could be done. President George H. W. Bush and his foreign policy team led by Secretary of State James Baker saw the world much like Lord Castlereagh had and felt the need to keep an eye on the big picture. As the Yugoslav federation began to split up in 1991, Baker – like Castlereagh in the Greek uprising a century

[28] Zimmerman, *First Great Triumph*, 257.

and a half earlier – pursued a conservative strategy that focused on the broader geo-strategic implications. He pushed back against the liberal forces in Slovenia and Croatia and urged them not to secede from the Yugoslav federation. Baker anticipated violence and feared that such a violent break-up might trigger a similar process in the USSR.

His pressure on Slovenia and Croatia not to secede was seen by many as a signal to Belgrade to launch a war to block the secession. In August 1991, the forces of the Serbian-led Yugoslav National Army intervened in both Slovenia and Croatia. The wars in Slovenia and Croatia were relatively short. Slovenia won its secession and ultimately independence after Serbian forces withdrew. In Croatia, however, Serbian forces gained control of nearly a third of the country before UN mediators were able to broker a ceasefire in January 1992.

In March 1992, war moved towards Bosnia as the republic's Muslim and Croatian population voted to secede from the rump Yugoslavia. Baker's approach was to keep the United States out of the conflict and to delegate it to Europe. The EU was formally created with the Treaty on European Union in Maastricht in February 1992 amid great fanfare, however, at the time it had no common foreign or security policy. The EU's response proved weak and ineffective because member states with deep and historic divisions in their relations with the Balkans failed to control the escalating violence.

Initially, the information flows on Bosnia were biased in favour of the Bush administration's views of the conflict. Furthermore, Bosnia's terrain, coupled with the inability by outsiders to distinguish one group from another, was seen as a significant deterrent to intervention. As the violence escalated, a number of elite communities emerged to demand more direct US engagement in the conflict. In the summer of 1992, these calls came from members of Congress, human rights organizations, Jewish communities, and others after the disclosure of Serbian-run concentration camps. This fuelled greater advocacy in Congress to lift the arms embargo that had been applied to the former Yugoslavia in the fall of 1991. Critics charged that the arms embargo locked in military advantages for the Serbs.

In November 1992, Arkansas Governor Bill Clinton defeated President Bush. Clinton had campaigned for stronger action on Bosnia. After the election and before Clinton's inauguration, President Bush and his Joint Chiefs of Staff reversed course on the humanitarian crisis happening simultaneously in Somalia and deployed the 10th US Mountain Division and others to Somalia to protect the distribution of humanitarian relief supplies. The decision effectively took Bosnia off the table for the incoming Clinton administration.[29]

Between 1993 and early 1995, the Clinton administration engaged Bosnia in fits and starts. Despite the escalating violence, the siege of Sarajevo, and daily news reporting of ethnic cleansing, public opinion on Bosnia remained relatively static. The public expressed concern for the civilians but generally concluded that there was not much the United States could do to stop the violence.

While public opinion alone did not directly contribute to demands for intervention, the combination of public and elite political opinion did play an indirect role in shifting the US position on intervention. Throughout the conflict, the United States had delegated the conflict management strategy to the UN and to NATO. The ongoing violence weakened the confidence of the public and the political elite in the effectiveness and credibility of both international organizations. Extensive restrictions on rules of engagement and cumbersome bureaucratic procedures limited the ability of either the peacekeepers or NATO aircraft from slowing the violence.

The Srebrenica massacre proved to be the tipping point. Srebrenica was declared a UN Safe Haven and the UN deployed a small contingent of peacekeepers to the village to protect it. In the spring of 1995, Croatian forces launched an offensive to reclaim territories in Croatia lost in 1991. This offensive coincided with a new push by the Bosnian army against Serbian forces. Sensing the endgame, Serbian forces withdrew from the Krajina region in Croatia and moved to shore up and consolidate control over territory it deemed necessary for a future Bosnian Serb political entity in eastern Bosnia. The Serbs pushed aside the UN peacekeepers and took control of Srebrenica. In doing so, they detained and eventually summarily executed more than 6,000 Bosnian Muslim men and boys in Srebrenica. Moreover, it appeared that the Serbs would undertake similar actions in two other safe havens in eastern Bosnia – Zepa and Gorazde.

For the Clinton administration, the atrocities at Srebrenica were both an affront to basic conceptions of human dignity and a threat to the broader international strategic landscape. The Clinton administration was simultaneously outraged by the massacre and distressed that the UN and NATO had been unable to do anything to stop the violence.

[29] Jon Western, 'Sources of Humanitarian Intervention: Beliefs, Information, and Advocacy in the U.S. Decisions on Somalia and Bosnia', *International Security*, 26, no. 2 (Spring 2002), 112–42.

On the latter point, Clinton feared that, if the United States did not respond to the violence, the integrity and credibility of the two leading multilateral institutions would be severely eroded. Intervention was needed not just to stop the violence against civilians but, in the aftermath of Srebrencia, to preserve the world's two most important global governing institutions.

It was the confluence of these two elements along with the changing military situation on the ground that finally compelled the administration to change course on Bosnia. In August, the United States initiated a more robust NATO airstrike campaign against Serbian targets in Bosnia. Less than a month later, the Serbs agreed to a ceasefire and to participate in peace talks in Dayton, Ohio, in November 1995.

Public opinion did not really change on Bosnia. In the end, it was the opinions of elites more than the public that moved American policy. Public opinion was always sympathetic to the plight of the Bosnians but not sufficiently moved to support US military action in support of intervention. Latent public opinion reflected a fairly entrenched view that was sceptical that the US military could really make a difference in the conflict.

CONCLUSION

The three cases here present some interesting, albeit preliminary, parallels and conclusions. In each case, the initial state position was a reluctance to intervene. However, both the humanitarian and strategic landscape changed over time and influenced intervention decisions. A number of factors contributed to these changes.

First, latent public opinion appeared largely predisposed to a position of non-intervention in the initial phase of the Greek and Bosnian crises. Public opinion accepted the initial dominant narrative for each crisis, namely that each case might be tragic but that core interests were not at stake and intervention would exacerbate rather than solve the problems. The Cuban case had deeper roots (it had been going on almost twenty years); hence, public predisposition appeared more sensitive to the plight of the Cubans and more open to intervention from the outset.

Second, the duration of the crisis was a significant factor in each case. Initial state propaganda and information advantages were lost as the crises continued year after year. The Greek crisis began in 1822 and continued for more than five years, leading to the intervention in 1827; the Cuban insurrection dated back to the early 1870s; and the Bosnian war lingered for more than three years prior to the US bombing campaign in August 1995. In addition, major atrocities reshaped the decision-making context over time. The massacre of Chios is often attributed as the catalyst for intervention in Greece. Proctor's report on the reconcentration policy and the massacre at Srebrenica were more explicit and proximate causes of the intervention decisions in the cases of Cuba and Bosnia, respectively.

What is less clear is whether the catalyst for intervention was public opinion per se or elite opinion and changing strategic elements that altered the political contexts. In all three cases, the increasing public and political demands corresponded with changing strategic landscapes. In the case of Greece, the protracted crisis convinced Canning and many other British elites that the Ottomans would not be able to reclaim control over the Greek territories and that preventing a Russo-Turkish war required endorsing Greek demands. In the case of Cuba, the sinking of the *USS Maine* transformed the crisis from a simple humanitarian question to a direct attack on the United States. In Bosnia, elite perceptions changed on the escalating damage to the integrity and legitimacy of the UN and NATO in the aftermath of Srebrenica.

In the end, public opinion in all three cases demonstrated elements of both outrage and prudence. The public is moved by images of mass violence against civilians and routinely sympathizes with the victims of mass violence, but those sympathies are often tempered by prudent concerns about the efficacy and utility of force. When those prudent concerns are mitigated with new information flows and mobilized advocacy that challenge and alter the dominant narrative, public opinion will move more clearly behind a humanitarian interventionist policy.

9

Non-state actors' humanitarian operations in the aftermath of the First World War

The case of the Near East Relief

Davide Rodogno

This chapter, based on archival sources often overlooked by historians, describes how an American humanitarian organization, the Near East Relief (NER) relieved and rehabilitated a select number of victims of 'crimes against humanity', specifically the ex-Ottoman Armenian civilians who were scattered across what would become Soviet Armenia, Syria and Lebanon (under French mandate), and Greece.[1] I highlight the ambitions and inconsistencies of NER politics and critically examine the paternalistic and quasi-colonial stance of NER relief workers and leaders. On the one hand, the chapter hints about how NER activities prefigured international development politics and practices undertaken by the United Nations Relief and Rehabilitation Administration (UNRRA) and other UN agencies in the aftermath of the Second World War. On the other hand, I argue that the international system that evolved out of the First

[1] NER documents are scattered throughout several archives and research centers. The most relevant are the National Archives, Washington DC; American Board Commission of Foreign Mission (ABCFM) Archives, Houghton Library, Harvard University (hereafter A-ABCFM); Rockefeller Archives Centre (hereafter RAC), Tarrytown, NY; New York Public Library Archives; League of Nations Archives; ICRC Archives, Geneva; the Library of Congress, Washington DC. Personal papers of several relief workers, directors, and campaigners who worked – on a voluntary basis or otherwise – for the NER are to be found in several US universities as well as the Library of Congress. Further information on the NER can be gathered by looking at the documents of the organizations with which it cooperated and those of its rivals, such as the American Relief Administration, whose main archives are at the Hoover Institute Archives at Stanford University, the America Women's Hospital, whose archives are in Philadelphia, and the Quakers' archives, also located Philadelphia as well as in London. This paper uses the sources found in the RAC and A-ABCFM.

World War was far from being propitious for humanitarian interventions of the kind that had taken place throughout the nineteenth century. Nevertheless, this very system fostered humanitarian actions by non-governmental actors, such as the NER.

As Fabian Klose states in the introduction of this book, the first half of the twentieth century seemed to experience a complete halt in the further development of the concept and practice of humanitarian intervention. Due to the heavy toll that the First World War took on Europe – socially, economically, and politically – nations became very wary of any proposed international military engagement on behalf of peoples in far-off lands. For this reason, the interwar period has been described as the 'eclipse of humanitarian intervention'.[2] In fact, dictators such as Benito Mussolini and Adolf Hitler gave an extremely bad name to humanitarian interventions, when they aggressed against Ethiopia and Czechoslovakia in the mid and late 1930s. However, the decline of humanitarian interventions was far from being ineluctable, and the idea of intervening in the internal affairs of sovereign states for humanitarian reasons did not vanish after 1918. It persisted in Western Europe and in the United States, taking on different shapes and forms.

The international order born after the end of the First World War and the creation of the League of Nations should have brought perpetual peace worldwide. The new international order would not have allowed humanitarian interventions to be undertaken by a self-appointed committee of powers that was allegedly acting in the interest of all members of the Family of Nations.[3] In theory, the League of Nations should have taken on the responsibility of humanitarian intervention as well as the protection of the most fundamental human rights all over the world.[4] The new 'Society of Nations' should have given the sanction of social solidarity, on an objective basis, to the hitherto purely sporadic, isolated acts of 'altruistic nations acting as enforcers of the law of nations'.[5] Being capable of

[2] Michael R. Marrus, 'International Bystanders to the Holocaust and Humanitarian Intervention' in Richard Ashby Wilson and Richard D. Brown (eds.), *Humanitarianism and Suffering: The Mobilization of Empathy* (Cambridge University Press, 2009), 164–68.

[3] Peter Haggenmacher, 'Pensiero Umanitario e Intervento in Gentili' in *Azione Umanitaria ed Intervento Umanitario. Il Parere del Comitato Internazionale della Croce Rossa. Pensiero Umanitario e Intervento Umanitario in Gentili, Atti del Convegno, Sesta Giornata Gentiliana, September 17, 1994* (Milan: Giuffré, 1994), 20–45.

[4] Malbone W. Graham, 'Humanitarian Intervention in International Law as Related to the Practice of the United States', *Michigan Law Review*, 22 (1924), 312–28, here 320.

[5] Ibid., 321.

formulating and enforcing international law, the new Society of Nations should have limited national sovereignty, abolished the inequality of states, and hence – as University of Texas professor Malbone W. Graham put it – prevented such 'crimes against humanity' as persecution, oppression, uncivilized warfare, injustice, and slave trade. In the long term, the League of Nations would have enforced 'the prevention and control of disease, the reduction of the opium traffic, and the mitigation of suffering throughout the world'.[6] In this idealistic view, the League of Nations and its members would have taken on the responsibility to protect humanity. Responsibility to protect is a term that I deliberately – not provocatively – use here, because the protagonists of the story I explore in this chapter referred to their actions in these terms.

In practice, as historian Mark Mazower points out, the new Society of Nations in Geneva still depended on the same civilizational hierarchies that had underpinned so much pre-1914 liberal thought.[7] Even though 'half-civilized' states such as Abyssinia, Siam, Iran, and Turkey were now members of the League of Nations, it remained exclusively the duty of only the 'civilized nations' to guide 'the less, or uncivilized, into the way of national self-realization'.[8] Many of the events I am about to examine revolved around the claim by humanitarians to have a duty (or a responsibility) to enlighten the 'uncivilized' populations of the Near East. This paternalist duty leaves no doubt about humanitarians' perceptions of local populations. From this perception was derived a specific vision of sovereignty, which derogated the sacrosanct principle of non-intervention in the internal affairs of a sovereign state. Representatives of Western European or American humanitarian organizations believed they had every right to interfere in the internal affairs of certain states. This moral right derived from their deeds during the First World War. Having rescued Belgian, French, and other European civilian populations, these organizations took it for granted that they would be welcome and did not doubt the positive consequences of their benevolent action. In this respect, I see an interesting continuity – not an identity – between

6 Ibid., 325.

7 Mark Mazower, 'An International Civilization? Empire, Internationalism and the Crisis of the Mid-twentieth Century', *International Affairs*, 82 (2006), 553–66, here 558. See also Eric D. Weitz, 'From the Vienna to the Paris System: International Politics and the Entangled Histories of Human Rights, Forced Deportations, and Civilizing Missions', *American Historical Review*, 113 (2008), 1313–43.

8 Mazower, 'International Civilization?', 559.

nineteenth-century, state-led humanitarian interventions and humanitarian actions undertaken by non-state actors in the 1920s.

I wish to briefly digress on the issue of sovereignty, which in my view is central to understanding how humanitarian organizations articulated their justification for action. Even if further research is needed on this specific point, my research in various US archives leads me to argue that American humanitarian organizations such as the NER, the American Red Cross (ARC), and the American Relief Administration (ARA) shared with the European powers similar views on selective and discriminatory sovereignty, on the self-declared latitude of interference in the internal affairs of newly independent states or of non-European states.[9] The institutionalization of a minority regime and of a mechanism of enforcing the rights of minorities, however imperfect or flawed, certainly encompassed the idea of protecting the most basic human rights (of European civilian populations). The minority regime was – at least as far as European territories were concerned – an attempt to prevent massacres and atrocities such as those that had victimized the Ottoman Christians in the past. The victorious powers promoted the rights of minority groups as 'obligations of international concern' – an echo of pre-war humanitarian intervention, but without commitment to act diplomatically or militarily. According to historian Michael Marrus, the peacemakers relinquished what might have been their commitments to humanitarian intervention in the preceding era and looked to the League of Nations to speak and act on behalf of them all.[10] The regime bestowed sovereignty upon new European nations; it was selective, partial, and discriminatory as far as it did not apply to Germany or to the victor states.[11] Minority rights were a badge of the new states' secondary status, manifested by their need for tutelage in the exercise of their own sovereignty.[12] To be sure, the victorious powers were reluctant themselves to be bound by such agreements, which created a standing grievance among the 'minority states' that festered over the period. Concern about minorities did not mean solicitude for them, and support for them was far from a transcendent humanitarian commitment. For instance, the victorious powers watched passively while hundreds of Jews were forcibly uprooted and tens of

[9] It is a fact that many members of the NER boards actively supported the idea of establishing the League of Nations.

[10] Marrus, 'International Bystanders', 166.

[11] André Liebich, 'Minority as Inferiority: Minority Rights in Historical Perspective', *Review of International Studies*, 34 (2008), 243–63.

[12] Mazower, 'International Civilization?', 560.

thousands lost their lives in pogroms and other anti-Jewish violence accompanying civil wars and regional conflicts in East Central Europe.[13]

Beyond Europe, the Covenant of the League of Nations set up the mandate system, which applied only to German colonial territories and to the Ottoman Empire territories beyond the boundaries of the newly independent state of Turkey. As Antony Anghie notes, the mandate system represented the international community's aspiration, through the League, to address colonial problems in a systematic, coordinated, and ethical manner.[14] 'At the highest level, it embodied the ideal policy of European civilization towards the cultures of Asia, Africa and the Pacific.'[15] On paper, the mandate system consisted of rudimentary normative and institutional processes for the protection of the indigenous populations. In fact, it did not result in a comprehensive body of law that could be designated as international human rights law.[16] It adapted the old concept of trusteeship in a new legal, scientific, and allegedly objective form, instituting a new form of colonial power based not on political but on economic control. Mandate territories were inserted into that economy in a subordinate role. As a result, those territories appeared to have been freed from political control, although they still remained subject to the control of the parties that exercised power within the international economy.[17] In the ex-Ottoman territories of Syria, Palestine, and Iraq, the enforcement of the mandate system had given the mandatory powers a chance to enforce the 'enlightened' and 'modern' reforms they had attempted in vain to impose on the Ottoman authorities. Very rapidly, however, their enthusiasm and optimism evaporated, to the disillusionment of local populations, whose subjugation was protracted under French or British rule, and to the disenchantment of the ruling authorities, who were now firmly convinced of the impossibility of exporting 'civilization'.

[13] Marrus, 'International Bystanders', 165, 167.

[14] Antony Anghie, *Imperialism, Sovereignty and the Making of International Law* (Cambridge University Press, 2005), 137.

[15] Quincy Wright, *Mandates under the League of Nations* (University of Chicago Press, 1930), vii; Susan Pedersen, 'Review Essay: Back to the League of Nations', *American Historical Review*, 112 (2007), 1091–117; Susan Pedersen, 'The Meaning of the Mandates System: An Argument', *Geschichte und Gesellschaft*, 32, no. 4 (2006), 560–82.

[16] Thomas Buergenthal, 'The Evolving International Human Rights System', *American Journal of International Law*, 100 (2006), 783–807, here 783.

[17] Anne Orford, *Reading Humanitarian Intervention* (Cambridge University Press, 2003), 25–6.

After 1918, several non-state actors, called international associations, the predecessors of today's non-governmental organizations (NGOs), operated in Central and Eastern Europe, Turkey, and other ex-Ottoman territories. They interfered in the internal affairs of newly independent states, and in the late 1910s and early to mid 1920s, they interacted (and clashed) with the League of Nations. As we know, they never had at its disposal the political and military capacity to enforce humanitarian intervention worldwide.[18] As we know, the ambitious idea never materialized of a League of Nations that was able to select and oversee the work of a single state, mandated by the international community as the agent of the organization, to remove 'unfortunate conditions violative of the most elementary human rights'.[19] The League of Nations did not provide for an extension of the mandate system or a 'policy of state-building' in circumstances related to humanitarian intervention. There was no mechanism entrusting the member states 'either to assume the burden of the administration of the territory, or to constrain the unworthy sovereign to mend his ways'.[20] As we know, the newfound international solidarity and increased integration and equality between states as well as the exercise of a new humanitarian intervention, for the general welfare of humanity, were never properly discussed by the League of Nations Council or Assembly. The alleged legality of humanitarian intervention through the development of new and enlightened standards of the social law of nations did not become a fruitful means for securing, through the international community, the redress of evils to which previous generations had been indifferent or blind. The aforementioned actors, including philanthropic foundations, attempted to set up these standards, which explains why some of them, like the NER, decided to go beyond relief.

The NER and other organizations acted in the space left by the unsettled territorial and political situations that existed in the aftermath of the First World War. They thrived wherever important sovereignty deficits persisted. From the Baltic States to Palestine, these non-state actors pursued a new kind of diplomacy, one that historian Dzovinar Kevonian has

[18] Ellery C. Stowell, 'Humanitarian Intervention', *American Journal of International Law*, 33 (1939), 733–6, here 733.

[19] Graham, 'Humanitarian Intervention', 326, argues that if the United States had undertaken a humanitarian intervention in the Ottoman provinces inhabited by Armenian populations such as it did in Cuba in 1898, such action would ultimately have led to the establishment of something like a type A mandate over those Ottoman provinces, regardless of the existence or nonexistence of the League itself.

[20] Ibid.

defined as 'humanitarian diplomacy'.[21] Of course, the NER's ability to operate abroad depended on the political authority it could harness. In Turkey, the Soviet Republic of Armenia, Greece, and Syria – under French mandate – the political conditions changed more or less rapidly. Systematically, the ability of the NER – and of other organizations – to intervene in these lands was inversely proportional to the ability of each of these states to exert its sovereign prerogatives. This is a meaningful difference between non-state actors' humanitarian actions and state-led humanitarian interventions. After all, the range of the NER's activities also depended on its relations with US diplomats, bankers, farmers, and on the contributions of US donors. I am not claiming that the NER was an extension of American foreign policy; I am making the point that the NER could not act independently of the US government and did not have at its disposal the coercive means to impose its views on recalcitrant or misbehaving governmental authorities.

Like the League of Nations, American and European international associations, and philanthropic foundations such as the Rockefeller Foundation, the NER understood humanitarianism as a permanent, transnational, institutionalized, and secular (though highly pervaded by Christian precepts and morals) means of understanding and addressing the causes of human suffering. NER leaders believed their humanitarian actions were intimately connected with international peacemaking, and they sympathized with the emerging concept of collective security as put forward by the League of Nations. The NER's ultimate objective was global peace.

The NER cared about the economic value of farms and industries, better agricultural methods, higher production per acre, highly skilled artisans and trained leaders, but it cared more about leaving a contribution of allegedly incalculable value to the Near East and the world. The NER's goal was to train orphaned children to be ambassadors of goodwill, unselfish service, and world peace.[22] Its ambition was to leave a permanent mark on the territories in which it operated. The NER identified uprooted orphaned children as agents of change; through the magic of some unspecified trickle-down effects, it hoped these children would enhance a virtuous spiral of progress and improvement in the Near East.

[21] Dzovinar Kevonian, *Réfugiés et diplomatie humanitaire: les acteurs européens et la scène proche-orientale pendant l'entre-deux-guerres*, (Paris: Publications de la Sorbonne, 2004).

[22] *Annual Report to Congress, 1923* (New York, 1924), RAC, NER, box 129.

James Barton, NER secretary and one of its most prominent figures, insisted on educating the leaders (i.e., elites) of the Near East. While acknowledging an education policy and vision typical of missionary societies, he anticipated the human capital theory of the early 1960s according to which education would lead to economic growth and development and eventually to overall societal development and modernization. This was one of the NER's most original contributions to interwar Western humanitarianism. In the 1930s, when the Near East Foundation (NEF) replaced the NER, the latter implemented technical assistance projects with exactly the same purpose on an even larger scale. This foundation hoped that the assistance given to Near East governments would trickle down and produce beneficial effects at local levels and, in turn, for entire nations. It believed in the possibility of socio-economic progress by means of planned technocratic and social-engineering interventions that would allow people in the non-Western parts of the world to enjoy the same fortunes from which Western nations had profited earlier in history.[23]

It is not my intention to claim that the way the NER interpreted humanitarian actions can be generalized to other groups. The NER coexisted with several other interpretations put forward by other international associations, such as the International Committee of the Red Cross, the Save the Children Fund and its international branch, the Union Internationale de Secours aux Enfants. Nevertheless, for Western humanitarians of all ilks, eastern, central, and south-eastern Europe and territories in the Middle East formed the fault lines of Western civilization, with areas devastated by war, epidemics, and hunger being the ideal setting for a growing number of private associations, philanthropic foundations – mainly American – and intergovernmental organizations, such as the League of Nations, to prove their purpose and usefulness to the world. Weak government was a common problem for countries in these geographic areas, either because they were newly independent, as was Poland, or because they were debilitated by war, regime change, governmental and economic crises, and the arrival of refugees, as was Greece. For many relief workers and leaders of the 'missions' to Greece, Syria, Lebanon, and Palestine, or Armenia, the recipients of aid and the beneficiaries of construction or rehabilitation programs were less civilized than

[23] Corinna Unger, 'The United States, Decolonization and the Education of Third World' in Jost Dülffer and Marc Frey (eds.), *Elites and Decolonization in the Twentieth Century* (Basingstoke: Palgrave Macmillan, 2011), 241–62, here 244.

Western Europeans, and they fantasized about how to resurrect the past glory of lands that had once been the cradle of Western/Christian civilization.

In the 1920s, the NER believed that relief would allow needy individuals and communities to help themselves in the short term and that further aid would lead these people to thrive economically, politically, and morally in the long term. Relief was inextricably related to 'rehabilitation', 'recovery', 'construction' and 'reconstruction', 'protection', 'prevention', and long-term aid; a panoply of terms that since the 1940s have been included under the term 'development aid'.[24] More recently, many of these have been included in scholarly debates on post-humanitarian interventions phases. Back in the 1920s, agrarian and education reform projects were not called 'development aid'; however, historian Corinna Unger claims that the often religiously inspired idea of helping other nations overcome their 'backwardness' was an important motive of non-governmental humanitarian undertakings at the time.[25]

THE NEAR EAST RELIEF, AN AMERICAN HUMANITARIAN ORGANIZATION

The NER's official records claim that, from 1918 to 1929, the organization spent over $116 million to save more than a million lives, mainly that of women and children. Its rehabilitation programs, they note, had enabled over 130,000 children to be housed, fed, and clothed, with the majority given a practical education that would enable them to earn a living.[26] In the mid 1920s, the NER moved from temporary emergency relief to 'constructive community service', as Barton termed it.[27]

[24] David Ekbladh, *The Great American Mission: Modernization & the Construction of an American World Order* (Princeton University Press, 2010). In his first chapter, Ekbladh argues that, after 1877, the term 'reconstruction' was given new meanings in an international conversation on progressive reform.

[25] Corinna Unger, 'Histories of Development and Modernization: Findings, Reflections, Future Research', H-Soz-u-Kult, 9 Dec. 2010, 1–41, here 7, www.hsozkult.geschichte.hu-berlin.de/ forum/2010–12–001.pdf (last accessed 14 Jan. 2014). Fred Cooper, 'Writing the History of Development', *Journal of Modern European History*, 8 (2010), 5–38.

[26] James L. Barton, *American Educational and Philanthropic Interests in the Near East*, undated (probably 1930), A-ABCFM, Barton Papers (hereafter B.P.), vol. 9.

[27] James Barton, *Near East Projects*, undated (probably 1929 or early 1930s), A-ABCFM, B.P., box no. 13. 'Service' and 'Administration' are terms that deserve to be examined

The amount of money the NER spent is certainly remarkable when compared to other European organizations. As to the focus on orphans, orphanages, and post-orphanage care, I intend to show some of its inconsistencies. The NER defined itself as an American humanitarian organization. In 1923, the NER General Secretary Charles Vernon Vickrey stated:

> Near East Relief is a humanitarian organization. It has saved, and we trust, will continue to save many lives. We are not content, however, with the saving of lives, if by so doing we merely prolong the physical existence of a certain number of human beings; we want not only to save life but to make life, bigger life, better life, for a better day of peace and international good will that is to be. It is believed that most of our workers overseas are dominated by this ideal of unselfish service of their fellowmen and the vision of a better world.[28]

The NER did not wish to save bare lives, in the meaning of Giorgio Agamben's *vite nude*. Their action aimed at making life bigger and better. The action of the NER was explicitly related to peace and implicitly related to trade. NER leaders adhered to the old liberal anthem that peace brought trade (and prosperity) and, vice versa, prosperity entailed peace. The NER interpreted short-term relief as being propaedeutic for rehabilitative programs based on education, public health, social welfare, and construction. In the 1930s, the NEF, the NER's successor, would increasingly offer technical assistance aid, which prefigured development programs and theories of human capital that would be fully developed after 1945.

The NER's leaders were not particularly original or unique. Their set of beliefs were very deeply rooted in many American – and European – secular and faith-based organizations. The most important, and one the most consensual – this is still largely the case today – was the principle of self-help. NER women and men on the ground would have found greatest satisfaction in seeing those they had helped able to help themselves. For NER humanitarians, self-help was a process: they would take those they sought to help by the hand and guide them along the path of moral and material improvement to self-reliance. NER workers believed that their

more thoroughly and connected to the history of Western humanitarianism. A comparative history of the American Relief Administration, NER, and ARC would be a very interesting means of understanding the nature of American humanitarianism during the interwar period.

[28] *Annual Report to Congress, 1923* (New York, 1924), p. 35, RAC, NER, box 129, author's emphasis.

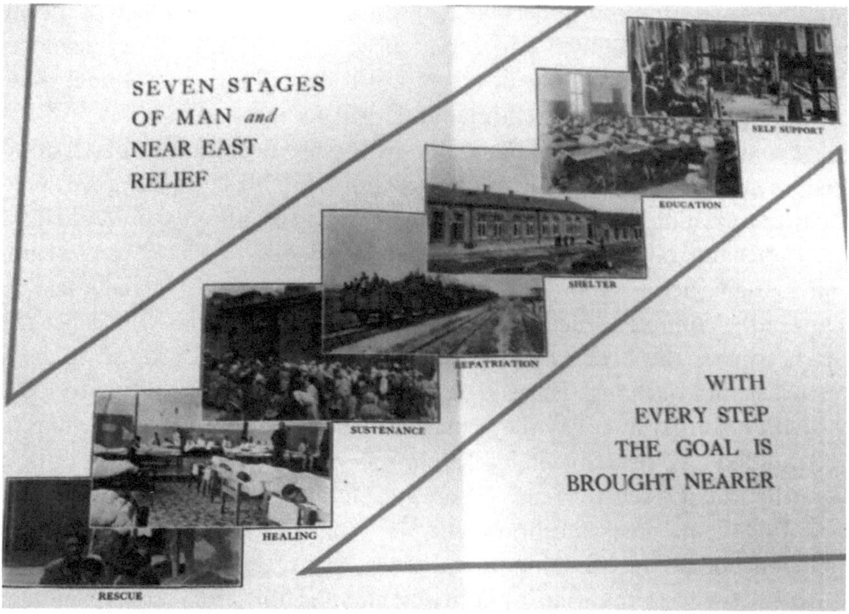

FIGURE 9.1 News Bulletin published by the American Committee for Armenian and Syrian Relief
Source: vol. IV, August–September 1919, no. 3, 6–7, A-ABCFM, Barton Papers, box no.12.

religious, that is, Protestant, background equipped them to read and interpret other cultures, societies, and religions, an engagement that was also shaped by their knowledge of modern science and access to technological innovations. NER humanitarians believed they could determine when a single individual, rural community, or entire state had reached that end point (as Figure 9.1 shows).

It exceeds the scope of this chapter to discuss the intellectual origins of the stages of civilization theory or its affinity with Walt Rostow's stages of economic growth. However, the figure is self-explanatory as to the posture of the NER with respect to the recipients of aid, and as to the relation between humanitarian actions and older state-led interventions of the kind the European powers or the United States had undertaken throughout the nineteenth century within the Ottoman territories or in Cuba or the Philippines. The NER presented itself as the indispensable means for local populations or entire states to reach self-reliance. Just as the main objective of nineteenth-century humanitarian interventions was to end massacre and to introduce reforms that would have 'enlightened' and 'civilized' Ottoman administration, early twentieth-century humanitarian actions such as those undertaken by the NER aimed at relieving needy civilian populations who had experienced the trauma of war, displacement, hunger, disease, and poverty, and to 'enlighten' and 'guide' these populations towards full self-reliance.

The approach of the NER to support the needy should be understood as construction rather than reconstruction, for NER workers assumed that pre-existing social, economic, or political conditions were unhelpful or irrelevant. NER humanitarians liked to pretend that they were beginning anew, acting upon a sort of tabula rasa, which allowed them to ignore the context of their action. In my view, this explains why, since the early 1920s, the NER oriented its action on uprooted groups, such as refugees and orphans. These groups had been cut off from their original societies, so that in a way they could be 'reset' and moulded according to NER ideology of achieving self-reliance or what was actually only a specific kind of self-reliance. Of course, just like humanitarian interventions of the nineteenth century, the beneficiaries of aid were not participants in the politics shaping their lives.

NER workers felt that a politically and socially ordered environment (not the restoration of order, for they believed proper order did not exist in the Near East) was the necessary context for this process, as images of regimented children in orphanages eloquently relate. Although they sometimes acted not unlike the military, NER humanitarians were primarily strict and demanding teachers, with education as their goal. Recipients of aid were not free to choose their own path to freedom and self-reliance. Trusteeship and self-help intertwined as the NER moved beyond relief to address the root causes of suffering. Recipients were to embrace help and rehabilitative support silently and with orderliness. They rarely raise their heads in the archives of the NER and of many other European and American humanitarian organizations. They are buried under piles of papers, objects, and very rarely subjects, and when they do emerge from obscurity, from the point of view of relief workers, they are little more than puppets. Recipients of aid could not be disempowered, for in NER narratives they had never had power. Agency would only be achieved when the NER deemed them sufficiently responsible, or sufficiently 'civilized', to become self-reliant.

Official documents indicate that the NER recognized a moral obligation to develop these orphans into useful citizens, for the sake of both the children themselves and the countries that had given them refuge. The NER claimed to have *the responsibility to protect* selected groups of peoples (I deliberately use this expression here). The decision to turn a short-term humanitarian endeavour into a long-term project gave the NER the moral upper hand when it came to donors and governments. It also legitimized the continued presence of the NER in several countries and closed the door on criticism of the foundation's activities.

The NER was organized according to criteria – for example, institutional, religious, fundraising – that were specifically American. To understand the ideology underpinning the organization's work and most of its practices, one must draw on the context of the so-called progressive era, with its many ambiguities and contradictions, and the cultural background of influential individuals associated with the NER, such as Paul Monroe, Thomas Jesse Jones, and James Barton.[29] A closer look at NER primary sources reveals that different visions of humanitarian aid coexisted and clashed within the organization. On the one hand, the main workforce of the organization was made up of missionaries who had a long experience in the Near East and spoke local languages. On the other hand, NER sources reveal a connection between the politics of the NER and educational programs in the states of the American South as implemented at the Tuskegee Institute in Alabama or at its mother institution, the Hampton Institute in Virginia. These institutions gained both reputation and financial support by philanthropic foundations such as the Rockefeller Foundation during the post–Civil War Reconstruction by exploiting a white preference for 'Negro education'. Advocates believed that education should have practical applications in the lives of black students, who would also learn to accept a socio-economic structure in which black people occupied the lowest places.[30] Many of these ideas would be transferred, though not necessarily adapted to the Near East. For NER leaders – with some exceptions, it is hard to know what workers on the spot thought – there was not a great difference between 'uncivilized' black Americans and local Near East populations. Of course, the NER put forward a discourse on civilizational differences between Christian Armenians and non-Christian populations; however, when it came to

[29] More on these individuals follows later in this chapter.

[30] Kenneth King, 'Africa and the Southern States of the U.S.A.: Notes on J. H. Oldham and American Negro Education for Africans', *Journal of African History*, 10, no. 4 (1969), 659–77; James D. Anderson, 'Northern Foundations and the Shaping of Southern Black Rural Education, 1902–1935', *History of Education Quarterly*, 18, no. 4 (1978), 371–96. Eric Anderson and Alfred A. Moss, Jr., *Dangerous Donations: Northern Philanthropy and Southern Black Education, 1902–1930*, with a foreword by Louis R. Harlan (Columbia, MO: University of Missouri Press, 1999).

educational programs, especially for uprooted populations, educational projects looked similar to those implemented in the southern states.[31]

NER leaders were closely connected with American philanthropic bodies such as the Phelps-Stokes or Rockefeller foundations. Since the mid 1920s, they had mimicked the principles and politics of the latter. When the financial and economic crisis heavily affected the funds at the disposal of the NER, its leaders sought to transform it into a foundation whose principal contribution was to offer technical assistance to governments and local authorities. Therefore, I claim that the history of the NER should be studied in connection to the history of American philanthropic foundations. The history of this organization is also intimately related to this history of public-private partnership. If during the humanitarian emergencies of the 1890s and 1900s, the US government participated hesitantly, then after 1914 an interventionist government joined forces with volunteers and associations. The work of historians Branden Little on the Commission for Relief in Belgium and Julia Irwin on the ARC are eloquent in this respect.[32] Government and private philanthropy worked hand in hand with assistance from the US Navy and other agencies. Last but not least, the NER embodied the coexistence and eventual transition from a religious – mainly that of Protestant and temperance reformers – American missionarism to a more secular one. As historian Ian Tyrell puts it, the ascendancy of the Rockefeller Foundation, the Young Men's/Women's Christian Association (YMCA, YWCA), and the Rotary was an extension of the work by missionaries and moral reform groups whose aspiration was to create a more Christian and moral world.[33]

[31] Adequate attention should be paid American colonial and educational experiences in the Philippines and Cuba, the transfer of such educational models to Africa, and their applications in the Near East. See Andrew W. Zimmerman, *Alabama in Africa: Booker T. Washington, the German Empire & the Globalization of the New South* (Princeton University Press, 2010).

[32] It would be interesting to compare and contrast the NER with other American organizations such as ARA or ARC. On the latter, see Julia Irwin, *Making the World Safe: The American Red Cross and a Nation's Humanitarian Awakening* (New York: Oxford University Press, 2013).

[33] Ian Tyrell, *Reforming the World: The Creation of American's Moral Empire* (Princeton University Press, 2010); Branden Little, 'Band of Crusaders, American Humanitarians, the Great War, and the Remaking of the World', Research Reports from the Rockefeller Archive Center, 2007 (Sleepy Hollow, NY: Rockefeller Foundation, 2008); Emily Rosenberg, 'Missions to the World: Philanthropy Abroad' in Lawrence Friedman and Mark McGarvie (eds.), *Charity, Philanthropy and Civility in American History* (New York: Cambridge University Press, 2003); Emily Rosenberg, *Spreading the American Dream:*

The NER was an expression of Protestant missionary humanitarianism that had been active in the Near East since the early 1820s.[34] When the First World War broke out, the work of the missionaries was disrupted. In the early 1920s, over 50 per cent of NER relief workers were missionaries of the American Board Commission for Foreign Missions (ABCFM or American Board), who must have seen the NER as the opportunity to continue the provision of elementary health services and education. Throughout the 1920s, even when the NER became a more secular organization, the influence of Protestant morals and precepts remained significant. During that decade, the organization's secretary James Barton, a missionary himself, claimed that, even though the NER was not a missionary society, it aimed at spreading Christian education to Near Eastern populations supposedly living in the dark.[35]

The intimate ties between Protestant missionaries and the NER explain the focus of the organization on Christian minorities and, more specifically, the attention to Ottoman Armenians. Moreover, the 'Armenian Question' and the massacres of Ottoman Armenians had been a hot topic in US press since the 1890s. American public opinion had shown a great interest on the fate of the Armenians, which in turns explains the rapid establishment of rescue committees starting in 1915. In fact, the NER was the result of the merger of the Persian War Relief, the Syrian-Palestine Relief Fund, and the Armenian Atrocities Committee, created in 1915 at the instigation of Ambassador Henry Morgenthau when news of the genocide reached America.[36] In response to Morgenthau's request,

American Economic and Cultural Expansion (New York: Hill and Wang, 1982); Emily Rosenberg, *Financial Missionaries to the World: The Politics and Culture of Dollar Diplomacy, 1900–1930* (Durham, NC: Duke University Press, 2004). Ludovic Tournès, 'Entre soft-power et société civile: Un siècle de diplomatie philanthropique en Europe' in Ludovic Tournès (ed.), *L'Argent de l'Influence. Les Fondations Américaines et leurs Réseaux Européens* (Paris: Autrement, 2010), 185–94; and Ludovic Tournès, 'La foundation Rockefeller et la naissance de l'universalisme philanthropique américain', *Critique Internationale*, 35 (2007), 173–97.

[34] Joseph Grabill, *Protestant Diplomacy and the Near East: Missionary Influence on American Policy, 1810–1927* (Minneapolis: University of Minnesota Press, 1971); Ussama Makdisi, *Artillery of Heaven: American Missionaries and the Failed Conversion of the Middle East* (Ithaca, NY: Cornell University Press, 2008).

[35] James L. Barton, *American Educational and Philanthropic Interests in the Near East*, undated (probably 1930), A-ABCFM, Barton Papers, vol. 9.

[36] Peter Balakian, *The Burning Tigris* (New York: Harper Collins, 2003); Jay Winter (ed.), *American and the Armenian Genocide of 1915* (Cambridge University Press, 2003); Hans-Lukas Kieser, 'Removal of American Indians, Destruction of Ottoman Armenians: American Missionaries and Demographic Engineering', *European Journal of Turkish Studies*, Thematic Issue, part I. [Online] 7 (2008), http://ejits.revues.org/index2873.html

Cleveland H. Dodge[37] and James L. Barton (foreign secretary of ABCFM and former president of Euphrates College, Harpoot) were joined by public figures such as Charles R. Crane (Chicago banker and a trustee of Constantinople Women's College), Samuel T. Dutton (professor at Teachers' College, Columbia University, New York City, and also a trustee of Constantinople Women's College) and a dozen church leaders with missionary or educational interests in the Near East. The three relief committees merged into the American Committee for Armenian and Syrian Relief (ACASR) in the fall of 1915 at the instigation of the Rockefeller Foundation.[38]

ACASR largely comprised Protestants, both ordained and lay, internationalists, and experienced public campaigners. The clergymen were church executives rather than pastors, mainly Presbyterians and Congregationalists, with many committeemen enlisted from interdenominational bodies such as the Federal Council of the Churches of Christ. The majority of the committee members were active in peace movements, such as the New York Peace Society and the Church Peace Union, or were trustees of the Carnegie Endowment for International Peace, the World's Court League, or the League to Enforce Peace. Some were officers of one or more institutions such as the YMCA, YWCA, the ARC, the New York Association for the Blind, the Hampton Institute, the General Education Board, and the National Recreation Association. Some were academics and others trustees of colleges and educational institutions in the Near East. Together they formed a close-knit group of like-minded members of the American (mainly New York) cultural, economic, and political elites. Their political connections reached as far as Dodge's friendship with Woodrow Wilson; they also had close ties to the press, both secular and Christian, a link that may explain their sensitivity to visual strategies, their investment in the publication of magazines and pamphlets, and their

(last accessed 14 Jan. 2014). Robert Leslie Daniel, 'From Relief to Technical Assistance in the Near East, A Case Study: Near East Relief and Near East Foundation', PhD thesis, University of Wisconsin (1953).

37 Cleveland H. Dodge was an official of the Phelps Dodge Corporation, a leading copper mining corporation. He was a Presbyterian and president of the board of trustees of Robert College. His family had a long-standing connection with the YMCA and YWCA. He created the Cleveland H. Dodge Foundation in 1917, while involved in the Near East. His son Bayard Dodge became president of the American University of Beirut in the mid 1920s and his daughter Elizabeth Dodge Huntington at Robert College in Constantinople. Dodge acted as treasurer of Near East Relief.

38 James Barton, *Twelve Years of Salvaging Life and Reconstruction*, unpublished paper, A-ABCFM, B.P., vol. 9.

funding of Hollywood movies such as *Ravished Armenia, the Story of Aurora Mardiganian*.[39] In 1918, ACASR was renamed the American Committee for Relief in the Near East and in 1919 became the NER. The founders of ACASR continued to work for the NER. The new organization enlisted Herbert Hoover, Franklin Roosevelt, and Charles Dawes; William Howard Taft and Charles Evans Hughes joined as trustees. American Catholic and Jewish representatives were invited to join, reinforcing ACASR's already strong ties with wealthy philanthropists and cultural, religious, and political elites. On 6 August 1919, the US Congress incorporated the committee known as the NER, providing official approval of the NER's efforts to organize food and medicine supplies and refugee administration in the Near East.[40] President Woodrow Wilson gave his complete support to the NER, as did President Harding. By 1919, the NER was large in comparison with other European organizations. Yet it was smaller in size and human resources than the ARA or the ARC, and its formal ties with the US government were less formal, although the NER was intimately connected to and dependent on the latter.

From 1919 to 1924 emergencies shaped the organization's plans. If official documents depict the NER as ready to face emergency thanks to it being a 'modern', scientific, efficient organization, confidential documents show that the NER improvised, postponed, or never implemented its original plans. Nevertheless, the organization kept some of its priorities, which reveal its ideology and the biased and selective nature of its humanitarianism. Even if a percentage of emergency aid reached Ottoman Muslim populations, the majority of NER relief was destined for Ottoman Christians, particularly Armenians. If circumstances dictated the NER's focus on refugees, an activity where the NER competed with other American and European international associations and organizations, orphan support became the NER's trademark. War made relief for adults necessary, but for the organization they were secondary recipients of aid. The records are evasive and fail to specify the organization's policy, for instance, on providing aid to refugees settled in camps, on

39 Anthony Slide, *Ravished Armenia and the Story of Aurora Mardiganian* (Lanham, MD: Scarecrow Press, 1997).

40 'NER was chartered by the Congress for the purpose of receiving what the public chose to give and carrying out as best it could the wished of its contributors.' B. Acheson, manuscript, ch. V, 11–12, RAC, NER, box 132.

the criteria of prioritization of geographical areas, or on the coordination/cooperation with other organizations.

In 1918–19, the NER focused on the food emergency in the Caucasus. The latter was a joint-operation of the Allies, the ARA, and the NER. It targeted surviving Armenians. The biggest operation of 1920 was the assistance the NER provided to Armenians evacuated from the region of Cilicia; many of them would become refugees in Syria and Lebanon, a territory under French mandate. In late 1922, after the fall of Smyrna and the defeat of Greece in the war against Turkey, the NER, like all other European and American humanitarian organizations, succoured, expelled, and exchanged populations. When Mustapha Kemal seized power, the NER found it difficult to operate within Turkish borders. On the one hand, there was no way the NER could enhance rehabilitation plans until 1923/24, with small exceptions. It had to focus on emergency aid operations, which were extremely expensive and frustrated many relief workers who wanted to go beyond (mere) relief. By 1923, other than in Constantinople, Christian minorities were no longer internally displaced peoples, but rather refugees, without any concrete prospect of being repatriated. This change represented an important turning point in NER politics. Starting in 1923, NER politics were related to sovereignty issues, and the organization had to decide whether to continue rehabilitation work inside Turkey (as suggested by some missionaries working for the NER) or gradually terminate that work, since Kemal made it clear that foreign institutions were *persona non grata*. Should the NER focus on Armenian refugees beyond Turkey?[41] What about non-Armenian refugees and local populations? Quite rapidly, NER leaders realized that the organization would not be able to continue relief for tens of thousands of individuals indefinitely. Since it could count on its members' expertise on education, it eventually terminated adult relief and continued rehabilitative aid for children. Furthermore, since the organization's funds were decreasing in the mid 1920s because of the donors' fatigue and the economic crisis, the NER decided to focus only on orphans. It is also worth noting further elements that eventually shaped these changes. First, even though it is never mentioned in NER sources, it is clear that refugee-orphans were the ideal recipients of aid: fundraising was relatively easy for this relatively small and easily identifiable group. Second, thanks to its special relationship with missionary schools, the NER had expertise,

41 A similar dilemma would be at the center of several discussions within missionary societies, especially the ABCFM; I do not deal with this issue here.

accumulated experience, and a clear advantage over any other international organization or association. This, in turn, might explain why the NER was so determined in 1922–3 to support the exchange of populations between Greece and Turkey.

A document from early 1922 – related to the aftermath of the evacuation of Cilicia by Armenians – illustrates that these choices were far from being unanimously accepted within the organization. Howard McAfee, NER director of the Beirut office, received a long letter from Nesbitt Chambers, a missionary and NER worker in charge of relief operations in Marash.[42] Chambers criticized a policy document entitled 'Marash and Adult Relief' previously sent by McAfee. The document specified that the NER should only focus on child welfare in general and on war orphans in particular. Chambers asked about the widow with several small children and no means of support. Did they come under the heading of 'war orphans'? Should the NER stop supporting children in their homes just because only one of their parents had been killed? 'Can't we kill the other parent and save the children?' asked Chambers sarcastically. On the issue of the NER's departure from Turkey, Chambers explained that widows and orphans had no means of travelling and could not pay for a passport. How did McAfee (and the NER) think of helping them?

Despite this criticism, the NER moved the heart of its activities in 1923 to three regions bordering Turkey: Syria (and Palestine), Greece, and Soviet Armenia.[43] The organization directed its aid on behalf of orphan children who had been moved out of Turkey. The NER focused on 57,000 orphans. Of these, 18,000 had been taken to Greece. According to NER statistics, half of these children were Armenian and half were Greek. The remaining 12,000 – mostly Armenians – were added to those already concentrated in Syria. In September 1923, when the 'child migration' – as Barclay Acheson, NER overseas director, referred to it – was still in progress, the NER listed its child dependents in all areas, including southern Russia and Persia, and found that it had 40,747 Armenian children in its orphanages. In addition there were 7,768 Greek children, 6,897 Bedouin, Tartar, Russian, Jewish, and Turkish children, and 850 Syrian children, making a grand total of 56,262 who were depending on America for food, clothing, and education.

42 Nesbitt Chambers, Marash, to Howard McAfee, 9 March 1922, 'Central Turkey Mission 1860–1927', vols. 27–9, A-ABCFM, ABC 16.9.5.

43 B. Acheson, manuscript, ch. VI, 8, RAC, NER, box 132.

Initial plans of relief *cum* rehabilitation were downsized further because, starting in 1923, a conspicuous decrease in donations deeply affected the NER's ability to implement them. From 1924 to 1930, discrepancy between the discourse on a bigger and better life and the reality of NER action grew larger. To underscore this point, I refer here to the organization's 'outplacing' program, according to which the greatest possible number of orphans were to be relocated to relatives or responsible caretakers as quickly as possible. The role of NER agents was in effect not rehabilitative; instead it was limited to supervising the living conditions of outplaced children. By 31 December 1924, the child welfare work had been downsized to the point that it covered only 38,300 children, of whom 21,292 were in NER institutions and 5,845 were in subsidized institutions; the remainder were referred to as post-orphanage children (2,203 boarded in families; 5,519 supervised in families; 3,442 fed by other means).[44]

CONCLUSION: FROM THE NER TO THE NEF

From 1923 to 1930 the NER reflected on its existence. The reflection took the form of 'surveys'. The organization's board entrusted external surveyors to advise on the work accomplished, to be accomplished, the termination of activities and the eventual direction the NER should take. The men commissioned with the first survey were Paul Monroe, director of the International Institute of Teachers College, Columbia University; R. R. Reeder, overseas commissioner of the Serbian Child Welfare Association for three years; and James L. Vance, former moderator of the Presbyterian Church in the South. Two further surveys were conducted from 1924 to 1927. The gentlemen (not a single woman was among them) in charge of these surveys were university professors, prominent experts in business, agriculture, education (e.g. Thomas Jesse Jones), and child welfare. They were partially responsible for the transformation of the NER that took place in 1929. Among the changes that occurred were, first, that the majority of missionaries who had been hired as relief workers terminated their collaboration with the NER. Second, the experts contributed to the organization's transformation into a foundation that would offer technical assistance to governments rather than operating with individuals. Third, with the economic crisis of the late 1920s, the organization's

[44] *Annual Report, 1924* (New York, 1925), 22–4, RAC, NER, box 134.

budget dwindled to a fraction of what it had been in the early 1920s. Therefore, a radical change of politics and actions was necessary if the aim of the NER was to survive. With the advent of the NEF the staff was reduced to a team of advisers who offered technical assistance to local and central governments to influence change. What about the children? What role were they to play in these countries? According to Barton – who remained a central figure in the new foundation – orphan children would become the 'nucleus with which to build an ever widening service to meet needs in communities in which the children are outplaced'. As he put it:

> America found starving, diseased child refugees. She healed them, fed them, trained them. For what? We do not propose to leave them now to revert to backward mental, physical and financial standards of their impoverishment environment. Instead we propose to use this young army of eager youth to set the peoples of the Near East on the pathway of progress.[45]

NER paternalism, its moral duty or 'mission' (a term still used today and deserving of further historical and interdisciplinary attention) to protect those who had received aid beyond the moment of relief, and its ambition to enable children to grow up to spearhead social, political, and economic change are clear. Towards the end of the 1920s, according to Barton, the NER was ready to lead 'an attack on the environment of the children to: A. Prevent their sinking to the low levels of health and economic conditions prevailing in the communities into which they have gone. B. Do what can be done to aid the community through the children.'[46]

In the 1930s, the NEF persisted in looking for the root causes of suffering. The new foundation did not distance itself from its predecessor the NER. Since there was a significant continuity in its personnel and leaders, the NEF did not mention the NER failure to address the root causes of poverty, poor health, and ignorance. The NEF blamed environments (households) where diseases, poverty, ignorance, and superstition prevailed. As Barton put it: 'Serving the child alone can hardly change the household's ways of living or materially influence the squalor of the village'. As a result, the child would run the danger of contracting disease again, thus increasing the welfare worker's burden.[47] To alleviate these conditions and prevent their recurrence, for the good of children as well as others in need, the NEF targeted Near East governments and local

[45] James Barton, *Near East Projects*, undated (probably 1929 or early 1930s), A-ABCFM, B.P., box no. 13.
[46] Ibid. [47] Ibid.

authorities. NEF technical assistance programs were as disproportionately ambitious as those of the NER. With only a fraction of the NER's human and financial resources, the NEF hoped to leave a mark in the Near East that was even greater than that intended by its predecessor. How a relatively modest amount of money would function as catalyst for modernization of entire societies is something that is not really explained in NEF documents.

The NEF's *modus operandi* was based on demonstration, with models showcased within local communities. The NEF's ultimate objective was to persuade local governments and peoples to adopt specific – American – development models. In this way, NEF paternalism intersected with modernization narratives in ways that recall the work of UNRRA, other UN agencies, and further organizations. The NEF, and its predecessor the NER, constructed and maintained a discursive and concrete separation between 'modern' NER donors and relief workers who dispensed aid and built model villages and houses and sanitation, on the one hand, and 'backward' sufferers and victims or helpless governments and local authorities, on the other. This distinction was a constitutive element of NER and NEF narratives. NER relief workers believed that God was at their side. In an unpublished typescript of 1940, NER/NEF overseas director Barclay Acheson eventually admitted:

> We know that oak trees will grow in temperate zones and palm tree in tropical climates, but we fail to realize that social, educational, financial and governmental institutions must fit the traditions, aptitudes and needs of the peoples they serve. Backward nations deeply resent cultural frustration and all institutions that are monuments to their inferiority – American religions, educational institutions and even her form of government are not necessarily suited to alien lands. We do not know enough to play God. Best method is to remove causes of retarded growth, stimulate indigenous growth and by slow process of trial and error evolve reforms.[48]

Acheson's admission that local culture and practices should be acknowledged and respected contained a continued paternalist sentiment that is evident in that final sentence when he refers to the 'retarded growth' and involvement in 'indigenous growth'. What I would like the reader to keep in mind is that Acheson and his acolytes believed that this change was possible. In conclusion, this brief account of the NER humanitarian vision and practices shows that, as the historian Johannes Paulmann has pointed

[48] B. Acheson, *Plowshares and Pruning Hooks*, unpublished typescript, 1940, ch. VII, RAC, NER, box 132.

out, emergency aid and development aid seem to have coexisted in the past.[49] This was certainly the case in the interwar period and as far as the NER was concerned.

[49] Johannes Paulmann, 'Conjunctures in the History of International Humanitarian Aid during the Twentieth Century', *Humanity: An International Journal of Human Rights, Humanitarianism, and Development*, 4, no. 2 (Summer 2013), 215–38.

10

Humanitarian intervention as legitimation of violence – the German case 1937–1939

Jost Dülffer

Humanitarian law and human rights law are different fields in international law, but the social, political, and cultural phenomena of the violation of basic needs and rights of individuals or collective groups pose a more universal question. Historians should address such phenomena without first considering the systematizations of their treatment in other disciplines. Thus, it may be correct that the notion of human rights only emerged in the wake of the horrors of the Second World War, but the underlying social processes, as well as reactions to them, are older and cannot be neatly separated. One might argue with Samuel Moyn that human rights violations always had to do with states, while the alleviation of humanitarian atrocities took place independently from the existence of states.[1] In my opinion, this means a relative scale of classification and not a strict partition of one from another, also with regard to the involvement of states.

Humanitarian intervention is mostly regarded as a positive action in the sense of the *Universal Declaration of Human Rights* of 1948.[2]

[1] Samuel Moyn, *The Last Utopia: Human Rights in History* (Cambridge, Mass.: Harvard University Press, 2010), 11–43. I would like to thank Claudia Kemper for her useful comments, Fabian Klose for providing further tips for literature and Dona Geyer as well as Peter Ridder for important technical assistance. A different German version concentrating on the Sudeten crisis in 1938: José Brunner, Doron Avraham, Marianne Zepp (eds.), *Politische Gewalt in Deutschland. Ursprünge – Ausprägungen–Konsequenzen*, (Göttingen: Wallstein, 2014), 91–110.

[2] Christian Tomuschat, 'Menschenrechtsschutz und innere Angelegenheiten,' http://tomuschat.rewi.hu-berlin.de/not (last accessed on 18 May 2015); good overviews include Stefan-Ludwig Hoffmann (ed.), *Moralpolitik: Geschichte der Menschenrechte im 20. Jahrhundert* (Göttingen: Wallstein, 2010), especially the chapters by Mark Mazower;

However, the topic has long been discussed, even if the language in which it is now framed was not used. There have been predecessors to humanitarian intervention because of the violation of basic rights, especially in the interwar period of the twentieth century. One of the most striking features in this period was the tension between self-determination, on the one hand, and minority rights, on the other.[3] The creation of new nation states in eastern Central Europe and the geographical shrinkage or dissolution of the vanquished great powers led to problems linked to large minority populations. 'The Paris peace treaties gave 60 million people a state of their own, but turned another 25 million into minorities.'[4] Compensation was to be provided by treaties obliging states to protect minorities. Although this was agreed upon, it was achieved only imperfectly. Especially in the new states, the ruling elites embraced the primacy of national consolidation, which the majorities tried also to achieve in economic, political, and sometimes even cultural terms. This created tension inside the states and also subsequently led in many cases to complaints from neighbouring states about the mistreatment of their related minorities. *Irredenta*, originally an Italian political catchword levelled against Austria-Hungary since the 1860s, received the implication of a potential intervention in favour of the suppressed. After the First World War, it became a political problem for large parts of central and eastern Europe. In some cases, *irredenta* was combined with the idea of enlarging the newly founded nation state into a greater one that included the entire ethnic population, even those enclaves existing outside its borders. Nevertheless, the political situation in this region remained relatively calm or at least did not develop into one with major violence. For the most part, the latent or sometimes manifest threat to intervene on behalf of suppressed minorities did not become an open problem during the 1920s. The League of Nations did not play a major part in these questions. The Covenant stressed the sovereignty of states very strongly

Jan Eckel and Samuel Moyn (eds.), *Moral für die Welt? Menschenrechtspolitik in den 1970er Jahren* (Göttingen: Vandenhoek & Ruprecht, 2012).

[3] Carol Fink, *Defending the Rights of Others: The Great Powers, the Jews, and International Minority Protection, 1878–1938* (Cambridge University Press, 2004); Mark Mazower, 'Minorities and the League of Nations', *Daedalus*, 126, no. 2 (Spring 1997), 47–63.

[4] Zara Steiner, *The Lights that Failed: European International History, 1919–1933* (Oxford University Press, 2005), 259; Mazower, 'Minorities', 50, quotes Jungjohann as citing the population size of minorities at 35 million, of whom only 8.6 million were living in Western Europe.

and thus left the League with little possibility to function as anything more than an arbiter, even in questions dealing with minorities.[5]

Germany's case can be seen also in this context of minorities living outside the shrunken Reich: the *Anschluss* of the newly founded state of Austria, originally proclaimed as '*Deutsch-Österreich*', was forbidden by the victorious powers because they did not want a territorial enlargement of the German Reich. A customs union between the two states, which had been planned in 1931, was equally interdicted by the *International Court of Justice*. The newly founded Czechoslovakian Republic contained a large German-speaking minority that had earlier been part of the Austro-Hungarian empire, but not of the German Reich. Also, the newly founded state of Poland included large German (and other) minorities, living especially in the so-called corridor between East Prussia and the rest of Germany. The minority treaties concluded by the Allies and the newly founded states in 1919 were less than clear in their outreach and not generally accepted. They did not speak about 'human rights' but about minority rights to be granted and guaranteed by the majority population. The first treaty was concluded with Poland and served as a kind of model for subsequent ones.[6] The Locarno treaties of 1925 did not guarantee the borders of Czechoslovakia and Poland but provided arbitration treaties between Germany, on the one side, and Poland and Czechoslovakia, on the other, which were meant to relax tensions and thus further reduce the danger of German revisionist intervention.

At first, the National Socialist seizure of power in 1933 did not alter these relations nor intensify problems on the level of daily diplomacy. Instead it rattled the fundaments of an accepted international order that was based on peaceful change. There has been extensive debate on the programmatic or situational foundations of Hitler's foreign policy.[7]

[5] Mark Swatek-Evenstein, *Geschichte der 'Humanitären Intervention'* (Baden-Baden: Nomos, 2008), 203–16; Harald Endemann, *Kollektive Zwangsmaßnahmen zur Durchsetzung humanitärer Normen: Ein Beitrag zum Recht der humanitären Intervention* (Frankfurt a. M.: Peter Lang, 1997), 101–7; F. X. de Limia, *Intervention in International Law* (The Hague: Uitgeverij Pax Nederland, 1971), 28–36; Sean D. Murphy, *The United Nations in an Evolving World Order* (Pittsburg: University of Pennsylvania Press, 1996), 57–64.

[6] Erwin Viefhaus, *Die Minderheitenfrage und die Entstehung der Minderheitenschutzverträge auf der Pariser Friedenskonferenz 1919: Eine Studie zur Geschichte des Nationalitätenproblems im 19. und 20. Jahrhundert* (Würzburg: Holzner, 1969); Steiner, *The Lights that Failed*, 361–3.

[7] Andreas Hillgruber, *Deutschlands Rolle in der Vorgeschichte der beiden Weltkriege* (Göttingen: Vandenhoek & Ruprecht, 1967); Klaus Hildebrand, *Deutsche Außenpolitik*

At any rate, basic axioms of National Socialist thinking were being permanently discussed in secret and sometimes even in public. One central axiom was to create living space in the east and a society based on a racial domination by the Germanic race. Hitler was sure that more than peaceful means were necessary to achieve this; war was needed and, prior to this, rearmament. To achieve this rearmament or '*Wiederwehrhaftmachung*' at the greatest possible speed was one of the guiding principles of the Nazi regime starting in 1933. The universally racist view was based on the idea that Jewish influences had to be fought not only domestically, but universally. In this worldview, Bolshevism meant full Jewish domination and Western democracies were in danger of falling prey to the Jews. The positive counterweight was the resolve of the Germanic race. 'There is only one people on earth which lives crowded together in great cohesiveness, with a homogeneous race and language, in the heart of Europe. This is the German people with its 110 million Germans in Central Europe ... and someday the world will and must belong to this cohesive Central European bloc', stated Hitler in a secret message to his generals on 22 January 1938.[8] In public, he spoke of 80 million Germans in Europe, although the Reich at the end of 1937 had only about 67 million inhabitants. The point behind this rhetoric was to propagate a way of racial thinking that turned minority problems into instruments for creating a greater Germany by annexation. Adding Germans to the people's community thus became an aim in which humanitarian motives played a role, but only in the form of rhetoric, of course.

Although this would mean a revolution, concrete National Socialist foreign policy had to operate carefully and in an interactive way within the framework of existing relations with the great powers. Thus it was a policy of systematic hypocrisy,[9] a policy that preached peace in order to better prepare for war without attracting too much attention and provoking counteraction by the other powers. It was a policy that used political

1993–1945: Kalkül oder Dogma? (Stuttgart: Kohlhammer, 1972); Gerhard L. Weinberg, *The Foreign Policy of Hitler's Germany [1933–1939]*, 2 vols. (Chicago University Press, 1970/80); Martin Broszat, *Der Staat Hitlers* (Munich: dtv, 1969); Frank McDonough (ed.), *The Origins of the Second World War: An International Perspective* (London: Continuum, 2011), especially the chapters by David Dutton, John Charmley, and Robert Young on British perspectives.

[8] Jost Dülffer, *Weimar, Hitler und die Marine: Reichspolitik und Flottenbau 1920–1939* (Düsseldorf: Droste, 1973), 547, author's translation.

[9] Hans-Adolf Jacobsen, *Nationalsozialistische Außenpolitik 1933–1938* (Frankfurt a. M.: Metzner, 1968), 328.

or even military blackmail to enhance the German potential without resorting to military force as long as possible. Under these circumstances, humanitarian arguments and motives gained a major importance in German foreign policy and in European international relations as such in the two years before the Second World War.[10] This will be demonstrated in the cases of Austria, Czechoslovakia, and Poland.[11]

AUSTRIA

Austria was the first example in which National Socialists 'learned' not to use revolutionary means openly. Hitler himself was convinced that his mother country with its 6 million inhabitants should belong to Germany.[12] In 1933, with help from the German motherland, Austrian National Socialist leader Theodor Habicht recruited an Austrian legion in Bavaria meant to intimidate the Austrian government as well as exert terror from within. It was the tactic of simultaneously eroding the country from within and pressuring it from without. At the time, the rebels did not strongly emphasize the idea of human suppression but argued instead for a revolution against a legitimate government that, in German eyes, did not really represent the people. This strategy failed twice: in 1933 and in 1934 when a coup d'état in Austria ended in the murder of Chancellor Engelbert Dollfuß and thus discredited the entire initiative nationally as well as internationally, especially in the view of Italian dictator Benito Mussolini. From that point on, the German government followed a course of slow evolution below the threshold of international attention. In 1936, a bilateral agreement between Germany and Austria was concluded that politically and economically rendered the Alpine republic

[10] There is a large scholarly literature on the international system and the way into war: Klaus Hildebrand et al. (ed.), *1939: An der Schwelle zum Weltkrieg* (Berlin and New York: de Gruyter, 1990); Donald C. Watt, *How War Came: The Immediate Origins of the Second World War, 1938–1939* (London: Heineman, 1988); Zara Steiner, *The Triumph of the Dark: European International History 1933–1939* (Oxford University Press, 2011), especially chapters 10–14; Joseph Maiolo, *Cry Havoc: How the Arms Race Drove the World to War* (London: Basic Books, 2010).

[11] For the argument as a provocative framework: Jacques Bricmont, *Humanitarian Imperialism: Using Human Rights to Sell War* (New York: Monthly Review Press, 2006).

[12] Norbert Schausberger, 'Österreich und die nationalsozialistische Anschluß-Politik', in Manfred Funke (ed.), *Hitler, Deutschland und die Mächte: Materialien zur Außenpolitik des Dritten Reiches* (Düsseldorf: Droste, 1976), 728–56; Norbert Schausberger, *Der Griff nach Österreich: Der Anschluß* (Vienna: Jugend und Volk, 1978), 451–558.

dependent on the Reich, which to an outsider might have seemed like a good permanent basis for peace.

Germany changed course again in late 1937. It was motivated primarily by the scarcity of raw materials, foreign currency, and labour in Germany, which escalated the situation and pointed the way towards direct annexation or *Anschluss*. As Hitler publicly announced one year later: 'In January 1938, I came to the definite decision to fight still in this year for the right of self-determination for the 6.5 million Germans in Austria.'[13] This right of self-determination, anchored in the Versailles system, was now interpreted as a basic human right being deprived to Austrians. Austrian National Socialists were encouraged to proceed more aggressively against their government. On 12 February 1938, Austrian Chancellor Kurt Schuschnigg was summoned to Berchtesgaden and forced to orient Austrian foreign policy even closer to that of the Reich, to grant not only amnesty but also unrestricted political freedom to National Socialists in his country, and to appoint their leader, Arthur Seyss-Inquart, as minister of the interior, responsible for domestic security. In Nazi terms this was seen as a kind of humanitarian intervention by direct political pressure. It created the opportunity for National Socialists to openly agitate and propagate their politics also in the direction of a political overthrow. In this sense, Joachim von Ribbentrop, the newly appointed German foreign minister, threatened the French ambassador:

> France and the world had to understand once and for all that, for a great power like Germany, it was in the long run impossible to view with complacency the incredible treatment that a part of the Germans living on her borders had been receiving in the in the last few years ... Should this, however, not prove to be the remedy, it would have to be understood that, in the protection of the interests and the lives of its racial comrades [*Stammesgenossen*], Germany would not shrink from the direst consequences, not even from a European war.[14]

From this point on, an all-out European war for humanitarian reasons became a threat used in National Socialist foreign policy, a policy of deterrence, nevertheless.

It was only after a last-minute attempt by Schuschnigg to rescue the remains of Austrian independence when announcing a plebiscite on

[13] *Archiv der Gegenwart* 1939, (30 January 1939), 3914.

[14] Memorandum by the Foreign Minister, 18 February 1938, Documents on German Foreign Policy, 1918–1945 [hereafter DGFP]: From the archives of the German Foreign Ministry, Series D, 1937–1945, Vol. I: From Neurath to Ribbentrop, September 1937 – September 1938, London: HMSO, 1949, no. 308, 529–31.

9 March that Hitler decided to intervene immediately by military means. Before doing this, the German chancellor tried to justify this step to Mussolini:

> For years the Germans in Austria have been oppressed and mistreated by a regime which lacks any legal basis. The sufferings of the innumerable tormented people know no bounds. Germany alone has so far received 40,000 refugees who had to leave their homeland, although the overwhelming majority of the people of Austria entirely share their ideology and their political views.

Not only Hitler but also the more traditionally oriented diplomats in the Wilhelmstrasse tried to mollify foreign governments: 'There was also talk of arms being handed out to the workers. In certain places in Austria there seemed to have been disturbances. I had read of shooting in Linz, in which 17 had been wounded and 1 killed.'[15] The Austrian talk of a plebiscite 'could only mean and was intended to mean doing political violence to the National Socialist part of the population'.[16] Hermann Göring, the second highest person in the Nazi hierarchy, made Seyss-Inquart send a telegram in which he was to write that he 'urgently requests the German Government to support it in its task and to help it to prevent bloodshed. For this reason he [Seyss-Inquart] asks the German government to send German troops at the earliest possible moment.'[17]

Consequently, the Wehrmacht occupied Austria peacefully and the *Anschluss* was proclaimed as the realization of a long-desired national aim, one supported by most Germans and Austrians (excluding the suppressed, of course). The arguments justifying this intervention were said to be bloodshed, the suppression of the National Socialist part of the Austrian population, as well as an impending civil war. Joseph Goebbels, too, lamented in a press conference about 'the intolerable oppression by a minority clique of the Austrians'.[18] Human rights violations and humanitarian reasons were the arguments used to spin a tight web of justification for the *Anschluss*.

This kind of argument and reasoning was not immediately accepted elsewhere in Europe at face value. However, since the traditionally

[15] Hitler to Mussolini, 11 March 1938, ibid., no. 352, 574–6, quote on 574.

[16] The German Foreign Ministry to Various German Diplomatic Missions, 11 March 1938, ibid., no. 357, 579, quote on 579.

[17] The Austrian Minister of the Interior (Seyss-Inquart) to the Führer and Reich Chancellor, telegram from Vienna, 11 March 1938, 9:40 p.m., ibid., no. 358, 580, quote on 580.

[18] Report by Ambassador Henderson, *Documents on British Foreign Policy*, 1919–1939 [hereafter DBFP], Third Series, Vol. 1: 1938, London: HMSO 1949, no. 50.

emotional relations between Germans and Austrians were obvious, this transgression of the international order of 1919/20 was accepted. In this context, another argument was also used: self-determination, the main catchword of the hated and derided Woodrow Wilson policy that had led to Versailles but was also a part of the human rights language that enjoyed a measure of popularity. It was said to have been finally achieved in this case.[19] Hitler even spoke about a 'human right' which people had to achieve on their own because it had been denied for a long time. In the logic of this internationally accepted legal basis of self-determination, a plebiscite was held in Austria on 10 April 1938,[20] which ended up with an overwhelming victory for the unification with Germany, although by then the oppressed already had little opportunity to utter their opinions. It was the formal acceptance of the habits of democratic legitimation by one of the fiercest opponents of such a system.

THE SUDETEN GERMANS IN CZECHOSLOVAKIA

The more than 3 million German-speaking people living in Czechoslovakia had little reason in general to complain about suppression.[21] Still, under the influence of National Socialist policy in the Reich, they and their politics radicalized. In 1933, after the fusion of several German parties, a Sudetendeutsche Heimatfront was founded. Because only parties could participate in elections, it was renamed as the Sudetendeutsche Partei (SdP) in 1935. All this led to a closer cooperation with

[19] Jörg Fisch, *Das Selbstbestimmungsrecht der Völker: Die Domestizierung einer Illusion* (Munich: Oldenbourg, 2010); Jörg Fisch, 'Adolf Hitler und das Selbstbestimmungsrecht', *Historische Zeitschrift*, 290 (2010), 94–118, here 103, 108–15. Fisch quotes several speeches by Hitler on this topic. These were given on 20 February, 12 March, 18 March (here the reference to a 'human right'), 25 March, and 12 September: all are taken – in chronological order – from Max Domarus, *Hitler: Reden 1932 bis 1945. Kommentiert von einem Zeitgenossen*, 4 vols. (Wiesbaden: R. Löwit, 1973), vol. 2, 801, 816, 827–9, 833, 901.

[20] Otmar Jung, *Plebiszit und Diktatur: Die Volksabstimmungen der Nationalsozialisten* (Tübingen: Mohr Siebeck, 1995), 109–24.

[21] Ronald M. Smelser, *Das Sudetenproblem und das Dritte Reich, 1933–1938: Von der Volkstumspoltitik zur Nationalsozialistischen Außenpolitik* (Munich: Oldenbourg, 1980), 188–215; Ralf Gebel, *'Heim ins Reich': Konrad Henlein und der Reichsgau Sudetenland (1938–1945)* (Munich: Oldenbourg, 2009), 51–61 (1937–38); René Küpper, *Karl Hermann Frank (1898–1946): Politische Biographie eines sudetendeutschen Nationalsozialisten* (Munich: Oldenbourg, 2010), 88–115; the classic book is Helmut K.G. Rönnefarth, *Die Sudetenkrise in der internationalen Politik*, 2 vols. (Stuttgart: Steiner, 1961).

German politics and shrinking loyalty to the Czechoslovak state. Significant for the radicalization of Nazi politics was Hitler's internal speech to the Wehrmacht commanders and the foreign minister on 5 November 1937, known as the Hossbach Protocol.[22] Hitler announced not only that Germany was under time pressure regarding the reaction of the European states against his policy of maximum armament, but also that the diagnosis of fading military superiority made it necessity to wage a major war in the coming years. As far as the next steps in his plans were concerned, he regarded both Austria and Czechoslovakia as the initial objects of expansion: 'For improvement of our politico-military position, our first objective, in the event of our being embroiled in war, must be to overthrow Czechoslovakia and Austria simultaneously in order to remove the threat to our flank in any possible operation against the west.'[23] This was a primacy of military strategy and geopolitics, which certainly was used with regard to this audience; ethnic arguments played no role at all: 'the Fuehrer ... wanted, while retaining his own independence of action, to exploit this favourable situation, which would not occur again, to begin and carry through the campaign against the Czechs. This descent upon the Czechs would have to be carried out with "lightning speed".'[24]

The interaction between SdP politics and guidance by the Reich cannot be depicted here in detail. It lasted until May 1938 when Germany decided to finally pursue the immediate course of a military attack on Czechoslovakia. The pretext was found in the so-called May crisis, when parts of the Czechoslovakian army mobilized in the wake of rumours about German troop concentrations. Hitler was upset and internally announced his firm resolution to solve the entire Czech – not just the Sudeten – problem once and for all by military means. Shortly before this escalation, in a directive for the Wehrmacht on 21 April, he had discussed causes for such an attack, including the following:[25] 'It is not my intention to smash Czechoslovakia by military action in the immediate future without provocation, unless an unavoidable development of the political conditions within Czechoslovakia forces the issue, or political events in Europe create a particularly favourable opportunity, which may perhaps

[22] Hossbach Protocoll, Berlin, 10 November 1937, DGFP, Series D, vol. I, no. 18, 25–32, quote on 29–31; on the economic reasons for this speech, see Dülffer, *Weimar, Hitler und die Marine*, 446–52.

[23] Memorandum, 11 November 1937, DGFP, Series D, vol. I, no. 19, 29–39, quote on 35.

[24] Ibid., quote on 37–8.

[25] Draft Weisung Grün, Attachment, 20 May 1938, DGFP, Series D, vol. II: Germany and Czechoslovakia, 1937–1938, London: HMSO, 1950, no. 172.

never recur.'[26] What he meant specifically became clearer when he added how the Reich might react with 'lightning action as the result of a serious incident which will subject Germany to unbearable provocation and which, in the eyes of at least a part of world opinion, affords the moral justification for military measures'.[27]

World opinion as a gauge for humanitarian intervention – this was indeed the nucleus of Hitler's use of this argument, but it was more difficult than might be assumed to undertake an annexation with an appeal to world opinion. Two months earlier, when planning further procedures, Foreign Minister von Ribbentrop had argued that

> it was a matter of drawing up a maximum program, the final aim of which would guarantee total freedom for the Sudeten Germans. It seemed dangerous to accept prematurely promises of the Czechoslovak Government, which, on the one hand, could give the impression abroad that a solution had been found and. on the other, would only partially satisfy the Sudeten Germans themselves.[28]

In this regard, Konrad Henlein and his SdP proved to be a reliable instrument for the tactics of German escalation politics. After a party rally – and now working in close cooperation with the Reich authorities – the SdP passed its *Karlsbad Programme* in which the party demanded not only full equal rights for the Sudeten Germans within the Czechoslovakian state, but also compensation for all injuries they were said to have suffered since the First World War. The party also affirmed its 'commitment to the German people' (*Bekenntnis zum deutschen Volkstum*).[29] This programme expressed the party's political will for much more than mere autonomy but nevertheless something less than *Anschluss* to the Reich. These demands formed the basis for the SdP's domestic negotiations with the Czechoslovakian authorities. Thus it pursued a tactic that Hitler expressly commanded to Henlein later on: 'Always negotiate and do not let the thread break. But always demand more than the opposing side can offer.'[30]

[26] Draft Directive 'Green', attachment to a letter from Keitel to Hitler, 20 May 1938, ibid., no. 175, 299–303; quote on 300.

[27] Ibid.

[28] Draft to Despatch by the Foreign Minister to the German Legation in Czechoslovakia, 29 March 1938, ibid., no. 109, 203–5, quote on 204.

[29] Memorandum of the Eight Demands Made by Konrad Henlein at the Sudeten German Party Congress at Karlsbad, DGFP, Series D, vol. II, no. 135, 242–3; an English summary is found in DBFP, Third Series, vol. I, no. 157, 182–86.

[30] Smelser, *Das Sudetenproblem*, 233.

The tactical use of the suppression of Sudeten Germans now became valuable in international politics. When British Ambassador Sir Neville Henderson complained to the German foreign minister during the May crisis about German measures of escalation, von Ribbentrop retorted:

> Lord Halifax [the British foreign minister] had taken note that I had told the British Ambassador that, if bloodshed occurred in Czechoslovakia as a result of the tension between Czechs and Germans, Germany would act ... I advised the British Government to take it up against Prague and not in Berlin. To have to exhort calmness on unarmed Germans, who today could no longer bicycle or walk in the streets without being exposed to the worst terror on the part of armed Czech, seemed to me a grotesque imputation, and I could not take this demand seriously.[31]

This was based on the assumption that especially the Western powers were aware of complaints about the abuse of human rights. Put differently: Paris and London became increasingly aware that Berlin might mean war and was only seeking reasons to legitimize it. Such awareness did not make things easier for them.

The French government was pledged to defend Czechoslovakia by virtue of a military alliance formed in 1935. Because the French military did not feel prepared to support its ally in the case of what would then be a European war, it was better to cling to any straw that might offer a solution or at least put off the necessity of harder decisions. As early as 1937, Great Britain had started to advise the Czechoslovakian government to grant or negotiate an acceptable solution with their minorities – especially the Germans, but to an extent also with the Slovaks, who were nominally also a constituent part of the combined republic.

British attempts to mediate the humanitarian question reached a climax in late July when Lord Runciman, who did not hold government office at the time, was appointed head of a mission to Czechoslovakia. Of course, the British government could not officially assume the role of mediator in the domestic affairs of a sovereign state, so the well-reputed lord formally acted as an independent 'investigator and mediator' between the Prague government and the Sudeten Germans.[32] In fact, everyone knew that the German government's attitude was decisive and that war might be imminent if the complaints of the Sudeten Germans

[31] DGFP, D II, No. 186, Memorandum by the Foreign Minister, 21 May 1938, DGFP, Series D, vol. II, no. 186, 315–17, quote on 315–6.

[32] Viscount Halifax to Ambassador Henderson/Mr. Newton, DBFP, Third Series, vol. II, no. 541/546 of 25/26 July 1938, 3 and 7.

were not satisfactorily answered. The Western powers seemed to be grasping at straws, and the French now more or less toed the line with the British. Nevertheless, British diplomats tried informally to advise Runciman on the kind of solution he might propose.[33] In the end, it was to no avail: Ribbentrop opined that such a mission would only prompt the Czechs to become more aggressive and tend to make them even more willing to follow Bolshevist ideas. Only Prague posed a hindrance for a 'settlement and the pacification of Europe'.[34]

After the *Anschluss* of Austria in March 1938, the Germans laid their cards on the table regarding Czechoslovakia in their game over the Sudeten Germans. Still, in the initial months after the *Anschluss*, German propaganda was very cautious. There was a sharp surveillance of the press, which was steered closely and carefully by the propaganda ministry or by Joseph Goebbels himself in press conferences held almost daily.[35] This does not mean that the fate of the Sudeten Germans was completely in the hands of the Berlin authorities, but the public sphere in which the issue was dealt could be manipulated almost at will. Notices about atrocities would be printed sometimes just in regional papers as rumours or facts, only to be mentioned later in nationally distributed media as incontestable but uncommented fact. In August 1938 – in accordance with the military plans for October – the tone got sharper. Hitler's speech at the Nuremberg party rally on 12 September finally accelerated and intensified the media coverage.[36] The *Führer* repeated his earlier demand 'that the Reich will not accept any longer further suppression and persecution of these three and a half million Germans'. On 19 September, journalists were reminded that they should no longer write about the

[33] Viscount Halifax to Viscounto Runciman, 18 August 1938, ibid., no. 643, 111–115; Ambassador to Germany, Henderson, to Viscount Halifax, 22 August 1938, ibid., no. 662, 129–30.

[34] Foreign Minister Ribbentrop to Viscount Halifax, 21 August 1938, ibid., no. 66, 127–9.

[35] Still a good survey for the sources: Walter Hagemann, *Publizistik im Dritten Reich: Ein Beitrag zur Methode der Massenführung* (Hamburg: Hansischer Gildenverein, 1948), 348–77 on the summer of 1938 (quote on 366, summary on 377); Engelbert Schwarzenbeck, *Nationalsozialistische Pressepolitik und die Sudetenkrise 1938* (Munich: Minerva, 1979). A fundamental and still useful publication of sources: Hans Behrmann et al. (eds.), *NS-Presseanweisungen der Vorkriegszeit: Edition und Dokumentation*, 7 vols. (Munich: Saur, 1984–2001), with comments; more recently, Bernd Heidenreich and Sönke Neitzel (eds.), *Medien im Nationalsozialismus* (Paderborn: Wilhelm Fink Verlag, 2010), especially the contribution by Joachim-Felix Leonhard.

[36] Max Domarus, *Hitler. Reden 1932 bis 1945: Kommentiert von einem Zeitgenossen*, 4 vols. (Wiesbaden: R. Löwit, 1973), vol. 2, 901.

7.5 cm artillery guns but prepare to report on the deployment of 21 cm ones in their propaganda.

More than sixty years ago, Walter Hagemann aptly summarized how the instrumentalization of the press was orchestrated with regard to this human rights question. The media guidelines that were handed down by the regime and set the tone on the issue were changed very often. The tone first became particularly virulent in May, then turned moderate again. However, after mid July, the number and aggressiveness of media reports swelled steadily until the final acts at Berchtesgaden, Godesberg, and Munich. The initiative was at first left solely to the Sudeten Germans but was amplified by German media. Only in the final phase did the Nazi leadership join in the campaign with rallies and speeches. Throughout the media campaign, the aim was always to steer German public opinion and intimidate other countries.

The ensuing steps to the incorporation of the Sudeten Germans into the Reich are well known: British Prime Minister Chamberlain visited Hitler three times between 15–30 September at Berchtesgaden, Bad Godesberg, and Munich. The last meeting took place as a western European summit including French Prime Minister Édouard Daladier and Italian Duce Benito Mussolini but no Czechoslovakian representative. After this, the Sudeten region was immediately ceded to Germany. Hitler had rhetorically used his readiness to risk a major war in order to blackmail the other great powers. Under this premise, he had confronted Chamberlain at Berchtesgaden with the complaint that 'the situation was very grave. On the basis of the latest information, 300 fatal casualties and many hundreds of injured were to be expected among the Sudeten Germans. There were entire villages from which the population had fled. Under these circumstances, a decision must be reached in some way or another within a very short time'.[37] Of course, this was no more than unconfirmed horror propaganda.

> In the case of the seven million Germans in the Ostmark, this demand had been met. The return to the Reich of the three million Germans in Czechoslovakia he (the *Führer*) would make possible at all costs. He would face any war, and even the risk of a world war, for this. Here the limit had been reached where the rest of the world might do what it liked, he would not yield one single step.[38]

[37] DGFP, Series D, vol. II, no. 487, Memorandum on the conversation between the Führer and Mr. Neville Chamberlain at the Obersalzberg, 15 September 1938, DGFP, Series D, vol. II, no. 487, 786–98, quote on 788.

[38] Ibid., quote on 790.

The Munich agreement marked a very precarious victory for Hitler. He had succeeded only because, on the surface, the argument about the suppression of the Sudeten Germans, that is, the ethnic arguments alleging violations of basic human rights, had been important. This coincided very well with the line of action put forth by State Secretary Ernst von Weizsäcker at the foreign ministry, starting after the May crisis, to foster a 'chemical solution' of the problem, accompanied by economic pressure, but not an act of open military aggression.[39] Only this procedure made the peaceful secession of the Sudeten area possible.

Nevertheless, Hitler was disappointed. He had wanted to achieve – perhaps even by way of a regional war – a military occupation of the entire the western part of Czechoslovakia, Czechia. Indeed, he had sought to engage in a short and isolated war so as to test the Wehrmacht, to mentally orient this instrument of aggression for greater tasks in the future, and to prepare the German public for what was to come. Yet, in a secret speech before German press correspondents on 10 November 1938, Hitler expressed his content with the relative success of the achievement 'to get a front of nearly 2,000 kilometres of fortifications without having fired a shot. Gentlemen, this time we acquired 10 million people and more than 100,000 square kilometres of territory only by the means of propaganda in the service of an idea'.[40] What Hitler here correctly called propaganda was not only propaganda in form, but also in substance, namely, the alleged violation of human rights.

PRAGUE, DANZIG, THE CORRIDOR, AND POLAND

In more than one regard, the Sudeten question turned out to be a singular and final success of the argument based on 'humanitarian intervention'. Hitler personally was not only convinced that he had to achieve the German struggle for living space and world dominion in his lifetime, he also perceived that counteraction by the international community, with its much greater war potential, only left him a rather narrow window of opportunity. Thus, a few weeks after the Munich summit, he told journalists expressly in his aforementioned speech that the 'pacifist record' had been played long enough. This also meant that ethnic arguments also had served their purpose and their use had basically come to an end. After

[39] Ernst von Weizsäcker, *Die Weizsäcker-Papiere*, ed. L. E. Hill (Frankfurt a. M.: Propyläen, 1974), 129, 131.

[40] Domarus, *Hitler*, 975.

the Berchtesgaden meeting in September, Chamberlain and French Prime Minister Daladier had again met to discuss their next steps; Chamberlain had assured his partner that 'no other solution than self-determination was now possible'.[41] Hitler had promised to stick to this principle of ethnic affiliation as a prerequisite for the Munich agreement. Yet as we know, the German government was not thinking in this direction, and only three weeks after Munich, Hitler ordered the military to prepare for a final crushing blow against what remained of Czechoslovakia.[42] Thus, what confidence had been generated in the words of the German dictator would all too quickly be destroyed once the Germans acted differently than promised.

In March 1939, the German government made the Slovaks intensify their complaints about Czech dominance in the Republic, and the German press was instrumental in raising accusations about the suppression of an ethnic minority, now of the Slovaks. This marked a new turn in propaganda: not only were the grievances of ethnic Germans placed in the forefront, but now, for the first time, the suffering of non-Germans was publicized in Reich propaganda. The target was clearly the new Czech government, which had tried in vain since October to accommodate German wishes. It had practically become a satellite, because the Western powers had abandoned it to its fate. In the final days before the occupation of Prague and the establishment of the 'Protektorat Böhmen und Mähren', the German press reported on violations but commented little on the situation of the Slovaks; diplomats were told that the 'old Benes spirit' had arisen once again in the Czech capital. The line of argument generally ignored the suffering of the minorities but emphasized instead a state in decay. In this sense, Czechoslovakian President Emil Hacha was summoned to Berlin and placed under severe psychological pressure by Hitler and his associates to finally put the 'fate of his state faithfully into the hands of the *Führer*'. In a 'proclamation to the German people',[43] which Goebbels read in the early morning of 15 March 1939, Hitler contended, 'since Sunday, fierce excesses have again occurred in many places in which many Germans fell victim ... Out of the densely

41 DBFP, Third Series, vol. II, no. 928, 378.

42 Directive by the Führer for the Wehrmacht, 21 October 1938, DGFP, Series D, vol. IV: The Aftermath of Munich, October 1938 – March 1939 (London: HMSO, 1951), no. 81, 99–100, quote on 99.

43 Quoted from Domarus, *Hitler*, 1096; see also Hagemann, *Publizistik*, 377–89; Martin Broszat, *Zweihundert Jahre deutsche Polenpolitik* (Frankfurt a. M.: Suhrkamp, 1972), 256–71.

populated German-language islands which German magnanimity last fall had left to Czechoslovakia, a stream of expellees who were deprived of their property again begins to pour into the Reich.' The task of the German Wehrmacht would only be 'to disarm the terrorist gangs and the supporting Czech armed forces and to protect the lives of all endangered people'. He added that this made sense in light of 1,000 years of German and Czech history.

However, this time Hitler had exhausted the patience of Great Britain: the argument of humanitarian intervention for ethnic reasons was no longer convincing. Hitler had broken his promise at Munich that Germany had no further ethnic claims. The first consequence of this breech was the British guarantee of the existence (though not the territory) of Poland on 31 March 1939, and the second consequence was a stronger determination not to give in when faced with the dictator's efforts at blackmail. 'Appeasement', with its economic or colonial stimuli, continued, but politics were now directed primarily against German dominance in Europe and aimed at stopping its policy. The British now tried to make it clear that they would accept war and would no longer remedy more or less legitimate German grievances in central Europe.

In Germany, Hitler ordered the Wehrmacht in early April to prepare for an assault on Poland, and on 28 April he cancelled the Anglo-German Naval Agreement, which should have been 'permanent', as well as the German-Polish Non-Aggression Pact of 1934. The latter happened only after the Polish government had refused to join Germany in her aggressive plans against the East earlier in the year.

It was a clear course for war, in which ethnic arguments no longer played a major role. Nevertheless, the German ethnic grievances against Poland were well known. Earlier they had not been regarded as real problems. One year earlier, Hermann Göring had declared to the British ambassador that 'apart from the Sudeten, everything else was of minor importance: Danzig was already practically German again; the problem of the corridor could be solved possibly by a corridor across a corridor; Memel would also have to come back to Germany, but these were all matters of comparatively easy adjustments'.[44] Although Göring was a master of hypocrisy, the tactical importance of ethnic arguments in Nazi politics can again be observed here. Relatively relaxed talks with Poland on the questions of Danzig and the corridor had continued until early

[44] Ambassador Henderson to Viscount Halifax, 20 April 1938, DBFP, Third Series, vol. I, no.152, 173–6, quote on 174.

1939, but since April, the strategy of complaining about the violation of human rights was intensified. In Gerhard Weinberg's words:

> The reason is easy to see: in this sphere his 1938 strategy simply had not worked. He had in 1938 been required to settle for his ostensible demands, and he was not about to take a chance on that happening again. If you did not want a negotiated settlement, and wished to avoid the risk of being nudged into one against your own preference, the safest thing to do was not to negotiate at all.[45]

That may be too much of a clear rationalization in a principally open historical situation, also from the perspective of a Hitler who now basically wanted an isolated war against Poland and hoped to avoid an all-out war for which the Wehrmacht was not prepared. Indeed, as he said when he addressed his generals on 23 May 1939: 'It is not Danzig that is at stake.'[46] Three months later, he is said to have argued to a similar audience: 'I hope this time there will be no swine (*Schweinehund*) with a plan for mediation' – in reference to the way the events leading to the Munich agreement were now being characterized.[47]

Thus the media were advised to remain relatively calm and only bring uncommented news on the fate of Danzig or the Germans in the corridor.[48] This time international diplomats closely followed these propaganda measures and tried to warn the German government against any unilateral action resembling that of the Sudeten crisis the year before. German agitation was intensified in the second half of July, but the order to the German press on 8 August still stipulated that 'Polish atrocities against ethnic Germans are still to be printed on page two'.[49] Only on the following day were Polish attacks against Germans to appear on the first page with prescribed commentary.

After the German assault on Poland on 1 September 1939, Hitler summed up the topic of ethnic and humanitarian intervention in his speech to the Reichstag: 'Danzig was and is a German city! The Corridor was and is German! … Danzig was separated from us! The corridor annexed by Poles! The German inhabitants mistreated in the most painful

45 Weinberg, *Foreign Policy*, vol. II, 561.

46 Minutes of a Conference, 23 May 1939, DGFP, Series D, vol. VI: *The Last Month of Peace* (London: HMSO 1957), no. 433, 574–80 (quote on 575).

47 Speech by the Führer to the Commanders in Chief, 22 August 1939, DGFP, Series D, vol. VII: *The Last Days of Peace* (London: HMSO 1956), no. 192 and 193, 200–6. See Wilfried Baumgart, 'Zur Ansprache Hitlers vor den Führern der Wehrmacht am 22. August 1939: Eine quellenkritische Untersuchung', *Vierteljahrhefte für Zeitgeschichte* 16 (1968), 120–49.

48 Hagemann, *Publizistik*, 389–412.

49 Ibid., 402.

way! More than a million people of German blood were forced to leave their homeland back in 1919/1920.'[50] The diplomatic notes to the Western countries were all similarly worded. In the German response to the British ultimatum, von Ribbentrop justified the German course: 'Moved by the suffering of the population tortured by the Poles and treated inhumanly', Germany had tried to solve the problem – the humanitarian problem – for five months with peaceful means. That time had now ended.[51]

CONCLUSION

Nazi foreign policy meant a policy towards war and the forming of an internationally competitive armed force able to fight permanently for living space and world dominion based on racial superiority. At first sight, this had nothing to do with human rights or intervention for humanitarian reasons.

A second and closer look reveals that the argument of humanitarian intervention got more than tactical use. The propagated aim to unite all Germans (ethnic Germans in the widest sense) in the German Reich shared some similarity with the right of self-determination as one of the guiding principles in the international order after the First World War. National Socialists did not believe in this as a guideline but argued instead for a self-determination derived from blood and not by free decision of citizenry. In this way, self-determination was ambivalent. It provided an argument for minority protection in a given state, but also for incorporation into the Reich. Despite this ambivalence, self-determination could be used in the European and international context as a tactic to calm concerns over Nazi foreign policy, which from 1933 deployed a 'strategy of grandiose self-belittlement'[52] and exploited the argument of self-determination as an internationally accepted principle. At the same time, German minorities became more or less inclined to favour a national union with the Reich. Nazi policy thus developed a pull-effect on minorities, which was reinforced by several Nazi agencies in the Reich and thus made the concession of better minority rights more and more obsolete. Even before the Second World War, German minorities functioned as a fifth column supporting German intervention. It is rather easy and morally noble to characterize this usage as misuse. Especially among jurists

[50] Domarus, *Hitler*, 1312. [51] Ibid., 1336–8.

[52] Jacobsen, *Nationalsozialistische Außenpolitik*, 328: 'grandiose Selbstverharmlosung'.

this argument is common. They only use it to reflect a bit on the misusers. Many of them also mention the Sudeten case (besides Italian or Japanese atrocities and their legitimizing strategies).[53] The well-known Holocaust historian Michael R. Marrus also speaks about 'the eclipse of humanitarian intervention in the interwar period'.[54] However, historians here and elsewhere should seriously take into consideration the language used: arguments matter and develop momentum in politics.[55]

The following points, drawn from different perspectives, may augment more general observations.

Besides arguments of self-determination, the fact that human rights violations or humanitarian atrocities against ethnic Germans were committed by the governments of some neighbour states provided a framework for propaganda by a Nazi regime harbouring expansionist aims. Regardless of real social, economic, or cultural grievances, propaganda exploiting the human rights and humanitarian theme could be intensified or abated as best served the political needs of the regime. Thus the topic became an instrument for domestic and foreign policy propaganda, as well as an issue in the formal diplomacy of the Reich, one that was first used against its neighbouring countries and later primarily against the Western powers.

The use of humanitarian intervention to incorporate territory into the German state was not an essential and unconditional part of German foreign policy in this period. On the one hand, the Saar plebiscite of 1935 was a remnant of the Versailles order, which coincided with both traditional German nationalist goals and special Nazi aims. On the other, the South Tyrolean ethnic Germans, who had become neighbours after the *Anschluss*, were sacrificed on the altar of German-Italian understanding in 1938, the same year of the *Anschluss*. South Tyrolean Germans would eventually be resettled elsewhere during the Second World War.[56]

53 See, for example, Ian Brownlie, *International Law and the Use of Force by States* (Oxford University Press, 1963), 340; Francis Kofi Abiew, *The Evolution of the Doctrine and Practice of Humanitarian Intervention* (The Hague: Kluwer, 1999), and most of titles from note 5; many more can be added.

54 Michael R. Marrus, 'International Bystanders to the Holocaust' in Richard Ashby Wilson and Richard D. Brown (eds.), *Humanitarianism and Suffering: The Mobilization of Empathy* (Cambridge University Press, 2009), 156–74 (quote in the subtitle on 164).

55 For a different period with a similar methodological approach, see Lora Wildenthal, *The Language of Human Rights in West Germany* (Philadelphia: University of Pennsylvania Press, 2013).

56 Macgregor Knox, *Common Destiny: Dictatorship, Foreign Policy and War in Fascist Italy and National Socialist Germany* (Cambridge University Press, 2000).

Similar observations can be made for the German-speaking minority in Alsace and Lorraine.[57] Until 1940, Nazi foreign policy maintained continually that the question was settled, so as to ease France's concern about German aims. Self-determination and the violation of human rights thus became a pretence for humanitarian intervention, or better, for aggression.

The cases presented here differ considerably in the way they were handled by Nazi politics. The Austrian case created a permanent intensification of German intervention from 1934 until a dependency on Germany in nearly all fields of political life had been achieved. Basically it was a policy of the 'chemical dissolution' that Ernst von Weizsäcker had propagated, in which arguments concerning humanitarian intervention played a relatively small role. Only in combination with the military invasion could the Austrian appeal for help function as a complementary side effect of demonstrative violence. Nevertheless, a plebiscite, something normally so contrary to Nazi ideas, produced an overwhelming majority in favour of the *Anschluss*. Such support had been demonstrated prior to the plebiscite at the mass rally on Vienna's *Heldenplatz* in a way that also impressed the Western powers.

The Sudeten German case was different. For more than a year, the claims of intolerable suppression and the need for self-determination were made and exploited at will by propaganda and diplomacy. Such a strategy was used even though the real intention of Hitler and his followers meant the military destruction of the Czechoslovakian state as such. This time a 'chemical solution', meaning a mixture of action from within and without, was only a secondary element that gained momentum during the summer of 1938 because of complaints about humanitarian abuse of Sudeten Germans, as the Runciman mission shows. Hitler was thus trapped by his pledge for 'only' humanitarian intervention and by the Munich agreement, in which he had to give in halfway in comparison with his real intentions.

The Nazi dictator was not willing to repeat this experience in 1939. In March of that year, National Socialist policy had supported Slovakian tendencies to claim independence using humanitarian arguments, but the German military invasion of Prague was primarily based on the argument of a failed state. As to Poland, the will to militarily crush this state could not be explained by humanitarian intervention, which at best would have

[57] Lothar Kettenacker, *Die nationalsozialistische Volkstumspolitik im Elsass während des Zweiten Weltkrieges* (Stuttgart: Deutsche Verlagsanstalt, 1973).

meant the occupation of Danzig, which had already undergone *Gleichschaltung*, or the Polish Corridor with its large German minority. International mediation on the basis of securing human rights for Germans had to be avoided for a long time, as it would not allow open military aggression against the Polish state as such. Only in the final weeks of August 1939 did the human suffering of Germans – but not self-determination – become another aspect of a political strategy which aimed at starting a regional, not an all-out European war, but which ended in a world war after 3 September 1939. Territorial gains, economic exploitation, and inhuman treatment of millions of people, culminating in the genocide of the European Jews, were the consequences, and it had been the instrumental use of humanitarian intervention and the evocation of human rights that had prepared the way for this structure of extreme violence.

The Nazi example of using human rights for the purpose of naked power politics and inhuman intervention, invasion, and war is an extreme one, but it is not singular. In the first place, it is strictly a case of the use of language.[58] As historians, we should not differentiate from the start between a 'good' use in the sense of our value system or our understanding of the Human Rights Convention in a common Western sense. Instead, we should take seriously the danger of exploitation and abuse of the concept of humanitarian intervention. We need to debate these different uses of the argument of humanitarian intervention in relation with – in a broad sense – political and very aggressive options to get a clearer picture of the opportunities and limitations of the humanitarian and human rights questions.

58 For the West German case after 1945, see Wildenthal, *The Language of Human Rights*.

PART IV

LIMITED OPTIONS OR FURTHER DEVELOPMENT? HUMANITARIAN INTERVENTION DURING THE COLD WAR

11

Cold War peacekeeping *versus* humanitarian intervention

Beyond the Hammarskjöldian model

Norrie MacQueen

The roots of what could be described as the traditional or 'classical' form of UN peacekeeping, which emerged in the 1950s, were both historical and more immediately political. Peacekeeping was not a UN innovation, although it came to be closely identified with the organization. In particular, it was associated with the UN's second Secretary-General, Dag Hammarskjöld of Sweden, who held the office from 1953 until his death in 1961 and who was responsible for the semi-formal conceptualization of this type of military intervention. Yet, when the UN adopted the purposes and techniques of peacekeeping, this occurred within a larger historical narrative, and the reasons were at least in part negative ones, associated with the failure of the much grander UN goal of establishing a global system of collective security. Cold War peacekeeping reflected the prevailing political constraints of the time. It involved, in essence, the use of armed forces without the use of armed force to address peripheral interstate conflicts in a deeply polarized international system.

By the early 1960s, this model had come under strain. Disobligingly, the conflicts in various parts of the world in which the UN was called on to intervene did not automatically conform to the 'ideal type' for which the peacekeeping model had been developed. In reality, the conflicts of the time rarely involved 'simple' straightforward confrontations between responsible sovereign states, which were at the centre of the original conception of peacekeeping. They were now frequently 'intra-state' in nature, fought out between armed factions rather than national armies and within rather than across national frontiers (although they almost always had critical international implications during this time of global polarization). The defining characteristics of 'peacekeeping' were therefore often not suitable to the task at hand by the 1960s. The shifting dynamics of complex conflict could throw into question the necessary consent of the protagonists of UN intervention. In some circumstances, adherence to principles of impartiality and the non-use of force circumscribed any meaningful humanitarian action by UN forces. Nor were the precise humanitarian objectives of UN interventions always clear. At times, the peacekeeping role revealed a contradiction between desirable political outcomes pursued in the interests of international stability, on the one hand, and the immediate goals of natural justice and 'human security', on the other.

Although the terms 'peacekeeping' and 'armed humanitarian intervention' have sometimes become synonymous in general public discussion, they actually describe quite different activities. The tensions between the two concepts have been evident in the post–Cold War period. The 'failure' of traditional peacekeeping in the conflicts of the 1990s in Bosnia, Somalia, and Rwanda, for example, was fundamentally a failure, for whatever reason, to engage in effective humanitarian intervention. Indeed, these specific peacekeeping ventures and the horrific violence surrounding them were explicitly cited by the authors of the original *Responsibility to Protect* report of 2001 as critical reasons to explore the possibilities of armed humanitarian intervention. By inference, when traditional 'peacekeeping' missions stood as silent witnesses to the deaths of countless thousands in their operational areas, then the model was in urgent need of re-examination.[1]

THE PRE-UN ORIGINS OF INTERNATIONAL PEACEKEEPING

The genesis of 'modern' peacekeeping after the Second World War can be found in the interwar years, when multilateral military operations first had a special prominence in international relations. In the 1920s, the post–Versailles frontiers of central and eastern Europe were redrawn, not always as a means of punitive 'victors' justice, as subsequently claimed, but often genuinely on the basis of morally grounded principles of self-determination. At this stage, the focus was on the rights of 'peoples' rather than those of the 'person'; the increasing primacy of the latter would develop later in the century (and form a large part of the

[1] International Commission on Intervention and State Sovereignty, *The Responsibility to Protect: Report of the International Commission on State Sovereignty and Intervention* (Ottawa: International Development Research Centre, 2001), vii, 1.

discussion on humanitarian intervention). The discourse in the post–First World War period associated the self-determined nation state with international stability and therefore considered it a precondition for world peace. This was reflected, for example, in the new colonial mandate system. This part of the League of Nations' responsibility marked an important step towards rethinking the nature of imperialism. Henceforward, colonial possessions taken from defeated states should not simply pass as spoils of war for the victors. Instead, their administration was to be the *responsibility* of the victorious powers under the supervision of the international community (embodied at that time by the League of Nations) until such time as they were prepared for independent statehood. A mandate was designed to be an intermediate stage on the way to independence, and the mandatory (the state now responsible for the territory) had a primary duty to effect this process.[2] Here too, Wilsonian morality with its rejection of old, self-defeating European ways of doing things was evident. In any event, the mandate system was an enduring advance (later adopted by the UN as the Trusteeship system).

Within Europe itself, which underwent its own internal process of 'decolonization' after the First World War, the new approach to the sovereign rights of nationality embraced the beginnings of a recognizable 'peacekeeping process'. Despite the fact that the United States did not ultimately take its place in the League as an institution (following the failure of Congress to ratify President Wilson's policy), the basic Wilsonian principle of the primacy of national self-determination in the post-war territorial settlement persisted. Its principal mechanism was the internationally regulated plebiscite in contested areas designed to determine the wishes of local populations. These potentially tense and unstable processes were overseen by various multinational military arrangements. The referendums to determine the shape of Germany's new borders with Poland – for example in the Allenstein and Marienwerder regions in 1920 and in Upper Silesia in the following year – were policed by British, French, and Italian contingents. In Silesia, the process was eventually placed under the full control of the League of Nations.[3] Following the evident success of these undertakings, a much more sophisticated League operation, involving a ten-nation multinational force, was planned for

[2] For an overview of the mandate system, see Michael D. Callahan, *Mandates and Empire* (Brighton: Sussex Academic Press, 2008).

[3] Alan James, *Peacekeeping in International Politics* (London: Macmillan, 1990), 27–32.

TABLE 11.1 *'Plebiscite Peacekeeping' in Europe, 1920–1935*[4]

Date	Region	Contending Actors	International Agency	Military Composition
1920	Schleswig	Germany, Denmark	PAAP	Britain, France
1920	Allenstein and Marienwerder	Germany, Poland	PAAP	Britain, France, Italy
1920	Klagenfurt Basin	Austria, Yugoslavia	PAAP	Britain, France, Italy, (Military Observers)
1921	Upper Silesia	Germany, Poland	PAAP superseded by League of Nations	Britain, France, Italy
1921	Vilna (Vilnius)	Poland, Lithuania	League of Nations	(Planned but not deployed) Belgium, Britain, Denmark, France, Greece, Italy, Netherlands, Norway, Spain, Sweden
1935	Saar	Germany, France (and League of Nations)	League of Nations	Britain, Italy, Netherlands, Sweden

Lithuania in 1921, although this plan was overtaken by events. Not all of these ventures were the primary responsibility of the League of Nations as an institution; some were carried out by the Principal Allied and Associated Powers (PAAP), the post-war victors acting as a collective. However, there was a general – and novel – consensus on the importance of the democratic element in territorial determination along with its international legitimization.

[4] A more detailed account of each of these plebiscite operations can be found in Norrie MacQueen, *Peacekeeping and the International System* (London: Routledge, 2006), 28–38.

The League of Nations undertaking that most obviously looked ahead to UN operations later in the century (and also into the next involved) the Saar territory on the Franco-German border between 1920 and 1935. Although the League's Saar involvement has received little attention from contemporary scholars of peacekeeping, it was a truly radical international departure.[5] Not only did the League become effectively the government of the Saar, it provided a carefully balanced and neutral multinational military force (composed of British, Dutch, Italian, and Swedish contingents) to supervise the tense and potentially violent period of the final plebiscite which determined the territory's return to German control. Remarkably, the plebiscite options were not restricted to a simple choice between German or French sovereignty; a third option was offered: the indefinite continuation of League of Nations government (a preference that gained about 10 per cent of the vote).[6]

The striking modernity of the Saar undertaking prefigured later multifunctional UN operations involving temporary executive authority such as those in Kosovo and East Timor/Timor-Leste in the post–Cold War period. Yet, as already noted, the Saar, along with the 'plebiscite peacekeeping' of the 1920s, has been largely overlooked by analysts of contemporary UN interventions. This apparent historical amnesia is, of course, part of a larger process of 'institutional forgetting' in the relationship between the two great global organizations of the twentieth century. The early UN tended to underplay, if not actively deny, the extent of its political and structural debt to the League of Nations system. After all, the 'failure' of the League had contributed to the world war that had brought the new UN into existence.

Yet a faint paper trail exists linking the new UN to the old discredited League in the early evolution of peacekeeping. For example, in a largely forgotten General Assembly document of January 1948, the UN Palestine Commission (which was then struggling with the consequences of Britain's relinquishment of the Palestine mandate) explored what it referred to as 'Precedents Concerning the Creation of an International Force'. The paper was designed 'to show that immediately after the First World

[5] Despite later neglect, the issue produced a wide range of contemporary accounts from differencing perspectives. Prominent among these were: Theodor Balk, *The Saar at First Hand* (London: Bodley Head, 1934); Michael T. Florinskey, *The Saar Struggle* (London: Macmillan, 1934); and Margaret Lambert, *The Saar* (London: Faber, 1934).

[6] On the organization of the international force, see F. P. Walters, *A History of the League of Nations* (Oxford University Press, 1960), 586–98. Walters was a senior member of the League Secretariat.

War ... it was possible to create international forces with a view toward assisting international commissions to fulfil the functions assigned to them' and to this end drew the General Assembly's attention to some of the missions we have just referred to.[7] However, this was a rare example of the UN acknowledging the potency of the precursors of peacekeeping in the League of Nations.

BIPOLARITY AND THE LIMITATIONS OF COLLECTIVE SECURITY

Beyond the models already established in the interwar years, the evolution of UN peacekeeping can also be traced to more immediate international conditions in the early post-war years. Put briefly, peacekeeping emerged as a UN activity in a space created by the failure of the organization's original – but politically unviable – ambition for a comprehensive system of global collective security.[8]

This larger aspiration was set out in Chapter VII (Articles 39–51) of the UN Charter dealing with 'Action with Respect to Threats to the Peace, Breaches of the Peace and Acts of Aggression'. Here responsibility for the UN's use of force in pursuit of international security was placed firmly in the hands of the five permanent members of the Security Council. The rest of the UN was required to provide them with whatever armed forces they might need in particular circumstances and undertook to do so by signing the Charter prior to becoming members.[9] Those requirements were to be assessed by a Military Staff Committee (MSC) composed of the chiefs of staff of the five permanent members and responsible to the Security Council. The MSC was then to direct UN operations, acting as a joint command.[10]

There was, of course, a fundamental problem with this process. Although the permanent members of the Security Council held a shared belief that the concentration of authority in their own hands was a good thing, they did not have anything resembling a shared view of the world,

[7] General Assembly document A/AC.21/W.18, 22 January 1948. Found at: http://unispal.un.org/UNISPAL.NSF/0/5C8A3A5D5F7129EE052566020045A8B3 (last accessed 13 December 2013).

[8] The most comprehensive account of the politics surrounding the construction of the Charter remains the now venerable one by Ruth Russell, *A History of the United Nations Charter: The Role of the United States, 1940 –1945* (Washington, DC: Brookings Institute, 1958).

[9] Charter of the United Nations, Articles 39 and 43.

[10] Ibid., Article 47.

a necessity if they were to exercise this power in any positive way. As the international system froze into bipolarity, conflicts, wherever in the world they occurred, were seen through the distinct ideological prisms of the opposing sides in the Cold War. The collective identification of 'aggression' requiring military intervention by the UN became utterly impossible. Aggressors and their victims would be defined according to ideological and diplomatic preference. With the power of veto available to each of the five permanently divided Security Council members, genuinely collective military enforcement by the UN became impossible.[11]

The inadequacy of these plans for 'conventional' military intervention was sharply exposed in 1950 with the outbreak of the Korean War. A Soviet boycott of the Security Council when the conflict began allowed the United States to co-opt the UN – or at least its name – to the Western side in the war. But the constitutional sleight of hand behind this was blatant and enhanced rather than diminished the perception of the failure of UN collective security.[12] Henceforward, the paralysis that the Cold War had imposed on the organization's ambitions was tacitly recognized. The UN would deploy military forces in various parts of the world during the rest of the Cold War, but these would be 'peacekeepers' and not enforcers of the collective will of the UN. Legally, the enforcement powers of Chapter VII of the Charter could have provided, in principle, a constitutional framework for humanitarian interventions, even in intra-state crises.[13] Yet in practical terms, the prospects for this were as distant as those for collective military action in the interstate conflicts which the chapter had been primarily designed to facilitate.

THE 1950S: PEACEKEEPING CONCEPTUALIZED

The UN had established something recognizable as a peacekeeping operation in 1948, shortly after its foundation, when it authorized a ceasefire

[11] The possibility of action by regional alliances within this framework was acknowledged, but only with the authority of the Security Council on a case-by-case basis. This question of the role of regional organizations would much later become an area of controversy for humanitarian intervention, for example in regard to NATO actions in Bosnia, Kosovo, and Libya. Ibid., Chapter VIII 'Regional Arrangements', Articles 52–3.

[12] See, in particular, Security Council resolutions S/RES/82(1950), 25 June 1950, and S/RES/84(1950), 7 July 1950. Found at: www.un.org/en/ga/search/view_doc.asp?symbol=S/RES/84(1950) (last accessed 13 December 2013).

[13] Although Article 2(7) of the Charter outlawed in principle UN intervention 'in matters which are essentially within the domestic jurisdiction of any state', it explicitly excluded 'the application of enforcement measures under Chapter VII' from this prohibition.

observation mission, the UN Military Observer Group in India and Pakistan (UNMOGIP), to oversee the agreement between India and Pakistan that ended the fighting over the disputed region of Kashmir.[14] Within weeks the UN had created a similar operation in the Middle East when international military observers were sent to the borders of the new state of Israel. This Truce Supervision Organization (UNTSO) was responsible for monitoring and reporting on the ceasefire agreed between Israel and the Arab states after the war that followed the declaration of establishment of the state of Israel.[15] The broader setting of both of these operations was not the Cold War as such, but the pressures placed on international regions by the process of decolonization (respectively, Britain's decolonization and simultaneous partition of India and the termination of its mandate for Palestine). This would remain a feature of UN peacekeeping operations in the 1950s and 1960s. However, as the polarization of world politics became ever more rigid during these years, the relationship between decolonization, regional instability, and the danger of Cold War 'infection' became ever more closely intertwined.

Initially these operations were regarded simply as *ad hoc* activities. The term 'peacekeeping' was not current and as yet there were too few operations to constitute a distinct 'project'. Soon though, both the Palestine and Kashmir operations would be encompassed by the new model of 'peacekeeping'. The catalyst for this conceptualization was the creation of the UN's first large-scale peacekeeping 'force', as opposed to a military observer mission. This came about in 1956 following the Anglo-French-Israeli attack on Egypt during the Suez Crisis. The United Nations Emergency Force (UNEF) took the idea of UN intervention by uniformed personnel much further than just military observation. UNEF involved an 'interposition' force that was more than 6,000-strong at its height, provided by ten UN member states. It was in place from November 1956 until the eve of the Six Day War in June 1967.[16] The initiative for

[14] The UN Military Observer Group in India and Pakistan (UNMOGIP) was initially authorized as a UN 'Commission' for the area by Security Council resolutions S/RES/30(1948), 30 January 1948, and S/RES/47(1948), 21 April 1948.

[15] The UN Truce Supervision Organization (UNTSO) was established by Security Council resolution S/RES/ 50(1948), 29 May 1948. Although authorized after the Kashmir operation, UNTSO military observers were deployed before those in the India–Pakistan conflict. Both operations remain in place up to the present.

[16] The Emergency Force was mandated by General Assembly resolution 1000 (First Emergency Session), 30 October 1956. Unusually, the operation was undertaken under the authority of the General Assembly rather than the Security Council.

this expansion of the UN's military role came from Secretary-General Dag Hammarskjöld, working closely with Lester Pearson, the foreign minister of Canada.

The broader lessons to be learned from the UNEF experience for the future of what was now emerging as a distinct peacekeeping project were drawn together by Hammarskjöld in 1958. These were then presented to the General Assembly in his *Summary Study of the Experience Derived from the Establishment of the United Nations Emergency Force*.[17] What were to become the defining characteristics of peacekeeping emerged from this document. These contrasted in virtually all significant aspects with the enforcement model of Chapter VII collective security. Enforcement required the identification and punishment of an 'aggressor'; peacekeeping, in contrast, followed the objective identification merely of a conflict. Enforcement action was designed to secure a military outcome; peacekeeping was concerned with neutral observation (as in the cases of UNTSO and UNMOGIP) or interposition (UNEF). Peacekeeping forces were drawn from states willing to provide contingents, while Chapter VII enforcement was, in principle, an obligation of UN membership (under the terms of Article 43 of the Charter). The peacekeepers themselves, in Hammarskjöld's view, should ideally come from small and middle-size powers rather than from big states whose presence might just further destabilize the situation into which a peacekeeping mission was deployed. From the *Summary Study* it is possible to distil what has been called the 'holy trinity' of peacekeeping characteristics: the consent of the 'host state', impartiality of the peacekeeping force, and use of force by the peacekeepers only in self-defence and as a last resort.

This conceptualization of peacekeeping was designed to navigate the UN through the reefs and sandbars of bipolarity while still permitting it to deploy military forces. Its fundamentally self-restricting character, however, pitched it against not just collective security by enforcement but also meaningful armed humanitarian intervention.

Despite the elaboration of peacekeeping as a distinct international activity in the *Summary Study*, its basis in international law remained opaque. Clearly, it was not the type of action envisaged by Chapter VII of the UN Charter; in a sense, peacekeeping emerged as a consequence of the *impossibility* of applying Chapter VII. Alternatively, Chapter VI, which deals with 'The Pacific Settlement of Disputes', might appear a more

[17] General Assembly document A/3943, 9 October 1958. Found at: www.un.org/depts/dhl/dag/docs/a3943e.pdf (last accessed 13 December 2013).

credible legal reference point, but the chapter made no reference to the use of military forces. From this situation there emerged an informal notion of peacekeeping as a 'chapter six-and-a-half' activity.[18] The legal basis of peacekeeping remained a contested area, however, and the debate intensified as the activity became increasingly complex in its objectives and multifunctional in its methods as it moved away from the classical model of interposition and observation.[19]

In addition to these severe operational limitations and the absence of a clear legal basis, the concept of peacekeeping as it emerged in the UN in the 1950s suffered a further severe impediment as a vehicle for humanitarian intervention: it was assumed to be appropriate in interstate and not in intra-state conflicts. In other words, peacekeeping interventions were primarily designed to keep the peace between the 'legitimate' forces of sovereign states in conflict with each other. Any 'civil' role would have placed it *prima facie* in conflict with the UN Charter's prohibition on intervention within states other than in the case of – the now redundant – Chapter VII arrangements. In short, the essential requirements for armed humanitarian intervention appeared to be withheld by self-denying ordinance on the part of the UN. These carefully constructed limits to peacekeeping, designed to evade the prohibitions of the Cold War, were soon to collide with the realities of humanitarian need.

Two UN interventions in the early 1960s, in the former Belgian Congo and in West New Guinea, illustrated these problems particularly clearly. In both operations the idealized peacekeeping model elaborated in the 1950s was severely tested and its limitations as a vehicle for effective humanitarian intervention became evident.

THE CONGO EXPERIENCE: PROBING THE BORDERS OF ENFORCEMENT

Known as ONUC, an abbreviation of its French name Opération des Nations Unies au Congo, the UN intervention in the vast former Belgian colony began in July 1960, just weeks after the country's independence. The operation remained in place until June 1964 and was by far the

[18] This expression is often attributed to Hammarskjöld himself, though there appears to be no clear evidence for this.

[19] For a concise discussion of Charter law concerning peacekeeping, see Alex J. Bellamy and Paul D. Williams, *Understanding Peacekeeping*, 2nd edn (Cambridge: Polity, 2010), 47–56.

largest UN peacekeeping venture up to that point (and for many years to come). At its height, it deployed almost 20,000 troops from twenty-eight UN member states.

Initially, ONUC was mandated as an interstate operation safely within the limitations of the Hammarskjöldian peacekeeping model. The original request for UN intervention (which provided the necessary 'consent') came from the new government of the Congo. Almost from the outset though the operation faced a raft of challenges which tested the key assumptions of the peacekeeping model itself. The Congo involved an 'interstate' crisis only in the formal terms of ONUC's initial mandate. The government requested a UN presence to be interposed between Congolese national forces and a Belgian military intervention provoked by an apparent breakdown of order following an army mutiny. The problem, according to the Congolese prime minister Patrice Lumumba and the president Joseph Kasavubu, was 'Belgian aggression'. Their joint telegram to Hammarskjöld requesting UN intervention asserted that the 'essential purpose of the requested military aid [was] to protect the national territory of Congo against the present external aggression which is a threat to international peace'.[20] The initial Security Council mandate for the operation reflected this,[21] but the dynamics of the crisis quickly saw ONUC confronting a multifactional civil conflict as well as a major crisis of secession. In these circumstances 'interposition' was meaningless. The principle of host state consent also soon became irrelevant when control of the state itself became uncertain. The Congo crisis therefore raised fundamental questions about Hammarskjöld's vision of peacekeeping as an alternative to goal-directed intervention. Virtually from its initial deployment, ONUC proved unequal to this political and humanitarian crisis in a country encompassing 2.3 million square kilometres and about 250 separate ethnic groups.

The extent and the rapid pace of the conflict in which UN forces found themselves became evident in the first weeks of the operation. Immediately following Congo's independence on 30 June, order had been threatened by parties and ethnic groups who felt excluded from power in the new state. On 4 July, the army mutiny began in the capital

[20] Telegrams dated 12 and 13 July 1960 from the President and the Prime Minister of the Republic of the Congo to the Secretary-General, Security Council document S/4382, 13 July 1960. Security Council Official Records Fifteenth Year, Supplement for July, August and September 1960, document S/4382.

[21] ONUC's 'first' mandate was given by Security Council resolution S/RES/143(1960), 14 July 1960. This was passed 8:0 with China, France, and Britain abstaining.

Léopoldville and quickly spread across the country. European residents were a particular target; murder and rape became widespread, and a white exodus began. Belgian forces (which were still stationed in the country by agreement) intervened; soon there were about 10,000 European troops confronting local forces. This provided the basis of the supposed 'international' conflict which justified UN intervention.

Amidst the chaos elsewhere, the situation in the mineral-rich and relatively developed province of Katanga was brought under control comparatively quickly. This however merely set the scene for a further, critical twist in the Congo crisis. The strongly European-influenced provincial-level administration of Moise Tshombe, backed by external mining and financial interests, now declared its independence. Thus, within two weeks of gaining statehood, the Congo presented the UN with a complex humanitarian crisis. It was a crisis within which a traditionally configured peacekeeping operation was essentially irrelevant.

The original international dimension to the conflict – the presence of Belgian forces in the country – was in fact largely resolved by mid-September 1960, by which time the troops had either been withdrawn or stood down. Yet in that same month, the central government effectively imploded as long-standing personal and ideological tensions burst to the surface between Lumumba and Kasavubu (who were, in loose diplomatic terms, anti- and pro-Western, respectively). A constitutional crisis resulted with each man claiming to have dismissed the other.[22] Simultaneously, the UN found itself entangled in a situation of contested legitimacy in Katanga, in which secession was supported by influential sections within the Western alliance but bitterly opposed by the Eastern bloc and most of the then emerging postcolonial world. In the meantime, the original 'host state', which had been the source of the 'consent' to the intervention required by the Hammarskjöldian model, had entirely disintegrated. In military terms, the Katanga situation was further complicated for the UN by the continued presence of around 200 Belgian soldiers after the withdrawal of their counterparts elsewhere in the territory.[23] Pressure on the UN operation to adopt an enforcement stance, both in respect of challenges to its authority within the country as a whole and specifically

[22] Published in the immediate aftermath of the crisis, the most thorough and insightful analysis of the tangled narrative of the Congo at this time remains that by Catherine Hoskyns, *The Congo Since Independence, January 1960–December 1961* (Oxford University Press, 1965).

[23] Alan James, *The Politics of Peacekeeping* (London: Chatto and Windus, 1969), 357.

in order to end the secession of Katanga, was growing by the day. In other words, each of the three elements of peacekeeping's 'holy trinity' – consent, neutrality, and the use of force only in self-defence – was being tested to destruction.

The response of the UN in the period that followed was to make successive adjustments of mandate, each of which took ONUC ever further from Hammarskjöldian peacekeeping and ever closer to an approach recognizable as armed 'humanitarian intervention'. The first of these shifts came in February 1961. This followed the abduction, forced transfer to Katanga, and murder of Patrice Lumumba, who, since losing the power struggle with Kasavubu, was supposed to be under the formal protection of ONUC. The fury with which this development was met by most of the nations in the Afro-Asian group at the UN and by the Soviet bloc galvanized Hammarskjöld and the Security Council to direct ONUC towards a greater degree of active intervention and away from the interposition model.[24] A new resolution now authorized the force to 'take immediately all appropriate measures to prevent the occurrence of civil war in Congo, including arrangements for cease-fires, the halting of all military operations, the prevention of clashes *and the use of force, if necessary, in the last resort*' (emphasis added).[25]

In a very real sense this was an historic resolution; for the first time in the UN's history, forces directly under its control were authorized to use force to achieve a set purpose. At least two of the elements of the 'holy trinity' had now been formally abandoned as the UN wavered on the critical frontier between peacekeeping and enforcement.

Although the new February 1961 mandate was robust in its acceptance of the use of force by UN personnel to achieve specific ends, it remained unclear whether it specifically authorized ONUC to end the secession of Katanga. In truth, had the draft been explicit in setting this as a UN objective, it would almost certainly have been vetoed by France and possibly Britain as well, both of which remained ambivalent on the issue of Katangese 'independence'. Hammarskjöld himself was, perhaps understandably, anxious not to depart too far from the traditional peacekeeping approach of which he had been, after all, the major architect. In the

[24] A detailed account of the Congo within the politics of the UN at this time can be found in Evan Luard, *A History of the United Nations*, vol. II: *The Years of Decolonisation, 1955–65* (London: Macmillan, 1989), 217–316.

[25] Security Council resolution S/RES161(1961), 21 February 1961. Found at: www.un.org/en/ga/search/view_doc.asp?symbol=S/RES/161(1961) (last accessed 13 December 2013). The Soviet Union and France abstained in the vote.

meantime, beyond Katanga, the situation across the huge country remained volatile. This of course was the essence of the UN's dilemma: there was no peace for peacekeepers to keep in the Congo.

The uncertainty over the degree of force that could be used by the UN was reflected in the actions of its officials on the ground. It would also lead, indirectly, to Hammarskjöld's death. Two inconclusive assaults by UN forces in Katanga directed by his representative there (the Irish diplomat Conor Cruise O'Brien) prompted Hammarskjöld to travel to Africa in September 1961 for crisis talks with the province's leaders.[26] In the course of his journey, his aircraft crashed in the British colony of Northern Rhodesia (Zambia) just across the Congo border, killing all on board.[27]

This new development brought a further shift in the tectonic plates of the conflict. Significantly, Hammarskjöld's successor as acting Secretary-General was from the postcolonial Afro-Asian world: U Thant of Burma. On one side of the Cold War divide, the Soviet Union was now constrained in its attacks on the UN over Congo – which it had pursued ferociously when Hammarskjöld had been in charge – in the broader interests of its diplomacy towards the postcolonial world. On the other side, France and Britain appeared, after the death of Hammarskjöld, to become aware of their increasing isolation on the Katanga issue within the UN as a whole. This realization was encouraged by the arrival of the Kennedy administration in the White House. The new US president was much more questioning than his predecessor towards standard 'Western' positions on Africa. Two months after Hammarskjöld's death, therefore, ONUC was given a 'third' mandate. This was even more robust than the February resolution that had first authorized the use of force. Now the

[26] Whether or not Hammarskjöld himself had approved such aggressive enforcement action by ONUC immediately became mired in controversy. O'Brien himself insisted that he was acting with full authorization. He makes his claim in his own account of the affair, *To Katanga and Back: A UN Case History* (London: Hutchinson, 1962). Hammarskjöld's biographer and UN official at the time, Brian Urquhart, argued that O'Brien acted without the knowledge of the Secretary-General. See his book *Hammarskjold* (London: The Bodley Head, 1973), 545–81.

[27] Controversy surrounded the circumstances of Hammarskjöld's death from the outset. There were claims that his plane was deliberately brought down either by a bomb on board or by enemy fire from the ground or the air (the Katangan secessionists deployed a small air force of French-made fighters). The weight of opinion lent towards the likelihood of an accident. In 2011, however, a closely researched and strongly argued book revived the assassination theory: Susan Williams, *Who Killed Hammarskjöld: The UN, the Cold War and White Supremacy in Africa* (London: Hurst, 2011).

secession of Katanga was explicitly condemned by the Security Council and ONUC was authorized 'to take vigorous action, including the use of the requisite measure of force' to detain and deport the ragbag of white mercenaries and Belgian officers that formed the backbone of Katanga's forces. The new resolution was much less ambiguous than its predecessor, declaring that 'all secessionist activities against the Republic of the Congo are contrary to ... Security Council decisions and [must] cease forthwith'.[28]

It would be another year before the UN made effective use of its new powers for forceful intervention. However, in December 1962, following a higher-than-usual level of provocation against UN personnel by foreign elements in Katanga, ONUC acted decisively. In the appropriately code-named 'Operation Grand Slam', the UN employed its ground forces along with extensive air power (involving Swedish and Ethiopian fighter squadrons and Indian bombers) to destroy completely the capacity of Katanga to resist reincorporation in the Congo republic. Within a few weeks the secession ended.[29]

This projection of international force, though long delayed, finally resolved the immobilizing tangle of interventionist thinking between traditional peacekeeping and its antithesis, namely goal-directed armed action. Yet, as is plain from even the most cursory survey of the Congo's subsequent history, this more muscular UN action did nothing to resolve the country's longer-term political and humanitarian problems.[30] Four decades later, UN forces would return to the Congo where, interestingly, they would once again find themselves positioned uncomfortably between the competing roles of traditional peacekeeping and armed humanitarian intervention. In 1999, following the effective collapse of the Congolese state amidst the regional war triggered by the Rwandan genocide of 1994, the Security Council mandated a new large-scale operation, the UN Mission in the Democratic Republic of Congo (MONUC, which became known in 2010 as the 'UN Stabilization Mission' or MONUSCO).[31] While these interventions were originally configured as traditional

[28] Security Council resolution S/RES/169(1961), 24 November 1961. Found at: www.un.org/en/ga/search/view_doc.asp?symbol=S/RES/169(1961) (last accessed 13 December 2013). The resolution was passed 9:0 with France and UK abstaining.

[29] See Michael Harbottle, *The Blue Berets* (London: Leo Cooper, 1975), 69–70.

[30] See Michael W. Doyle and Nicholas Samabanis, *Making War and Building Peace: United Nations Peace Operations* (Princeton University Press, 2006), 179.

[31] MONUC was established by Security Council resolution S/RES/1279(1999), 30 November 1999, and MONUSCO by A/RES/1925(2010), 28 May 2010.

peacekeeping operations, the complexity of this later Congo crisis and the logic of external intervention in it rendered this approach more or less irrelevant. As in the early 1960s, the UN mission crept towards enforcement (now involving the use of helicopter gunships against anti-government forces rather than fighter-bombers).[32] Once again, decades on, the UN's experience in the Congo highlighted the limitations of Hammarskjöld's carefully elaborated peacekeeping model.

WEST NEW GUINEA: THE VARIABLE MORALITY OF INTERVENTION

Nested within the timeframe of the Congo operation, a second UN intervention began and ended in another part of the postcolonial world. Of much shorter duration than ONUC – it lasted only from October 1962 to May 1963 – the United Nations Temporary Executive Authority (UNTEA) and its subordinate United Nations Security Force (UNSF) in West New Guinea nevertheless took the organization into equally new and challenging territory. This intervention prefigured the UN's later role in assuming temporary governmental control in contested territories in the post–Cold War world. In both Kosovo and East Timor, UN administrations followed armed humanitarian interventions (by NATO and by an Australian-led 'coalition of the willing', respectively). In contrast, the West New Guinea operation also harked back to the aforementioned role of the League of Nations in the Saar. This type of venture constitutes what might be seen as the most radical form of international intervention: nothing less than the assertion of sovereign power in the area in question. However, the outcome in West New Guinea raised important questions that could and should be put to the UN about the purposes of its intervention in the shifting mores of international politics. The involvement in West New Guinea pointed up an uncomfortable truth: not all peacekeeping interventions by the UN, even when 'successful', need necessarily be 'humanitarian' in outcome.

Historically, West New Guinea ('Irian Jaya' in Bahasa Indonesia) had been located at the eastern edge of the Dutch East Indies. With the creation of Indonesia after the Second World War, the Netherlands insisted on retaining this part of its old empire on the grounds that it was culturally, politically, and economically in a different condition than

32 The UN's own account of MONUSCO and its enforcement actions can be found at http://monusco.unmissions.org/ (last accessed 13 December 2013).

the other components of the new independent state and that West New Guinea's ethnically distinct Papuan Melanesian population required extended colonial 'mentoring' in preparation for a separate independence. This position was, of course, consistent with the principles underlying the mandate and trusteeship philosophies of the League and the UN, respectively. However, it was not acceptable to President Sukarno's radical nationalist regime in the new Indonesia. The result was protracted diplomatic conflict which by the beginning of the 1960s had escalated to involve Indonesian military infiltration into the territory and clashes with the Dutch colonial forces.[33]

Although overshadowed by events in the Congo, the situation in West New Guinea was nevertheless serious by 1962, and in that year American pressure and mediation produced a general agreement by the Netherlands to relinquish the territory.[34] Amidst the realities of world politics at the beginning of the 1960s, the Dutch position had simply become untenable. The influx of new Afro-Asian members to the General Assembly as a result of the surge of decolonization at the time meant that the prevailing culture in the UN – and throughout much of the world – was strongly anti-imperialist. In this environment, Western states were anxious not to compromise their tenuous standing with this new power bloc in the face of the challenge posed by the Soviet Union's anti-colonialist and internationalist rhetoric. If the logic of this Western position required the diplomatic abandonment of one of their own, then that was a price that had to be paid.

According to the American-brokered agreement, sovereignty over West New Guinea was to be transferred initially from the Netherlands to the UN. The Temporary Executive Authority would administer the territory on behalf of the UN for a transitional period, after which power would be transferred to Indonesia.[35] The UN's role in the process was managed personally by Secretary-General Thant with the support of the

[33] On Indonesia's post-independence relations with the Netherlands, see Stephen Drakeley, *The History of Indonesia* (Westport, Conn.: Greenwood Press, 2005); Donald W. Fryer and James L. Jackson, *Indonesia* (London: Benn, 1977).

[34] The text of this 'Agreement between the Republic of Indonesia and the Kingdom of the Netherlands Concerning West New Guinea' can be found in Rosalyn Higgins, *United Nations Peacekeeping 1946–67: Documents and Commentary*, vol. II: *Asia* (Oxford University Press, 1970), 101–6.

[35] The General Assembly ratified the role assigned to the UN in the Dutch-Indonesian agreement in General Assembly resolution 1752 (XVII), 21 September 1962. This authorized 'the Secretary-General to carry out the tasks entrusted to him in the Agreement'.

General Assembly. Interestingly, the Security Council had no direct involvement. This arrangement indicated how Thant's standing contrasted with that of Hammarskjöld and had thereby already changed the international dynamics of the Congo crisis. It would have been inconceivable for the Soviet Union to give such latitude to Hammarskjöld, who had become deeply distrusted in Moscow. Thant however represented, in a sense, the emerging Afro-Asian bloc and was not to be thwarted.[36]

UNTEA would have its own security force (UNSF), composed of 1,500 military personnel provided almost entirely by Pakistan. UNSF performed the traditional peacekeeping function of monitoring the ceasefire between Indonesian and Dutch forces pending the withdrawal of the latter. Its more significant role was as the quasi-national military force of the transitional 'UN state' of West New Guinea. The iconography of the arrangement was carefully constructed: the UN flag flew beside that of the Netherlands over official buildings until 31 December 1962, after which the UN and the Indonesian flags would fly together until the final transfer of sovereignty. Then, a so-called 'act of free choice' – the precise form of which remained 'constructively' undefined – was to be overseen by the UN. This was to take place before the end of 1969 and was to determine definitively the wishes of the indigenous Papuan people for their long-term political future.[37]

The period of UN administration in West New Guinea passed with only isolated incidents of political violence. Under Indonesian pressure, the transfer of power took place ahead of schedule in May 1963, and Irian Jaya was absorbed as a new province of the Republic of Indonesia. Ostensibly, this far-reaching UN intervention was completely successful. In reality, the West New Guinea operation saw UN power and authority directed at goals which were, to say the least, morally questionable. The aftermath of the transfer of power validated the claims of those, the Dutch government among them, who feared the human consequences of West New Guinea's annexation by Indonesia. The territory became subject to Indonesia's internal migration programme, which brought wholesale population transfers to Irian Jaya from the more crowded parts of the national archipelago. As a result, the alienation of land from its traditional owners became widespread. Simultaneously, the territory's vast

[36] The moral and humanitarian basis of the venture was in fact questioned in the General Assembly by a number of newly independent Francophone African states, twelve of which abstained on Resolution 1752 along with Haiti and France itself.

[37] For a relatively recent background study on the legal basis of the UN intervention, see Daniel Gruss, 'UNTEA and West New Guinea' in A. Von Bogdandy and R. Wolfrum (eds.), *Max Planck Yearbook of United Nations Law* (2005), vol. IX, 97–126.

mineral potential was exploited by companies that had been licensed by the Indonesian government in the interests of the (non-Papuan) Indonesian elite and that worked hand in hand with multinational mining companies. Over the following decades, Papuan nationalist agitation, at times involving armed conflict, was ruthlessly suppressed by the Indonesian military.[38]

In 1969, Indonesia, after considerable prevarication, arranged the 'act of free choice' required under the terms of the 1962 agreement. Despite UN supervision, the process was deeply flawed. It involved merely a 'consultation' among government-controlled 'representative councils', which voted unanimously to maintain West New Guinea as a province of Indonesia, just as the regime (now under Sukarno's successor, the military strongman General Suharto) had planned. The UN approved the process, perhaps in view of the huge implications of any other course of action.

In other words, UN interventions during the Cold War did not always immediately serve humanitarian and 'moral' causes. The intervention in West New Guinea was a demonstration that the use of UN power could be as pragmatic as that of any sovereign state pursuing its interests in the international system. A defence of the UN position could be offered on the basis that pragmatism itself has a long-term 'humanitarian' function. In this view, the primary objective of UN intervention is to stabilize relations between states in order to prevent armed conflict, even if the making of this particular 'Westphalian' omelette can only be achieved by occasionally breaking some local humanitarian eggs. The consequences of reopening the entire issue of West New Guinea's international status would indeed have been enormous. There would have been a clear danger of widespread violence both by and against Indonesia. Yet the result of UN action and inaction from 1962 onwards had been to deny the people of West New Guinea the opportunity of genuine self-determination, in plain breach of the UN's own Charter.

BEYOND THE HAMMARSKJÖLDIAN MODEL: A GOOD PLACE TO BE?

The Congo operation demonstrated the *limitations* of the peacekeeping model when the only prospect of progress towards peace required a more

[38] A detailed analysis of the West New Guinea crisis (though a fundamentally anti-Indonesian one) is provided by John Saltford, *The United Nations and the Indonesian Takeover of West Papua, 1962–1969: The Anatomy of a Betrayal* (London: Routledge, 2002).

robust form of intervention. The case of West New Guinea highlighted the dangers inherent in going *beyond* the peacekeeping model by putting UN intervention at the service of contested state interests.

Fortunately, perhaps, challenges to the underlying principles and objectives of UN interventions of those types did not reappear during the remainder of the Cold War. Subsequent peacekeeping operations in the 1960s and 1970s saw a reversion to the minimalist model of observation and interposition. In 1964, another large UN force was deployed, this time to Cyprus. Although the conflict there was an intra-state one rather than directly international in nature and despite widespread apprehensions about 'another Congo' at the outset, the operational characteristics of the UN Force in Cyprus (UNFICYP) stayed comfortably within the criteria of classical peacekeeping.[39] Similarly, the UN operations between Israel and Egypt in Sinai, and Israel and Syria in the Golan Heights after the 1973 Middle East war (the Second UN Emergency Force and the UN Disengagement Observer Force, respectively), provided classic buffer forces that were free from any threat of the 'mission creep' of the Congo operation. The UN Interim Force in Lebanon (UNIFIL), deployed in 1978, had a potentially more problematic mandate, one similar to the original tasks set for the UN in the Congo.[40] On the ground, however, the force's actions were closely circumscribed by the web of regional and global interests involved in Lebanon.

After the establishment of the Lebanon force there was a period of dormancy in UN interventions. This coincided with the unravelling of détente and a consequent wariness on the part of the superpowers towards multilateral interventions they could not fully control.[41] No new UN operations would be authorized until 1989, when the Cold War was already ending. Then, suddenly, the capacity of the UN to intervene in the plethora of conflicts that ignited in the new post-bipolar world order was stretched to the limit. Most of these new post–Cold War

[39] For a careful and detailed account of the background to the UN intervention, see Alan James, *Keeping the Peace in the Cyprus Crisis of 1964* (London, 2002).

[40] UNIFIL was to confirm 'the withdrawal of Israeli forces, [restore] international peace and security and [assist] the Government of Lebanon in ensuring the return of its effective authority'. Security Council resolution S/RES/425(1978), 19 March 1978. Found at: www.un.org/en/ga/search/view_doc.asp?symbol=S/RES/425(1978) (last accessed 13 December 2013).

[41] New non-UN multinational interventions were mounted during this period – for example, in Sinai and Lebanon – but these were purely Western in conception and composition. See Norrie MacQueen, *The United Nations, Peace Operations and the Cold War*, 2nd edn (London: Longman Pearson, 2011), 86–9.

conflicts were intra-state in nature and confronted the UN once again with the problems inherent in the traditional peacekeeping model. Interventions from Bosnia to Somalia to Rwanda faced this fundamental identity crisis, which had first become evident in Congo decades before.[42]

By the end of the 1990s, the dilemma appeared to have been resolved to some extent. The UN had simply removed itself from the dangerous borderlands between peacekeeping and armed humanitarian intervention. In a sense, the UN retreated to the minimalist approach of the 'classical' period of peacekeeping. Coercive interventions had now become the responsibility not of the UN directly but of other agencies acting with UN authorization and legitimization. This development appeared to begin in the later phase of the Bosnian war. After the UN's failure to prevent the Srebrenica massacre in 1995, NATO (which had already been present in the war theatre in a dual key arrangement with the UN) moved decisively to the foreground and effectively imposed an outcome to the conflict through the revealingly named 'Operation Deliberate Force'.[43] Four years later, in 1999, NATO acted first and sought UN legitimization only retrospectively when it intervened against Serbia in Kosovo. Later that same year, an Australian-led 'coalition of the willing' brought an end to the violence in East Timor and created the conditions for the resumption of a more traditional form of peacekeeping there by the UN.[44] Events in Sierra Leone in 2000, where there was a British intervention parallel with but separate from a continuing UN operation, and in Libya in 2011, where NATO action was authorized by a Security Council resolution, were further examples of this 'multi-agency' approach to intervention, which permitted the UN to stay within the safer hinterland of traditional peacekeeping.

In some ways, this double-layered approach to humanitarian intervention is an ungainly model, but in general terms it has been effective in

[42] This 'new peacekeeping' of the 1990s is explored in Bellamy and Williams, *Understanding Peacekeeping*, 93–120.

[43] On the insurmountable challenges facing UN 'peacekeeping' in Bosnia, see Spyros Economides and Paul Taylor, 'Former Yugoslavia' in Mats Berdal and Spyros Economides (eds.), *United Nations Interventionism, 1991–2004* (Cambridge University Press, 2007), 65–107.

[44] The Australian led enforcement operation, the International Force in East Timor (INTERFET), was deployed in September 1999 and then supplanted the following year after the situation was stabilized by the military component of the United Nations Transitional Administration in East Timor (UNTAET). See Ian Martin and Alexander Mayer-Rieckh, 'The United Nations and East Timor: From Self-determination to State-Building', *International Peacekeeping*, 12, no. 1(2005), 125–45. On East Timor see also Chapter 13 by Bradley Simpson in this book.

most cases. The continued authority of the UN under international law is implicit in the 'requirement' for Security Council authorization for these ventures. The approach skirts round the continued absence, even after the end of the Cold War, of sufficient Security Council consensus to permit full-scale Chapter VII enforcement directly by the UN itself. The international politics of the Syrian crisis during 2013 re-emphasized this reality. The inter-agency approach acknowledges the legitimacy – and potential value – of regional special interests (whether NATO in the Balkans and the Mediterranean or Australia in the Asia-Pacific area). Finally, it permits the UN to maintain a peacekeeping role of its own that is still based on the general principles of consent, impartiality, and the use of force only for self-defence as set out by Dag Hammarskjöld in the 1950s. In the 1950s, this contemporary joint approach was simply not available. During the Cold War there was no prospect of Security Council authorization of such arms-length interventions by regional agencies. This resulted in the destructive confusion around peacekeeping operations in the Congo and elsewhere, which at times pulled the UN itself towards existential crisis.

12

From the protection of sovereignty to humanitarian intervention? *Traditions and developments of United Nations Peacekeeping in the twentieth century*

Jan Erik Schulte

After the end of the Cold War, various military interventions were undertaken to protect the civilian population during times of armed conflict and to facilitate the distribution of humanitarian aid. Especially the operations in the Balkans and in Somalia, which are generally seen as disastrous failures, and the highly controversial Kosovo air campaign in 1999 sparked a debate about the function and legitimization of 'humanitarian intervention' that is still under way today.[1]

Within this debate, historical examples are used to underline the rightfulness and necessity of humanitarian intervention, or they are portrayed as prototypes that have only become fully developed in the present. It was not until recently that historical research entered this debate. Research started to discuss continuities and shed light on early forms of humanitarian intervention. Depending on its scope of investigation, historical research regularly traces lines of development at least as far back as the early modern period.[2]

While the modern discourse on humanitarian intervention obviously includes the UN, it widely disregards the organization's major military organ, the Blue Helmets. Most studies simply do not discuss a possible relationship between Cold War peacekeeping and humanitarian

[1] *The Responsibility to Protect.* Report of the International Commission on Intervention and State Sovereignty, published by the International Development Research Centre, Ottawa, December 2001, 1–2; D. M. Malone and K. Wermester, 'Boom and Bust? The Changing Nature of UN Peacekeeping', *International Peacekeeping*, 7, no. 4 (2000), 37–54, here 49; T. B. Seybolt, *Humanitarian Military Intervention: The Conditions for Success and Failure* (Oxford University Press, 2007), 1–15.

[2] See Chapter 1 by Fabian Klose in this book.

intervention. The one notable exception to this limited approach ignoring UN peacekeeping is Norrie MacQueen's book *Humanitarian Intervention and the United Nations*, published in 2011.[3]

If, however, a meaningful history of humanitarian intervention intends to discuss precedents and continuities, then the development of UN peacekeeping has to be included. It is in this context that the following four major theses will be discussed.

1. Although there has been no linear development in UN peacekeeping, its operations during the Cold War present a major precondition for the genesis of the concept and the practice of humanitarian intervention since the 1990s.
2. The changes in UN peacekeeping and the development of the complex and multidimensional missions of the 1990s were gradual. Sovereignty was neither sacrosanct – not even before 1989 – nor effectively given up.
3. The motives and practices of traditional troop providers, such as Canada, reveal that there was an opportunity for robust humanitarian intervention even under the UN flag.
4. In reality, however, large-scale armed humanitarian interventions have been undertaken only on behalf, but not under the control, of the UN. Even after the end of the Cold War, the only surviving superpower – the United States – and the only surviving powerful military organization – NATO – were both unwilling to delegate their supreme military power.

PROBLEMS OF DEFINING PEACEKEEPING AND HUMANITARIAN INTERVENTION

Before beginning with the historical analysis of UN peacekeeping, it is necessary to discuss the scope of the term 'humanitarian intervention' as well as the current understanding of the term 'peacekeeping'. It seems that the failure to include the Blue Helmets in the narrative of humanitarian intervention is a direct result of a largely ahistorical use of terminology. Currently, several schematic classifications exist that divide the history of UN peacekeeping into several phases. They all see 1989/90 as a dividing point. The UN missions conceived in the preceding period of roughly

[3] N. MacQueen, *Humanitarian Intervention and the United Nations* (Edinburgh University Press, 2011). See also Chapter 11 by Norrie MacQueen in this book.

forty years tend to be called 'first-generation peacekeeping' or more often 'classical peacekeeping'. These terms suggest that the operations of the Cold War period were more or less identical and non-confrontational.[4] This picture is not entirely incorrect. However, it provides no leeway for a nuanced analysis that takes into account the different characters of the various UN missions. Consequently, we need to bypass these homogenizing descriptions in order to recognize and evaluate the various traditions that extended beyond 1989/90.[5]

In 1958, Secretary-General Dag Hammarskjöld produced a paper in which he reflected upon the first large-scale peacekeeping operation of the UN. In so doing, he devised what eventually was heralded as the major principles of traditional peacekeeping: consent, neutrality, and the use of force only in self-defence. Hammarskjöld's paper marks an important moment in the history of UN peacekeeping, but it did not become its blueprint. It simply provided some guidelines, which were then followed rhetorically more often than practically.[6]

While the definition of 'classical peacekeeping' is too narrow, that of 'humanitarian intervention' can be either narrowed even further or expanded to the point that it becomes very broad and imprecise.[7] For the purpose of our argument, let us turn to a more narrow definition by Ramesh Thakur, a former commissioner on the International Commission on Intervention and State Sovereignty, as found in the *Oxford*

[4] S. Gareis and J. Varwick, *Die Vereinten Nationen: Aufgaben, Instrumente und Reformen*, 4th edn (Bonn: Bundeszentrale für politische Bildung, 2007) 118–21; M. W. Doyle and N. Sambarnis, 'Peacekeeping Operations' in T. G. Weiss and S. Daws (eds.), *The Oxford Handbook on the United Nations* (Oxford University Press, 2008), 322–48, here 324–34. For a detailed discussion of 'traditional peacekeeping', see P. F. Diehl, *International Peacekeeping* (Baltimore and London: The John Hopkins University Press, 1994), 4–14. An official definition provides UN Department of Peacekeeping Operations, *United Nations Peacekeeping Operations: Principles and Guidelines* (New York: United Nations, 2008), 17–18.

[5] For an approach that does not see any real continuity between Cold War and post–Cold War peacekeeping, see F. H. Fleitz, Jr., *Peacekeeping Fiascoes of the 1990s: Causes, Solutions, and U.S. Interests* (Westport, CT and London: Praeger, 2002), 8–10.

[6] It should be borne in mind that the report was to comfort potential troop providers in making stand-by arrangements for UN purposes. Furthermore, the various topics were open for discussion. Contrary to the report, less than two years later UN peacekeepers were in the Congo 'employed … in situations of an essentially internal nature'. See 'Summary Study by the Secretary-General, 9 October 1958' in R. C. R. Siekmann (ed.), *Basic Documents on United Nations and Related Peace-keeping Forces* (Dortrecht: Martinus Nijhoff Publishers, 1985), 50–5, here 52.

[7] J. M. Welsh, 'Introduction' in J. M. Welsh (ed.), *Humanitarian Intervention and International Relations* (Oxford University Press, 2006), 1–7, here 3.

Handbook on the United Nations. He sees humanitarian intervention as 'the use of military force on the territory of a state without its consent with the goal of protecting innocent victims of large scale atrocities'.[8] A similar definition is given by J. L. Holzgrefe and others.[9] However, since Thakur's definition still appears to be somewhat more compact, it will serve as the starting point for the following discussion.

The four parameters of Thakur's description of humanitarian intervention seem to be clear: first, the site of humanitarian intervention is a foreign state; second, the sovereignty of the state has to be violated without its consent; third, the intervention is a military one; fourth, its goal is to rescue 'innocent' victims of large-scale acts of violence.

While the first point is uncontested, the problem begins with point two. Admittedly, a certain amount of compulsion or pressure seems to be a necessary ingredient, but the scope and nature of this pressure are difficult to define. Furthermore, in contrast to point three of Thakur's definition, the intervention does not have to be military in all cases. For example, a state could give in and accept humanitarian intervention as a result of escalating forms of diplomatic pressure. It is interesting that Holzgrefe, for example, includes the 'threat to use force' in his definition of humanitarian intervention but explicitly excludes diplomatic pressure.[10] Finally, contrary to point four, humanitarian interventions do not only deal with large-scale atrocities. Humanitarian interventions might tackle human rights violations in general, or, on a much larger but more imprecise scale, they might be used to topple tyrannical regimes.[11]

Our final point refers to the major goal of the action. This, however, is not easy to analyse. Humanitarian intervention is more than a legal concept or a mode of description. It appears as a moral norm and is used as a political argument. The rhetoric of humanitarian intervention certainly does not always reveal the true nature of the military endeavour.

[8] R. Thakur, 'Humanitarian Intervention' in T. G. Weiss and S. Daws (eds.), *The Oxford Handbook on the United Nations* (Oxford University Press, 2008), 387–403, here 388.

[9] J. L. Holzgrefe, 'The Humanitarian Intervention Debate' in J. L. Holzgrefe and R. O. Keohane (eds.), *Humanitarian Intervention: Ethical, Legal, and Political Dilemmas*, 3rd edn (Cambridge University Press, 2004) 15–52, here 18.

[10] Holzgrefe, 'Humanitarian Intervention Debate', 18.

[11] F. K. Abiew, *The Evolution of the Doctrine and Practice of Humanitarian Intervention* (The Hague: Kluwer Law International, 1999), 31–2; B. Simms and D. J. B. Trim, 'Towards a History of Humanitarian Intervention' in B. Simms and D. J. B. Trim (eds.), *Humanitarian Intervention: A History* (Cambridge University Press, 2011), 1–24, here 2–7; *The Responsibility to Protect*, 8.

The labelling of an intervention as humanitarian helps legitimize the breach of state sovereignty and violent action in general.[12]

In order to evaluate military intervention and classify it as being humanitarian, it is important to find a way to evaluate the goals. What is the role of the contemporary rhetoric used by the actors? What are the true and underlying motives? What is the relative importance of various motives? Finally, what are the results of the intervention? Because of the problems that have surfaced in current political debates with regard to defining what humanitarian intervention is, the International Commission on Intervention and State Sovereignty suggested in its final report of 2001 to replace the term 'humanitarian intervention' with the concept of the 'responsibility to protect',[13] a suggestion that has been adopted repeatedly.

For our purposes here, it is sufficient to outline some of the problems and the varying dimensions of the definitions of humanitarian intervention. The very latitude afforded by the various definitions makes it much easier to discuss some overlaps between humanitarian interventions and UN Blue Helmet operations. On this basis, we can evaluate the importance of various UN missions for the development of humanitarian intervention in the twentieth century. To facilitate our comparison of 'humanitarian intervention proper' and 'Cold War peacekeeping', we shall concentrate on the four points discussed above: the site of intervention, the reaction of the targeted state regarding intervention, the type of action, and the aim of intervention.

UN PEACEKEEPING: AN OVERVIEW

Surprisingly, the UN Charter does not provide any legal foundation for the most important instrument of UN conflict resolution. Nonetheless, for sixty years, UN peacekeeping has been used to restrain conflicting enemies, end conflicts, and help rebuild war-torn societies. UN peacekeeping has developed as a result of the paralysation experienced by the UN Security Council during the East–West confrontation. To cope with conflicts between states, the Charter has given the UN various options. Chapter VI outlines the process of peaceful conflict resolution. By contrast, the following Chapter VII allows a more assertive approach, in

[12] *The Responsibility to Protect*, 9, 16; Fleitz, *Peacekeeping Fiascoes*, 170; Thakur, 'Humanitarian Intervention', 400–1.

[13] *The Responsibility to Protect*, 9, 17–18.

which the UN Security Council can take forceful action even against the will of the conflicting parties. Because of the antagonistic interests of the two superpowers, Chapter VII was hardly used during the Cold War. As a reduced form of military engagement, both the UN Security Council and the UN General Assembly used lightly armed soldiers under the direct control of the UN Secretariat. UN peacekeeping therefore filled a vacuum left by the unavailability of certain instruments prepared for by the UN Charter but not used during the Cold War. Informally, UN peacekeeping established a so-called chapter six and a half, that is, an instrument halfway between consent-orientated conflict resolution and coercion.[14]

According to official reports, thirteen missions were established from 1948 to 1988.[15] The first two observer missions, for which the name peacekeeping initially did not exist, were conceived in 1948/49. One became operational in the Middle East and one in the border region between India and Pakistan. UN peacekeeping proper, however, did not come into being until 1956. During the Suez Crisis, the first large UN force was positioned as a buffer between the belligerents. This 6,000-man contingent was named the United Nations Emergency Force (UNEF). Established in November 1956, its soldiers wore the well-known light-blue headgear for the first time, which then became the symbol of UN peacekeeping.

Depending on the relationship between the two superpowers in the following years, several UN peacekeeping missions were established. They included four large operations. Besides the first UNEF mission (1956–1967), there was the Congo mission (1960–1964), the Cyprus mission (first set up in 1964), and the second UNEF mission (1973–1979), which was deployed again at the border between Egypt and Israel. Because of the so-called second Cold War, no new deployments were ordered between 1978 and 1988. Of the thirteen missions established during the Cold War era, five were never terminated and are still operational today.

[14] For an overview, see N. MacQueen, *Peacekeeping and the International System* (London and New York: Routledge, 2006); for detailed case studies see W. J. Durch (ed.), *The Evolution of UN Peacekeeping: Case Studies and Comparative Analysis* (New York: St Martin's Press, 1993); W. J. Durch (ed.), *UN Peacekeeping, American Politics, and the Uncivil Wars of the 1990s* (New York: St Martin's Press, 1996).

[15] List of Peacekeeping Operations 1948–2013 (sic 2014), www.un.org/en/peacekeeping/documents/operationslist.pdf (last accessed 4 July 2015).

The year 1988 marked the renaissance of UN peacekeeping. This situation was caused by the change in the international climate. The two superpowers in particular were willing to cooperate on a much larger scale than ever before since the Second World War. In 1988 and 1989, five new missions were started. A second wave of expansion continued into the mid 1990s. During that time, however, UN peacekeeping also experienced its most horrific failures. They bear the names of three countries: Somalia, Yugoslavia, and Rwanda. Surprisingly, there was no real decline in the number of operations following these devastating experiences. However, the operations became politically less prominent. Furthermore, troop withdrawals were undertaken especially by the Western states. Today, Bangladesh, Pakistan, India, Ethiopia, and Rwanda are the major providers of troops. Among the Western states, Italy deploys the largest contingent, ranking just twenty-sixth on the list of UN troop providers.[16]

According to an official overview, sixty-nine missions were established between 1948 and 2014. Of these, sixteen are still operational. This includes five deployments from the Cold War period, only one from the major expansion phase after 1988/89, and ten established since 1999.[17] In April 2015, a total of 107,565 soldiers and policemen were being deployed.[18] This figure is much higher (about 30,000 more men) than in the heyday of UN peacekeeping during the first half of the 1990s. As seems obvious, peacekeeping is still a viable concept of international conflict resolution.[19]

FACETS OF UN BLUE HELMET OPERATIONS DURING THE COLD WAR

Against this background and with a focus on Cold War peacekeeping, it is possible to return to the analysis of the four major components of humanitarian intervention as listed earlier.

[16] Ranking of Military and Police Contributions to UN Operations, 31 May 2015 http://un.org/en/peacekeeping/contributors/2015/may15_2.pdf (last accessed 4 July 2015).

[17] List of Peacekeeping Operations 1948–2013 (sic 2014), www.un.org/en/peacekeeping/documents/operationslist.pdf (last accessed 4 July 2015).

[18] Peacekeeping Fact Sheet (30 April 2015), www.un.org/en/peacekeeping/resources/statistics/factsheet.shtml (last accessed 4 July 2015).

[19] R. Thakur, *The United Nations, Peace and Security: From Collective Security to the Responsibility to Protect* (Cambridge University Press, 2006), 44–7.

Site of intervention

Other than the definition of classical peacekeeping suggests, UN soldiers were not solely and primarily used as a buffer in interstate wars. Not unlike operations that are labelled humanitarian interventions, UN Blue Helmet missions were deployed on the soil of sovereign states or in territories whose actual statehood was challenged or only recently established.

The first UN observer missions were conceived in the context of state-building wars and the associated process of decolonization. This was the nature of the observer mission established in 1949 in the border region between India and Pakistan. Both were successor states of the former British India. The conflict centred on the territory of Kashmir, which was claimed by both countries. The war between the two sovereign states, however, was only the result of internal turmoil in Kashmir. In reality, the interstate war superseded a violent intra-territorial conflict. Because of this, the UN Security Council deployed not only an observer force, the United Nations Military Observer Group in India and Pakistan (UNMOGIP), to monitor the ceasefire. It also sent a commission assigned to prepare the upcoming plebiscite in Kashmir. The plebiscite never materialized, so the UN commission was disbanded in 1950, but UNMOGIP continued and still exists today.[20]

The Congo operation from 1960 to 1964 was one of the most obvious examples of UN intervention into the realm of a sovereign state. At the outset, the Opération des Nations Unies au Congo (ONUC) was designed as an enlarged observer force monitoring the retreat of the troops of the former colonial power, Belgium. As a supplementary task, ONUC was ordered to support the central government in Kinshasa on a limited scale. This unspecific mandate proved to be the gateway to an enlargement of both the commitment and the force. ONUC became entangled in the internal political power conflicts, the broadening civil war, and the separatist movement in the Congolese province of Katanga. The results of UN intervention were mixed. Not the least of which was the cost of the entire operation: it nearly bankrupt the UN. However, at the time the prevailing view assessed the operation positively for having prevented the break-up

[20] K. T. Birgisson, 'United Nations Military Observer Group in India and Pakistan' in W. J. Durch (ed.), *The Evolution of UN Peacekeeping: Case Studies and Comparative Analysis* (New York: St Martin's Press, 1993), 273–84.

of the Congo. This perception underscored the understanding that the mission represented a major UN intervention in an intrastate conflict.[21]

Less well-known but eventually an important precedent for similar missions that mushroomed after the end of bipolarity was a UN intervention in West New Guinea in 1962/63. The United Nations Temporary Executive Authority (UNTEA) and the subordinated UN Security Force (UNSF) actually administered the territory for about seven months. As scheduled, it was handed over to Indonesia on 1 May 1963. The plebiscite, which the Indonesian government had promised to hold, was never truly monitored by the UN. It can therefore rightfully be asked whether UN intervention failed to fulfil humanitarian goals and ultimately violated human rights.[22]

Only a short time after this, in 1964, the UN established another large-scale force, this time on the island of Cyprus. First and foremost, UN Blue Helmets were deployed to fence in the conflict and prevent an outbreak of war between the two NATO partners Turkey and Greece. Yet, in reality, the task of the United Nations Force in Cyprus (UNFICYP) was somewhat different. UN soldiers had to intercede between two belligerent factions of an intercommunal strife, namely between the Greek-speaking and the Turkish-speaking population of the island. Until 1974, UNFICYP was indeed used as a buffer force, but not in an interstate conflict with clear borders. It was a civil-war situation with unclear frontlines.[23]

To sum up, two of the four large-scale peacekeeping operations during the Cold War (in the Congo and on Cyprus) intervened in intra-state conflicts and were deployed on the territory of sovereign but deteriorating states. Beyond that, other UN soldiers were stationed in regions of conflict that were not only, or only partially, the result of tensions between sovereign states.[24]

[21] K. A. Spooner, *Canada, the Congo Crisis, and UN Peacekeeping, 1960 –64* (Vancouver and Toronto: University of British Columbia Press, 2009), 212–13. Also A. J. Bellamy and P. D. Williams, *Understanding Peacekeeping*, 2nd edn (Cambridge and Malden: Polity Press, 2011), 86–7 argue that ONUC was 'largely successful in terms of accomplishing its mandate'.

[22] W. J. Durch, 'UN Temporary Executive Authority', in W. J. Durch (ed.), *The Evolution of UN Peacekeeping: Case Studies and Comparative Analysis* (New York: St Martin's Press, 1993), 285–98. See also Chapter 11 by Norrie MacQueen in this book.

[23] A. James, *Keeping the Peace in the Cyprus Crises of 1963–64* (Houndmills, Basingstoke: Palgrave, 2002).

[24] See, for example, the UN mission in the Lebanon in 1958.

Reaction of the targeted state vis-à-vis intervention

Conditio sine qua non of the founding of the UN was the sovereignty of the member states. This was set out specifically in Article 2 of the UN Charter. This article made it clear that the UN had no right to interfere in the internal affairs of a member state. Only if peace was threatened or already breached, or a member state was attacked as stipulated in Chapter VII of the Charter, could the culprit state potentially forfeit it sovereign rights. Since Chapter VII was not explicitly used in the context of UN Blue Helmet operations during the Cold War, it appears at first sight that the sovereignty of the states in question was not affected. Ergo, peacekeeping units should have been deployed only with the consent of the governments of the countries on whose territory they were stationed.

An example of this procedure was the establishment of the first UNEF mission. Not only did the Egyptian government accept the resolution of the General Assembly, which established the first Blue Helmet force, but the Secretary-General explicitly stated in one of his reports that UN soldiers were only 'to enter Egyptian territory with the consent of the Egyptian government'.[25]

Similarly, when the UN established the second UNEF mission in October 1973, the Egyptian government again explicitly allowed the UN to deploy troops on Egyptian soil: 'The Government of the Republic of Egypt considers that the presence of the United Nations Emergency Force on its territory is of a temporary nature and is, moreover, governed by the Charter of the United Nations, its purposes and principles and the general principles of International Law which safeguard Egypt's sovereignty and territorial integrity.'[26]

In reality, the situation was not always so clear. Indeed, quite often various mandates stressed the fact that the states on whose territory peacekeeping troops were to be deployed were sovereign states. In some mandates, however, the dangers that the volatile crisis posed for international peace were also mentioned. They therefore used formulations that implicitly referred to Chapter VII of the UN Charter. This stated that

[25] 'Second and final report of the Secretary-General on the plan for an emergency international United Nations force requested in the resolution 998 (ES-I), adopted by the General Assembly on 4 November 1956' (UN Doc. A/3302 of 6 November 1956), in Siekmann (ed.), *Basic Documents*, 4–5, here 5.

[26] Letter dated 27 October 1973 from the representative of Egypt to the Secretary-General (UN Doc. S/11055 of 27 October 1973), in ibid., 185.

the sovereignty of member states could be violated in order 'to maintain or restore international peace and security' (Articles 39 and 42).

On 4 March 1964, the UN Security Council adopted a resolution that established a UN force for Cyprus. The resolution stated that the situation on the Mediterranean island 'is likely to threaten international peace and security and may further deteriorate unless additional measures are promptly taken to maintain peace and to seek out a durable solution'.[27] While elsewhere in the resolution the territorial integrity of Cyprus was stressed, a similar passage was notably absent in the Security Council resolution concerning an earlier case: on 21 February 1961, the mandate for the UN troops in the Congo was manifestly broadened. It was argued that the civil war in the Congo had become dangerous for international peace and security.[28]

However, the semantics of the mandates only give a limited idea of whether governments willingly or unwillingly accepted peacekeeping troops. In order to answer this question, it is equally important to review the international context and especially the diplomatic negotiations that preceded the actual deployment of troops.

A closer look reveals that only in a minority of cases were UN missions established without one of the superpowers, most notably the United States, forcing state actors to comply with UN actions. Sometimes, one of the parties in a conflict asked for UN help, while the other had to be coerced into accepting UN troops.

From the four large-scale peacekeeping operations, two (Congo and Cyprus) were established after the responsible government officials had requested UN help. As the conflict dragged on and became more and more confusing, the disintegrating Congolese government lost its influence on the UN contingent – even though ONUC still more or less supported the central government under President Joseph Kasavubu. After Prime Minister Patrice Lumumba was murdered, the notoriously weak position of the government became obvious. As already mentioned, the new and broadened mandate of 21 February 1961 practically disregarded the Congolese government and Congolese sovereignty.

Similarly, the government of Cyprus had only limited influence on the establishment of the UN force. It came into being more or less as a reaction to a British proposal. London first wished to deploy a peacekeeping formation made up of NATO troops. While Nicosia favoured a UN

[27] Security Council Resolution 186 (1964) of 4 March 1964 [S/5575], in ibid., 147.
[28] Security Council Resolution 161 (1964) of 21 February 1961, in ibid., 77–8.

force, it was only deployed because the guaranteeing powers of Cyprus, Greece, Turkey, and Great Britain accepted this idea. Again, this case study displays the mixed nature of the situation. Nicosia was not in a position to make a free and independent decision.[29]

Even both UNEF missions were the result of massive interventions by the superpowers. In the case of the first UNEF mission, it was mainly the United States that used its weight to coerce the various parties into complying with the UN resolutions. Later, in 1973, Israel and Egypt approved the second UNEF mission only after US foreign minister Henry Kissinger started his shuttle diplomacy. It was obvious that pressure from Moscow and Washington was behind the reluctant concessions made by the regional opponents. So, the ceasefire and the deployment of UN soldiers were ultimately the work of the two superpowers.

Type of action

During the Cold War, UN Blue Helmets were generally only lightly armed for the purpose of self-defence. The observer missions never assumed any military role. Similarly, the large-scale undertakings with hundreds or thousands of soldiers usually restricted the use of arms to cases where UN soldiers were attacked.

However, this rule also had its exceptions. At the request of the UN civil authorities, the relatively unknown UN Security Force in West New Guinea could be called on to maintain public order. If action was taken, the local police also came under the control of UNSF. While there were no concrete regulations how order was to be restored, one could at least potentially visualize a broad interpretation of the existing instructions.

Arms were used differently in two major UN operations. During the Turkish invasion of Cyprus in 1974, UN Blue Helmets used their allotted firepower to safeguard the lives of innocent civilians. Furthermore, they declared Nicosia airport a 'UN protected area'[30] and therefore directly confronted the invading army.

Of course, the major example for the mandated and large-scale use of lethal weapons is the Congo mission. As mentioned earlier, the renewed mandate of 21 February 1961 explicitly ordered 'that the United Nations

[29] James, *Keeping the Peace.*

[30] Excerpts from Force Commander's Directives to Force and District Commanders, UNFICYP, 27 September 1974, Library and Archives Canada (LAC), RG 25, vol. 10646, file 21–14–6-UNFICYP-1, pt. 27.

take immediately all appropriate measures to prevent the occurrence of Civil War in the Congo, including arrangements for ceasefires, the halting of all military operations, the prevention of clashes, and the use of force, if necessary, in the last resort'.[31] Especially when ONUC wanted to end the secession of Katanga and to expel the foreign mercenaries, it had to use lethal force. Extraordinarily, ONUC even used fighter jets on the one and only occasion in the history of UN peacekeeping. The UN mission in the Congo was obviously the first to receive a 'robust mandate' – a term coined in the 1990s to describe missions that were allowed to use military force.

Aims of intervention

Until the détente of the two superpowers at the end of the 1980s, humanitarian tasks were not high on the agenda of UN peacekeeping. Political and military considerations dominated. Peacekeeping was a niche product of the Cold War. Blue Helmets were deployed where no existential interests of the superpowers were involved, or where they were hoping to contain regional conflicts.

Two major international crises occurred in 1956. They made it clear that UN engagement could not take place against the vital interests of one of the superpowers. The Soviet crushing of the Hungarian uprising sparked nothing more than verbal condemnation by the UN Security Council and the UN General Assembly. At the same time, the UN was preparing the first large-scale peacekeeping mission. It was deployed in the Middle East to end the widely criticized French and British intervention in the Egyptian and Israeli war of October/November 1956.[32]

Furthermore, UN peacekeeping tried to reduce the fallout of postcolonial territorial conflicts. Basically this meant that the UN pulled the chestnuts out of the fire for the Western colonial powers. It was against this background that major missions were sent, for example, to Kashmir, the Congo, West New Guinea, Cyprus, and last but not least, the Middle East. The various missions in the Middle East resulted from the founding of the state of Israel after Britain had hastily retreated from its commitments.[33]

[31] Security Council Resolution 161 (1964) of 21 February 1961, in Siekmann (ed.), *Basic Documents*, 77.

[32] W. Heinemann and N. Wiggershaus (eds.), *Das internationale Krisenjahr 1956: Polen, Ungarn, Suez* (Munich: R. Oldenbourg Verlag, 1999).

[33] Bellamy and Williams, *Understanding Peacekeeping*, 85.

It is clear that humanitarian considerations did not play a prominent role. There were other reasons for initiating and legitimizing peacekeeping operations. However, as time progressed, several missions were given additional humanitarian tasks.[34] The Cyprus conflict is an early example of what was seen as a humanitarian crisis.[35] 'Innocent' victims were suffering because of the civil war, although the official mandate of 1964 did not reflect humanitarian considerations.[36] Nevertheless, in the years that followed, UNFICPY tried not only to calm down the political and military conflict, it also helped rebuild both the economy and the social texture of the country.

UNFICPY officially assumed humanitarian responsibilities, especially during the fighting that followed the Turkish invasion of 1974, when it was ordered to protect the local population. In the narrow sense, the activities of the UN troops did not constitute a humanitarian intervention, because the peacekeeping force was already on location when the fighting started. Nonetheless, the task of protecting the civil population was clearly and indisputably humanitarian. As it happened, the UN soldiers did use force to fulfil their obligations when they declared Nicosia airport a 'UN protected area'. This was the first time UN Blue Helmets established and protected such a security zone.

After 1974, humanitarian tasks were still part of the duties of UN peacekeepers on Cyprus. Summarizing the Secretary-General's report of 2 December 1986, Karl T. Birgisson wrote: 'Humanitarian functions include facilitating the visits south of the buffer zone for Greek Cypriots living in the northern part of the island; support for the refugee assistance efforts of the UN High Commission for Refugees, including delivery of foodstuffs; and cooperation with the UN Development Program, World Health Organization, and other agencies working on Cyprus.'[37]

[34] Notably the Congo mission and UNEF II.

[35] Geoffrey S. Murray, Head United Nations Division, Canadian Department of External Affairs, to Arnold Smith, Assistant Under-Secretary, 12 February 1964, LAC, RG 25, vol. 10130, file 21–14–1-CYP, pt. 2.

[36] Nevertheless the second part of the mandate wasn't confined to the narrow task of securing the island. The force was actually ordered to help rebuild the country: 'the function of the Force should be, in the interest of preserving international peace and security, to use its best efforts to prevent a recurrence of fighting and, as necessary, to contribute to the maintenance and restoration of law and order and a return to normal conditions', Security Council resolution 186 (1964) of 4 March 1964 [S/5575] in Siekmann (ed.), *Basic Documents*, 147.

[37] K. T. Birgisson, 'United Nations Peacekeeping Force in Cyprus', in W. J. Durch (ed.), *The Evolution of UN Peacekeeping: Case Studies and Comparative Analysis* (New York: St Martin's Press, 1993), 219–36, here 236, n. 14.

Still, it might be somewhat shortsighted to search for specific humanitarian tasks performed by one or the other of the UN missions. Such a targeted search would probably overshadow a more important integration of UN peacekeeping into the history of humanitarian intervention. Yet it might be worth asking whether or not UN peacekeeping performed a particularly humanitarian task while helping to end wars, to prevent armed conflicts, to reduce intercommunal tension, and to stabilize states. It was not always the case, but in more than one instance, the UN Blue Helmets did help to secure, or at least tried to secure, the basic rights of the civil population.

GRADUAL TRANSITION: POST–COLD WAR PEACEKEEPING

At the end of the Cold War there was not an instant revision of the previous practice of UN peacekeeping. Initially, the new détente in the superpower relationship only opened a way for the deployment of Blue Helmets in regions hitherto unavailable for UN engagement, and, of course, it set the stage for the establishment of new missions – something that had not happened for a full decade.

In 1988/89, five UN missions were initiated. They were deployed in regions that, just a few years earlier, had been seen more or less as the backyards of the Soviet Union or the United States. The United Nations Good Office Mission in Afghanistan and Pakistan (UNGOMAP) facilitated the retreat of Soviet troops from Afghanistan. Halfway around the globe, in the US area of interest, the first Blue Helmets mission started in 1989: the United Nations Observer Group in Central America (ONUCA) was mandated to supervise the peace process in various Central American states. These two operations in Asia and Central America, as well as the observer mission in the Iran–Iraq border region (UN Iran–Iraq Military Observer Group, UNIIMOG), were similar to Cold War observer missions. At least in the beginning, unarmed military observers monitored a ceasefire, troop withdrawals, or a peace process upon which the parties had agreed.

In the period from 1988–89, two other missions were established in Namibia and Angola. They were the first in Africa since the end of the Congo operation in 1964. In comparison with the three observer missions aforementioned, the two African deployments were much larger and had a multidimensional character. With the UN missions' support, impartial and free elections were held in Namibia that resulted in the country becoming independent in 1990. As had been the case during the Cold

War era, it was not primarily the initiative of the contesting parties that brought them to accept the UN intervention. It was the pressure mounted by the United States and the Soviet Union that moved the peace process forward, facilitated UN engagement, and brought about Namibia's independence.[38]

In the analysis of these five new missions, it becomes obvious that the changes from Cold War peacekeeping to post–Cold War peacekeeping were gradual. At this stage, humanitarian goals, at least in a narrower sense, were not given priority.

It was not the end of the Cold War but the First Gulf War of 1991 that marked a major turning point in the history of peacekeeping and humanitarian intervention. Authorized by the UN Security Council and based on Chapter VII of the UN Charter, an international coalition led by the United States re-established the sovereignty of Kuwait. The war fostered the impression that, under the umbrella of the UN, successful military actions were possible. At the same time, however, even a casual observer became aware that the UN was clearly capable of authorizing an operation. The troops on the ground would nonetheless be under the control of individual states. Therefore, there was a clear difference between this UN-authorized action in the Gulf and UN-controlled peacekeeping missions. Not only were the mandates and structures different, but even more importantly, the Allied forces of 1991 were much more loosely integrated into the UN system than they had been in any prior peacekeeping mission. This limitation of UN control would become an important precedent.[39]

In 1992, a multidimensional peacekeeping operation was installed in Cambodia. It was the most complex and largest peacekeeping mission undertaken to that point. Its ambitious objectives were to rebuild a state and its political system as well as to guarantee free elections and a plural democracy. Militarily, the mission was a huge challenge. At one stage, around 20,000 soldiers and policemen were deployed in Cambodia. The military experienced a broadening of its mandate. Again, this development did not amount to a complete reversal of already established practices. The major goals were primarily political. Given the country's

[38] See the respective chapters in Durch, *UN Peacekeeping*, and MacQueen, *Peacekeeping*, passim.

[39] Security Council Resolution 678 (1990), 29 November 1990, S/RES/678 (1990). According to MacQueen, *Humanitarian Intervention*, 48 the new humanitarian interventionism emerged from the older UN peacekeeping rather 'than from that of enforcement'.

previous bloody history, the mission nonetheless had a major humanitarian impact on Cambodia.[40]

In June 1992, parallel to the Cambodian experiment, UN Secretary-General and former Egyptian Foreign Minister Boutros Boutros-Ghali published his own views on the future of UN peacekeeping. His study *An Agenda for Peace* suggested a broadening of the tasks and responsibilities of UN peacekeeping. This included less limiting rules for the use of force as well as new opportunities for intervention that ultimately would affect the sovereignty of states.[41] Still, because there was no independent UN military, troops for these missions had to be provided by individual states – which meant that Boutros-Ghali's suggestions would be discussed separately in each individual case. *Agenda for Peace* – similar to Hammarskjöld's study of 1958 – was therefore only a guideline for discussion, not a program to be implemented.

Soon the operations in Somalia, Yugoslavia, and even more so Rwanda, confirmed that member states possessed only a limited willingness to provide troops for more robust peacekeeping missions under UN authority.

Although 1992 was not the turning point of UN peacekeeping, this year did set the course for the future. It started out as a year of hope, but – with the benefit of hindsight – it proved to be the beginning of several major disasters. In February 1992, the UN mission in Yugoslavia, called United Nations Protection Force (UNPROFOR), was initiated. In the following month, the United Nations Transitional Authority in Cambodia (UNTAC) became operational. Another month later, in April, the United Nations Operation in Somalia (UNOSOM, later named UNOSOM I), was established. In June, as already mentioned, Boutros-Ghali published his *Agenda for Peace*.

In Yugoslavia, UNPROFOR did begin as a more or less typical Blue Helmet operation. It was deployed in an area where civil war had ultimately evolved into a war of independence. As in various missions before, UN soldiers were to monitor and secure a ceasefire upon which the parties to the conflict had agreed. This conflict, in which the peacekeepers were to mediate, was undeniably larger and more complicated than many of its predecessors, but it was far from unprecedented. UN troops had had

[40] J. A. Schear, 'Riding the Tiger: The United Nations and Cambodia's Struggle for Peace' in W. J. Durch (ed.), *UN Peacekeeping, American Politics, and the Uncivil Wars of the 1990s* (New York: St Martin's Press, 1996), 135–91.

[41] MacQueen, *Humanitarian Intervention*, 50–60.

similar experiences in Cyprus. There were also some similarities to the Yemen operation of the Cold War period. At first, UNPROFOR was only deployed in Croatia. The objective here was to keep apart the various combatant groups of the civil war. Leaving the political and military tasks aside, the UN troops were also ordered to protect the civil population against persecution and ethnic cleansing. To fulfil this portion of its mandate, UNPROFOR established so-called UN Protected Areas. They were controlled by UN soldiers and their local administrations were helped and monitored by UN civilian police and UN civilian advisers. Humanitarian tasks and administrative responsibilities were an integral part of the operation in Croatia. Thus, Norrie MacQueen labels this mission as a humanitarian intervention, despite the fact that there was at least a rhetorical acceptance of the UN role by the parties of the conflict and that the use of force by UN soldiers was still highly restricted.[42]

Two months later, in April 1992, the UN operation in Somalia got underway. From the beginning, it was clearly organized as a humanitarian intervention. As a result of the internal turmoil, no Somalian state or government existed that could give its consent to UN intervention. The prime goal of UNOSOM was to protect transports of relief supplies for the starving population, but it soon became evident that this outwardly straightforward task could not be performed under the restrictions of the UN mandate. The troops were not allowed to confront the Somali militias directly when they repeatedly harassed the relief convoys. UNOSOM appeared to struggle with an impossible situation. To withdraw from the mission was not feasible due to the strength of public pressure. At the same time, to broaden the mandate seemed to carry uncalculated risks for decision-makers at the UN headquarters in New York.

In this situation, the United States offered to help. For a limited period, it was to provide a military battle group meant to protect UN Blue Helmets while they, in turn, provided a safe environment for the relief initiatives. Looking back, the US offer was an ambivalent one. On the one hand, the militias were deterred by the so-called Unified Task Force (UNITAF) only at the beginning. It soon became obvious that the deployment of UNITAF was more of a propaganda measure than an effective military one because it neither confronted nor disarmed the militias.

[42] W. J. Durch and J. A. Schear, 'Faultlines: UN Operations in the Former Yugoslavia' in W. J. Durch (ed.), *UN Peacekeeping, American Politics, and the Uncivil Wars of the 1990s* (New York: St Martin's Press, 1996), 193–274, here 205–12; MacQueen, *Humanitarian Intervention*, 144–5.

On the other hand, there was an even more far-reaching realization: at least theoretically, a robust mandate under Chapter VII of the UN Charter was not first given to Blue Helmets under UN control, but to a task force of an independent UN member state. With this, a practice was established that foreshadowed the reality and problems of UN peacekeeping in the coming years.

It was only after the withdrawal of UNITAF that the eventually expanded UN operation in Somalia, now called UNOSOM II, received a robust mandate. It was the first time since 1989/90 that UN peacekeepers were officially allowed to apply force under Chapter VII of the Charter. Despite this, the UNOSOM II operation was still not large enough to actually fulfil its mandate. To make the situation even more complicated, the United States continued to maintain a strong military presence in the conflict zone. This force was also designed to protect the relief efforts. The result was complete chaos in leadership and assignments, and the lack of clarity led to multiple and ever-increasing attacks on UN Blue Helmets and US soldiers alike. The climax was reached after the so-called Black Hawk Down incident in October 1993, in which several US soldiers who had been killed were put on public display and their bodies mutilated. Because of the public outcry in the United States – a reversal of the 'CNN effect' – the US government felt it could no longer put its soldiers in harm's way in Somalia. Consequently, the US force withdrew. In turn, this led to a complete breakdown of the no longer adequate UN operation.[43]

US authorities blamed the UN for the failure in Somalia. This was unjust but had far-reaching consequences nonetheless. Henceforth, the United States would be even more reluctant to provide US soldiers for UN-controlled peacekeeping operations. Only days after the final incident in Somalia, President Bill Clinton remarked: 'My experiences in Somalia would make me more cautious about having any Americans in a peacekeeping role where there was any ambiguity at all about what the range of decisions were, which could be made by a command other than an American command with direct accountability to the United States here.'[44]

[43] I. H. Daalder, 'Knowing When to Say No: The Development of US Policy for Peacekeeping' in W. J. Durch (ed.), *UN Peacekeeping, American Politics, and the Uncivil Wars of the 1990s* (New York: St Martin's Press, 1996), 35–67; W. J. Durch, 'Introduction to Anarchy: Humanitarian Intervention and "State-Building" in Somalia' in ibid., 311–65.

[44] Cited in Daalder, 'Knowing When to Say No', 56. For an evaluation of US peacekeeping policy, see Fleitz, *Peacekeeping Fiascoes*, 104–22, 130–4; J.-M. Coicaud, *Beyond the*

In Yugoslavia, UNPROFOR experienced a similar extension of the area of operation and an expansion of the mandate. Until June 1992, the area of operation was mainly Croatia. It was then extended to Bosnia and Herzegovina. This territory was also caught up in the bloody civil war. Like in Croatia, the parties involved in the conflict first gave their albeit rather reluctant consent to the deployment of UN troops. The main objective of UN peacekeepers was humanitarian in nature. The peacekeepers were especially tasked to deliver relief supplies to Bosnia's besieged capital city, Sarajevo. As in Somalia, the initially limited objectives were constantly modified and enlarged. This resulted in the expansion of the operation and an increased entanglement in the Bosnian civil war. In Bosnia, UNPROFOR developed into a typical example of 'mission creep'.

Protecting the civilian population became the top priority for UNPROFOR B-H (Bosnia and Herzegovina). In order to fulfil its mandates, it not only organized relief transports but also established 'Safe Areas', which were not to be attacked by the conflicting parties. This specific mandate was adopted on 16 April 1993 (Resolution 819). Although the Security Council was acting under Chapter VII of the Charter, UN soldiers on the ground were not given the clear order to protect the Safe Areas by force, if required. There was therefore a major discrepancy between the level of protection offered and the limited resources provided to guarantee the security of the Safe Areas – a discrepancy that was highlighted by the failure of UN peacekeepers to safeguard the inhabitants of Srebrenica and that remained in place until the end of UN peacekeeping in Bosnia.

A more robust course of action on the ground was prevented by the United States, which did not want to commit ground troops. In turn, France and Britain, as major providers of UNPROFOR troops, rejected the idea of airstrikes, which were preferred by the United States. The two European powers feared, rightly as it turned out, that their soldiers would be easy targets for Serbian retaliatory strikes. Again, the sole surviving superpower and the two major West European powers were the ones who set the course for UN peacekeeping. It was only after British and French peacekeeping soldiers were removed from dangerous areas in 1995 that NATO airstrikes compelled the Serbs to return to the negotiation table.[45]

National Interest: The Future of UN Peacekeeping and Multilateralism in an Era of U.S. Primacy (Washington, DC: United States Institute of Peace Press, 2007) 111–38.

45 Durch and Schear, 'Faultlines'.

Unlike the missions in Yugoslavia and Somalia, the United Nations Assistance Mission for Rwanda (UNAMIR), which was conceived in October 1993, started out as a rather small yet equally inadequate endeavour. Nonetheless, it developed into one of the most notorious failures of the UN system as a whole. Not by accident, Holzgrefe begins his discussion of the legality and necessity of humanitarian intervention by turning the spotlight on Rwanda.[46] The UN Secretariat ignored early warnings about an impending massacre issued by the UN force's Canadian commander Roméo Dallaire in January 1994. Furthermore, in the middle of the genocide, which claimed approximately 800,000 lives starting on 6 April 1994, UN headquarters dramatically reduced the strength of the UN force on the ground. This decision was a follow-up to the Belgian government's order to completely withdraw its contingent from UNAMIR, following the murder of ten of its soldiers. At the same time, even as the death toll climbed, the Security Council avoided any further commitment and avoided calling the mass killings by their proper name of 'genocide'. Only after Tutsi rebel forces had crushed Hutu government resistance and virtually stopped the massacre did the international community react. Belatedly, a UN-authorized but French-commanded intervention force and a large contingent of reinforcements for a renewed UNAMIR II were sent to Rwanda. This case study especially shows, as Norrie MacQueen argues, that major UN powers or troop contributors will abstain from risking the lives of their soldiers when they have no political interest in a region – which in turn leaves the UN impotent.[47]

By the middle of the 1990s, the prospects and limitations of humanitarian intervention in the context of the UN were quite obvious. These were highlighted by the Gulf War of 1991, the military actions of the

[46] Holzgrefe, 'Humanitarian Intervention Debate', 15–17. Indeed, in studies on humanitarian intervention Rwanda serves as a major example. See N. J. Wheeler, *Saving Strangers: Humanitarian Intervention in International Society* (Oxford University Press, 2000), 208–41; J. Mayall,'Humanitarian Intervention and International Society: Lessons from Africa' in Welsh, *Humanitarian Intervention*, 120–41, here 135–7; Seybolt, *Humanitarian Military Intervention*, 70–7.

[47] MacQueen, *Humanitarian Intervention*, 114–128. For the UN involvement, see Report of the Independent Enquiry into the actions of the United Nations during the 1994 genocide in Rwanda, 15 December 1994, S/1999/1257, www.un.org/news/dh/latest/rwanda.htm (last accessed 8 January 2014); B. D. Jones, *Peacemaking in Rwanda: The Dynamics of Failure* (Boulder and London: Lynne Rienner Publishers, 2001); R. Dallaire with B. Beardsley, *Shake Hands with the Devil: The Failure of Humanity in Rwanda* (New York: Carroll & Graf Publishers, 2005).

United States and NATO in Somalia and Yugoslavia, and the missed opportunity to intervene in the 1994 Rwandan genocide. The United States, its Western allies, and NATO as a whole were not prepared to subordinate their military power for robust interventions under UN control.[48] Whether the UN would have been capable of leading combat troops in action is a purely rhetorical question. The UN never really had to face the test, since all major peace enforcement operations during the 1990s were carried out by individual states or military alliances. Although the states that provided the troops were leading members of the UN, their operations and soldiers were actually only loosely connected with it. This, of course, resulted in a major dilemma: UN-controlled humanitarian intervention could not be conducted with or without the political and military support of the major powers.

A DIFFERENT PATH: THE EXAMPLE OF CANADA

In the early 1990s, the ultimately distant relationship that the great powers had with UN peacekeeping did not necessarily represent the consensus of the international community. At least Canada, one of the major supporters of UN peacekeeping during the Cold War, followed a different path. It would be interesting to discover whether other traditional troop providers, such as the Scandinavian states, Austria, and India, showed similar tendencies.

Since the 1950s, Canada had been one of the major troop providers for UN peacekeeping. In fact, Canadian soldiers participated in virtually every Blue Helmet operation until the mid 1990s. Canadian governments displayed a variety of motives for supporting UN peacekeeping, including military-political considerations vis-à-vis the Atlantic alliance. At the same time, successive Canadian governments tried to conduct a more or less independent foreign policy, not least because they wanted to distance themselves from their powerful neighbour down south. Equally important was that Canadian foreign politics increasingly embraced multilateralism starting in the 1950s, and the UN was therefore considered a cornerstone of Canadian international relations. Starting in the 1960s and even more so during the 1970s, Canadian society accepted peacekeeping

[48] K. von Hippel, 'NATO, EU, and ad hoc Coalition-led Peace Support Operations: The End of UN Peacekeeping or Pragmatic Subcontracting?', *Sicherheit und Frieden* (S+F: Security and Peace), 22, no. 1 (2004), 12–18; MacQueen, *Humanitarian Intervention*, ch. 5.

as a major element of national self-definition. Canadian peacekeepers were to act as ambassadors to the world on behalf of Canada's peaceful and multicultural traditions. In this context, it was seen as natural that Canadian Blue Helmets assisted in peace processes, helped nation-building endeavours, and supported humanitarian activities. While these considerations did not necessarily dominate Ottawa's foreign-policy rhetoric, they were still important elements in the national peacekeeping discourse and helped shape the political decision-making process.[49]

Canadian motives went beyond those officially named in the context of Cold War peacekeeping mandates. Consequently, one might ask whether the motives of troop-providing countries established important criteria for determining the true nature of UN peacekeeping interventions. The sum of the motives of the individual states might have differed from those dictated by the powers dominating the Security Council, and they might have differed from the declarations given by the UN Secretariat, too.

As a case study, let us take Ottawa's policy towards Yugoslavia. Based on its past experience, Canada tried to expand the objectives and mandates of UN peacekeeping. In contrast to the major powers, Canada's government first urged the international community to intervene early in the intra-state conflict in the Balkans. Second, it called for a robust mandate. It was even prepared to put its own soldiers in harm's way in order to end or restrain the bloody civil war in Yugoslavia. Starting in July 1991, Canadian Foreign Minister Barbara McDougall in particular became a vocal advocate for intervention, even if this meant disregarding Yugoslavian sovereignty. On 25 September she said: 'A collapse of effective governmental authority in Yugoslavia, if it continues, could ... endanger peace and security in neighbouring countries. So the concept of sovereignty must respect higher principles, including the need to preserve human life from wanton destruction.'[50] Further, she urged that the time had come for the UN to 'open our horizons a bit on what

[49] N. Hillmer, 'Peacekeeping: Canada's Inevitable Role' in M. A. Hennessy and B. J. C. McKercer (eds.), *War in the Twentieth Century: Reflections at Century's End* (Westport, CT and London: Praeger, 2003), 145–65; A. W. Dorn, 'Canadian Peacekeeping: Proud Tradition, Strong Future?', *Canadian Foreign Policy*, 12, no. 2 (Fall 2005), 7–32. The best historical study on early Canadian Cold War peacekeeping is S. M. Maloney, *Canada and UN Peacekeeping: Cold War by Other Means, 1945–1970* (St Catherines, Ontario: Vanwell Publishing Limited, 2002).

[50] N. Gammer, *From Peacekeeping to Peacemaking: Canada's Response to the Yugoslav Crisis* (Montreal and Kingston: McGill-Queen's University Press, 2001), 82.

peacekeeping and peacemaking means'.[51] In Canada, this position was capable of winning a majority. Lloyd Axworthy, at the time foreign affairs critic for the opposition Liberal Party and later Canadian foreign minister, demanded: 'It is time for a new ethic of intervention, one that will move us beyond where we are now.'[52]

It looks as if middle powers, which traditionally provided troops for UN peacekeeping, had more to gain than the major powers. The latter apparently wanted to limit UN agency to certain peacekeeping politics and to keep full control over their troops. In the medium term, it was this policy that prevailed. Because of the UN peacekeeping disasters in Somalia, Yugoslavia, and Rwanda and because of NATO's growing role as the world's police force, even traditional peacekeepers such as Canada retreated from UN peacekeeping.[53]

CONCLUSION

Since its inception, UN peacekeeping has been subjected to constant change. Its history, rather than featuring clear-cut breaks and turning points or definitive changes of operational objectives, displays more gradual alterations and temporary setbacks. We cannot distinguish a phase where state sovereignty was the sole or paramount objective. Equally, there was never a period when sovereignty was completely neglected and humanitarian intervention dominated. This said, Cold War peacekeeping displayed various elements that, after 1989/90, were seen as constitutive of humanitarian intervention. The post–Cold War interventions, however, were often authorized by the UN, but they were not controlled nor carried through by UN peacekeepers. As the UN is not a supranational but an international body, more often than not its failures are indeed failures of its member states.

Would an independent military organization directly controlled by the UN be a solution? In the 1940s and 1950s there was some talk of a UN force, but it never materialized. At the most, several of the traditional peacekeepers established national stand-by forces ready for UN duty. An independent UN force would certainly give additional and perhaps badly

51 Ibid., 83. 52 Ibid., 89.

53 C. Létourneau and J. Massie, 'Un symbole à bout de souffle? Le maintien de la paix dans la culture stratégique canadienne' *Études internationals*, 37, no. 4 (2006), 547–73, here 567–8; for a more general discussion of Canadian strategic culture, see Stéphane Roussel (ed.), *Culture stratégique et politique de défense: L'expérience canadienne* (Outremont, Québec: Athéna éditions, 2007).

needed legitimization to humanitarian interventions, but it would not change the system. Still, the UN was ultimately an amalgamation of independent states with mostly independent national objectives, and the Security Council, as the ultimate decision-making body, would deploy or avoid deploying UN soldiers according to the national interests of the veto powers. Thus, the legitimacy of any future intervention labelled as humanitarian will continue to be questioned, because of the motives of both the decision-makers and the troop providers.

PART V

A NEW CENTURY OF HUMANITARIAN INTERVENTION?

13

A not so humanitarian intervention

Bradley Simpson

On 8 September 1999, US President Bill Clinton announced that the United States was severing military ties with the government of Indonesia and called on Indonesian President B. J. Habibie to accept the introduction of armed international peacekeepers into the territory of East Timor. Just nine days earlier, East Timor had voted overwhelmingly for its independence in a UN-sponsored referendum, after twenty-four years of brutal Indonesian occupation. Immediately following the announcement of the results of the referendum, Indonesian soldiers and proxy Timorese militias razed the territory to the ground, killing more than 1,500 Timorese and driving a third of Timor's population from their homes. Facing overwhelming international condemnation, Habibie reluctantly acceded to the introduction of peacekeeping forces, and two weeks later, the first Australian-led International Forces for East Timor (INTERFET) disembarked in the capital of Dili. They would stay for the next three years as the UN attempted to prepare East Timor for eventual independence in May 2002.

Many scholars have treated the international community's involvement in East Timor in 1999 as a paradigmatic case of humanitarian intervention, owing both to its timing (coming in the aftermath of Rwanda and Kosovo) and to the justifications offered by international policymakers, who explicitly invoked humanitarian concerns.[1] Yet a

[1] James Cotton, 'Against the Grain: The East Timor Intervention', *Survival*, 43, no. 1 (2001), 127–42; Nicholas J. Wheeler and Tim Dunne, 'East Timor and the New Humanitarian Interventionism', *International Affairs*, 77, no. 4 (2001), 805–27; Leonard C. Sebastian and Anthony L. Smith, 'The East Timor Crisis: A Test Case for Humanitarian

closer examination of the events of 1999 suggests a more complicated picture. While some countries – or at least their publics – were motivated by a genuine humanitarian impulse, this chapter will argue that most governments, including Australia and the United States, were motivated more by fears that the devastation of East Timor might fatally undermine both Indonesian political stability and the credibility of the UN. The lessons that East Timor holds for both the history and future of humanitarian intervention are therefore more limited, and more sobering, than the humanitarian rhetoric surrounding it would suggest.

THE INDONESIAN INVASION OF EAST TIMOR AND INTERNATIONAL RESPONSE

The island of Timor is located 400 miles north of Australia in the southeastern end of the Indonesian archipelago. For more than 400 years, the eastern half of Timor languished as a backwater of the Portuguese empire, while the western half became part of the Netherlands East Indies and later Indonesia.[2] Following the fall of Portugal's quasi-fascist government in 1974, political parties formed in the colony and spurred a vigorous independence movement. The Indonesian armed forces launched a campaign to annex the territory, coveting its potentially valuable resources and fearing that an independent East Timor might spark separatist tendencies elsewhere in the archipelago. In August 1975, Indonesian intelligence operatives provoked a brief civil war from which the progressive, pro-independence party Fretilin emerged victorious. This failure prompted the Indonesian National Armed Forces (ABRI) to initiate full-scale military operations.

Facing the prospect of an imminent invasion, Fretilin declared East Timor's independence on 28 November 1975. Two days later Indonesia invaded. On the eve of the invasion, US President Gerald Ford and Secretary of State Henry Kissinger visited Indonesian President Suharto in Jakarta, where they offered explicit American approval.[3] The US defeat

Intervention', *Southeast Asian Affairs* (January 2000), 64–83; more generally, see J. L. Holzgrefe and Robert O. Keohane, *Humanitarian Intervention: Ethical, Legal, and Political Dilemmas* (Cambridge University Press, 2004).

[2] Sanjay Subrahmanyam, *The Portuguese Empire in Asia, 1500–1700: A Political and Economic History* (Books Britain: London, 1993).

[3] 'East Timor Revisited: Ford, Kissinger and the Indonesian Invasion, 1975–1976', A National Security Archive Electronic Briefing Book, edited by William Burr and Michael Allen, http://nsarchive.gwu.edu/NSAEBB/NSAEBB62/ (last accessed on 18 May 2015).

in Vietnam, Laos, and Cambodia had reinforced the Ford Administration's determination to shore up anti-communist regimes around the world, no matter how odious, and Kissinger was hardly inclined to challenge Indonesia over a place seemingly as insignificant as Timor.[4] An estimated 60,000 Timorese were killed by Indonesian forces or died of forced starvation and disease in the months following the invasion. However, fierce East Timorese guerrilla resistance persisted for another six years, during which time between 108,000 and 180,000 Timorese died from massacre, starvation, and disease.[5]

International reaction to the invasion of East Timor was muted. The UN Security Council condemned the invasion and called for East Timorese self-determination but the United States prevented the UN from enforcing this and subsequent resolutions.[6] The State Department wrote President Ford that the United States 'has no interests in Portuguese Timor' and should 'follow Indonesia's lead on the issue'.[7] The global press apparently agreed, and coverage of East Timor quickly evaporated.[8]

Western governments quickly accommodated Indonesia's invasion and occupation, treating the 1976 annexation of East Timor as a *fait accompli*, although Indonesian forces struggled until 1980 simply to establish military control over the territory. In 1986, Australia became the first (and only) government to legally recognize the annexation in spite of considerable public opposition, while Washington continued to

[4] For recent accounts see Peter Kornbluh, *The Pinochet File: A Declassified Dossier on Atrocity and Accountability* (New York: New Press, 2003); 'State Department Opens Files on Argentina's Dirty War', National Security Archive Electronic Briefing Book, edited by Carlos Osorio, assisted by Kathleen Costar, http://nsarchive.gwu.edu/NSAEBB/NSAEBB104/ (last accessed on 18 May 2015).

[5] For more, see Brad Simpson, '"Illegally and Beautifully": The United States, the Indonesian Invasion of East Timor and the International Community', *Cold War History*, 5, no. 3 (August 2005), 281–315; John G. Taylor, '"Encirclement and Annihilation": The Indonesian Occupation of East Timor' in Robert Gellately and Ben Kiernan (eds.), *The Specter of Genocide: Mass Murder in Historical Perspective* (Cambridge University Press, 2003), 163–89; *Chega! Final Report of the Commission for Reception, Truth and Reconciliation in East Timor (CAVR)*, (Dili, 2006), Executive Summary, 47–55.

[6] Roger S. Clark, 'The "Decolonization" of East Timor and the United Nations Norms on Self-determination and Aggression' in *International Law and the Question of East Timor* (London: Catholic Institute for International Relations, 1995): 65–103.

[7] Telegram 286596, US State Department to US Delegation Secretary's Aircraft, 7 December 1975, NSA Country Files, East Asia and the Pacific, Indonesia Box 6, Gerald Ford Library.

[8] Noam Chomsky and Edward S. Herman, *The Political Economy of Human Rights*, (Boston: Pantheon, 1979), vol. I, 129–205.

'accept the de facto incorporation of East Timor without maintaining that a valid act of self-determination has taken place'.[9] The defeat of Falintil guerrilla forces in the early 1980s made the territory's chances for independence appear extremely remote. Throughout the decade, international commentary generally focused on the narrow issue of human rights under Indonesian occupation rather than the broader question of self-determination. By the late 1980s, East Timor seemed 'the quintessential lost cause, followed only by a tiny fringe of hard core activists'. Western support for Jakarta, the predictable result of Cold War politics and Indonesia's strategic and economic importance, continued unquestioned throughout the period.[10]

Nearly fifteen years after Indonesia's invasion and annexation of East Timor, a combination of factors in the international system, in Indonesia, and in East Timor fostered a resurgence of activism both within the territory and internationally. In 1989, the Suharto regime concluded that East Timor was sufficiently pacified to open up the territory to journalists and foreign tourists.[11] The partial opening of East Timor allowed for a freer flow of information to international supporters, who revived a somewhat dormant international solidarity movement.

Shifts in the international system also created new space for challenging both the Indonesian occupation and Western support for Jakarta. The end of the Cold War in 1989 offered the possibility of divorcing Indonesia's invasion and occupation of East Timor from Jakarta's role as a bastion of anti-communism in Southeast Asia, especially among Indonesia's erstwhile supporters in the US Congress. Moreover, the emergence of the Baltic States from Soviet control contrasted sharply

[9] Telegram 5366, Jakarta to the State Department, 25 April 1978, declassified through FOIA request by author; Telegram 6209, Jakarta to the State Department, 12 May 1978, ibid; CIA National Foreign Assessment Center Weekly Military Review, 26 July, 1978, ibid; 'At the Decolonization Committee', *Tapol Bulletin*, (London) no. 89 (October 1988), 8–16; 'East Timor Campaign in Japan Gathers Momentum', *Tapol Bulletin* (London), no. 91 (February 1989), 17–18.

[10] Quoted in Charles Scheiner, 'Grassroots in the Field – Observing the East Timor Consultation' in Richard Tanter et al. (eds.), *Bitter Flowers, Sweet Flowers: East Timor, Indonesia, and the World Community* (New York: Rowman & Littlefield, 2001), 109; see also 'Solidarity Groups Meet in Copenhagen', *Tapol Bulletin* (London), no. 92 (April 1989), 17–18.

[11] Constancio Pinto and Matthew Jardine, *East Timor's Unfinished Struggle: Inside the Timorese Resistance* (Boston: South End, 1997), 106–21; Arnold S. Kohen, *From the Place of the Dead: The Epic Struggles of Bishop Belo of East Timor* (New York: St. Martin's Press, 1999), 130–59.

with East Timor's continued subjugation, a point made with repeated frequency at the time.[12]

Although East Timor gained more attention between 1989 and 1991, this visibility did not translate into policy changes on the part of Indonesia's chief supporters: Britain, Australia, and the United States, or its neighbours in the Association of Southeast Asian Nations (ASEAN), all of whom prized good relations with Jakarta over self-determination for East Timor. In November 1991, however, Indonesian forces launched a major crackdown in East Timor, culminating in a massacre in the capitol city of Dili in which at least 270 Timorese were killed.[13] The Dili massacre helped spur increased mobilization among grassroots activists in many countries, who began targeting Western military support for Indonesia as a way of pressuring Jakarta to withdraw from East Timor.

By 1996, the East Timor solidarity movement, working with church activists and more mainstream non-governmental organizations (NGOs) dedicated to human rights and peace, had successfully inserted East Timor at the centre of the Indonesian bilateral relationship with the United States, Australia, Britain, and many other countries. This success was, in turn, made possible by the work of thousands of ordinary Timorese who rebuilt the civilian resistance to Indonesian occupation in the 1990s. What the transnational East Timor solidarity network had not yet done was shift public discourse in many countries from the narrow terrain of human rights to the broader terrain of self-determination.[14] This shift took place when the Nobel Committee awarded the 1996 Nobel Peace Prize to Bishop Belo and de facto Foreign Minister José Ramos-Horta for their efforts to bring about a peaceful end to the Indonesian occupation.[15]

In the wake of the Nobel Prize, public discourse in the United States regarding East Timor slowly shifted to include self-determination as well as human rights. Canada, Australia, Japan, Britain, and other European

[12] Quoted in Scheiner, 'Grassroots in the Field', 111; 'Baltics Parallel East Timor?', *Reuters*, 12 September 1991.

[13] 'East Timor: Forgotten Case of Annexed Isle Resurfaces', *Agence France Press*, 12 November 1991; 'U.S. Reporter, Badly Beaten in East Timor, Says Saw Dozens Killed', *Reuters*, 12 November 1991.

[14] 'East Timor Solidarity Worldwide', *Tapol Bulletin* (London), no. 130 (August 1995), 1–16.

[15] Michael A. Salla, 'Creating the "Ripe Moment" in the East Timor Conflict', *Journal of Peace Research*, 34, no. 4 (November 1997), 449–66.

countries with active East Timor solidarity networks witnessed similar shifts. The Indonesian government, however, continued to dismiss calls for a referendum, with the support of its Western backers.[16]

Again, international forces intervened. The Asian economic crisis in 1997 increased international pressure on Jakarta to seek a negotiated solution to its occupation of East Timor. Even observers sympathetic to Indonesia now viewed the East Timor issue both as a major drain on vital national resources and as a major obstacle to international support for Indonesian economic recovery.[17] A few months later, on 21 May 1998, President Suharto was swept from power by the forces of economic collapse and popular mobilization as hundreds of thousands of Indonesians braved the threat of army repression and poured into the streets demanding his resignation.

Suharto's resignation sparked immediate calls by East Timorese leaders for a referendum on the territory's future and spurred a massive mobilization among Timorese youth who demanded a referendum as well as the release of jailed independence leader Xanana Gusmao. Indonesian military and intelligence officials responded by organizing paramilitary militias to terrorize independence supporters. US officials seeking to restore political and economic stability in Jakarta now faced an emboldened Timorese resistance, the escalation of Indonesian military terror, and an effective grassroots opposition in the United States demanding strict conditions on the provision of any assistance to Jakarta. Correspondingly, the Clinton Administration began signaling to interim Indonesian President B. J. Habibie the need for a resolution of the East Timor conflict, in part because stiff Congressional and activist opposition was frustrating its efforts to maintain ties to the Indonesian National Armed Forces, still viewed by US officials as guarantors of domestic order. On 22 May 1998, the day after Suharto resigned, the US Senate unanimously called on President Habibie to support democratic and economic reforms in Indonesia and East Timor and to 'support an internationally supervised referendum on self-determination'.[18]

16 Nick Cohen, 'Making a Killing out of Indonesia', *The Observer*, 11 December 1996; Doug Mellgren, 'Nobel Peace Prize Once Again Prods Totalitarian Regimes', *Associated Press*, 11 December 1996; Wheeler and Dunne, 'East Timor'.

17 On the crisis in Indonesia, see Andrew McIntyre, 'Political Institutions and the Economic Crisis in Thailand and Indonesia' in T. J. Pempel (ed.), *The Politics of the Asian Economic Crisis* (Ithaca, NY: Cornell University Press, 1999), 143–63.

18 Michael Richardson, 'U.S., Australia and Portugal Call for the Release of Resistance Leader', *International Herald Tribune*, 22 May 1998; Allan Nairn, 'Our Men In Jakarta',

Following Suharto's overthrow, interim Indonesian President B. J. Habibie announced that Jakarta might support increased autonomy for East Timor and that he was intensifying negotiations with Portugal, under UN auspices, aimed at a political settlement. On 5 May 1999, Indonesia and Portugal reached an agreement to hold a UN-sponsored popular ballot on East Timor's future at the end of August. Voters would choose to accept or reject an Indonesian proposal for increased autonomy, with rejection of autonomy seen as a de facto vote for independence. Shortly after UN officials announced the vote, Indonesian military forces and paramilitary proxies accelerated a campaign of intimidation and violence against independence supporters.[19]

The deeply flawed agreement left Indonesia in charge of security during the pre-ballot period. Australian and US intelligence and embassy reporting revealed the absurdity of this arrangement, concluding as early as April 1999 that Indonesian army, intelligence, and special-forces units were organizing, training, and equipping Timorese militias with the goal of terrorizing the population into voting against independence.[20] But when he met with the chief of the Indonesian National Armed Forces, General Wironto, on 9 April 1999, Commander in Chief of the Pacific Fleet Admiral Dennis Blair did not mention Indonesian military support for paramilitary terror in East Timor and told Wironto that he 'looks forward to the time Indonesia will resume its proper role as a leader in the region'. Blair expressed both sympathy for 'the difficulty of the challenges faced by Wironto and the TNI' (as the ABRI had been renamed) and opposition to recent Congressional restrictions on US assistance to Indonesia on human rights grounds.[21]

Australian Foreign Minister Alexander Downer later suggested that US Assistant Secretary of State Stanley Roth raised the possibility of US support for international peacekeepers in East Timor as early as February,

The Nation, 15 June 1998, 12–15; 'U.S. Urges Elections Soon & Resolution to E. Timor Issue', *Associated Press*, 6 June 1998.

19 'With Suharto Gone, Hope for Change Grows in East Timor', *Associated Press*, 10 June 1998; Bob Lowry, 'East Timor: An Overview of Political Developments' in Chris Manning and Peter Van Diermen (eds.), *Indonesia in Transition: Social Aspects of Reformasi in Crisis* (London: Zed Books, 2000), 91–109.

20 See, for example, US State Department of Intelligence and Research (hereafter INR), Report, *Indonesia: Festering East Timor*, 10 April 1999, declassified through FOIA request by author.

21 Telegram 1778, Jakarta to State Department, 'Admiral Blair meets with General Wironto', 9 April 1999, declassified through FOIA request by author; Telegram 1815, Jakarta to State Department, 13 April 1999, ibid.

in the midst of ongoing conversations between Australian and US civilian and military planners. In the wake of the April 6 Liquica massacre, in which Indonesian-sponsored militias massacred more than fifty pro-independence supporters outside of a church, Australian Prime Minister John Howard also pressed President Habibie to allow an international peacekeeping force into East Timor. Habibie, however, politically vulnerable to pressure from Indonesian army commanders as well as nationalist politicians such as Megawati Sukarnoputri, flatly rejected such calls.[22] Jakarta's allies in Washington, meanwhile, refused to press for the introduction of UN security forces to ensure a fair vote. Clinton Administration officials believed that pressure on Indonesia might destabilize the fragile government. Throughout the spring and summer, the Pentagon, which still maintained close ties to the TNI, remained resolutely opposed to the introduction of peacekeepers, though at White House direction military planners did begin developing contingency plans for their possible deployment.[23] Roth argued for the introduction of peacekeepers again in July, warning that a major human rights and humanitarian crisis was in the offing.[24] But the Assistant Secretary was in a distinct minority, and most US and Australian officials dismissed humanitarian concerns as irrelevant to the broader goal of maintaining close ties to Indonesia at a time of great political instability in Jakarta.

The Clinton Administration's political reluctance to pressure Indonesia for the introduction of UN peacekeepers did not, however, preclude the Pentagon from undertaking detailed contingency planning for a possible military intervention in East Timor. US Pacific Command (USPACOM) planning initially involved the mere evacuation of US personnel from the territory, but by July it had been expanded to include possible military intervention under the banner of the UN or a regional coalition including Australia.[25] Contingency planning, however, does not signify political will, and, as one USPACOM official put it, 'they [USPACOM] certainly had no authority from Washington for peacekeeping'. Australian, New Zealand, and British military officials engaged in similar planning for possible military intervention, but likewise expressed deep scepticism at

[22] John Ballard, *Triumph of Self-Determination: Operation Stabilise and United Nations Peacemaking in East Timor* (Westport, CT: Praeger, 2008), 41.

[23] Telegram 2533, Canberra to State Department, 10 August 1999, declassified through FOIA request by author.

[24] Geoffrey Robinson, *'If You Leave Us Here, We Will Die': How Genocide Was Stopped in East Timor* (Princeton University Press, 2011), 187–91.

[25] Ballard, *Triumph of Self-Determination*, 55–6.

the prospect of pressuring their Indonesian counterparts to accept armed UN peacekeepers prior to the vote or after.[26]

Between 5 May and 30 August 1999, the UN Assistance Mission for East Timor (UNAMET) registered nearly every eligible voter in East Timor, amid an unfolding campaign of 'militia' terror waged against independence supporters. Even before the 5 May agreement was signed, on 6 April Indonesian-backed militia killed more than thirty refugees sheltered in a church in Liquica, a town on the outskirts of the capital Dili, and murdered fifteen others at the home of high-profile independence supporter Manuel Carrascalao; several hundred were killed before the referendum took place. Over the ensuing months, Timorese militia, working openly with Indonesian military and police support, also drove tens of thousands of independence supporters from their homes, creating a refugee crisis in the midst of voter registration efforts.[27]

The abysmal security situation, which raised serious questions as to whether Indonesia would even allow the ballot to take place, prompted UNAMET officials to request a delay in the vote, which was postponed from 8 August to 30 August. Even the overwhelming evidence of Indonesian control of militia violence, now buttressed by Australian intelligence leaks indicating that the Indonesian armed forces were considering a scorched-earth retreat in the event that they lost the ballot, did not shift the political dynamics in Washington, Canberra, or other Western capitals.[28] In spite of mounting evidence to the contrary, Western governments continued to insist that Indonesian security forces could be relied upon to maintain security and that the Habibie government could exert control over an armed forces establishment still firmly opposed to the 30 August referendum.

THE VOTE AND INTERVENTION

The presence of international observers, UN workers, and international media bolstered the courage of the East Timorese, who defied Indonesia's

[26] David Connery, *Crisis Policymaking: Australia and the East Timor Crisis of 1999* (Canberra, ACT: Australian National University Press, 2010), 89–90.

[27] Gerry Van Klinken, *Masters of Terror: Indonesia's Military and Violence in East Timor* (Lanham, MD: Rowan & Littlefield, 2006).

[28] State Department Memo for NSC Deputies Committee, 30 August 1999, appendix to USGAO report *UN Peacekeeping-Executive Branch Consultation With Congress Did Not Fully Meet Expectations in 1999–2000*, GAO-01–917. Washington, DC: Government Accountability Office, September 2001, declassified as a result of FOIA request by author.

terror campaign and turned out in world historic numbers (more than 98 per cent of registered voters) to decide their future. Still, the Indonesian army had no intention of recognizing the results of the referendum. Immediately after the results of the vote were announced, with 78.5 per cent of Timorese rejecting Indonesia's autonomy proposal, the army and its paramilitary proxies began carrying out a scorched-earth campaign of terror and destruction. Between 4 September and 10 September, the Indonesian army, intelligence, special forces, and police units, working closely with their Timorese militia proxies, looted and razed East Timor to the ground, destroying approximately 70 per cent of the country's infrastructure, forcing nearly 300,000 people across the border into neighbouring West Timor, and killing perhaps 2,000 others.[29] As part of this campaign, militias terrorized journalists, NGO workers, and UNAMET personnel – besieged at their compound in Dili – in an attempt to drive all foreigners out of the territory.

Scholars and intelligence analysts continue to disagree on the Indonesian army's motives for engaging in such actions, in full view of the international community. Some argue that the army hoped to send a signal to restive provinces such as Aceh and West Papua that their demands for self-determination might meet a similar fate if carried to their logical conclusion.[30] Others suggest that the Indonesian army hoped to goad Falantil – the armed wing of the Timorese resistance – into responding to militia attacks and thereby justifying Indonesian claims that violence in the territory was the result of warring Timorese factions rather than state-sponsored terror. Analysis of Indonesian documents suggests that Indonesian military officials such as Minister of Defence General Wironto, as well as commanders on the ground, having failed to predict the level of support for independence, hoped to discredit the results of the referendum and provide a pretext (through the generation, for example, of massive flows of refugees who could be portrayed as 'pro-autonomy') for keeping all or part the territory under Indonesian control.[31]

[29] John Roosa, 'The Indonesian Military's Last Years in East Timor: An Analysis of Its Secret Documents', *Indonesia* 72 (October 2001), 9–43; Gerry Van Klinken (ed.), *Masters of Terror: Indonesia's Military and Violence in East Timor in 1999* (Canberra: Strategic and Defence Studies Centre, Australian National University, 2002).

[30] CIA Senior Executive Intelligence Brief, 27 September 1999, declassified through FOIA request by author.

[31] Roosa, 'Indonesian Military's Last Years', 9–44.

Though the US Congress had successfully terminated most US military assistance to Jakarta on human rights grounds by 1999, Indonesian military officials were confident that they could employ massive violence in East Timor without fear of sanction, so long as their neighbours in the region and Indonesia's allies remained supportive or neutral. Indonesia's ASEAN neighbours, as they had since Jakarta's invasion of the territory in 1975, continued to treat the crisis in East Timor as a domestic matter, in line with the organization's long-standing position against interference in the internal affairs of member states. Southeast Asian governments such as Thailand and the Philippines worried that support for Timorese independence would provide succor to local separatist movements and feared Indonesia's possible disintegration, however remote. They were also reluctant to acknowledge a UN right to intervention that might trump ASEAN norms and presumptions of sovereignty.[32]

To Indonesia's surprise, many Western governments (especially Portugal and the Netherlands) and their publics responded with genuine outrage as the scope and intensity of the violence in East Timor became apparent. Just as important, UN Secretary General Kofi Annan played an 'unusually active role' in pushing for international intervention. The Secretary-General announced that he was sending a special mission from the UN Security Council (UNSC) to investigate the situation in Dili and called President Habibie on 5 September to urge him to accept peacekeepers. Habibie pressed for time and responded by announcing that he would have General Wironto declare martial law in an effort to restore order. At the same time, however, UN officials repeatedly tried to organize an evacuation of the UN compound in Dili in response to Indonesian and militia attacks, backing down only in the face of a revolt by a number of foreign journalists and UNAMET staff who refused to abandon the nearly 2,000 Timorese refugees who had taken shelter there.[33]

To the outrage of observers around the world, however, both the US and Australian governments continued to reject international demands for Indonesia to allow a UN peacekeeping force to enter the territory. On 7 September, Pentagon spokesperson Kenneth Bacon insisted that the United States would 'continue to encourage the Indonesian authorities

[32] Alan Dupont, 'ASEAN's Response to the East Timor Crisis', *Australian Journal of International Affairs*, 54, no. 2 (2000), 163–70.

[33] Robinson, '*If You Leave Us Here, We Will Die*', 191; Jamsheed Marker, *East Timor: A Memoir of the Negotiations for Independence* (London: McFarland, 2003); Ian Martin, *Self-Determination in East Timor: The United Nations, the Ballot, and International Intervention* (Boulder, CO and London: Lynne Rienner Publishers, 2001).

to provide security', while National Security Advisor Sandy Berger quipped to reporters that 'my daughter has a messy apartment up in college, maybe I should intervene to have that cleaned up. I don't think anyone ever articulated a doctrine which said that we ought to intervene wherever there's a humanitarian problem'.[34]

Two days later, however, with Dili still in flames, both the United States and Australia abruptly changed policy and pressed Indonesia to immediately support the introduction of armed peacekeepers. On 9 September, President Clinton, while at an Asia Pacific Economic Cooperation summit in Auckland, New Zealand, told reporters: 'If Indonesia does not end the violence it must invite the international community to assist in restoring security.' Perhaps more important, he announced the suspension of military ties with Jakarta and threatened the suspension of international economic assistance, without which the Habibie government would almost certainly have collapsed. Within twenty-four hours, General Wironto, who had previously declared that Indonesian troops would resist the introduction of any foreign forces, bowed to American pressure and announced his acceptance of US demands. Ten days later the first INTERFET forces, representing eighteen nations, began to land in East Timor, where they would stay for the next three years.

So what happened? What explains the rapid turnaround in the US and Australian position and their endorsement of armed intervention in East Timor? Numerous scholars attribute the policy shift to a 'new normative context of humanitarianism' that 'constrained [the] exercise of Indonesian sovereignty' following the clear victory for pro-independence forces in the 30 August referendum.[35] But there is no single, simple answer to this question. The decision to intervene in East Timor was highly contingent and could have easily gone the other way; it does not produce hard and fast lessons for scholars of humanitarian intervention.

[34] Alex Keto, 'White House Talks Loudly with No Stick On E. Timor', *Dow Jones Newswire*, 7 September 1999; Elizabeth Becker and Philip Shenon, 'U.S. Priority Is to Maintain Good Ties With Indonesia, Officials Indicate', *New York Times*, 8 September 1999; Gay Alcorn, 'Media Critics Have Administration "Bastards" on the Defensive', *Sydney Morning Herald*, 9 September 1999; Press Briefing by the National Security Advisor and the National Economic Advisor, 8 September 1999, the White House; State Department Background Briefing Paper, 7 September 1999, declassified as a result of FOIA request by author.

[35] Cotton, 'Against the Grain'; Sebastian and Smith, 'East Timor Crisis', 65; Anne Orford, *Reading Humanitarian Intervention: Human Rights and the Use of Force in International Law*, (Cambridge University Press, 2003), 1–4, 19–25; Geoffrey Robertson, *Crimes Against Humanity: The Struggle for Global Justice* (New York: New Press, 2007), 127.

One important factor in the decision to intervene was the active personal diplomacy of UN Secretary-General Kofi Annan. Annan signalled his early interest in the success of the referendum by assigning two of his most trusted officials, Jamsheed Marker and Ian Martin, to oversee the UNAMET mission. He viewed the Indonesian challenge to UNAMET as a threat to the credibility of the UN itself, as well as to the future of its election monitoring and peacekeeping capacity. In addition to speaking directly with Indonesian President Habibie, Annan called dozens of world leaders in early September asking for commitments to an anticipated peacekeeping force. More forcefully, Annan stated publicly that if Indonesia did not accept the help of the international community, it could not escape responsibility 'for what could amount, according to reports reaching us, to crimes against humanity'.[36]

The Secretary-General's job was made easier by the worldwide media coverage of the terror and destruction caused by the Indonesian army and the militias. Hundreds of journalists from all over the world had converged on East Timor and provided extensive coverage of the violence leading up to the ballot, as well as the remarkable courage of the Timorese who nevertheless turned out in record numbers to vote for their independence. Indonesian military commanders on the ground in East Timor knew this – hence their and the militias' determined efforts in the days after the referendum to terrorize foreign correspondents and foreigners more generally into leaving, so that the campaign of violence to follow could take place in a media vacuum, just as it had after 1975.

As Geoffrey Robinson has noted, however, mass media coverage of East Timor would likely have had little effect without a pre-existing, worldwide network of NGOs and church and solidarity groups who could exploit the available window of opportunity to mobilize public pressure in favour of intervention. During the first week of September, solidarity groups held demonstrations in more than twenty countries, including a massive demonstration of perhaps 400,000 in Lisbon, Portugal, that prompted the Portuguese prime minister to threaten to withdraw from Kosovo and restrict US access to the Azores airbase. In the United States, grassroots activists bombarded the White House and Congress with tens of thousands of phone calls demanding an immediate severing

[36] UNSG, Statement on East Timor, 8 September 1999, United Nations Press Center.

of military ties with Jakarta.[37] In Australia, long home to the most active and well-organized solidarity movement and a sizeable Timorese refugee community, trade unionists organized boycotts of Indonesian shipping, mail service, airline travel, and trade with overwhelming public support. It amounted to 'the strangest and most inspiring event' that opposition leader Kim Beasley claimed he had seen in Australian political life (and therefore arguably an aberration). One Canadian diplomat remarked that 'the media was not as important as NGOs' long-term access to Foreign Minister Lloyd Axworthy', which kept lines of communication open at the moment when supporters of East Timor most needed them.[38]

Moreover, the international political system in 1999 was unusually, if perhaps only temporarily, receptive to arguments in favour of humanitarian intervention. The international community's inability or unwillingness to respond effectively to the Rwandan genocide and the massacres at Srebrenica, among other 1990s episodes of mass killing, began to erode the presumption in favour of sovereignty and non-intervention (a particularly important principle for ASEAN nations) even in the face of gross human rights abuses.[39] President Bill Clinton had just recently authorized the NATO bombing of Kosovo, widely considered at the time to be a successful example of armed humanitarian intervention, in spite of the heavy civilian cost. James Cotton argues that, in Australia at least, 'a growing awareness of bad faith of the past' had 'touched the national conscience', making it possible for an Australian government that had previously prioritized strategic and trade relations with Indonesia to accommodate itself to the extraordinary outpouring of public support in favour of intervention.[40] The following year, many of these Western governments and certain policymakers, such as former Australian Foreign Minister Gareth Evans, would establish the International Commission on Intervention and State Sovereignty, which developed the concept of responsibility to protect.

[37] 'East Timor solidarity protests in Portugal', topic 23120 on reg.easttimor, 9 September 1999; 'CONGRESS: Senators Reid, Feingold, Kennedy on East Timor', topic 23131 on reg.easttimor, 9 September 1999.

[38] Clinton Fernandes, *Reluctant Saviour: Australia, Indonesia, and the Independence of East Timor* (Location: Scribe Publications, 2004), 86–95.

[39] Sebastian and Smith, 'East Timor Crisis'; more generally, see Bernard Kouchner, 'Establish a Right to Intervention Against War, Oppression', *Los Angeles Times*, 18 October 1999, 12.

[40] Wheeler and Dunne, 'East Timor', 807, 815; Cotton, 'Against the Grain', 135.

Indonesia was also unusually susceptible to international pressure in 1999. An inexperienced civilian president was still seeking to establish a modicum of political stability following the resignation of President Suharto just fifteen months earlier. Moreover, the Indonesian economy was still reeling from the aftereffects of the Asian Financial Crisis, making the government highly dependent upon Western financial and political support. The international political environment in 1999 contrasted sharply with 1975, when not a single Western nation raised serious objections to Indonesia's invasion of East Timor and many simply denied reports of massive atrocities, which dwarf in scale those committed by Jakarta and its proxies twenty-four years later.

The Clinton Administration's decision to support the deployment of an armed international force to East Timor, however, simply cannot be explained as the product of a newfound humanitarian sensibility. Although the experiences of Rwanda and the intervention in the Balkan wars had altered sensibilities in Washington and elsewhere about the possibilities of humanitarian intervention, they had also strained the capacities of military planners, created tension between civilian and military officials wary of open-ended peacekeeping operations, and generated a certain amount of 'war weariness' among members of Congress who were dubious of the strategic rationale for humanitarian intervention. General John Castellaw of USPACOM later observed that the Pentagon

> viewed this very reluctantly. If you look at that period there we are talking about, 1999, we had come out of Desert Storm and we were still doing no-fly zones in Iraq. We'd done Bosnia-Herzegovina and Kosovo ... we were tired by this time in the decade and the Clinton Administration was [tired] too. It became apparent to me ... that the policymakers and senior leadership were very reluctant to get involved in the effort.

UNAMET head Ian Martin similarly noted the false analogy between Kosovo and East Timor, observing that 'no country suggested following the Kosovo precedent for unauthorized intervention, although sensitivity to the comparison or contrast with Kosovo may have intensified the diplomatic efforts of some countries'.[41]

Moreover, in discussions with their Indonesian counterparts throughout the period leading up to and following the referendum, US officials

[41] Interview with David Castellaw, cited in Connery, *Crisis Policymaking*, 89; Martin, *Self-Determination in East Timor*, 104; see also, Ian Martin, 'International Intervention in East Timor' in Jennifer M. Welsh (ed.), *Humanitarian Intervention and International Relations*, (Oxford University Press, 2006), 142–62.

continued to frame their interests squarely in terms of preserving close relations with Jakarta, though the evidence of the Indonesian military's role in organizing, arming, and directing militia violence in East Timor was overwhelming. In Washington's view, the Indonesian army's destruction of East Timor in September 1999 was important not for its moral or humanitarian implications but for the political costs it might impose elsewhere. In repeated meetings with Minister of Defence General Wironto, President Habibie, and others, US officials never addressed the humanitarian implications of Indonesia's attempt to thwart the will of the Timorese for independence, but rather emphasized the need for Indonesia to maintain its regional standing and avoid taking provocative actions that might prompt sanctions by Congress or multilateral organizations such as the IMF and World Bank.[42] Recently declassified State Department and National Security Council documents suggest that the Clinton administration was less influenced by humanitarian concern for the suffering of the Timorese than by the concern that the Indonesian army's actions would leave the administration no choice but to isolate Indonesia diplomatically and further undermine the political stability of an already weak post-authoritarian regime.

US officials also worried that a failure to act on East Timor would harm important bilateral and multilateral relationships. Between September 7 and September 9, when Clinton publicly called on Habibie to accept international peacekeepers, Australian officials warned that US refusal to support intervention in East Timor would profoundly undermine public confidence in the US–Australian bilateral relationship. Portugal's prime minister threatened to withdraw from the international coalition then intervening in Kosovo and restrict US access rights to the strategically vital Azores air base if the United States did not act decisively.[43] US Ambassador to Indonesia Stapleton Roy perhaps best explained Washington's reluctance to sanction Jakarta, even as its troops and militia proxies were burning East Timor to the ground in full view of the world, when he pointed out 'the dilemma' faced by the great powers: 'Indonesia matters and East Timor doesn't.'[44]

[42] Telegram 03045, Canberra to State Department, 10 September 1999, declassified as a result of FOIA request by author; Telegram 04662, Jakarta to the State Department, 22 September 1999, ibid.

[43] Interview with José Ramos-Horta, May 2002.

[44] Matthew Jardine, 'East Timor, the United Nations, and the International Community: Force Feeding Human Rights into the Institutionalized Jaws of Failure', *Pacifica Review*, 12, no. 1 (February 2000), 47–62, here 47; Sander Thoenes, 'What Made Jakarta Accept

CONCLUSION

So what lessons or implications does the international intervention in East Timor in 1999 hold for scholars of humanitarian intervention? In many ways, humanitarianism served as a substitute for human rights or self-determination as a justification for international involvement in East Timor. Those nations – such as the United States and Australia – which had long backed the Indonesian invasion and occupation of the territory could elide the political implications of intervening to halt a possible genocide by framing their decision (for public consumption, at least) in apolitical terms as a response to a humanitarian crisis rather than a human rights crime. Second, humanitarian intervention, as James Cotton suggests, 'was at best a trigger for addressing international and regional issues of longer standing'. Indonesia's continued occupation of East Timor was an anomaly from a period of heightened Cold War anxieties in Southeast Asia. Its allies and neighbours, especially Australia and Japan, had no stake in supporting the occupation once the Habibie government itself displayed a willingness to change policy. Australia's position in particular, with the deep and broad public support for East Timorese self-determination and an Australian peacekeeping role, was unusual for the region. Furthermore, regional support for intervention in East Timor did not in any important way undermine the resistance of ASEAN nations to humanitarian intervention as a principle or their commitment to doctrines of state sovereignty and non-interference more generally. The long and tortured path towards the adoption of an ASEAN human rights covenant would seem to confirm this observation.[45] Moreover, Indonesian diplomats and observers voiced similar scepticism over the claim that humanitarian concerns animated intervention in East Timor. Indonesia's ambassador to Australia, Arizal Effendi, among others, denounced 'the jingoism of using humanitarian pretexts to justify unilateral armed intervention into the internal affairs of a developing country, including by way of a coalition of nations outside the framework of the United Nations'.[46]

Peacekeepers', *Christian Science Monitor*, 14 September 1999. Shortly after writing this article, Thoenes was murdered by Indonesian soldiers in Dili.

45 INR, Intelligence Assessment, 'UN/East Timor: Human Rights Geopolitics,' 22 September 1999, declassified as a result of FOIA request by author.

46 Dupont, 'ASEAN's Response', 164–5.

The surest sign that the international community's support for humanitarian intervention in East Timor did not signal a newfound moral sensibility (to the Timorese or anyone else) was the tepid support of countries such as the United States and Australia for holding Indonesia accountable for the crimes committed there.[47] Both countries pivoted with embarrassing speed to 'rehabilitating' Indonesia's tarnished image, resuming military assistance, opposing vigorous prosecution of Indonesian perpetrators of mass human rights abuses, and pressing the Timorese to forgive and forget. To the extent that a genuine support for humanitarian intervention existed, it was among the engaged publics of those nations with long-established solidarity groups, who viewed intervention as a necessary but preliminary step towards finally securing East Timor's independence, and, eventually, pressing for accountability in Indonesia so that its armed forces could not commit similar human rights crimes elsewhere. In this respect, as in many others, the 'humanitarian moment' which international intervention in East Timor in 1999 appeared to herald was fragile, fleeting, and highly unlikely to be repeated elsewhere.

[47] Mohamed Othman, 'East Timor: A Critique of the Model of Accountability for Serious Human Rights and International Humanitarian Law Violations', *Nordic Journal of International Law*, 72 (2003), 448–54.

14

The responsibility to protect

Foundation, transformation, and application of an emerging norm

Manuel Fröhlich

The immediate reaction to the decision of the United Nations Security Council to pass Resolution 1973 on 17 March 2011, regarding the situation in Libya, was remarkable. On the same evening, UN Secretary-General Ban Ki-moon called it 'historic',[1] and a few weeks later this was echoed by the leaders of the United States, France, and Great Britain.[2] Barack Obama, Nicolas Sarkozy, and David Cameron stressed the fact that this resolution contained an 'unprecedented international legal mandate' authorizing the use of force 'to protect civilians' that were threatened by their own ruler with mass atrocities. Notwithstanding the subsequent controversies over the implementation of Resolution 1973, it was also remarkable because its reference to the 'responsibility to protect' (R2P) signalled the actual use of a concept that only ten years before had entered the international arena as a phrase coined by an international commission trying to find a new balance between state sovereignty and the legitimacy and rules of intervention. R2P can, in fact, be seen as an attempt to reframe and reform the concept and practice of what hitherto has been termed 'humanitarian intervention'. This makes it a rather special case of normative change in international relations. Against this background, this chapter first traces the origin and foundations of R2P and then looks at the transformation of the concept from its publication

[1] K.-M. Ban, *Statement on Libya*, 17 March 2011, www.un.org/sg/statements/?nid=5145 (last accessed 26 Aug. 2013).

[2] B. Obama, D. Cameron, and N. Sarkozy, 'Libya's Pathway to Peace', *New York Times*, 14 April 2011, www.nytimes.com/2011/04/15/opinion/15iht-edlibya15.html?_r=0 (last accessed 26 Aug. 2013).

in 2001 to its first implementation in 2011. It then turns to the still rather new empirical record of R2P, focusing particularly on the case of Libya, before it concludes with a discussion of R2P in terms of normative change in international relations.[3]

CONCEPTUAL FOUNDATION

The legitimate use of force is defined in rather clear words in Article 2.4 of the UN Charter: 'All Members shall refrain in their international relations from the threat or use of force against the territorial integrity or political independence of any state, or in any other manner inconsistent with the purposes of the United Nations.' The rationale for this provision can be seen in the centuries-long experience that the threat or use of force against that very integrity and independence of states had been one of the main drivers of conflict in the international system. The general prohibition of force in Article 2.4 is reinforced in Article 2.7: 'Nothing in the present Charter shall authorize the United Nations to intervene in matters which are essentially within the domestic jurisdiction of any state or shall require the Members to submit such matters to settlement under the present Charter; but this principle shall not prejudice the application of enforcement measures under Chapter VII.' This article once again safeguards the principle of sovereignty as an ingredient of a peaceful world order. With the general rule or principle thus spelled out, Chapter VII does hold two exceptions to this rule. In the first of these, it details the procedure for the use of force 'in the common interest' (Preamble): The Security Council

[3] This chapter draws on earlier work dealing with these issues, most notably M. Fröhlich, 'Responsibility to Protect: Zur Herausbildung einer neuen Norm der Friedenssicherung' in J. Varwick and A. Zimmermann (eds.), *Die Reform der Vereinten Nationen: Bilanz und Perspektiven* (Berlin: Duncker and Humblot, 2006), 167–86; and M. Fröhlich, 'Der Fall Libyen und die Norm der Schutzverantwortung', *Zeitschrift für Politikwissenschaft. Journal of Political Science*, 21 (2011), 135–51. For further orientation in the growing literature on R2P, see also E. Strauss, *The Emperor's New Clothes? The United Nations and the Implementation of the Responsibility to Protect* (Baden-Baden: Nomos, 2009); C. Verlage, *Responsibility to Protect. Ein neuer Ansatz im Völkerrecht zur Verhinderung von Völkermord, Kriegsverbrechen und Verbrechen gegen die Menschlichkeit* (Tübingen: Mohr Siebeck, 2009); A. J. Bellamy, *Responsibility to Protect: The Global Effort to End Mass Atrocities* (Cambridge: Polity, 2009); G. Evans, *The Responsibility to Protect: Ending Mass Atrocity Crimes Once and for All* (Washington, DC: Brookings Institution Press, 2009); A. Hehir, *The Responsibility to Protect: Rhetoric, Reality and the Future of Humanitarian Intervention* (London and New York: Palgrave, 2012); D. Peters, *Die Responsibility to Protect als Maßstab im Umgang mit schwersten Menschenrechtsverbrechen* (Münster: Lit, 2013).

'shall determine the existence of any threat to the peace, breach of peace, or act of aggression [and] decide what measures shall be taken ... to maintain or restore international peace and security' (Article 39). Article 42 explicitly states the option to take 'action by air, sea, or land forces' for that purpose. The second exception to the general prohibition of force under the Charter is the right of individual and collective self-defence as laid down in Article 51 of the Charter. This right can be understood as a provisional scope of action for member states who need not wait for the Security Council to authorize specific actions 'if an armed attack occurs' (Article 51).

Simple as these provisions may sound, they do contain quite some room for interpretation and contestation and have clearly not been observed as strictly as they were conceived. Looking at the practice of (humanitarian) interventions since the founding of the UN, one special challenge to the UN rules emerges: these rules were written against the background of interstate conflict with one state attacking another. The majority of conflicts today are, however, intra-state conflicts between government and opposition forces, rebel groups, etc.[4] In this context, sovereignty – the ingredient of a peaceful international order – can be transformed into an impediment of a peaceful international order when governments refer to their sovereign rights to shield off any outside interference when planning, for example, mass crimes or ethnic cleansing.[5]

Two examples from the 1990s stand out as bleak illustrations of this phenomenon: the 1994 genocide in Rwanda (resulting in about 800,000 deaths in a matter of weeks) and the 1995 massacre of 8,000 people in what had been declared the 'safe area' of Srebrenica.[6] Experiences such as Rwanda and Srebrenica triggered a new debate on the need to rebalance the relationship between sovereignty and intervention. Another event of the 1990s further intensified that debate: in 1999, NATO carried out a military intervention in Kosovo that had not been authorized by the UN Security Council. While Rwanda and Srebrenica epitomized the tragic results of inaction, Kosovo showed that action to stop mass atrocities

[4] Human Security Center, *Human Security Report 2005: War and Peace in the 21st Century* (Oxford University Press, 2005).

[5] M. Fröhlich, 'Zwischen Friedensformel und Kriegsgrund: Der Kampf um Souveränität', *Osnabrücker Jahrbuch Frieden und Wissenschaft*, 11 (2004), 157–65.

[6] See M. Fröhlich, 'Keeping Track of UN Peace-keeping: Suez, Srebrenica, Rwanda and the Brahimi Report' in J. A. Frowein and R. Wolfrum (eds.), *Max Planck Yearbook of United Nations Law* 5 (2001), 185–248.

might have serious consequences for the general prohibition of the use of force in international law and international relations. Kosovo also illustrated the existence of a gap between the proscribed legality and the perceived legitimacy of intervention.

This gap was also identified by then UN Secretary-General Kofi Annan, who (partly motivated by his own experience as Under-Secretary-General for peacekeeping operations during the events of Rwanda in 1994) had tried to put this issue on the international agenda with a series of interviews, articles, speeches, and lectures.[7] Fully aware that a discussion of the sovereign rights of its member states was a very sensitive issue, he nonetheless used the presentation speech for his 1999 annual report to the General Assembly of the United Nations to confront member states with a number of considerations regarding the relation between sovereignty and intervention by citing the cases of Rwanda and Kosovo, but also Sierra Leone, Angola, or East Timor, as new challenges for the international community.[8] Behind these cases Annan discerned a more general challenge, namely the need to reconcile two transformations and indeed two types of sovereignty:

> State sovereignty, in its most basic sense, is being redefined by the forces of globalization and international cooperation. The State is now widely understood to be the servant of its people, and not vice versa. At the same time, individual sovereignty – and by this I mean the human rights and fundamental freedoms of each and every individual as enshrined in our Charter – has been enhanced by a renewed consciousness of the right of every individual to control his or her own destiny.

In this context, he speaks of a 'developing international norm in favor of intervention to protect civilians from wholesale slaughter'. In his speech, the Secretary-General was, however, keenly aware of the fact that he could not confront the members states of the UN with a specific answer to these problems single-handedly, as this would most probably be regarded as overstepping his mandate. He wanted to initiate further debate. This initiative was taken up by the Canadian government, whose Foreign Minister Lloyd Axworthy advocated the instalment of an international commission of experts on the topic.[9] The idea was realized with

7 See M. Fröhlich (ed.), *Kofi Annan: Die Vereinten Nationen im 21. Jahrhundert. Reden und Beiträge 1997–2003* (Wiesbaden: Verlag für Sozialwissenschaften, 2004).

8 UN Doc. SG/SM/7136, 20 Sept. 1999.

9 See L. Axworthy, *Navigating a New World: Canada's Global Future* (Toronto: Vintage Canada, 2003), 177–99.

the creation of the International Commission on Intervention and State Sovereignty (ICISS). This commission was chaired by former Australian Foreign Minister Gareth Evans and Algerian diplomat and former UN Envoy Mohamed Sahnoun. In its composition, the commission wanted to defy the impression that its work would be dominated by Western or Northern views.

The report focuses on the protection of the individual as the main purpose of national and international politics.[10] Protecting people thus becomes a constitutive feature of sovereignty. The report argues that this has been part of the 'obligations inherent in the concept of sovereignty'[11] from the very beginning of the term in the seventeenth century. One can trace this debate to the origin of the term in the work of Jean Bodin.[12] Therefore, the notion that sovereignty could be conceived as a shield to defend rulers who commit crimes against their own population has never been an authentic reading of the history of this idea. Based on these considerations, the report states: '[T]he idea [is] that sovereign states have a responsibility to protect their own citizens from avoidable catastrophe – from mass murder and rape, from starvation – but that when they are unwilling or unable to do so, that responsibility must be borne by the broader community of states.'[13] In cases where the primary responsibility of a state vis-à-vis its own population does not bring about the necessary protection, the international community has to engage in a kind of secondary or complementary responsibility: 'Where a population is suffering serious harm, as a result of internal war, insurgency, repression or state failure, and the state in question is unwilling or unable to halt or avert it, the principle of non-intervention yields to the international responsibility to protect.'[14] This statement represents a substantial change in the discourse on sovereignty and intervention. The argument here is not about a right of states to intervene but about a responsibility to protect individual human beings. At the same time, the ICISS report (in a distinct echo of the agenda laid down by Annan) stressed its understanding that this responsibility is not only and not even primarily about military

10 International Commission on Intervention and State Sovereignty (ICISS), *The Responsibility to Protect: Report of the International Commission on Intervention and State Sovereignty* (Ottawa: International Development Research Centre, 2001), www.responsibilitytoprotect.org/ICISS%20Report.pdf (last accessed 26 Aug. 2013) (hereafter ICISS 2001); see also Fröhlich, 'Responsibility to Protect', 167–86.

11 ICISS 2001, xi.

12 M. Fröhlich, 'Lesarten der Souveränität', *Neue politische Literatur* 50 (2005), 19–42.

13 Ibid., viii. 14 Ibid., xi.

action. The responsibility does encompass a threefold spectrum of action that ranges from a 'responsibility to prevent' mass murder and loss of life to a 'responsibility to rebuild' after the immediate outburst of conflict and violence has ended. Confronting violence by military means (but also by non-military sanctions, such as embargos) is coined the 'responsibility to react' – and only one of three responsibilities that the report discusses as part of a comprehensive concept.[15] The report even argues that military means are only suitable in 'in extreme cases', while prevention is declared to be 'the single most important dimension of the responsibility to protect'. Measures dealing with 'both the root causes and direct causes of internal conflict and other man-made crises putting populations at risk' have to be tried and exhausted 'before intervention is contemplated'.[16]

Trying to find principles that could guide this contemplation is another important task that the commission wanted to address. The point of departure of any discussion of R2P is phrased as a just-cause threshold consisting of two kinds of 'serious and irreparable harm occurring to human beings': 'A. large scale loss of life, actual or apprehended, with genocidal intent or not, which is the product either of deliberate state action, or state neglect or inability to act, or a failed state situation; or B. large scale 'ethnic cleansing', actual or apprehended, whether carried out by killing, forced expulsion, acts of terror or rape.'[17] These threshold cases are then combined with a set of 'precautionary principles' to judge the legitimacy of military intervention: 'right intention', 'last resort', 'proportional means', and 'reasonable prospects'.[18] In the explanation of all of these principles, the perspective of possible victims of violence is the point of reference.

Two additional sets of principles complete the comprehensive approach of the ICISS report. A section on 'right authority'[19] states that there is 'no better or more appropriate body than the United Nations Security Council' to authorize military intervention 'for human protection purposes', but the Council should also 'deal promptly with any request' and 'seek adequate verification of facts'. While these suggestions address the responsibility of states in general and the Council members in particular, the next suggestion calls upon the permanent members of the Council 'not to apply their veto power, in matters where their vital state interests are not involved, to obstruct the passage of resolutions authorizing military intervention for human protection purposes for which there is

[15] Ibid. [16] Ibid. [17] Ibid., xii. [18] Ibid. [19] Ibid.

otherwise majority support'. If the Council fails to deal with a situation, the ICISS report lists two 'alternative options': the involvement of the General Assembly under the 'Uniting for Peace' procedure (the 'Korea' or 'Suez' model) or action by regional or subregional organizations under Chapter VIII of the Charter 'subject to their seeking subsequent authorization' from the Council (the 'Kosovo', 'Sierra Leone', or 'Liberia' model).[20] As for the scope of flexibility in looking for alternative options, this has been one of the highly contested issues in the work of the commission.[21]

The last suggestion concerning right authority once again underlines the special responsibility of the Council but warns that 'if it fails to discharge its responsibility to protect in conscience-shocking situations … concerned states may not rule out other means [and] the stature and credibility of the United Nations may suffer thereby'. Finally, the ICISS report discusses a number of operational principles that should be observed in the application of R2P, including clear mandates, sufficient resources, and rules of engagement that 'reflect the principle of proportionality' with 'the objective being protection of a population, not defeat of a state'.[22]

In this statement on R2P in the ICISS report, a number of elements surface from the history of ideas concerning both the notion of sovereignty and intervention. The report does, however, combine and integrate them in a new way. Several lines of thought are discussed in the report itself, but the following five elements are of special relevance.

The first and most obvious element is the tradition of just-war thinking. To a great part, the R2P principles echo the classical elements of *causa iusta*, *recta intentio*, *debitus modus*, and *legitima auctoritas* that were introduced as criteria for the just use of force beginning in medieval times.[23] The similarity of terms and concepts also means that R2P entails two ambivalences that were already present in the medieval concept of

[20] ICISS 2001, 54. For the background of these cases and procedures, see V. Lowe et al. (eds.), *The United Nations Security Council and War: The Evolution of Thought and Practice since 1945* (Oxford University Press, 2008).

[21] ICISS 2001, vii. [22] Ibid., xiii.

[23] See A. J. Bellamy, *Just Wars: From Cicero to Iraq* (Cambridge: Polity, 2006); M. Walzer, *Just and Unjust Wars: A Moral Argument with Historical Illustrations*, 4th edn (New York: Basic Books, 2006); M. Fixdal and D. Smith, 'Humanitarian Intervention and Just War', *Mershon International Studies Review*, 42 (1998), 283–312; as well as S. Chesterman, *Just War or Just Peace? Humanitarian Intervention and International Law* (Oxford University Press, 2001).

just war. The first ambivalence is that the concept wants to legitimize and limit the use of force at the same time. The second ambivalence stems from the fact that beyond the identification of certain principles and criteria lie a number of unsettled questions, such as what would define the '*ultima*' in *ultima ratio* and also who should decide when any of these criteria have been met. Regarding the definition of *legitima auctoritas*, one can observe a central difference between the just war tradition and R2P: whereas the former assigned the wisdom to decide on the applicability of a just-war situation to the minds of individual rulers deciding unilaterally while obeying what they perceive to be the will of God, the latter assigns this decision to a multilateral process. The crucial importance of the Security Council and also the problems of its decision-making process have already been mentioned, but even the alternatives discussed would imply a multilateral decision.

The second element present in the R2P concept is the idea of sovereignty as responsibility. As has already been mentioned, the idea that the protection of its citizens constitutes the main reason for the establishment of sovereign power can be traced back to the seventeenth century and various models of contractual theory. The report argues for a shift in understanding from 'sovereignty as control to sovereignty as responsibility'.[24] This conceptual link between sovereignty and responsibility received additional emphasis and indeed practical relevance from the experience of humanitarian work in the 1980s and 1990s.[25] Among others, it was the work of Francis Deng – both academically as a fellow with the Brookings Institution and politically as Special Representative of the UN Secretary-General – that advocated and established the link between sovereignty and responsibility against the background of the plight of internally displaced persons, which has become symptomatic for many African conflicts.[26] The report argues that '[s]overeignty as responsibility has become the minimum content of good international citizenship'.[27]

The third and even more recent element present in the R2P concept is the concept of human security that was first introduced to the political discourse in the 1994 human development report issued by the United

[24] ICISS 2001, 13.

[25] See F. Deng et al., *Sovereignty as Responsibility: Conflict Management in Africa* (Washington, D.C.: Brookings Institution Press, 1996).

[26] See T. G. Weiss and D. A. Korn, *Internal Displacement: Conceptualization and Its Consequences* (New York and London: Routledge, 2006).

[27] ICISS 2001, 8.

Nations Development Programme (UNDP).[28] The report, developed under the aegis of former Pakistani Finance Minister Mahbub ul Haq, argues that threats to human life do not only and maybe not even primarily lie with military threats reaching across the border of different states. It is the concrete security and life chances of individuals that need to be at the centre of security policy. The 1994 report distinguished seven dimensions of security: economic security, food security, health security, environmental security, personal security, community security, and political security. In that sense, the UNDP concept is an example of the broadening and widening of the notion of security in international relations, in which the term is broadened (horizontally) by adding new dimensions beyond military security, and widened (vertically) by identifying the individual and not only the state as a whole as the referent object of security policy.[29] In this context it is no coincidence that Canada ventured to take on the initiative by Kofi Annan. Under its Foreign Minister Lloyd Axworthy, Canada had pursued various initiatives and strategies in order to strengthen a human security approach – exemplified in its engagement for the Ottawa process, which resulted in the Treaty on the Ban of Land Mines.[30] Apart from Canada it was Japan that most prominently promoted and pursued various efforts to pursue human security, also with a view to better economic or health conditions. The existence of the human security network, a cross-continental group of states that committed themselves to the promotion of human security, is further evidence that this concept is not a purely 'Western', 'liberal', or 'Northern' invention.[31] While the human security agenda is diverse, there is no doubt that a clear link exists between the concept of human security and R2P. In a section devoted to human security issues, the ICISS report also recalls the fact that Annan's initiative in 1999 challenged member states to 'address the prospects for human security and intervention in the next century'.[32]

[28] See United Nations Development Programme, Human Development Report (New York: United Nations, 1994) as well as F. O. Hampson et al, *Madness in the Multitude: Human Security and World Disorder* (Oxford University Press, 2002); S. N. MacFarlane and Y. F. Khong, *Human Security and the UN. A Critical History* (Bloomington and Indianapolis: Indiana University Press, 2006); M. Fröhlich and J. Lemanski, 'Human Security: The Evolution of a Concept and Its Doctrinal as well as Institutional Manifestations' in C. Schuck (ed.), *Security in a Changing Global Environment: Challenging the Human Security Approach* (Baden-Baden: Nomos, 2011), 21–49.

[29] See also D. Caldwell and R. E. Williams, *Seeking Security in an Insecure World* (Lanham, MD: Rowman and Littlefield 2006).

[30] See Axworthy, *Navigating a New World*, 126–55.

[31] See www.humansecuritynetwork.net (last accessed on 18 May 2015).

[32] ICISS 2011, 15.

Closely associated with the human security approach is the fourth element of R2P: the notion of individual responsibility in international criminal law. Here again, Canada (among others) played a leading role in the establishment of the International Criminal Court (ICC). The crimes that the Court deals with do not only stem from conflicts between states but also from massacres against civilians within a given state: war crimes, crimes against humanity, genocide, and aggression. The work of the ICC focuses not only on the plight of individuals as victims of these crimes but also on the individual responsibility of military commanders or even state representatives who, under the ICC Statute, can now be held accountable as individuals under criminal law.[33] This rather new development once again has its roots in the debate on the prevention and prohibition of genocide that was led most intensively after the experience of Nazi terror but also has antecedents before the twentieth century.[34] Mirroring in a way the new focus on the human being as associated with human security, the debate on international criminal law presupposes a focus on humanity as a point of reference and indeed on an actor whose consciousness can be shocked and who has certain responsibilities in upholding the very basis of human existence and dignity.[35]

Last but not least R2P builds upon the concept of humanitarian intervention. Cases of the twentieth century are discussed in the accompanying research volume of the report.[36] Examples of earlier interventions in history are briefly mentioned in a critical way and the point is made that cases from the nineteenth century were usually 'motivated by strategic, economic, or political interests' in the spirit of 'paternalism of intervening powers', who saw themselves as 'self-appointed custodians of morality and human conscience'.[37] There are obvious similarities between

[33] See W. A. Schabas, *An Introduction to the International Criminal Court*, 3rd edn (Cambridge University Press, 2007).

[34] See W. A. Schabas, *Genocide in International Law: The Crime of Crimes*, 2nd edn (Cambridge University Press, 2009), 17–58.

[35] See M. Fröhlich, 'Crimes against Humanity, Humankind and the International Community', *Development Dialogue* 55 (2011), 33–45.

[36] See ICISS, *The Responsibility to Protect: Research, Bibliography, Background* (Ottawa: International Development Research Centre, 2001), www.idrc.ca/EN/Resources/Publications/Pages/IDRCBookDetails.aspx?PublicationID=242 (last accessed 26 Aug. 2013), 47–126 (hereafter ICISS Research 2001); Chesterman, *Just War or Just Peace?*; T. G. Weiss, *Humanitarian Intervention: War and Conflict in the Modern World* (Cambridge: Polity, 2007).

[37] ICISS Research 2001, 16–17.

R2P and humanitarian intervention. According to Holzgrefe's definition, humanitarian intervention is to be understood as 'the threat or use of force across state borders by a state (or group of states) aimed at preventing or ending widespread and grave violations of the fundamental human rights of individuals other than its own citizens, without the permission of the state within whose territory force is applied'.[38] Measured against this definition, R2P tries to establish or accentuate some new elements that account for its special character and the claim that it offers better chances to avoid the pitfalls of traditional notions of humanitarian intervention.

First, R2P does not primarily aim at establishing new international law but to structure the political debate. It offers guidelines that – over time – should establish more systematic practice. Although the threshold criteria name a number of triggers for R2P, there is no automatism in these triggers because further criteria (especially the 'reasonable chance of success in halting or averting suffering . . . with the consequences of action not likely to be worse than the consequences of inaction'[39]) offer elements that also need to be taken into account.

Second, R2P wants to shift the debate from a state-centred 'right to intervene' to a people-centred 'responsibility to protect'.[40] In that context it does not argue from the perspective of a particular political ideology or represent a specific group of states. It is the human experience of suffering that is at the centre of R2P. It also does not address primarily questions concerning the protection of particular human rights (or particular readings of those rights), although standards and practices of human rights are an essential basis for R2P.[41] Its concern is restricted, plain and simple, to 'large scale loss of life'.

Third, the concept seeks to strengthen international law and multilateral procedures. The decision on when to intervene is not put into the hands of individual rulers but subject to a multilateral decision-making process in accordance with the UN Charter. These procedures should in a way temper the tendency for 'self-appointed custodians of morality and conscience'[42], as witnessed in some historical examples of humanitarian

[38] J. L. Holzgrefe, 'The Humanitarian Intervention Debate' in J. L. Holzgrefe and Robert O. Keohane (eds.), *Humanitarian Intervention: Ethical, Legal, and Political Dilemmas* (Cambridge University Press, 2004), 18. See also Fabian Klose, Chapter 1 in this book.

[39] ICISS 2001, xii. [40] Ibid., 11. [41] Ibid., 14. [42] ICISS Research, 17.

intervention. However, this argument does imply close scrutiny of the UN Security Council, its membership, and its procedure.

Fourth, R2P is not only about intervention by military means for it also includes prevention and reconstruction efforts as part of the international community's comprehensive responsibility and approach to intervention.[43] R2P thus presents the chance to debate, argue, and decide on matters involving sovereignty and intervention with a new vocabulary. Beyond the cases of Kosovo and Rwanda, there seems to be some need for that effort to establish a new vocabulary, because the majority of humanitarian interventions in R2P-like situations before 1990 (most notably the cases of the Indian intervention in East Pakistan, Tanzanian intervention in Uganda, or Vietnamese intervention in Cambodia) were presented in the language of 'self-defence'. For the governments concerned, this seemed to be the safest way to legitimize action in lieu of a legally established principle of humanitarian intervention.[44] In this context, it is also noteworthy that the responsibility to prevent and rebuild need not necessarily be enacted without the permission of the state concerned but can be met with its consent or even invitation.

In addition to these differences, the commission has consciously decided not to use the term 'humanitarian intervention' because of the way it is perceived: humanitarian agencies oppose the link of 'humanitarian' with 'military', and state representatives have argued that the positive adjective 'humanitarian' forecloses the debate whether the intervention in question is really good or feasible. So R2P is understood to be 'a rather larger language change, and associated reconceptualization of the issues'.[45] The report is based on the observation that there has been a 'remarkable, even historic, change that has occurred in the practice of states and the Security Council in the past generation'[46] with respect to 'evolving international standards of conduct for states and individuals'[47] regarding the protection of human security. It does not claim, however,

[43] In that sense it is more compatible with the definition by Trim and Simms that does not limit itself to military action (although it emphasizes coercion) and that explicitly accounts for prevention as one feature of humanitarian intervention. See D. J. B. Trim and B. Simms, 'Towards a History of Humanitarian Intervention' in B. Simms and D. J. B. Trim (eds.), *Humanitarian Intervention: A History* (Cambridge University Press, 2011), 1–4.

[44] Chesterman, *Just War or Just Peace?*, 63–83.

[45] ICISS 2001, 9.

[46] Ibid., 75.

[47] Ibid., 6.

that R2P has already become customary international law. The aim of the report is stated more in political than in legal terms and uses dynamic, not static, vocabulary when it speaks of an 'emerging guiding principle'[48] or the willingness to 'break new ground in a way that helps generate a new international consensus on these issues'[49] while 'clarify[ing] and focus [ing] the terms of the debate'.[50] Once again eschewing the debate of the legal nature of R2P, the report recommends that the General Assembly adopt a declaratory resolution including the idea of R2P, its three main components (prevent, react, rebuild), its threshold principles and its precautionary principles.[51] The Security Council, for its part, should define a 'set of guidelines' regarding military intervention, including the restriction of the veto as outlined in the report.[52] In sum, the ICISS report encompasses the following elements: 1. the idea of sovereignty as responsibility; 2. a threefold distinction between responsibilities to prevent, react, and rebuild; 3. a rather unspecific but focused definition of the threshold for R2P situations; 4. a number of precautionary principles; 5. proposals to strengthen Security Council responsibility; 6. the adoption of declaratory resolutions and guidelines by the General Assembly and the Security Council; and 7. operational principles for the use of force.

CONCEPTUAL TRANSFORMATION

The report of the commission was officially presented to the UN Secretary-General and informed the debate on intervention on sovereignty from that point on. Because of the sensitive nature of the issue it addressed, it is quite remarkable that a concept presented by experts in 2001 was included into the text of the landmark resolution of the General Assembly in 2005, which was the largest gathering of heads of state and government up to then, and even became part of a Security Council resolution authorizing the use of force in 2011. Along the way, the concept of R2P was, however, substantially transformed. This transformation is indicative of the contested subject matter, but it also further illustrates the debate on sovereignty and intervention. Discussions about the wording of R2P therefore mirror different understandings of the issues at stake and shall be outlined here in a short overview.[53]

The process that started with the ICISS report and ended in the outcome document of the General Assembly encompasses various steps

[48] Ibid., 15. [49] Ibid., viii. [50] Ibid., 74. [51] Ibid., 74–5. [52] Ibid., 75.
[53] See Fröhlich, 'Responsibility to Protect', as well as Bellamy, *Responsibility to Protect.*

that range from another report by a high-level panel in 2004 and a further report by the Secretary-General through various drafts of a negotiated document issued by the president of the General Assembly and finally the officially adopted wording of the resolution in 2005. Each of these steps will now be measured against what has been established as constitutive features of the comprehensive concept of R2P according to the ICISS report. Table 14.1 briefly illustrates the transformation.

The ICISS report was finished just three weeks after the events of 11 September 2001. The focus on Rwanda and Kosovo now shifted to the question of how to fight terrorism. In the months after 9/11, the fear of terrorist attacks overlapped with a growing feeling that the fight against terrorism could become a new reason for interference and indeed intervention by Western countries in the Global South. The fight against terrorism thus revived many of the arguments against humanitarian intervention: fighting terrorism trumped concerns of national sovereignty; protection from terror attacks could curtail human rights. A number of countries from the South feared that R2P would infringe upon their sovereignty and be a thinly veiled disguise for great-power intervention.[54] The experience of the Iraq war set the stage for the further debate of R2P, which was being discussed amidst concerns over unilateral action breaking up the system of collective security of the UN Charter. The question of when to use force now was dominated by options of pre-emption and a wide interpretation of the right of individual and collective self-defence. For Annan, the international community had reached 'a fork in the road' regarding the future development of collective security.[55] Once again he resorted to a mechanism that he had used before: trying to initiate a debate on the reform of the UN that would address both the concerns about terrorism and the disintegration of the system of collective security, he installed a high-level panel to work on reform proposals for the UN.

Drawing from the ICISS report, the 'High Level Panel on Threats, Challenges and Change' (HLP),[56] whose members included ex-ICISS co-chair Gareth Evans, also introduced in its report from December 2004 a paragraph on 'sovereignty and responsibility', which stressed that sovereignty included the imperative 'to protect the welfare of its own peoples and meet its obligations to the wider international community'.[57] In the

[54] Weiss, *Humanitarian Intervention*, 124. [55] UN Doc. SG/SM/8891, 23 Sept. 2003.

[56] 'High Level Panel on Threats, Challenges and Change', UN Doc. A/59/565, 02 Dec. 2004 (hereafter HLP).

[57] HLP, para. 29.

TABLE 14.1 *Transformation of R2P elements from the ICISS report to the General Assembly Outcome Document*

	ICISS 2001	HLP 2004	ILF 2005	PING I	Ping II	PING III	OD 2005
1. Sovereignty as responsibility	*Yes*	*Yes*	*Yes*	*Yes*	*Yes*	*Yes*	*Yes* but tied to specific crimes
2. Responsibilities to prevent, react, and rebuild	*Yes*	*Implicit*	*Implicit*	*No*	*No*	*Partly* with reference to prevention	*Partly* with reference to prevention
3. Unspecific but focused definition of the threshold for R2P situations	*Yes*	*Yes* genocide and other large-scale killing, ethnic cleansing, or serious violations of international humanitarian law	*Yes* genocide, ethnic cleansing, and other such crimes against humanity	*Yes* genocide, war crimes, ethnic cleansing, and crimes against humanity	*Yes* genocide, war crimes, ethnic cleansing, and crimes against humanity	*Yes* genocide, war crimes, ethnic cleansing, and crimes against humanity	*Yes* genocide, war crimes, ethnic cleansing, and crimes against humanity
4. Precautionary principles	*Yes*	*Yes*	*Yes*	*Implicit* consideration by the General Assembly	*Implicit* consideration by the General Assembly	*Implicit* consideration by the General Assembly	*No*

Table 14.1 (*cont.*)

	ICISS 2001	HLP 2004	ILF 2005	PING I	Ping II	PING III	OD 2005
5. Proposals to strengthen Security Council responsibility	*Yes*	*Yes* refrain from veto	*No* reference to restriction on veto	*No* reference to restriction on veto	*No*	*Yes*	*No*
6. Declaratory resolutions/ guidelines by the General Assembly and the Security Council	*Yes*	*Yes*	*Yes* but only SC	*Implicit* only call for consideration by the SC	*No*	*No*	*No* only further debate by the GA
7. Operational principles for the use of force	*Yes*	*Partly* less detailed	*No*	*No*	*No*	*No*	*No*

chapter on collective security, there is an even stronger echo of the ICISS report endorsing 'the emerging norm that there is a collective international responsibility to protect'.[58] In varying degrees, the panel echoes the crucial elements of the ICISS report. It does not, however, limit their applicability to cases of military force in humanitarian interventions, but rather to the use of military force in a larger sense, including cases like the contested Iraq war.

HLP served Annan as a resource to formulate his own reform proposals, which he did in a report entitled *In Larger Freedom* (ILF) in April 2005. He reinforces his support for R2P in a section titled 'Rule of Law', citing the HLP statement, and adds that this responsibility lies 'first and foremost'[59] with the state, but that it 'shifts' to the international community when the state is 'unable or unwilling' to protect. While there are also references to prevention, peacebuilding, and operational principles, the Secretary-General obviously pays respect to the centrality and autonomy of the Security Council in authorizing the use of force and leaves out a statement on the use of the veto. Annan understood his report as an offer 'for consideration by Heads of State and Government' at the 2005 millennium+5 summit.[60]

The diplomatic process to draft the resolution of the General Assembly shows that the concept of R2P was an issue that initiated considerable debate and controversy. With the help of the various drafts by the president of the General Assembly, Jean Ping, one can trace the development of the argument leading up to the adoption of the ultimate text in the resolution.[61] Ping issued three main drafts. The first one (PING I) from 3 June contained a section on the 'Responsibility to Protect'.[62] The first paragraph used the language of ILF but with some variations.[63] Although the core argument was clearly present in Ping's draft, other elements of the ICISS concept were less visible. Some diplomatic formulations (for example, 'as necessary') were combined with repeated citation of the

58 Ibid., para. 203.

59 "In Larger Freedom: Towards Development, Security and Human Rights for All. Report of the Secretary-General" (New York, 2005) (hereafter ILF), para. 135.

60 ILF, para. 221.

61 All the documents can be accessed via at the website titled 'UN Documents, Speeches, Position Papers and Press Releases on the Millennium Summit and Its Follow-Up', www.globalpolicy.org/msummit/millenni/m5outcomedocindex.htm (last accessed on 18 May 2015).

62 'Draft Outcome Document of the Millennium+5 Summit', 3 June 2005 (hereafter Ping I).

63 Ping I, para. 72.

Charter provisions as a signal to rule out any deviation of its procedure. The threshold criteria were specified and war crimes were added to the list.

Although the whole spectrum of diplomatic interaction cannot be reconstructed here, the text of Ping's once again informal second draft, dated 22 July (PING II) is quite telling as far as the reactions of member states to the draft are concerned.[64] There were some small but significant changes, for example, when the potential help and support by states through the international community was to be provided in cases where it was deemed 'as appropriate' instead of the more urgent label 'as necessary'.[65] The resort to military means was also specified as being tied not only to the exhaustion of all non-military means but to the determination that 'national authorities be unwilling or unable to protect their populations'. Once again, the need for further discussion of the criteria was repeated,[66] but even a vague reference for consideration by the Council was omitted.

Negotiations dragged on and prompted Ping to introduce a third draft on 10 August (PING III).[67] Apart from some changes in wording, three substantial novelties emerged. First, the 'responsibility to protect' now also entailed 'the prevention of such crimes, including their incitement'[68] and led to the demand to establish an 'early warning capability' of the UN. Second, what was termed the 'responsibility' to use non-military means was now phrased more specifically as an 'obligation'. Third, the crucial demand to refrain from using the veto was reintroduced.[69] While the second draft was very cautious as compared to the first one, the wording and substance of the third draft changed direction: it was much more assertive than the preceding drafts. However, this need not be understood as an indication for more leeway and support for R2P. The contrary could be true: since even the cautious formulations of the second draft had encountered a number of objections, the third draft enlarged the scope of negotiation by indicating more assertive R2P positions, so as to create some room for compromise that could still entail core elements of the concept. Not surprisingly, the third draft evoked further opposition – not the least from the United States, whose newly appointed permanent representative to the UN, John Bolton, had issued a series of letters with

[64] See UN Doc. A/59/HLPM/CRP.1/Rev.1, 22 July 2005 (hereafter Ping II).
[65] Ping II, para. 113. [66] Ibid., para. 76.
[67] See UN Doc. A/59/HLPM/CRP.1/Rev.2, 10 August 2005 (hereafter Ping III).
[68] Ping III, para. 119. [69] Ibid., para. 120.

dozens of corrections of the draft.[70] Referring to the R2P section, Bolton showed support for the general idea but emphasized that anything that would limit or bind the authority of the Council (and especially its permanent members) was not acceptable to the United States. China issued a position paper in which, surprisingly, it included the concept[71] but emphasized the primary responsibility of states to their people and warned against outside interference: 'Prudence is called for in judging a government's ability and will to protect its citizens. No reckless intervention should be allowed.' On the one hand, Beijing, with its generally sovereignty-dominated reading of R2P, stressed the Charter procedure and peaceful means, while on the other, it acknowledged that 'massive humanitarian crisis' is a 'legitimate concern of the international community'.

Ping worked on yet another draft that was negotiated among a group of 32 countries (PING IV).[72] This draft from 6 September referred to the veto in brackets, indicating that there was no consensus on this issue.[73] There was obviously a proposal to further document a sovereignty-dominated reading of R2P because a bracketed extension added that discussion in the General Assembly should not only bear in mind relevant provisions of the Charter and international law but also 'the principle of non-interference in internal affairs of States'.[74] In another draft, circulated on 12 September (PING V) just before the final adoption of the resolution, the appeal to limit the use of the veto had been deleted – as had the further reference to the principle of non-interference.[75] That very last draft shows that the final negotiations over the text were still very controversial. Bracket-options in that draft included proposals to change or even delete the formula R2P altogether, suggesting instead the section titles 'Responsibility to protect civilian populations' or even 'Responding to

[70] See for instance Bolton letter, 30 August 2005, www.responsibilitytoprotect.org/files/US_Boltonletter_R2P_30Aug05%5b1%5d.pdf (last accessed on 18 May 2015); the version with US amendments to the revised draft outcome document of 10 August 2005 is found at www.globalpolicy.org/images/pdfs/0825usproposal.pdf (last accessed on 18 May 2015).

[71] 'Position Paper of the People's Republic of China on the United Nations Reforms', 7 June 2005, at www.china-un.org/eng/xw/t199101.htm (last accessed on 18 May 2015).

[72] 'President's Draft Negotiating Document for the High-Level Plenary Meeting of the General Assembly of September 2005, submitted by the President of the General Assembly, 6 September 2005', www.globalpolicy.org/images/pdfs/0906coregroup.pdf (last accessed on 18 May 2015) (hereafter Negotiating Document).

[73] Negotiating Document, para. 128. [74] Ibid.

[75] 'Draft Negotiated Outcome Document', 12 September 2005, www.globalpolicy.org/images/pdfs/0912draftnegotiated.pdf (last accessed on 18 May 2015) (hereafter Negotiated Outcome Document).

genocide, war crimes, and crimes against humanity'.[76] In a rather typical compromise, the final formulation then emerged as 'Responsibility to protect populations from genocide, war crimes, ethnic cleansing and crimes against humanity'. The two crucial paragraphs obtained a number of interesting details.[77] However, in sum, the outcome document represents both the adoption and transformation of the original ICISS concept: 1. the idea of sovereignty as responsibility is clearly stated; 2. of the threefold distinction between responsibilities to prevent, react, and rebuild, reaction is framed in the context of Chapter VII measures and there are some references to prevention; 3. the broad focus of the threshold has been specified to concrete situations regarding genocide, war crimes, ethnic cleansing and crimes against humanity; 4. the precautionary principles, which had been injected into the general discussion of the use of force, are not mentioned at all; 5. the proposals to strengthen Security Council responsibility are omitted; 6. the adoption of declaratory resolutions and guidelines by the General Assembly and the Security Council is only present in the form of an appeal to further discuss the issue in the Assembly; and 7. operational guidelines have also been left out. So the R2P of the outcome document is quite different from the R2P

[76] Negotiated Outcome Document, para. 127.

[77] UN Doc. A/RES/60/1, 24.10. 2005, para. 138–9: 'Responsibility to protect populations from genocide, war crimes, ethnic cleansing and crimes against humanity:138. Each individual State has the responsibility to protect its populations from genocide, war crimes, ethnic cleansing and crimes against humanity. This responsibility entails the prevention of such crimes, including their incitement, through appropriate and necessary means. We accept that responsibility and will act in accordance with it. The international community should, as appropriate, encourage and help States to exercise this responsibility and support the United Nations in establishing an early warning capability.139. The international community, through the United Nations, also has the responsibility to use appropriate diplomatic, humanitarian and other peaceful means, in accordance with Chapters VI and VIII of the Charter, to help protect populations from genocide, war crimes, ethnic cleansing and crimes against humanity. In this context, we are prepared to take collective action, in a timely and decisive manner, through the Security Council, in accordance with the Charter, including Chapter VII, on a case-by-case basis and in cooperation with relevant regional organizations as appropriate, should peaceful means be inadequate and national authorities manifestly fail to protect their populations from genocide, war crimes, ethnic cleansing and crimes against humanity. We stress the need for the General Assembly to continue consideration of the responsibility to protect populations from genocide, war crimes, ethnic cleansing and crimes against humanity and its implications, bearing in mind the principles of the Charter and international law. We also intend to commit ourselves, as necessary and appropriate, to helping States build capacity to protect their populations from genocide, war crimes, ethnic cleansing and crimes against humanity and to assisting those which are under stress before crises and conflicts break out.'

of the ICISS report. At the same time, a number of observers argue that the remarkable thing about the outcome document is that R2P managed to survive as part of that resolution of the General Assembly. Forces of support and opposition clearly became discernible in the debates, and while R2P was taken from the level of academic report to that of political resolution, its existence was anything but established. A presentation of the further conceptual debate and the positions of various governments exceeds the scope of this article. Suffice it to say that the controversy around the instalment of a Special Adviser to the UN Secretary-General on R2P and a General Assembly debate that merely noted and not even endorsed a report on the further development of R2P illustrate the divisions among the UN membership and the still looming contestation of the very idea of R2P.[78] The report prepared by Special Adviser Edward Luck had indeed anticipated the concerns of member states and proposed a three-pillar strategy for the report of the Secretary-General. This would include, first, the protection responsibilities of the state; second, international assistance and capacity-building; as well as, third, timely and decisive response. R2P[79] was introduced as 'an ally of sovereignty, not an adversary', but the debate on the report about the issue was very controversial nonetheless, and the General Assembly only decided to continue its consideration of R2P.[80] Even these supporters of R2P would probably not have expected the highly contested concept to be included in a binding resolution of the Security Council authorizing the use of force only about one and a half years after this compromise by the General Assembly. This brings us to the empirical application of R2P with a special focus on the situation in Libya.

EMPIRICAL APPLICATION

Beginning with its formulation in 2001, R2P was referred to by various actors in various situations. Significantly, the concept was not only taken up by state representatives but was also adopted by a number of organizations from civil society. Some of these NGOs, supported by funds

[78] See S/2007/721, 07.12.2007. For an overview of the General Assembly debate, see www.responsibilitytoprotect.org (last accessed 26 Aug. 2013), and the concluding document UN Doc. A/63/677, 12 Jan. 2009.

[79] The Special Adviser prefers to use the acronym RtoP to signal the understanding of the UN and distance this reading from an equation with the acronym R2P that was created with the ICISS report. This said, this chapter uses the established acronym throughout.

[80] UN Doc. A/RES/63/308, 07 Oct. 2009.

from national governments, have built up an international coalition for R2P in recent years that tries to raise awareness, monitor, and advocate for R2P.[81] The concept also found broad appeal in academic circles, which resulted in the founding of research institutions and the establishment of a journal specifically devoted to R2P issues.[82] Regarding concrete situations and crises, R2P was invoked from different sides regarding the crisis in Darfur, the post-election violence in Kenya, the humanitarian crisis after cyclone Nargis in Myanmar, or the unrest in Kyrgyzstan.[83] Once again, it would be beyond the scope of this article to deal with all of these references. For reasons both of practicality and relevance, the following section will focus on the application of R2P by the UN Security Council.

A complete search for references to the concept and term of 'responsibility to protect' in all resolutions since 2001 (and indeed since the beginning of the UN) results in twenty-five resolutions that used this exact wording (see Table 14.2). Without going into the details of all these resolutions, some features of Security Council reference to R2P emerge. First, references to R2P are part of the usual repetition in follow-up resolutions (see the examples of Mali, Libya, and Georgia). The case of Georgia, or more specifically the situation in Abkhazia, is noteworthy, not only because it precedes the 2005 outcome document. The resolutions stress the 'responsibility to protect' on the part of Abkhazia regarding the refugees and returnees of the conflict. It is unclear but not very probable that we are witnessing here a conscious initial reference to the whole concept of R2P.[84] However, the context the situation of refugees and internally displaced persons recalls one of the fundamental elements of R2P, as discussed earlier. Second, if one leaves aside the case of Georgia, roughly half of the other references to R2P are made in the more declaratory, preambular paragraphs of the resolutions, and the other half are made in the operative clauses of the resolutions. Even there, the wording is regularly one of a communicative nature (reaffirming, recalling, etc.). Third, as the case of Sudan shows, R2P may imply international

[81] See www.responsibilitytoprotect.org (last accessed 26 Aug. 2013).

[82] See www.brill.com/global-responsibility-protect (last accessed 26 Aug. 2013).

[83] See, for example, Strauss, *The Emperor's New Clothes?*; Bellamy, *Responsibility to Protect*, and C. Kreuter-Kirchhof, 'Völkerrechtliche Schutzverantwortung bei elementaren Menschenrechtsverletzungen: Die Responsibility to Protect als Verantwortungsstruktur', *Archiv des Völkerrechts*, 48 (2010), 338–82.

[84] S. Chesterman, 'Leading from Behind: The Responsibility to Protect, the Obama Doctrine, and Humanitarian Intervention after Libya', *Ethics & International Affairs*, 25 (2011), 279–85.

TABLE 14.2 *'Responsibility to protect' in UN Security Council Resolutions, 1946–2013 (as of 15 July 2013)*

Resolution	Situation	Reference
S/RES/ 1393 (2002)	Georgia	Para 11: *Recalls* that the Abkhaz side bears a particular responsibility to protect the returnees and to facilitate the return of the remaining displaced population
S/RES/ 1427 (2002)	Georgia	Para 12: *Recalls* that the Abkhaz side bears a particular responsibility to protect the returnees and to facilitate the return of the remaining displaced population
S/RES/ 1462 (2003)	Georgia	Para 14: *Recalls* that the Abkhaz side bears a particular responsibility to protect the returnees and to facilitate the return of the remaining displaced population
S/RES/ 1494 (2003)	Georgia	Para 15: *Recalls* that the Abkhaz side bears a particular responsibility to protect the returnees and to facilitate the return of the remaining displaced population
S/RES/ 1524 (2004)	Georgia	Para 16: *Recalls* that the Abkhaz side bears a particular responsibility to protect the returnees and to facilitate the return of the remaining displaced population
S/RES/ 1554 (2004)	Georgia	Para 16: *Recalls* that the Abkhaz side bears a particular responsibility to protect the returnees and to facilitate the return of the remaining displaced population
S/RES/ 1564 (2004)	Sudan	Preamble: *Recalling* that the Sudanese Government bears the primary responsibility to protect its population within its territory
S/RES/ 1582 (2005)	Georgia	Para 18: *Recalls* that the Abkhaz side bears a particular responsibility to protect the returnees and to facilitate the return of the remaining displaced population
S/RES/ 1615 (2005)	Georgia	Para 19: *Recalls* that the Abkhaz side bears a particular responsibility to protect the returnees and to facilitate the return of the remaining displaced population
S/RES/ 1653 (2006)	Great Lakes region	Para 10: *Underscores* that the governments in the region have a primary responsibility to protect their populations, including from attacks by militias and armed groups

Table 14.2 (*cont.*)

Resolution	Situation	Reference
S/RES/ 1674 (2006)	Protection of civilians in armed conflict	Para 4: *Reaffirms* the provisions of paragraphs 138 and 139 of the 2005 World Summit Outcome Document regarding the responsibility to protect populations from genocide, war crimes, ethnic cleansing and crimes against humanity
S/RES/ 1706 (2016)	Sudan	Preamble: *Recalling* [resolution] 1674 ... which reaffirms the provisions of paragraphs 138 and 139 of the 2005 United Nations World Summit outcome document
S/RES/ 1894 (2009)	Protection of civilians in armed conflict	Preamble: *Reaffirming* the relevant provisions of the 2005 World Summit Outcome Document regarding ... the responsibility to protect populations from genocide, war crimes, ethnic cleansing, and crimes against humanity
S/RES/ 1970 (2011)	Peace and security in Africa	Preamble: *Recalling* the Libyan authorities' responsibility to protect its population
S/RES/ 1973 (2011)	Libya	*Preamble: Reiterating* the responsibility of the Libyan authorities to protect the Libyan population and *reaffirming* that parties to armed conflicts bear the primary *responsibility* to take all feasible steps *to ensure the protection* of civilians
S/RES/ 1975 (2011)	Cote d'Ivoire	Preamble: *Reaffirm* the primary responsibility of each State to protect civilians
S/RES/ 1996 (2011)	South Sudan	Para 3: Advising and assisting the Government ... in fulfilling its responsibility to protect civilians
S/RES/ 2014 (2011)	Yemen	Preamble: *Recalling* the Yemeni Government's primary responsibility to protect its population
S/RES/ 2016 (2011)	Libya	Para 3: *Underscores* the Libyan authorities' primary responsibility for the protection of Libya's population
S/RES/ 2040 (2012)	Libya	Para 4: *Underscores* the Libyan authorities' primary responsibility for the protection of Libya's population

Table 14.2 (*cont.*)

Resolution	Situation	Reference
S/RES/ 2085 (2012)	Mali	Para 9: To support the Malian authorities in their primary responsibility to protect the population
S/RES/ 2093 (2013)	Somalia	Preamble: *Recognizing* that the Federal Government of Somalia has a responsibility to protect its citizens
S/RES/ 2040 (2012)	Libya	Para 5: *Underscores* the Libyan authorities' primary responsibility for the protection of Libya's population
S/RES/ 2100 (2013)	Mali	Para 24: *Reiterates* that the transitional authorities of Mali have primary responsibility to protect civilians in Mali
S/RES/ 2109 (2013)	Sudan/South Sudan	Preamble: *Recalling* the Presidential Statement of 12 February 2013 that recognized that States bear the primary responsibility to protect civilians

assistance, such as a peace operation. Overall, R2P is predominantly referred to in the context of a state's primary responsibility to its people, whereas the complementary responsibility of the international community is not explicitly stated. Fourth, two thematic resolutions on the protection of civilians in armed conflict, an issue that coined its own acronym PoC, show a link between R2P and the inclusion of protection tasks in the mandate of already existing peacekeeping operations.[85] Other than R2P (but surely associated with it), PoC is a consequence of the reform process in peacekeeping operations. PoC is not so much about sovereignty and the question of when to intervene, but about one aspect in the planning and conduct of peace operations. So references to R2P in Security Council decisions up until Libya had been existent but were rather muted or tended to focus on state responsibility.

The case of Libya, which shall be treated in more detail here, is one that clearly was not about PoC but – to recall the phrase 'historic' cited at the

[85] See M. Fröhlich, 'Die Vereinten Nationen am Scheideweg' in Bundesakademie für Sicherheitspolitik (ed.), *Sicherheitspolitik in neuen Dimensionen*, supplementary vol. I, (Hamburg: Mittler, 2004), 427–48; and V. Holt and G. Taylor, *Protecting Civilians in the Context of UN Peacekeeping Operations: Successes, Setbacks and Remaining Challenges* (New York: UN Department of Peacekeeping Operations and UN Office for the Coordination of Humanitarian Affairs, 2009).

beginning of this chapter – clearly concurred with the argument of R2P. When the events in Libya unfolded, the initial reaction of the Council was expressed in Resolution 1970, which, in line with former resolution references, reiterated 'the Libyan authorities' responsibility to protect its population'.[86] That resolution immediately installed a number of sanctions under Article 41 and also stated that 'the widespread and systematic attacks currently taking place in the Libyan Arab Jamahiriya against the civilian population may amount to crimes against humanity'. In part, this recalled the specific threats that the outcome document had listed, but again, the complementary responsibility of the international community was not explicitly stated (although implicitly present in that the Council was dealing with the situation).

When we turn our attention then to Resolution 1973 on Libya, it is surprising to see that the exact term 'responsibility to protect' was not mentioned in this resolution. Yet, the concept was clearly present, starting with a perambulatory paragraph reiterating the responsibility of the Libyan authorities and reaffirming that 'parties to armed conflict bear the primary responsibility to take all feasible steps to ensure the protection of civilians'.[87] Furthermore, the Council expressed its determination 'to ensure the protection of civilians and civilian populated areas'. The resolution was replete with references to protection: it called for a ceasefire and the end of all attacks on civilians,[88] supported the mission of a UN envoy to work on a political option to resolve the crisis in accordance with the concerns of the population,[89] and appealed again to the Libyan authorities to take 'all measures to protect civilians'. This spectrum echoed the dual character of R2P as being a national and international responsibility. The comprehensive set of measures also echoed the triad of prevention, reaction, and rebuilding, as discussed earlier. Paragraph 4 of the resolution offered a number of special features. It authorized individual member states as well as regional organizations, after consultation with the Secretary-General, 'to take all necessary measures ... to protect civilians and civilian populated areas under attack'. The wording of 'all necessary measures' hinted at the use of force in the sense of Article 42 of the Charter. It was rather unusual for the Council to grant so loosely such an authorization to a group of states. Paragraph 4 also excluded the option to deploy an occupation force – wording that precludes the establishment of a presence like in Iraq but left open the option to deploy

[86] UN Doc. S/RES/1970, 26 Feb. 2011. [87] UN Doc. S/RES/1973, 17 Mar. 2011.
[88] Ibid., para. 1. [89] Ibid., para. 2.

special forces for a limited time period and scope of action. Paragraphs 6 and 8 of the resolution dealt with the establishment of a no-fly zone. Again, the wording included references to 'all necessary measures'. The resolution additionally reaffirmed the referral of the situation in Libya to the International Criminal Court (which brings to mind the element of international criminal justice in R2P) and the imposition of non-military sanctions. The text of the resolution also contained the provision that assets frozen as a result of the sanctions in place should be made available 'for the benefit of the people of the Libyan Arab Jamahiriya' as soon as possible.[90] Projecting beyond the current government in Libya, this already alluded to a 'responsibility to rebuild'. Notwithstanding the fact that the concept was not used as a wording trademark in the resolution, the broad range of references clearly indicate that R2P was a crucial element of the debate on how to confront the situation in Libya. Again, a detailed description of the diplomatic process that led to the adoption of the resolution goes beyond this chapter,[91] but the reference to the concept merits attention.

Although its substance has been transformed and surpassed by more recent UN publications and texts, the ICISS report in its entirety offers at least some explanation of why the heavily contested concept became a guideline for action in this context. The situation in Libya involved nearly all of the elements and principles that the commission had contemplated.[92] Concerning 'just cause', the situation clearly fulfilled the threshold criteria of 'large scale loss of life, actual or apprehended, with genocidal intent or not, which is the product either of deliberate state action, or state neglect or inability to act, or a failed state situation'.[93] At the beginning of March 2011, several international organizations estimated that violence in the country had caused several thousand casualties.[94] The declared intention to attack densely populated areas, such as the city of Benghazi with a population of roughly 600,000 people, entailed the prospect of a substantial increase in casualties. In contrast to several other cases

[90] Ibid., para. 20.

[91] See an initial overview by E. O'Brien and A. Sinclair, *The Libyan War: A Diplomatic History. February – August 2011* (New York: Center on International Cooperation, New York University, August 2011).

[92] See Fröhlich, 'Der Fall Libyen und die Norm der Schutzverantwortung'.

[93] ICISS 2001, xii.

[94] See H. Müller, *Ein Desaster: Deutschland und der Fall Libyen. Wie sich Deutschland moralisch und außenpolitisch in die Isolation manövrierte*, HSFK Statement 2, (Frankfurt a. M.: Hessische Stiftung für Friedens-und Konfliktforschung, 2011).

where there had been no explicit evidence of the intention of rulers to commit atrocities, the situation in Libya was rather clear. Both Muammar al-Gaddafi and his son Saif al-Islam had explicitly threatened revenge and massacres – in front of microphones and cameras.[95] In doing so, they underlined the fact that here was a case of 'national authorities manifestly fail[ing] to protect' their own citizens – to use the words of the 2005 outcome document. Hence, the situation in Libya was rather clear and also exceptional. Unlike the situation in Darfur, here was a dictator bluntly announcing his intention to massacre. Unlike the situation in Rwanda, even the Libyan UN delegation had broken with Gaddafi and supported the establishment of a no-fly zone. Under 'right intention', the ICISS report had asked that any operation must be 'clearly supported by regional opinion and victims concerned'.[96] The opposition groups had, for the large part, united behind the call for a no-fly zone. Support also came from the region with votes and declarations by the Arab League, the Organization of the Islamic Conference, as well as the Gulf Cooperation Council. As for the 'last resort' principle, there had been several attempts at mediation, although they probably would have needed more time to have an effect. The immediate threat to Benghazi tipped the scale for the argument that there were 'reasonable grounds for believing lesser measures would not have succeeded'.[97] Consideration of the principle of 'reasonable prospects' also was no impediment to an application of the responsibility to react: the terrain in Libya allowed for several military options, the areas of Gaddafi forces and rebel forces were easy to identify, and the military means of the government not insurmountable. All these considerations – together with the dynamic of the diplomatic negotiations for the text – resulted in the fact that the 'right authority' principle did not pose a problem once a sufficient majority in the Council had supported adoption of the resolution and no vetoes were cast. To be sure, the Council did not need a reference to the responsibility to protect in order to pass such a resolution. Its authority to order military action is not dependent upon identifying specific triggers, nor does it (and did it) use the references to protection in a legal sense of a principle that would have

[95] See The Editors, 'What Qaddafi Said: Excerpts from Libyan Leader Muammar al-Qaddafi's Last Televised Address', Foreign Affairs Report *Libya in Crisis*, www.foreignaffairs.com/articles/67878/the-editors/what-qaddafi-said?page=show (last accessed 26 Aug. 2013); *Euronews*, 'Saif al-Islam Gaddafi: "In 48 Stunden ist alles vorbei"', Interview on 16 Mar. 2011, http://de.euronews.net/2011/03/16/saif-al-islam-gaddafi-in-48-stunden-ist-alles-vorbei-/ (last accessed 26 Aug. 2013).

[96] ICISS 2001, xii. [97] Ibid., xii.

given its decision more weight. Although R2P is not an element of Resolution 1973 in a technical sense of the wording, we cannot understand the striking fact that members of the Council agreed on this resolution in such a short amount of time without taking into account the context of the conceptual foundation and transformation of R2P, as outlined earlier.

An account of the Libya case in R2P terms cannot, however, overlook that ultimate implementation of the operation also shows incompatibilities with the operational principles and the requirement of proportional means. There were some ambiguities in the mandate and command structure, and the primary emphasis on air power led to collateral damage and a concentration on certain kinds of military targets. The R2P requirement of 'gradualism in the application of force, the objective being protection of a population, not defeat of a state'[98] also was not mirrored in the reality of the operation, which aimed at maximum speed in order not to strain public support among the states that had agreed to participate in the operation. Without questioning the success of having saved the lives of thousands with the military operation in Libya, the R2P concept also would have required the world community to consider protecting some of the villages in which Gaddafi had allegedly hidden in the final days of the operation. These villages had been surrounded by rebels, and a just application of the R2P principle would have called for a strong and principled effort to quell any options of revenge or retaliation. Having said this, one also has to underline that inaction would have led to the fall of Benghazi and would also have thus terminated the further development of R2P.[99]

CONCLUSION

This remarkable development of R2P can be understood in terms of normative change in international relations. There are obvious links to what Finnemore and Sikkink have described as elements of a 'norm life cycle'.[100] According to this norm life cycle model, the initiative by the ICISS and Kofi Annan could be understood as the efforts of 'norm

98 Ibid., xiii.

99 R. Thakur, 'UN Breathes Life into Responsibility to Protect', *Toronto Star*, 21 March 2011 (last accessed 26 Aug. 2013).

100 M. Finnemore and K. Sikkink, 'International Norm Dynamics and Political Change', *International Organization* 52 (1998), 887–917; E. Luck, 'Building a Norm: The Responsibility to Protect Experience' in R. I. Rotberg (ed.), *Mass Atrocity Crimes:*

entrepreneurs'[101] whose work is typical of the first phase of the life cycle: norm emergence. This phase then leads up to a 'tipping point' that, in turn, leads to the second phase: 'norm cascade'. Finnemore and Sikkink do not believe that it is only the power of norms in a constructivist perspective on social action that accounts for their proliferation. They also underline that rational choice theory accounts for the decisions of member states (and their leaders) to promote and adopt a specific norm. This ties in with the argument made by ICISS that, 'whatever other motives intervening states may have', the protection intention should at least be the dominant one.[102] After a critical mass of actors (in this case mostly states) have agreed upon a new norm, it cascades to other levels of actions and groups of actors, a development that finally leads to the third phase of the life cycle: 'internalization'. In that last phase, the norm is established as some kind of self-evident standard of behaviour. The 2005 document of the General Assembly – in such a reading – can be seen to be an equivalent of the 'tipping point'. However, the reality of the R2P case is not completely compatible with the elements of the norm life cycle. On the one hand, the resolution is 'more' than the required group of critical states because all members of the UN agreed to the incorporation of R2P into that document. On the other, the document is 'less' than the required 'tipping point' because a resolution of the General Assembly is not binding international law, and member states had used the negotiations on the text to substantially change the content of the R2P concept, which still remained contested.

In this perspective, the example of R2P offers a number of lessons for normative change in international relations. It is rather symptomatic that a political actor in the R2P process, UN Special Adviser Edward Luck, reflected on his own work on the emergence of R2P by applying the norm life cycle.[103] Although he affirms that the model can be applied, he argues: 'There have been more stops, starts, detours, and regeneration in R2P's young life than any chart could properly depict.'[104] He adds that 'the model fails to incorporate the interactive and sometimes even dysfunctional nature of international politics, assuming an overly linear conception of progress'.[105] The reality is obviously not ordered strictly according

Preventing Future Outrages (Washington, DC: Brookings Institution Press, 2010), 108–27.

101 Ibid., 896–9. 102 ICISS 2001, xii. 103 Luck, 'Building a Norm', 110.

104 Ibid.

105 Ibid., 112; see also J. Welsh, 'Implementing the Responsibility to Protect: Where Expectations Meet Reality', *Ethics & International Affairs*, 24 (2010), 415–30.

to the model. The conceptual foundation and transformation depicted earlier clearly illustrate movements back and forth as well as contradictions and compromise along the way. In this context, Luck argues that the fact that a tipping point is reached (as in the outcome document 2005) is no guarantee that the norm will progress forward – it can also tip backwards.[106] The contestation of norms is therefore not unusual, but rather a standard feature of new norms emerging in the international realm.[107]

Against this background, Resolution 1973 may mark yet another 'tipping point' that again raises the question whether the norm will gain further ground or will roll back. The case of Syria in this context is quite remarkable in many ways: the death toll is even larger than in the Libyan case, but the reaction has not been as quick and decisive as it was in Libya. There are several reasons for this difference. Nearly all of the enabling factors in place in Libya – ranging from the terrain to the unity of opposition forces – were not in place in Syria. In addition, Russia and China framed Syria in the context of what they depicted as a betrayal of their acquiescence with the Libyan decision. The Russian foreign minister clearly stated that Russia would not 'allow the Libyan experience to be reproduced in Syria'.[108] For the ICISS report, opposition by permanent members of the Security Council is one of the crucial impediments to the application of R2P. The report clearly states that R2P may not be applied in all cases in which it should be applied, but 'the reality that interventions may not be able to be mounted in every case where there is justification for doing so, is no reason for them to be mounted in any case'.[109] Such an argument is, however, dangerous for a normative concept that – according to its ethical core – aims to protect all people at risk and not only those who live in certain countries. This has opened the doors for a new line of criticism against R2P. Besides those who claim that R2P is a type of free ticket for neocolonial military suppression, some commentators would argue that R2P is mere rhetoric that does not live up to its promise because its conceptual overreach is not balanced by concrete reforms of the political and legal procedures to address atrocities. Instead

[106] Luck, 'Building a Norm', 117.

[107] A. Wiener, 'Enacting Meaning-in-Use: Qualitative Research on Norms and International Relations', *Review of International Studies*, 35 (2009), 175–93.

[108] Interview at http://en.rian.ru/russia/20121209/178024186.html (last accessed 26 Aug. 2013).

[109] ICISS 2001, 37.

of putting effort in its further development, one should revert to the concept of humanitarian intervention.[110] The argument presented here takes a middle road: R2P has succeeded not only in changing but even in raising the level of debate in a way that enhances the value of former debates on humanitarian intervention. Its development from concept to practice has been astonishingly fast, and this is because the range of problems that confronts the international community is closely tied to the main concern of R2P. While R2P obviously holds the potential of instrumentalization, the debate on the concept and its transformation have also shown that criticism directed at R2P can also be instrumentalized – to discredit the idea of human rights and human security. Although this experience is also present in the history of humanitarian intervention, the foundation, transformation and application of R2P offers a new language and new potential to reconcile or balance sovereignty and intervention in the twenty-first century. As the history of humanitarian intervention shows, no normative claim and concept can take away the ambivalences and dilemmas that seem to be inherent in any effort of the international community or humanity to try and find an appropriate reaction to massacre.

[110] A. Hehir, *The Responsibility to Protect*, 3–12.

15

Humanitarian interventions, past and present

Andrew Thompson

Today everyone is a humanitarian, or at least that is how it seems. Humanitarian crises are rarely absent from the global media. They call forth large-scale campaigns designed to mobilize donor publics and to persuade or pressurize governments into action they might otherwise avoid. In many of the world's most troubled regions, humanitarian interventions have become a substitute for political interventions, with the emphasis more on the containment of conflict than its prevention or resolution. There is in fact much gnashing of teeth over an ongoing 'crisis of humanitarianism', fuelled by the more routine interaction of humanitarians with military forces and by resistance from non-Western powers to humanitarian missions widely perceived to serve Western interests.[1] In the wake of military intervention in Iraq, which produced a bigger

I would like to thank Jean-Luc Blondel, Fabian Klose, Robert Peckham, and Annabel Lenton-Thompson for their perceptive comments on an earlier draft of this essay. The author is proud to be an Honorary Professor in the College of Graduate Studies at the University of South Africa in Pretoria, and grateful for UNISA's friendship and support.

[1] For the debate, see Mary Anderson, *Do No Harm: How Aid Can Support Peace – Or War* (Boulder, CO: Lynne Rienner Publishers, 1999); Didier Fassin and Mariella Pandolfi (eds.), *Contemporary States of Emergency: The Politics of Military and Humanitarian Interventions* (New York: Zone, 2010); David Kennedy, *The Dark Sides of Virtue: Reassessing International Humanitarianism* (Princeton University Press, 2004); Jonathan Moore (ed.), *Hard Choices: Moral Dilemmas in Humanitarian Intervention* (Lanham: Roman & Littlefield, 1998); Fiona Terry, *Condemned to Repeat? The Paradox of Humanitarian Action* (Ithaca, NY: Cornell University Press, 2002); Peter Walker and Daniel Maxwell, *Shaping the Humanitarian World* (New York: Routledge, 2009).

humanitarian disaster than it set out to resolve, some question whether aid may not be doing more harm than good.[2]

These problems have become all too familiar in recent times. Yet there is a much longer and richer history of humanitarian action and intervention, which is explored in this book. The greater prominence of humanitarian issues in international affairs is a defining characteristic not only of the last two decades but of the last two centuries. The precise origins of this transformation may be open to debate. Its effects are however plain to see. Starting in the early 1800s, humanitarian movements became more widespread and popular. They were driven by a mixture of secular and religious concerns, redefined norms in the regulation of armed conflict, and promoted an unprecedented change in the breadth of knowledge within Western societies about the sufferings of people elsewhere in the world, however selective the resulting interventions may have been.

In their preoccupation with the here and now, humanitarians are said to be ignorant of their own history.[3] There are signs that this is changing, however.[4] Leading humanitarian organizations have been delving back into their past in order to look forward to the challenges of the future. Tracing the arc of modern humanitarianism – from the anti-slavery movements of the early nineteenth century to twenty-first-century peacekeeping missions, counter-insurgency campaigns, and internationalized civil wars – is not only of academic interest therefore. With the publication in 2011 of Michael Barnett's *Empire of Humanity: A History of Humanitarianism* and Brendan Simms' and David Trim's *Humanitarian*

[2] For a trenchant critique, arguing that recipients of aid are not better but worse off as a result, see Dambisa Moyo's, *Dead Aid: Why Aid Makes Things Worse and How There is Another Way for Africa* (London: Penguin, 2009).

[3] For the view that aid agencies need to pay more attention to the history of contemporary ideas and interventions, see David Lewis, 'International Development and the "Perpetual Present": Anthropological Approaches to the Re-historicization of Policy', *European Journal of Historical Research*, 21 (2009), 32–46. For the insights to be gained, see Monica Van Beusekom and Dorothy Hodgson, 'Lessons Learned? Development Experiences in the Late Colonial Period', *Journal of African History*, 41 (2000), 29–33.

[4] Randolph Kent, Justin Armstrong, and Alice Obrecht, *The Future of Non-Governmental Organisations in the Humanitarian Sector: Global Transformations and Their Consequences*, Humanitarian Futures Programme discussion paper (Kings College London, 2013), esp. 5–6. For an example see C. Magone, M. Neuman and F. Wiseman, *Humanitarian Negotiations Revealed: the MSF Experience* (Hurst, 2011). This would equally be true of the International Committee of the Red Cross, with which I am organizing a conference in September 2015 to mark the 50th anniversary of its 'Fundamental Principles' and to explore the history of the principles from the beginning of the Red Cross / Red Crescent Movement.

Intervention: A History, there is a palpable sense of a new research landscape opening up before our eyes, the contours of which are so ably delineated by the contributors to this book.[5] Collectively, they make a compelling case for the study of humanitarian interventions in the past in order to better understand the problems faced in the present.

The preceding chapters range widely across three centuries of humanitarian history and many different types of conflict in many different parts of the world. Four overarching themes nevertheless emerge. The first – to which we shall return – is the definitional difficulties that arise from the terms 'humanitarian' and 'intervention'. It is these definitional difficulties which lie at the heart of many of the debates about humanitarian interventions whether in the academic literature or between politicians and in the press. Another is the differing perceptions of the lawfulness and legitimacy of this *particular* mode of humanitarian activity, and the consequent challenge of building of a consensus around protecting international humanitarian norms by force, even as those norms are themselves in flux. Third, many of the contributors explore the respective roles of state and non-state bodies in response to large-scale loss of life and human rights violations and how this has shifted over time. Finally, and crucially, there is the question of the broader geopolitical environment in which conflict takes place, and how geopolitics has affected the nature of the humanitarian interventions undertaken in conflict and the type of justification they require.

For the book as a whole, a key point to grasp is that histories of humanitarian intervention do not stand alone. Rather they are entangled with broader historiographies of humanitarianism and of human rights. The intensifying critical scrutiny to which forcible humanitarian interventions have lately (and rightly) been subjected must not be viewed in isolation from other forms of humanitarian aid. Humanitarian interventions have taken place in the context of a wider international humanitarian system, of which 'armed humanitarianism' was merely one, if very visible, component.[6] Take, for example, the unease surrounding the

[5] Michael Barnett, *Empire of Humanity: A History of Humanitarianism* (Ithaca, NY: Cornell University Press, 2011); Brendan Simms and David J. B. Trim (eds.), *Humanitarian Intervention: A History* (Cambridge University Press, 2011).

[6] For the view that governments have fabricated moral motives in order to secure public support for military campaigns that would not otherwise have been forthcoming, see Mark Curtis, *Unpeople: Britain's Secret Human Rights Abuses* (London: Vintage, 2004), esp. chs. 7 and 8. Curtis reprises the argument popularized by Naomi Klein in *The Shock Doctrine: The Rise of Disaster Capitalism* (New York: Metropolitan Books,

conflation of military and humanitarian roles in conflict during and after the 1990s. The militarization of humanitarian aid is widely viewed by humanitarians as a chief cause of the 'crisis' referred to earlier. But the militarization of aid is itself part of a much bigger debate surrounding humanitarian action – its purpose, its inadequate means, and its questionable consequences. Indeed, the increased frequency, severity, and unpredictability of emergencies as a result of global economic instability, climate change,[7] and the rise of sectarian violence has presented as many problems for 'peaceful' humanitarian operations as it has for their 'forcible' counterparts. As we enter the twenty-first century, international NGOs, multilateral agencies, and governments are all having to ask whether emergency aid and relief may not have to be conceived and delivered very differently in future if the international humanitarian system is not repeatedly to fail those most in need.

The 2011 report *Humanitarian Emergency Response Review* of Lord (Paddy) Ashdown is a case in point. The Ashdown report was at pains to set its findings in a longer-term perspective. It depicts humanitarians as being caught in a race between the growing size of the challenge and their ability to cope: a race they are deemed not to be winning.[8] Part of the problem is felt to lie with an international humanitarian system that, over the last 150 years, has evolved haphazardly and inconsistently, repeatedly failed those in need, and suffered from numerous gaps, overlaps, and inefficiencies as well as lack of accountability, leadership, and coordination. In the words of the report: 'Merely improving upon what has been done in the past will not be enough to meet the challenges of the future.'[9] Interestingly, the report draws no hard and fast distinction between humanitarian interventions and other types of humanitarian action. Instead, it reflects the current zeitgeist around the problem of 'shrinking humanitarian space' by insisting that there will be times when military force, mandated by the UN, is vital to protect the increasingly 'fragile'

2007), in particular that humanitarian crises are opportunities for the power of the state (or private capital) to expand.

7 For the relationship between climate change and conflict, see S. M. Hsiang, M. Burke and E. Miguel, 'Quantifying the Influence of Climate Change on Human Conflict', *Science*, 341 (2013), 1212–26.

8 *Humanitarian Emergency Response Review*, 28 March 2011, Chaired by Lord (Paddy) Ashdown, available from the website of the Department for International Development: https://gov.uk/government/uploads/system/uploads/attachment_data/file/67579/HERR.pdf (last accessed 5 August 2015).

9 Ibid., 12.

environment into which humanitarian agencies are admitted and times when it is not.

Like many other such publications the Ashdown report treats humanitarianism as a stable and singular concept. In this book, by contrast, the reader repeatedly encounters the question of how widely or narrowly the concept should be defined.[10] Defined too widely, humanitarianism lacks precision; defined too narrowly, we lose sight of 'the broader ways in which humanitarian ideology intersected with various forms of coercive ... diplomacy'.[11]

A further – and central – definitional difficulty arises from the interplay between the 'national' and the 'international' in humanitarian policy and practice. Humanitarians present what they do as universal – they are a territorially boundless community transcending nation states. Yet few would deny that today's international humanitarian system remains tied to particular parts of the Western world at the expense of humanitarianism's non-Western equivalents. To understand why this is the case we need to delve back into the nineteenth as well as the twentieth century. Take the care of the poor in Africa. In precolonial times this was largely a matter of individual largess and distributed through highly personal networks.[12] The idea of institutionalized welfare provision was very much a colonial innovation. Precisely because African generosity was not easily channelled into large European organizations, indigenous welfare traditions were easily overlooked. In China, meanwhile, the state has long been regarded as a legitimate and positive humanitarian actor. Less value is therefore placed on civil society actors and there is also much less debate in China about the political manipulation of aid.[13]

Even within the West, humanitarian movements are remarkably diverse. Over the last century the range of activities they have undertaken has expanded almost exponentially. It now includes the provision of water, food aid, shelter, medical and health services, refugee services, rehabilitation and welfare projects, human rights advocacy, and full-scale military intervention. Because of this ever-widening range of activities judging whether interventions are predominantly for humanitarian purposes is considerably more complex. A diversity of missions has produced

[10] Jan Erik Schulte, Chapter 12, 254, in this book.
[11] Quote taken from Abigail Green, Chapter 7, 145, in this book.
[12] John Iliffe, *The African Poor: A History* (Cambridge University Press, 1987), ch.11.
[13] Miwa Hirono, 'Three Legacies of Humanitarianism in China', *Disasters*, 37 (2013), 202–20.

a diversity of requirements and a corresponding need to separate out humanitarianism's different strands in order to better gauge what an appropriate 'intervention' might be.[14]

Histories of humanitarian intervention turn around the questions of who intervenes, for what reasons, through what relationships, and with what results.[15] On the face of it, the essential features of a humanitarian *intervention* are well established. They are uninvited and unwelcome interventions by one or more states in the affairs of another state, infringing on the sovereignty of that state, involving the use of force, and undertaken for the purpose of humanitarian protection and assistance.[16] But beyond the slippery question of what are considered to be valid humanitarian objectives, there is equally, as Jan Erik Schulte points out, the matter of how much and what type of compulsion is required. In the preceding chapters we have encountered two main scenarios in which the roles of the military and humanitarians have become blurred. One is the limited deployment of a strong military presence to clear the ground for humanitarians to act, either by removing blockades imposed on relief or by protecting its distribution, as was the case in Somalia and the Balkans during the early 1990s (and is again the pressing issue in Syria today).[17] The other scenario is the co-optation of medical, welfare, and education programmes within counter-insurgency operations, as part of a broader strategy for winning the loyalty of local people, as was the case in Iraq and in Afghanistan a decade later.[18]

Such engagement of the military with relief operations is by no means a uniquely contemporary phenomenon. A recurring theme in the history of

[14] I am grateful to Corinna Hauswedell, who expressed this point very forcefully at the conference from which this book emerged.

[15] Fred Cooper makes this point with reference to development, see 'Writing the History of Development', *Journal of Modern European History*, 8 (2010), 5–23.

[16] The term 'humanitarian intervention' is defined at various stages in this book: see Fabian Klose, Chapter 1, 7–8; Schulte, Chapter 12, 255–56; and Norrie MacQueen, Chapter 11, 232. For an important contribution from the wider historiography, see J. L. Holzgrefe and Robert Keohane, *Humanitarian Intervention: Ethical, Legal and Political Dilemmas* (Cambridge University Press, 2004).

[17] On Somalia, see Jon Western, Chapter 8, 181–82, in this book; on the Balkans, see Schulte, Chapter 12, 272, 275–76.

[18] Marcos Ferreiro, 'Blurring of Lines in Complex Emergencies: Consequences for the Humanitarian Community', *The Journal of Humanitarian Assistance*, 24 December 2012, http://sites.tufts.edu/jha/archives/1625 (last accessed 5 August 2015). For a case study of post-war counter-insurgency operations that explores their links to welfare and development programmes, see David French, *The British Way in Counter-Insurgency, 1945–67* (Oxford University Press, 2011), ch. 6.

modern humanitarianism is that of its cooperation, complicity and collusion with state power. The dilemma faced by humanitarians – past and present – is whether they can ever share common goals with the military. Many think not. Humanitarian intervention is either regarded *a priori* as a misnomer – the military, it is argued, can never be genuinely humanitarian – or joint military-humanitarian operations are felt to be far too vulnerable to pressures to deploy aid according to strategic assessments of military threat rather than impartial humanitarian need. Either way, there is a fundamental ambivalence to the concept of humanitarian intervention, as noted by Manuel Fröhlich – a concept that wants to legitimize yet limit the use of force at the very same time.[19]

Maintaining a distinction between the military and humanitarian components of emergency interventions is, as we have noted, all the more difficult as a result of the expansion of the scope of humanitarianism itself.[20] As the aid community has moved beyond the traditional task of distributing emergency relief to try to prevent acts of ethnic cleansing, or to support processes of post-conflict reconstruction and transformation, so it has become harder to distinguish its goals from those of donor states' security and stabilization agendas. The concept of humanitarian interventionism has come to look suspiciously like a post-Cold War concept of 'liberal interventionism': international stability is equated with the Western export of democratic freedoms, human rights, and neo-liberal economic values to 'failing' non-Western regimes.

Much of the legitimacy of humanitarian interventions hangs in the balance of this question of right motivations. Yet, as Michael Ignatieff argues, humanitarian motives are not discredited simply because they are mixed. Otherwise, almost all interventions would be suspect.[21] Genuine grievances have always been exploited for reasons of state interest. The real issues are, first, whether *non-humanitarian* considerations prevent the possibility of any positive humanitarian outcome? Second, how do we

[19] Fröhlich, Chapter 14, 303–4.

[20] See, especially, Geoff Loane, who, while observing how humanitarianism's base 'is as broad as the multiplicity of actions that go to represent its interventions', notes how the resulting ambiguities can complicate humanitarianism's mandate, blur the boundaries between relief and development operations, and make the presence of aid agencies more open to manipulation by belligerents: Geoff Loane and Tanja Schümer (eds.), *The Wider Impact of Humanitarian Assistance: The Case of Sudan and the Implications for European Union Policy* (Baden-Baden: Nomos, 2000), 19–20, 24–5.

[21] M. Ignatieff, *Empire Lite: Nation-Building in Bosnia, Kosovo and Afghanistan* (London: Vintage, 2003), 59; see also Simms and Trim, *Humanitarian Intervention*, 398, 400.

judge humanitarian value in the light of the inevitable compromises that humanitarianism's involvement with these other – more overtly political – considerations entail?[22]

The study of motivation requires sensitivity to the consequential use of language – namely, how the categories through which people have thought about human suffering in the past shaped what they actually did.[23] Because the labelling of an intervention as *humanitarian* is ultimately the basis upon which the breach of state sovereignty is justified and the deployment of force legitimized, it is vital to try to disentangle different impulses to act in order to understand why states have previously intervened when they did and in the way they did. Purity of humanitarian motivation has probably never existed.[24] Terms like 'genuine humanitarianism' must therefore be suspect. What the contributors to this book suggest is that, scratching beneath the surface, genuine humanitarian impulses are invariably entangled with (and sometimes side-lined by) a wider set of geopolitical, diplomatic, and security concerns.[25]

At their worst, humanitarian interventions have merely provided pretexts for military conquest, the control of natural resources, and the assertion of great power status, largely or wholly divorced from the human suffering they claim as their primary concern. Mairi MacDonald's study of the Brussels Anti-Slavery Conference (1890) exposes the conceit that colonial rule was the best or the only way to protect Africans against the slave trade. Anti-slavery ends and humanitarian rhetoric were 'used to justify means that were not far from the worst of the abuses the Brussels Treaty sought to eliminate'. The close links between humanitarianism and the colonial projects of European powers are further highlighted by Fabian Klose. During the nineteenth century, humanitarians were sometimes vociferous advocates of imperial expansion, with missionary activity leading to calls for protectorates to shield indigenous populations from the ravages of settler occupation.[26] Yet, as MacDonald shows, Leopold

[22] Thomas Weiss, *Humanitarian Intervention: Ideas in Action* (Cambridge: Polity Press, 2012), 7; Nicholas J. Wheeler, *Saving Strangers: Humanitarian Intervention in International Society* (Oxford University Press, 2000), 133; Ignatieff, *Empire Lite*, 23.

[23] On the importance of language, see Didier Fassin, *Humanitarian Reason: A Moral History of the Present* (Berkeley: University Of California Press, 2012).

[24] Klose, Chapter 1, 13.

[25] This point comes across powerfully in Bradley Simpson's contribution in Chapter 13 of this book; see also Western on the American response in Cuba, Chapter 8, 177-80.

[26] A. Lester, *Imperial Networks: Creating Identities in Nineteenth Century South Africa and Britain* (London: Routledge, 2001); Jane Sansom, *Imperial Benevolence: Making British Authority in the Pacific Islands* (Honolulu: University of Hawai'i Press, 1998);

was more cynical: to exploit Congo's resources, he wrapped up commercial self-interest in the language of European civilization: an abuse of the term 'humanitarian' which 'provided cover for decidedly inhumane and uncivilized behaviour'.[27]

In a similar vein, Jost Dülffer reveals how a long tradition of political obfuscation among the great powers persisted well into the twentieth century, as the appeal to higher moral purposes served as little more than a Trojan horse for the projection of state power. His salutary essay on the 'dark sides' of intervention demonstrates how humanitarian language paraded as altruism under the Nazi regime. Like Leopold, Hitler cynically appropriated such language for aggressive and expansionist purposes. The fight for living space in Central and Eastern Europe may at first seem a far cry from humanitarianism. But the aim to unite all Germans in a single Reich not only evoked the principle of self-determination: it raised the question of the protection of minorities, the violation of whose rights and freedoms had been a long-standing humanitarian concern. There was nonetheless an inherent danger in the use of such rhetoric. The logic upon which it was based – minority rights – exposed Hitler's foreign policy to charges of having suppressed one ethnic group in favour of another. The use of the concept of humanitarian intervention by the Nazi regime for ethnic reasons was increasingly unconvincing therefore.[28]

Parsing out 'humanitarian' from other impulses is a tricky task.[29] The chapters by Norrie MacQueen and Jan Erik Schulte explore why humanitarian operations have been sometimes more, sometimes less prominent on the agenda of UN peacekeeping. During the Cold War, humanitarian operations were of secondary importance: other reasons for initiating peacekeeping operations prevailed. Humanitarian tasks were, however, grafted onto existing missions, most notably the UNFICYP in the Cyprus conflict after the 1974 Turkish invasion; the UNOSOM in Somalia in 1992 – a UN operation clearly organized as a humanitarian intervention; and UNPROFOR in Yugoslavia after its mission was extended from Croatia to Bosnia and Herzegovina in the same year.[30] For all that, the risk of conceptual confusion remains. Peacekeeping missions, unlike

Z. Laidlaw, *Colonial Connections, 1815–45: Patronage, the Information Revolution and Colonial Government* (Manchester University Press, 2005); Ian Tyrrell, *Reforming the World: The Creation of America's Moral Empire* (Princeton University Press, 2010).

[27] Mairi MacDonald, Chapter 6, esp. 122, 136–38, 140–41; quote from 140, in this book.

[28] See Jost Dülffer's contribution, Chapter 10, in this book.

[29] As recognized by Western, Chapter 8, 177.

[30] Schulte, Chapter 12, 266, 270, 272.

humanitarian interventions, have historically required the consent of the host state, the impartiality of the peacekeeping force, and the use of force in self-defence only as a last resort. Indeed, for MacQueen, the 'fundamentally self-restricting character' of peacekeeping pitches the concept 'against not just collective security by enforcement but also meaningful armed humanitarian intervention'.[31] It is also worth noting how, in response to the large-scale loss of life in conflict, the UN has been willing to act pragmatically in its own self-interest just as much as any member state – and arguably all the more so when its reputation and credibility as a multilateral institution have been on the line.[32]

The remainder of this chapter will pursue five avenues of enquiry which are critical to a more integrated analysis of the history of humanitarian interventions – an analysis which bridges the nineteenth, twentieth, and twenty-first centuries; state and non-state actors; Western and non-Western practices and perceptions; and the relationship between humanitarian interventions and related discourses, especially those on religious persecution, 'civilization', and 'human rights'.

First: many of the chapters in this book grapple with what we might call the dynamics of commitment of proponents of humanitarian intervention. Humanitarianism has never stood alone: it is a doctrine dependent on an array of other beliefs and ideals. It is these beliefs and ideals that are in turn the key to understanding why public narratives of suffering have taken particular forms and why they have been mobilized on behalf of some peoples and not others.[33] Of particular interest is the interface between humanitarianism and anti-slavery, as well as anti-Semitism and Philhellenism, discourses closely tied to those 'solidarity', 'advocacy', and 'exile' communities that lobbied states to protect their kith and kin.[34] These communities portrayed the sufferings of their own peoples in a universal language of humanity, recasting the violence inflicted upon like-minded religious, ethnic, or linguistic groups as crimes offending

[31] MacQueen, Chapter 11, 239.

[32] This was also true of other multilateral institutions, including NATO and the Commonwealth. For the concerns of the Clinton administration for the UN and NATO after the atrocities at Srebrenica, see Western, Chapter 8, 182–83.

[33] Richard Wilson and Richard Brown, 'Introduction' in Richard Wilson and Richard Brown (eds.), *Humanitarianism and Suffering: The Mobilization of Empathy* (Cambridge University Press, 2009), 1–30.

[34] On anti-slavery, see Klose, Chapter 5; on anti-Semitism, see Green, Chapter 7; on Philhellenism, see Western, Chapter 8; on advocacy communities, see Simpson, Chapter 13.

international society as a whole. In this way, a wide range of civil and religious liberties were advanced under the symbol of the moral progress that humanitarianism embodied.

These constellations of different moral and ideological precepts which together have constituted humanitarianism explain why it has proved so difficult to separate the religious from the secular, the ethical from the political, and the rhetorical from the epistemological in humanitarian policy and practice. Humanitarian sensibilities have, at various times, been refracted through languages of 'civilization', 'trusteeship', 'self-determination', and 'human rights'. As people expressed solidarity with their fellow human beings, within their own countries and across international borders, we need to ask how far such empathy was a product of humanitarian concern? Put another way, was humanitarianism essentially a function of other commitments and hence reliant upon the hospitality provided by other movements and vulnerable to their priorities and preoccupations? Or was humanitarianism – as a global discourse, backed by global institutions – able to harness these other discourses for its own ends?

Of particular interest here is what Michael Geyer aptly describes as the 'troubled rapport' between humanitarianism and human rights – at once convergent and competitive concepts.[35] Human rights violations have triggered humanitarian interventions. Humanitarian interventions have reinforced human rights discourse. Beyond that, the element of universality, rooted in the Enlightenment, underpins human rights and humanitarian thinking. They share a view of 'humanity' as a unified international community: basic rights and fundamental needs are to be enjoyed by all people in the world by virtue of that humanity. They suffer from similar shortcomings too. The common humanity that humanitarians and human rights activists invoke is not always as common as they suggest. Humanity is defined so as to give rights to some while withholding them from others; aid and relief are distributed to certain places while neglecting humanitarian needs elsewhere. As one commentator shrewdly observes, 'the "human" part of human rights' – and, we might add, of humanitarianism, too – 'has always been unstable, variable in scope and inclusiveness'.[36]

[35] Michael Geyer, Chapter 2, in this book.

[36] Joanna Bourke, *What It Means To Be Human: Reflections from 1791 to the Present* (London: Virago, 2011), 136.

Such is their convergence. That said, the fusion of humanitarianism and human rights is analytically difficult,[37] and the promotion of the one has sometimes been (or at least perceived to have been) at the expense of the other.[38] Encompassing the sacred as well as the secular, humanitarian discourse has long been based on the alleviation of suffering rather than the defence of rights. Faced with the destitution and oppression of others, humanitarians appeal as much to the heart as to the head – pity, charity, and compassion are the sentiments they seek to evoke. Why, then, in recent times the fashion for eliding humanitarianism and human rights?

Kofi Annan's assertion that a global age calls for a new type of global security is a striking example of this category conflation.[39] In a clear riposte to non-interventionists, Annan called for the UN to take seriously its responsibility to protect people against egregious violations of human rights. His deliberate linking of the protection of human rights with humanitarianism was not new. As Bradley Simpson observes, the temptation to substitute the one for the other has long been present. Over the decades, the act of intervening in humanitarian crises has frequently been regarded as less political than that of responding to human rights crimes.[40] (In a similar fashion proponents of development aid have represented large-scale agricultural projects as *technical* solutions to problems of deprivation and poverty, thereby ignoring how they entrench state power.) Indeed, by focusing attention on the interests of victims rather than states, humanitarianism has sometimes lent an aura of morality to interventions far less disinterested than their sponsoring states suggest.[41]

Nor is it only states that have succumbed to such temptations. There is just as pressing a need to investigate when and why non-state humanitarianism has adopted a language of inalienable and universal rights.[42] Some agencies, such as the International Red Cross / Red Crescent Movement,

[37] Geyer, Chapter 2.

[38] A. Dirk Moses, 'The United Nations, Humanitarianism and Human Rights: War Crimes / Genocide Trials for Pakistani Soldiers in Bangladesh, 1971–1974' in Stefan Ludwig Hoffman (ed.), *Human Rights in the Twentieth Century* (Cambridge University Press, 2011), 277.

[39] Kofi A. Annan, *We the Peoples: The Role of the United Nations in the 21st Century* (New York: United Nations. Department of Public Information, 2000).

[40] Simpson, Chapter 13, 297.

[41] Didier Fassin and Mariella Pandolfi, 'Introduction: Military and Humanitarian Government in the Age of Intervention' in Fassin and Pandolfi (eds.), *Contemporary States of Emergency*, 13.

[42] Matthew Hilton, 'International Aid and Development NGOs in Britain and Human Rights since 1945', *Humanity*, 3, no. 3 (Winter 2012), 449–72.

remain firmly of the view that humanitarianism is non-political.[43] The International Committee of the Red Cross (ICRC), in particular, has been prepared to sacrifice the right to speak out in order to protect its proximity to the victims of armed conflict and to gain access to places often off-limits to other organizations. This is a principled stance in so far as the ICRC has a clear mandate given by states under the Geneva Conventions; human rights are covered by a separate body of international law and regarded by the ICRC and others as part of political decision-making. But it is also pragmatic, as the public condemnation of human rights abuses runs the risk of jeopardizing the ICRC's operations in the field. That said, 'public silence' does not equate to silence in negotiations, while repeated violations of humanitarian law by states may lead to the ICRC to take a more public stand.[44] Other agencies, however, such as Oxfam and Christian Aid, have strenuously sought to incorporate the human rights concept into their work by representing emergency relief and development aid as a matter of survival or socio-economic rights.[45] In their view, humanitarianism's quest to be apolitical is not only naïve but positively harmful, in so far as it draws public attention away from the political reasons for victimization and the violation of rights.[46]

The relationship between humanitarianism and human rights is further complicated by the more integrated way of thinking about the legal protection of victims of armed conflict that has emerged over the last half century. International humanitarian law has slowly expanded towards the concerns of the human rights community partly as a result of the

[43] The ICRC, the National Red Cross and Red Crescent Societies, and their International Federation formally codified their 'fundamental principles' of humanity, impartiality, neutrality, and independence in Vienna in 1965. In practice, within the movement there are strong differences: some national societies are very close to their governments, some are more international in their outlook and operation.

[44] See, for example, the ICRC's policy on reports on political detention, where the rule of confidentiality may be suspended in such circumstances. Nor are private negotiation and public condemnation necessarily antagonistic. It can be argued that the success of humanitarian and human rights NGOs is precisely contingent on a real articulation between quiet diplomacy and moral persuasion, on the one hand, and public pressure and denunciation, on the other.

[45] A criticism of such moral approaches to human rights is that they undermine legal approaches without seriously challenging the violence and exploitation that give rise to economic and social vulnerability: see Geoff Loane and Céline Moyroud (eds.), *Tracing the Unintended Consequences of Humanitarian Assistance: the Case of Sudan* (Baden-Baden: Nomos, 2001).

[46] R. A. Wilson (ed.), *Human Rights, Culture and Context: Anthropological Perspectives* (London: Pluto Press, 1997).

increase of internal conflicts and civil wars after 1945. Such 'protracted social conflicts', characterized by conditions of indiscriminate warfare, have seen repeated denials of humanitarian assistance by warring parties and generated growing international concern about the treatment of civilian bystanders.[47] They have thus underscored the necessity of extending elementary principles of protection for civilian populations in international humanitarian law. Article 3 of the 1949 Geneva Conventions was meant to address these situations. Almost before the ink had dried on Article 3, however, it was widely apparent that its sixteen lines of text would not be sufficiently strong. From the 1950s onwards a succession of expert commissions and conferences sought to strengthen this aspect of international humanitarian law, culminating in the two additional protocols to the Geneva Conventions of 1977. Yet Protocol II, intended to provide greater protection to the victims of 'non-international' armed conflicts, was in reality a poor help.[48] The legal basis of the work of humanitarian agencies in internal or 'non-international' armed conflicts remains problematic to this day.

The bitter and bloody internal or intra-state conflicts of the 1990s – Bosnia, Iraq, Liberia, Rwanda, Somalia, Southern Sudan, and Zaire – were very much a part of this longer chain of events. This type of conflict had been testing the limits of international humanitarian and human rights law for at least four decades. What was new about the 1990s was the shift in attitudes within the UN – especially its Security Council; in particular the UN's greater readiness to undertake military intervention in civil war situations for humanitarian purposes. The 1990s recorded the largest number of countries involved in civil conflict at any time since the

[47] Christopher Weeramtry, *Universalising International Law* (Leiden: Nijhoff, 2004), 169–71. Fabian Klose, *Human Rights in the Shadow of Colonial Violence: The Wars of Independence in Kenya and Algeria* (Philadelphia: University of Pennsylvania Press, 2013), 120–37. For the idea of a 'protracted social conflict', see Edward Azar, Paul Jureidini, and Ronald McLaurin, 'Protracted Social Conflict: Theory and Practice in the Middle East', *Journal of Palestine Studies*, 8, no. 1 (1978), 41–60.

[48] Article 3 expanded the scope of the Geneva Conventions to 'non-international armed conflicts' in which all parties involved were expected to observe basic humanitarian principles, including the respect for persons not participating in the conflict, and the prohibition of torture, taking hostages, and irregular convictions and executions. But its sixteen lines of text entailed only a minimum set of humanitarian rules and, moreover, presupposed the existence of a 'non-international *armed conflict*' without defining the threshold beyond which a conflict would be considered such. See François Bugnion, *The International Committee of the Red Cross and the Protection of War Victims* (Oxford: Macmillan, 2003), 330–6, 447–51.

Second World War.[49] The resultant blurring of distinctions between combatants and civilians also produced by far the largest number of Security Council resolutions on humanitarian issues at any time since the UN's founding.[50] (This may also be the reason for the sharp increase in the proportion of international aid agency budgets allocated to civil conflict during this decade.)

A second theme to emerge from this book is that of periodization. What are the origins of the concept of humanitarian intervention? What were its formative moments? Humanitarianism's psyche of rupture and regeneration can pose problems here.[51] Despair at the failure of present generations to address the problems of poverty, injustice, and senseless violence is counterbalanced by the hope invested in the future to bring miraculous improvements to people's lives. It is a psyche that has tended to cut off current practices from previous experiences out of which later humanitarian praxis evolved. The opening chapters in this book exploring the earliest episodes of humanitarian intervention[52] and its early legal justifications[53] are particularly valuable therefore in charting how ideas about who deserves protection, the rationale for protection, and the rhetoric deployed to justify protection all changed over time.[54] During the nineteenth century, humanitarian interventions promoted by churches on the ground of religious affinity stood alongside anti-slavery and abolitionist action based around the language of 'civilization', chauvinistic as that language could be.[55] A subsequent twentieth-century shift from a language of civilization to that of a common humanity is more difficult to

[49] C. Blattman and E. Miquel, 'Civil Wars', *Journal of Economic Literature*, 48, no. 1 (2010), 3–57.

[50] A. Roberts, *Humanitarian Action in War: Aid, Protection and Impartiality in a Policy Vacuum*, (Oxford University Press, 1996), 15.

[51] Guillaume Lachenal and Bertrand Taithe, 'A Missionary and Colonial Genealogy of Humanitarianism: The Aujoulat Case in Cameroon, 1935–73'. Copy supplied by Professor Bertrand Taithe.

[52] Fabian Klose, Chapter 5, and Abigail Green, Chapter 7, in this book.

[53] Daniel Marc Segesser, Chapter 3; Stefan Kroll, Chapter 4, both in this book.

[54] David Trim, 'Conclusion: Humanitarian Intervention in Historical Perspective' in Simms and Trimm, *Humanitarian Intervention*, 387.

[55] Bronwen Everill, *Abolition and Empire in Sierra Leone and Liberia* (Basingstoke: Palgrave Macmillan, 2013), Richard Huzzey, *Freedom Burning: Anti-Slavery and Empire in Victorian Britain* (Ithaca, NY: Cornell University Press, 2012), and the study by Alan Lester and Fae Dussart, *Colonization and the Origins of Humanitarian Governance. Protecting Aborigines across the Nineteenth-Century British Empire* (Cambridge University Press, 2014).

pin down.[56] It does not appear to have been the product of any single interest or ideology, but was a feature of the interwar era – a moment when humanitarians combined liberal internationalism with imperial rule and when an informal world of extra-parliamentary pressure gradually gave way to the more formal and structured international NGO environment that would entrench itself after the Second World War.

Periodization is also important because of the way the humanitarian sector has lived by stories of its previous engagement with the world. It is a frequent refrain today that a new era of humanitarian aid and humanitarian intervention was ushered in by the 1990s. This is partly predicated on a rather nostalgic view of the 1960s and 1970s – a time when there were supposedly clear rules of engagement for humanitarians in war zones and combatants respected humanitarian missions.[57] It is true that the events of the 1990s led to a renewed focus on the politics of Western humanitarianism. But this book brings home a deeper, more complex history of humanitarian intervention, which, as its contributors show, has long proved itself to be a flexible, malleable, and polycentric concept. If there was something particular about the pairing of the 'humanitarian' with the 'military' during the 1990s, it is the emergence from within the international community of new arguments about the *locus* of sovereignty (in particular, the idea of sovereignty in part residing below or above the level of the state) at the very same time as the notion of 'failed' or 'fragile' states was emerging.[58] Interestingly, international development NGOs and the UN specialized agencies, faced with inefficient, unwieldy, and

[56] Mark Mazower, 'The End of Civilization and the Rise of Human Rights: The Mid-Twentieth-Century Disjuncture', in Stefan Ludwig Hoffman (ed.), *Human Rights in the Twentieth Century* (Cambridge University Press, 2011), 29–44.

[57] See, for example, Lord Malloch-Brown, former administrator of the UN Development Programme and former UN deputy secretary-general, at a symposium organized by the Institute for Government, 12 March 2013: www.instituteforgovernment.org.uk/events/politics-humanity-john-holmes (last accessed 21 May 2014).

[58] The language of 'failing', 'fragile', 'collapsed', and 'quasi' states was popularized at this time. For 'failing states', see Gerald Helman and Steven Ratner, 'Saving Failed States', *Foreign Policy*, 89 (1992–93), which defined the term as a 'situation where governmental structures are overwhelmed by circumstances', quote on 5; for 'collapsed' states, see I. William Zartman (ed.), *Collapsed States: The Disintegration and Restoration of Legitimate Authority* (Boulder, CO: Lynne Rienner, 1995); for 'quasi' states, see Robert Jackson, *Quasi-states: Sovereignty, International Relations and the World* (Cambridge University Press, 1990); for 'fragile' states, see Tim Besley and Torsten Persson, *Fragile States and Development Policy* (London: Centre for Economic Policy Research, 2011). Although they have their own nuances, each of these terms rests on a view of certain states not being able to discharge some or all of the functions of truly sovereign powers. They carry the implication that, in situations where good governance has partly or wholly

corrupt governments, were likewise grappling with the problem of whether to bypass the apparatus of developing states and deliver their anti-poverty programmes through civil society actors or community groups.[59]

Third, there is the question of how to situate the state in histories of humanitarian intervention. How, across the last few centuries, have state and non-state actors come together to respond to atrocities and to fashion the legal instruments and ideological defences required to sanction forceful interventions? To what extent has state-sponsored armed force proved a necessary factor in protecting the environment in which relief agencies operate and in ensuring their access to populations at risk?

Humanitarian organizations have long agonized over their relationship to government. Yet they exist because of, not despite of, the state; many aid agencies in fact perform state-like functions.[60] In the second half of the nineteenth century, humanitarian circulations of many kinds helped to hold expanding Western European empires together, even as they challenged these empires' practices and underlying premises. Humanitarians could be vociferous advocates of imperial expansion, with missionaries calling for protectorates to shield indigenous populations from the ravages of settler occupation.[61] But in becoming part of colonial governance, humanitarian principles were also heavily circumscribed by it. In Congo, what MacDonald aptly describes as the 'breathtaking cynicism' of the Brussels Treaty of 1890 was based on the pretence that colonial rule was the surest way to provide humanitarian protection – a pretence that justified Leopold's actions to an international community

broken down, protecting the populations of such states may require the sovereign will of one or more external powers.

59 The roots of this shift in thinking could be quite different: the dominant, market-driven ideology of the World Bank, IMF, and US Treasury in the so-called Washington Consensus period contrasted with the emphasis on grassroots initiatives and community empowerment by many NGOs.

60 Peter Willetts (ed.), *Pressure Groups in the Global System: The Transitional Relations of Issue-Oriented Non-Governmental Organizations* (London: Pinter, 1982), 1–15, and Clare Saunders, 'British Humanitarian Aid and Development NGOs, 1949–Present' in N. Crowson, M. Hilton, and J. McKay (eds.), *NGOs in Contemporary Britain: Non-state Actors in Society and Politics since 1945* (Basingstoke: Palgrave Macmillan, 2009), 38–58.

61 A. J. Lester, *Imperial Networks: Creating Identities in Nineteenth Century South Africa and Britain* (London: Routledge, 2001); Jane Sansom, *Imperial Benevolence: Making British Authority in the Pacific Islands* (Honolulu: University of Hawai'i Press, 1998).

and allowed his Belgian agents to ruthlessly exploit their Congolese subjects in the name of European civilization.

For well over a century, humanitarians have feared becoming ensnared by state-sponsored interventions. The threat to their independence posed by counter-insurgency operations in Iraq and Afghanistan is only the latest if pronounced manifestation of this fear. The degree of their discomfort has depended on the nature of the intervention in question. The further one travels from the more limited aim of emergency relief towards a broader transformation of society, the greater the scope for the confusion of political, military, and humanitarian aims.

If the type of force exerted in any given intervention may vary, so too may the perception of that intervention by its 'beneficiary' state. Humanitarians can be slow to appreciate that *any* type of intervention in a war has a strategic military significance. Take the Nigerian–Biafran War (1967–70) – perhaps the most widely publicized African conflict of the last century and one of the greatest tests for the international humanitarian system that emerged from the Second World War.[62] Doctors Without Borders (Médecins Sans Frontières) eventually emerged from the experience of this conflict, if not quite in the way its founder Bernard Kouchner would later recall. Kouchner – a young French doctor with the Red Cross – was appalled by what he had seen, as indeed were other ICRC aid workers in Biafra. He returned home to reject the principles of neutrality and non-interference in favour of a new more activist brand of humanitarianism which saw the exercise of state power and the right of states to intervene as critical to the humanitarian creed.[63]

Few in the West regarded – or referred to – the massive relief operation mounted by the ICRC and the churches as a humanitarian

[62] My analysis of the Nigerian–Biafra War is based on as yet unpublished research in the archives of the International Red Cross Movement. A key text remains John Stremlau, *The International Politics of the Nigerian Civil War, 1967–70* (Princeton University Press, 1977). For the wider literature, see Suzanne Cronje, *The World and Nigeria: A Diplomatic History of the Biafran War, 1967–70* (London: Sidgwick & Jackson, 1972); Alvin Edgell, 'Nigeria/Biafra' in Morris Davis (ed.), *Civil Wars and the Politics of International Relief: Africa, South Asia and the Caribbean* (New York: Praeger, 1975); Michael Gould, *The Biafran War: The Struggle for Modern Nigeria* (London: I.B.Tauris, 2013); John Okpoko, *The Biafran Nightmare: The Controversial Role of International Relief Agencies in a War of Genocide* (Enugu, Anambra State, Nigeria: Delta of Nigeria, 1986); Godwin Alaoma Onyebbula, *Memoirs of The Nigerian–Biafran Bureaucrat: An Account of Life in Biafra and within Nigeria* (Ibadan: Spectrum Books, 2005).

[63] MSF was born in 1971 as a merger of Groupe d'Intervention Médical et Chirurgical d'Urgence (formed in response to Biafra) and Secours Médical Français (formed in response to a flood disaster in eastern Pakistan).

'intervention',[64] but the Nigerian Federal Military Government (FMG) certainly did. It argued that the airlift of aid into Biafra, flown at night rather than during the day, and in defiance of its wishes, was illegal under international humanitarian law. In a war fought with relatively small armies and budgets, the Federal Military Government also pointed out that a relief operation on such a scale would inevitably have political repercussions, for example in providing an increasingly beleaguered Biafra with much needed foreign exchange or by Biafra taking advantage of relief flights as cover for bringing in ammunition and arms. Meanwhile, the Organization of African Unity recognized the conflict as one that should primarily be resolved by the Nigerians themselves.[65] In the perception of the majority if not all African governments, non-Africans had set about changing the course of a war whose consequences for postcolonial Africa, where most newly independent countries had their own minority problems, were far-reaching.[66] The fact that Biafra controlled Nigeria's oil reserves made non-African involvement on its behalf even more suspect. What in Europe and North America had the appearance of a non-forcible, non-state humanitarian mission looked rather different from the perspective of Nigeria and many other African states, which were keenly aware that the major donors of aid to Biafra were the UN and Western governments.

Such differences of perspective between Western and non-Western powers as to what constitutes a humanitarian *intervention* point to a deeper, more fundamental and unresolved tension inherent in contemporary humanitarianism.[67] On the one hand, humanitarians espouse a

[64] There were, however, arguments, framed in terms of international law, for a 'humanitarian intervention' to be undertaken by the Organization of African Unity or the UN. In some ways, these arguments prefigured the later R2P doctrine in their assertion that sovereignty was conditional and depended on the observance by the Nigerian authorities of minimum standards of human rights, which were regarded as fundamental to the maintenance of international peace and security, and which the Nigerians were said to have violated by their treatment of the Ibo people. See Michael Reisman and Myres S. McDougal, 'Humanitarian Intervention to Protect the Ibos' in Richard B. Lillich (ed.), *Humanitarian Intervention and the United Nations* (Charlottesville, VA: University Press of Virginia, 1973), 167–95.

[65] Klass van Walraven, *Dreams of Power: The Role of the Organisation of African Unity in the Politics of Africa, 1963–1993* (Aldershot: Ashgate, 1999), 307–11.

[66] The exceptions were Ivory Coast and Gabon, with close ties with France (which supported Biafra), and Zambia and Tanzania, whose motives appear to have been humanitarian.

[67] David Forsythe, 'Contemporary Humanitarianism' in Wilson and Brown (eds.), *Humanitarianism and Suffering*, 59.

cosmopolitan solidarity. Rising above the narrow provincialism of state interest, they imagine themselves as community that is coterminous with mankind. On the other, they have long been reliant upon donor states and under pressure to become more accountable to beneficiary populations. In the growth of the UN's specialist agencies some identify a more genuinely or authentically *international* field of humanitarian action. Yet humanitarians did not suddenly cease to serve national objectives after 1945. Rather, humanitarian power and state power continued to advance each other's interests as well as their own: bilateral and multilateral aid coexisted, and state and non-state actors cooperated, competed and not infrequently collided.[68] 'Humanitarian nationalism' and 'international humanitarianism' may in theory be distinct; yet rarely are they so in practice.

Why is there so much talk of the shrinking of 'humanitarian space' today?[69] The notion of 'humanitarian space' refers to the environment in which humanitarians carry out their work. In its physical dimensions, it refers to the ability of humanitarians to gain access to the people they wish to help; in its operational dimensions, to the type of activity they are able to undertake. In many of the conflicts studied in this book such 'space' was sharply circumscribed by donor governments and host states. There never was a 'golden age' when the freedom of humanitarians to deliver aid and relief was widely or universally respected. It is more fruitful to think of humanitarian space as expanding and contracting over time, according to how vigorously the principle of state sovereignty is asserted and the success of humanitarians in negotiating access with states.[70] Understood this way, 'humanitarian space' is the product of the political transactions required for aid to be delivered and atrocities to be addressed. Humanitarian principles meanwhile are part of the rhetorical armoury of humanitarians by which they seek to preserve for

[68] This is particularly evident from research on American humanitarianism. See Julia Irwin, *Making the World Safe: The American Red Cross and a Nation's Humanitarian Awakening* (Oxford University Press, 2013); and Heike Wieters' research on the Co-operative for American Remittances to Europe (CARE), 'On Money and Missions', a paper given at the workshop 'Humanitarianisms in Context: Histories of Non-state Actors, from the Local to the Global', Potsdam, 28–9 November 2013.

[69] Cynthia Brassard-Boudreau and Don Hubert, 'Shrinking Humanitarian Space? Trends and Prospects on Security and Access', *The Journal of Humanitarian Assistance*, 24 November 2010, http://sites.tufts.edu/jha/archives/863 (last accessed 5 August 2015).

[70] Richard Falk, 'Dilemmas of Sovereignty and Intervention', *Foreign Policy Journal*, 18 July 2011, www.foreignpolicyjournal.com/2011/07/18/dilemmas-of-sovereignty-and-interven tion/ (last accessed 5 August 2015).

themselves sufficient freedom of action. What *may* be distinctive about recent times is the 'willingness ... of humanitarian organizations to operate in more risky environments than they did in the past' and the implications of this for humanitarians' reliance upon military force.[71]

Fourth, there is the question of paternalism and power.[72] Humanitarianism's western origins and orientation are increasingly felt to be a barrier to effective action. The credibility of humanitarianism has been badly damaged by recent interventions that have primarily served the strategic interests of the intervening powers. In the hands of some critics, this translates into the argument that humanitarianism in Africa and Asia in the late twentieth century and early twenty-first century has simply been a rerun of colonialism. As with their predecessors, the moral obligation of today's generation of humanitarians to improve the lives of others is said to stem from the assumed superiority of their own culture.[73] There is indeed a paradox here. The very encounters that bring into closer view the suffering of the developing world – or Global South – and that have forged new patterns of responsibility, frequently portray those in need of help as technologically, economically, and culturally backward, a backwardness which can only be made good by following in the footsteps of Western powers. 'They' need to become more like 'us'.

This view of humanitarianism as an imposition over others – something that exercises power over the very people it seeks to emancipate – takes me to my fifth and final point about the justification for interventions. In arguing that the doctrine of humanitarianism intervention serves principally to defend the projection of American power in order to hold other nations in its thrall, critics – most famously Noam Chomsky – are tapping into a deep sense of unease as to who decides what counts as a

[71] For this claim, see Brassard-Boudreau and Hubert, 'Shrinking Humanitarian Space?', para. 35, preceding para. 38.

[72] For the power exercised by aid agencies, see R. L. Stirrat and Heiko Henkel, 'The Development Gift: The Problem of Reciprocity in the NGO World', *Annals of the American Academy of Political and Social Science*, 554 (1997), 66–80. For the continuity, in thought and action, of the work of contemporary NGOs in Africa with that of their colonial predecessors, see Firoze Manji and Carl O'Coill, 'The Missionary Position: NGOs and Development in Africa', *International Affairs*, 78 (2002), 567–83.

[73] For the classic statement, see Arturo Escobar, *Encountering Development: The Making and Unmaking of the Third World* (Princeton, NJ: Princeton University Press, 1995). For a nuanced critique, see Emma Crewe and Richard Axelby, *Anthropology and Development: Culture, Morality and Politics in a Globalised World* (Cambridge University Press, 2013), 8–10, 12–15, 38–40, 77–86, 131–56.

humanitarian intervention.[74] Who judges its credentials? Is this left to states? Or is there a role for non-state actors? Are humanitarian norms to be enforced by force only with a UN mandate and Security Council authorization? Or can convincing criteria be established for interfering in the internal affairs of another state when such a mandate is lacking?[75] What happens when the use of force specified in the initial language of authorization is stretched to and beyond its limits by subsequent military action, as happened in Libya under Security Council Resolution 1973?[76] These are, in essence, the dilemmas with which the concept of 'responsibility to protect' (R2P) has grappled.

How should the international community respond to situations when people are subjected to appalling cruelty by their governments? The question is all the more problematic because of humanitarianism's selective – some would say blatantly selective – gaze. Why do interventions happen in some locations and not others? Why is the public outraged by some atrocities yet apparently indifferent to others? To what extent are different norms and standards applied to 'first' and 'third' world conflicts? There are no transcendent humanitarian commitments. Rather humanitarian sensibilities reside in the mind. Interest, circumstance, and opportunity dictate where and when human suffering is recognized, as does the likelihood of humanitarian interventions provoking dissent by a great power or military opposition by warring parties.[77] As the contributors to this book show, states have chosen *not* to undertake interventions on as many or perhaps more occasions as they have. Such selectivity turns partly on the strategic interests of intervening powers, partly on the types of people felt to be deserving of protection, and partly on what we might call 'moral geographies' or 'emotional economies' of care – lines of emotive and empathetic

74 See the works by Noam Chomsky, *World Orders, Old and New* (London: Pluto, 1994), *Hegemony or Survival: America's Quest for Total Dominance* (New York: Metropolitan Books, 2003), and *Imperial Ambitions: Conversations with Noam Chomsky on the Post 9/11 World, Interviews with David Barsamian* (New York: Metropolitan Books, 2005). For a spirited argument against, see Elizabeth Cobbs Hoffman, *Playing Umpire: America and the World* (Cambridge, MA: Harvard University Press, 2013).

75 Wheeler, *Saving Strangers*.

76 Intervention in Libya was initially justified by reference to an emergency situation endangering the lives of many Libyan civilians. It was later converted operationally by NATO into regime change in Tripoli, but without having secured a broader mandate from the Security Council. See also Fröhlich, Chapter 14.

77 Roberts, *Humanitarian Action in War*, 24–5.

connection that allow some localities to become the focus of protection and assistance, while others are ignored.[78]

This brings us to the intractable yet inescapable issue of *sovereignty*, and we historicize it. Those opposing humanitarian interventions pitch the respect for state sovereignty against defence of humanity. The humanitarian imperative, they insist, must not be allowed to trump the inviolability of national sovereign rights. (Hence the controversy surrounding the 1992 Security Council resolution 794 regarding Somalia.)[79] For the UN, founded on the bedrock principle of the sovereignty of its member states, humanitarian interventions have thrown into sharp relief the tensions between maintaining a system of state sovereignty and maintaining international peace and order. In fact, until the 1980s, the UN's marked reluctance to interfere in the domestic affairs of its member states resulted in a very restricted engagement with humanitarian or any other types of emergency.[80] This, then, is the basic dilemma interventionists have long confronted. Under what circumstances, if any, might the classical rule of non-interference be qualified? And what are the implications of such qualifications for the view that a system of stable interstate relations rests on the sovereignty of those states?

Here, as Daniel Segesser reminds us, we need to consider carefully what was meant by sovereignty at different points and by different actors in the past.[81] Much of the period covered by this book was as much (or more) an age of empire states as an age of the nation state. The normative status achieved by the nation state after 1945 turned sovereignty into an absolute and indivisible principle.[82] Yet for much of human history, sovereignty was viewed quite differently – a conditional concept, capable of being qualified, exercised over certain aspects of statehood and not others, and diminished by degrees. Different levels of sovereignty could thus be invested in 'civilized' and 'uncivilized' powers, or in 'major

78 This theme is picked up by several contributors, see Kroll, Chapter 4; Green, Chapter 7; Dülffer, Chapter 10; and Rodogno, Chapter 9 in this book.

79 The Security Council authorized the creation of a Unified Task Force to create a 'secure environment' in order to provide humanitarian assistance to the civilian population. Its resolution determined that 'the magnitude of human tragedy caused by the conflict in Somalia, further exacerbated by the obstacles being created to the distribution of humanitarian assistance' constituted a threat to international peace and security.

80 M. Duffield, *Development, Security and Unending War: Governing the World of Peoples* (Cambridge: Polity, 2007), 70.

81 Segesser, Chapter 3.

82 For the force of this point, see John Darwin, *After Tamerlane: The Rise and Fall of Global Empires, 1400–2000* (London: Allen Lane, 2007).

powers', 'minor powers', and 'non-powers'. Sovereignty could be held in trust by imperial states acting on behalf of the international community, or shared between states in jointly administered occupied territories, or fiercely contested between rival ethnic groups in newly liberated colonies. Empires – and their mental maps of civilization – provide a crucial context in which past debates about state sovereignty and intervention occurred.[83]

The latest move by proponents of the R2P concept to reframe sovereignty as a question of the responsibility of states to protect their own citizens is, therefore, part of a much longer sequence of debates among international lawyers, diplomats, humanitarian policymakers, and human rights activists regarding the obligations of states to the international community of which they are part.[84] As Stefan Kroll shows, it is the 'consciousness of that collectivity' that has led successive generations of interventionists – humanitarian and otherwise – to argue for the right of collective interference as an extension of the principle of sovereignty from the domestic to the international sphere – a *sine qua non* of a functioning community of states.[85]

The history of empires also speaks to a related and persistent problem, namely that of conflict definition: how violence is named, and who gets to do the naming. War, it has been said, 'is the violent expression of a complex set of opposing interests and aspirations'.[86] The labelling of wars is inherently controversial because the way conflict is defined shapes perceptions of the moral status of combatants and who are their victims. Conflict definition is, in fact, as much a crux of the matter as sovereignty and a question no less 'recalcitrant'.[87] Intra-state conflicts, secessionist

[83] I would like to acknowledge here an important contribution from Martin Aust during discussions at the conference.

[84] Kennedy, *The Dark Sides of Virtue*, 254. For the basis of the R2P concept, its four specified violations (genocide, war crimes, ethnic cleansing, and crimes against humanity), its three pillars (the responsibility of individual states to protect, the role of the international community to assist states in discharging that responsibility, and the circumstances in which collective action against states failing in their duty of protection might be envisaged), and the argument that 'responsibility' should be seen as an ally of 'sovereignty', see 'Responsibility to Protect: Timely and Decisive Response', Report of the United Nations Secretary-General, General Assembly, 66th Session, 25 July 2012, www.globalpolicy.org/humanitarian-intervention.html (last accessed May 2014). The report also warns against the dangers of humanitarian action being used as a substitute for political action and reaffirms the need to defend 'humanitarian space' by respecting the so-called fundamental principles of 'neutrality, independence, humanity and impartiality'.

[85] See Kroll, Chapter 4. [86] Roberts, *Humanitarian Action in War*, 11.

[87] On the 'recalcitrance' of the question of sovereignty in the debate about humanitarian interventions, see Trim, 'Conclusion', 381.

movements and ethnic conflagrations are widely referenced by contributors to this book. What are the processes by which conflicts are classified either as civil wars, liberation movements, or terrorist campaigns, with all the implications these descriptions then carry for the mobilization of humanitarian sympathies and the harnessing of such sympathies to calls for military intervention?[88] The risks of humanitarian double standards here have not been lost on recent commentators. Humanitarian interventions may be an expression of the growing interdependence and fragility of a globalizing world. Yet, as Michael Geyer argues, the questions of sovereignty and accountability provoked by humanitarian interventions are ultimately part and parcel of an argument for power and order in the international system.[89] They point to the stark inequalities between states and to the lack, not the realization, of a comprehensive system of global collective security.[90] The interveners are invariably those who are able to enforce their own rules of order on others – the 'law of the strongest' is as much a characteristic of humanitarian interventions as it is of peacekeeping or other types of military operation.[91]

If interventions have their critics, it is worth remembering that the consequences of non-intervention are agonized over, too. Lurking behind much recent commentary on humanitarian intervention is the question painfully posed by the survivors of Srebrenica towards the UN Blue Helmets: 'why did they not protect us?' At the time of writing the question is being transferred to Syria. Three years into a complex civil war, nearly half of the population are in need of humanitarian aid, a quarter of a million are living in besieged areas where they are unable to access help, and a staggering 2.4 million refugees have been displaced into five neighbouring states.[92]

Participants at the conference from which this book emerged spoke eloquently of the 'intrinsic dilemmas' and 'irreconcilable character' of the concept of humanitarian intervention – the contrary pulls of good intentions and hard-core power politics. Humanitarians hope to change the world, but the world profoundly shapes what humanitarianism is and

88 See Western's observation that 'whether or not these broad views translate into expressed support for *direct military intervention* on behalf of victims and against perpetrators is often a function of how the conflict is framed and understood', Chapter 8, 169.

89 Geyer, Chapter 2, 35. 90 MacQueen, Chapter 11, 236.

91 Viewed from the perspective of the Ottoman Turks, David Rodogno notes how the history of such interventions speaks of an 'exclusionary control' by the West in the setting of humanitarian norms.

92 These are the figures currently in the public domain. See *Christian Aid Magazine*, (Winter/Spring 2014), 16–17 and (Spring/Summer 2014), 5.

what it is able to do.[93] History can help to reconstruct the contexts and constraints under which humanitarian interventions have previously occurred. The experience of the past can shed light on how interventions in the present are likely to be perceived. Moreover, without history we cannot fully understand the legal frameworks in which humanitarian interventions have come to be sanctioned, or the underlying moral codes created for and inscribed into humanitarian work. At whom do you aim interventionist policies? What do you do about sovereignty? How do you work through and respect local institutions? How do you make judgements about proportionality, necessity, reasonable prospects of positive outcomes, collateral damage, unintended consequences, and right motivations? Such moral codes – and their attendant 'moral hazards'[94] – lay at the heart of decisions to intervene in the affairs of other states. Whether humanitarians occupy a position of distant sympathy, professional mediation, critical solidarity, or protective support, squaring up to these questions will be as important to the pursuit of their goals in the future as it has been in the past.

[93] For an eloquent recognition of this fact, see Barnett, *Empire of Humanity*.
[94] MacDonald, Chapter 6, in this book.

Index